Canada in Question:
Federalism in the Seventies
SECOND EDITION

McGraw-Hill Ryerson Series in Canadian Politics

General Editor — Paul W. Fox

Politics: Canada; 3rd ed. Paul Fox
Canadian Foreign Policy; D.C. Thomson & R.F. Swanson
The Constitutional Process in Canada; 2nd ed. R.I. Cheffins & R.N. Tucker
Political Party Financing in Canada; K.Z. Paltiel
One Man-One Vote; W.E. Lyons
Nationalism in Canada; P. Russell
Political Parties and Ideologies in Canada; W. Christian & C. Campbell
Canada: A Socio-Political Report; R. Manzer
Pressure Group Behaviour in Canadian Politics; A. Paul Pross
Canada in Question: Federalism in the Seventies; 2nd ed.; D.V. Smiley
Political Parties in Canada; C. Winn & J. McMenemy
Government in Canada; T.A. Hockin

Forthcoming

Canadian Politics: Exercises in Analysis; J. Jenson & B. Tomlin
Politics: Canada, 4th ed.; Paul Fox

Canada in Question:
Federalism in the Seventies
SECOND EDITION

Donald V. Smiley

Professor of Political Science
Erindale College
University of Toronto

McGRAW-HILL RYERSON

Toronto   Montreal   New York   London
Sydney   Mexico   Panama   São Paulo
Johannesburg   Düsseldorf   New Delhi
Kuala Lumpur   Auckland

Canada in Question: Federalism in The Seventies

ISBN -0-07-082371-5

    3 4 5 6 7 8 9   AP   5 4 3 2 1 0 9 8 7

Printed and bound in Canada

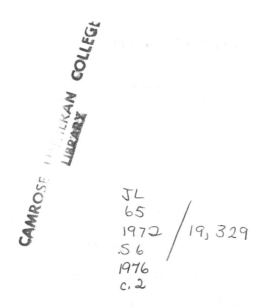

CONTENTS

This book is dedicated to Henry Angus, Dean Emeritus of Graduate Studies of the University of British Columbia, whose study of the Canadian Confederation extends for over sixty years of its history. His lucidity in analysis and exactness in expression are standards which I should like sometime to meet.

FOREWORD TO
THE SECOND EDITION

It is a testimonial both to the continuing rapid change in Canadian federalism and to Professor Smiley's quality as a scholar that he has decided to revise his book *Canada in Question: Federalism in the Seventies* within three years of the date of its original publication. Few books, especially in Canadian government, are revised so thoroughly in such a short time, particularly when the original has been received as favourably and sold as well as Professor Smiley's first edition.

The author has not altered the entire book, of course. He has left almost untouched the first few chapters, which deal with the constitutional structure and the evolution of Canadian federalism, although he has brought the text up to date where necessary. He has also not revised one of my favourite chapters, which deals with the role that political parties play in Canadian federalism. Although not many readers have said that they agree with me — except the author, fortunately — I still think that this is one of the most original, perceptive, and significant chapters in the book.

The remainder of the book — that is to say, the bulk of it — has been revised thoroughly. Professor Smiley has not merely updated his text; he has completely rewritten, and in some cases recast, his chapters on executive federalism, federal-provincial fiscal relations, and cultural duality, and added new material and reflections on some other aspects of federalism. His final chapter asks, and seeks to answer, the provocative question, "Is Canada a National Community?"

In my view the author's revisions are excellent. What I believed to be initially a first-class book on Canadian federalism has been made even better. The evidence that has been used is more voluminous and more revealing. Professor Smiley also deals with some "hot" contemporary issues, such as the dispute over energy resources. Finally, he has explained some difficult aspects of current Canadian federalism, for example, intergovernmental fiscal relations, even more clearly than he did the first time. I also appreciate the fact that in his final chapter he does not hesitate to state his own position with clarity and vigour, with a few shafts flung with typical Smiley deftness at the theories and the academics with whom he disagrees.

Professor Smiley has a gift for explaining difficult and complicated subjects in easily readable prose. He also has the ability to make his writing lively and interesting by infusing it with his own convictions.

Perhaps the highest compliment I can pay to his new edition is to say that I wish I had it available to use with my students immediately.

Paul Fox,
General Editor.

University of Toronto,
October 3, 1975.

INTRODUCTION TO
THE SECOND EDITION

I approach the second edition of *Canada in Question* with some ambivalence. It is of course gratifying that there has been enough demand for the original book to cause the publishers and the general editor of the McGraw-Hill Ryerson Series in Canadian Politics to ask me to undertake this revision. On the other hand, a more adequate analysis of the Canadian federal system would not have required up-dating after less than five years. However that may be, once the decision to do the revision was made I undertook to go about the task thoroughly. In general, the first two chapters and the chapter on political parties do not differ significantly from those in the earlier book but the rest of the analysis is completely re-cast. This expanded treatment was possible only by McGraw-Hill Ryerson agreeing to publish a book significantly longer than the original, and I am grateful for this concession.

This revision attempts to incorporate three changes of the past half-decade — changes in my outlook on the Canadian Confederation, in the academic and other literature pertinent to the subject and in the federal system itself. Of these, the first is by far the least consequential. Almost all the reviews of *Canada in Question* made note of what was regarded as my gloominess about Confederation — one spoke rather poetically of an analysis "studded with the thorns of pessimism" — and several quoted the sentence in the Introduction to the effect that the completion of the book had been "delayed by two periods in which I ceased to work because of the judgement that the federation would not last as long as it would take to finish the manuscript". If anyone is still interested, these interruptions were directly after the October Crisis of 1970, and after the breakdown of constitutional negotiations in June of the next year. Yet the statement was heedless, and if indeed Confederation was in process of disintegration this should have been made clear by my analysis rather than by a cryptic and gratuitous statement about my emotional responses to ongoing developments.

The analytical literature on Canadian federalism continues to expand. In the past five years, two excellent book-length studies by Richard Simeon[1] and by J. Stefan Dupré and his colleagues[2] have vastly enhanced our understanding of the processes of federal-provincial decision. Significant articles in a collection of essays edited by Paul Pross shed new light on the relation between interest groups and the working of the federal system.[3] Paul Weiler's recent book on the Supreme Court of Canada contains a brilliant and iconoclastic formulation of the role of judicial review in umpiring the relations between the federal and provincial governments.[4] And in addition, issues of such academic publications as the *Canadian Journal of Political Science*, *Canadian Public Administration*, the *Journal of Canadian Studies* and the *Canadian Historical Review* continue to make contributions to our knowledge of the Canadian federation. This academic concern parallels, of course, the preoccupation of policy-makers and the informed public with federal matters, and the American scholar Daniel Elazar has remarked that Canada is perhaps the only country where a traveller can buy a paperback on federalism in any major airport.[5]

More than in the past, the recent academic literature on Canadian affairs is focussed on provincial and regional rather than national development. The 1967 history text *Canada: Unity in Diversity* by Paul G. Cornell, Jean Hamelin, Fernand Ouellett and Marcel Trudel[6] has such an orientation, distinguishing it from both the nation-building emphasis of such scholars as Donald Creighton and A.R.M. Lower and from the two-nations formulation of the "Montreal School", whose most influential figures have been Michel Brunet and Maurice Seguin. Several young historians are engaged in studies of Ontario; although the results of this work remain for the most part as unpublished doctoral dissertations, excellent examples of the enterprise are contained in a collection of essays edited by Donald Swainson, *Mowat's Ontario*.[7] H.V. Nelles' superb book on the development of natural resources and hydro-electric power in Ontario between 1849 and 1941[8] is full of insights for the students of federalism as is, in a very different way, Neil McKenty's biography *Mitch Hepburn*.[9] Morris Zaslow's book on the history of the Canadian North between 1870 and 1914[10] gives much attention to the policies of the provinces as well as the Dominion in the development of their respective frontiers.

Among political scientists, Edwin R. Black and Alan C. Cairns in an article published in 1965[11] argued that the development of Canadian federalism had been characterized by province-building as well as nation-building and urged scholars to a concern with the provinces. Yet during the 1960s the preoccupation with cultural duality frustrated sustained attention from students of government to provinces other than Quebec. However, we now have useful political histories of Newfoundland and Saskatchewan by S.J.R. Noel[12] and David Smith[13] respectively, and a collection of essays on the latter province edited by Duff Spafford and Norman Ward.[14] Although a useful start in its field, the collection of essays on the politics of the ten provinces edited by Martin Robin[15] vary greatly in quality and were not written within a common conceptual framework to facilitate comparative analysis. Two articles in the September 1974 issue of the *Canadian Journal of Political Science*, by John Wilson[16] and by David Elkins and Richard Simeon,[17] have this comparative thrust, and Wilson has evolved a highly original formulation of the relation between provincial party systems and levels of economic development. The 1974 book by J.E. Hodgetts and D.P. Dwivedi[18] on public personnel administration in the provinces is, one would hope, a harbinger of future studies on provincial administrative institutions. It is thus as certain as any such thing can be that comparative provincial politics and government will emerge as a sub-field of the political science enterprise in Canada. However, we still lack comprehensive and contemporary accounts of particular provinces. Fred Schindeler's excellent analysis *Responsible Government in Ontario*[19] limits itself to the cabinet and the legislature and the earlier books of a more comprehensive nature on Prince Edward Island,[20] Nova Scotia,[21] New Brunswick[22] and Manitoba[23] are somewhat out of date.

There is no logical necessity that their enhanced concern with provincial history and politics should lead Canadian scholars to support the contemporary ascendancy of the provinces in the federal system. Yet fragmentary evidence suggests this is happening, and if my English Canadian colleagues are not following the election returns they appear to be responding to current shifts in the balance of powers in the Canadian Confederation with complacency and in some cases gratification. This emergent conventional wisdom is asserted in its most categorical form by the historian Christopher Armstrong in the conclusion of his essay on Oliver Mowat and federal-provincial relations ". . . [Mowat's] vision of Canadian development was different from Macdonald's, but time has proved him more far-sighted".[24] John Wilson ends his essay to which I have already referred with the judgement that the "radically different political cultures" of the provinces create a situation in which "our national leaders will be incapable of speaking to the national collectivity except in times of crisis" and thus "We must either abandon the search for national unity altogether or redefine its meaning in a way which recognizes that our 'limited identities' constitute the essence of what it is to be Canadian."[25] This then is the new conventional wisdom of the Canadian academy, and like any other orthodoxy, established or emergent, it needs to be treated with scepticism.

Apart from analyses directly related to federalism, my recent thinking about Canada has been very much influenced by the writings of S.D. Clark, Harold Innis and Karl Polanyi. Belatedly I have read and found very helpful M.J.C. Vile's *Constitutionalism and the Separation of Powers*[26] and in particular his argument that political scientists should turn their attention to "the complex inter-relationships of groups and structures" in contradistinction to the neglect by behavioralists of constitutional and institutional factors. The spirit of Vile's conclusion in a general and inadequate way informs this book. "The study of politics must, therefore, very largely consist of the examination of the ways in which constitutional and political institutions, and the social forces and movements in a particular society, interact with each other; of the limits upon the extent to which stable constitutional modes of behaviour can be developed and maintained; and of the effects they can have on molding behaviour."[27] I have elsewhere designated this kind of political analysis as "neo-institutionalism".[28] Its ablest expression in the literature of Canadian politics and government is J.R. Mallory's *Social Credit and the Federal Power in Canada*,[29] in my view the best book on Canadian federalism that has ever been written.

An honest scholar acknowledges even as he cannot repay his intellectual debts. Specific acknowledgements are contained in the footnotes at the end of each chapter. But in a more direct and personal way my studies are helped along every week of the year by colleagues and students at the University of Toronto. In the original book and this revision I have been assisted in big ways and small by the good humour and good judgement of the General Editor of this Series, Paul Fox. I have learned a great deal about many aspects of Canadian politics and government from my association with Kenneth Bryden, Steve Clarkson, Ted Hodgetts and Frank Peers in teaching the core graduate course in that subject. Each in his own way Steve Dupré, Richard Day and Jack McLeod have instructed me in the political economy tradition. Peter Russell has contributed much to my still amateurish grasp of the legal foundations of Canadian federalism. I continue to learn much from my association with graduate students in the Department of Political Economy, of whom I should like to mention three in particular — Douglas Bennett, Robert Campbell and John McDonough.

Ms. Mary-Lynn Maltby of Erindale College typed this manuscript with great pleasantness and efficiency and put me very much in her debt.

Finally, my wife and daughters have shown their love by their tolerance of my preoccupations with this revision.

I end with the conventional statement that I am responsible for anything wrong with this book.

Donald V. Smiley.
Toronto, August 1975.

Notes

[1]*Federal-Provincial Diplomacy: The Making of Recent Policy in Canada*, University of Toronto Press, 1972.
[2]J. Stefan Dupré, David M. Cameron, Graeme H. McKechnie and Theodore B. Rotenberg, *Federalism and Policy Development: The Case of Adult Occupational Training in Ontario*, University of Toronto Press, 1973.
[3]*Pressure Group Behaviour in Canadian Politics*, McGraw-Hill Ryerson Series in Canadian Politics, Toronto, 1975. See particularly articles by Dawson, Bucovetsky and Kwavnick.
[4]*In the Last Resort: A Critical Study of the Supreme Court of Canada*, Carswell, Toronto, 1974.
[5]"Federalism in Multiple Dimensions", 4 *Publius: The Journal of Federalism*, Summer 1974, p. 1.
[6]Holt, Rinehart and Winston of Canada, Toronto/Montreal, 1967. See particularly William Kilbourn's Introduction for an analysis of the place of this book in Canadian historiography.
[7]Macmillan of Canada, Toronto, 1972.
[8]*The Politics of Development: Forests, Mines and Hydro-Electric Power in Ontario 1849-1941*, Macmillan of Canada, Toronto, 1974.
[9]McClelland and Stewart, Toronto, 1967.
[10]*The Opening of the Canadian North 1870-1914*, The Canadian Centenary Series, McClelland and Stewart, Toronto.

[11]"A Different Perspective on Canadian Federalism", *IX Canadian Public Administration*, March 1966, pp. 27-45.

[12]*Politics in Newfoundland*, University of Toronto Press, 1971.

[13]*Prairie Liberalism: The Liberal Party in Saskatchewan 1905-'71*, University of Toronto Press, 1975.

[14]*Politics in Saskatchewan*, Longman Canada, Toronto, 1968.

[15]*Canadian Provincial Politics*, Prentice-Hall of Canada, Scarborough, 1972.

[16]"The Canadian Political Cultures: Towards a Redefinition of The Nature of the Canadian Political System", pp. 438-483.

[17]"Regional Political Cultures in Canada", pp. 397-437.

[18]*Provincial Governments as Employers*, Canadian Public Administration Series, McGill-Queen's University Press, Montreal and London, 1974.

[19]University of Toronto Press, 1969.

[20]Frank Mackinnon, *The Government of Prince Edward Island*, University of Toronto Press, 1951.

[21]J. M. Beck, *The Government of Nova Scotia*, University of Toronto Press, 1957.

[22]H.G. Thorburn, *Politics in New Brunswick*, University of Toronto Press, 1961.

[23]M.S. Donnelly, *The Government of Manitoba*, University of Toronto Press, 1963.

[24]"The Mowat Heritage in Federal-Provincial Relations", *Mowat's Ontario, op. cit.*, p. 118.

[25]*ibid.* p. 483.

[26]Oxford University Press, 1967.

[27]*ibid.* p. 314.

[28]"Must Canadian Political Science be a Minature Replica?" *Journal of Canadian Studies*, February 1974, p. 39.

[29]University of Toronto Press, 1954.

POSTSCRIPT

Less than two weeks after the manuscript of this book had been delivered to the publishers the federal Minister of Finance introduced into the House of Commons Bill C-73, "An Act to provide for the restraint of profit margins, prices, dividends and compensation in Canada". This is the kind of experience which makes me wish that I had chosen to become a student of something that stayed put, say medieval history or microeconomics. The new federal policies for the time being at least have arrested the trends toward provincialism that set in during the late 1950s. Further, these policies appear to be dividing Canadians on axes other than those of language/culture or province/region; the incidence both of inflation and of measures to control inflation are complex and the emergent cleavages may well be of a kind unprecedented in the Canadian experience — for example, as the guidelines are directed rather specifically towards John Kenneth Galbraith's planning sector where competitive forces are weak, it is not improbable that we will see new forms of cooperation between big business and organized labour against the federal program.

The provinces have been uncharacteristically compliant in the face of the new federal initiatives. The Trudeau government apparently made a rather abrupt decision to support mandatory guidelines and this was taken without consultation with the provinces, whose premiers were informed of this decision after being summoned peremptorily to Ottawa for the Thanksgiving weekend. Provincial governments have their own reasons for wishing inflation abated and are willing for the time being at least to let their federal counterparts run the hazards of such action, even in respect to matters which are unequivocally provincial or local. The federal enactment provides that the cabinet may sign agreements with the provinces to apply the guidelines to provincial and local government agencies. Some of the provinces believe that the three-year period under which the controls are operative is too long and Ottawa is, it seems, willing to enter into such agreements for shorter periods. On the whole, the provinces have been cooperative and are themselves beginning in some cases to control forms of income such as rents which are outside the federal guidelines.

It is likely that the constitutionality of the federal program will soon be challenged in the courts. The federal case would in all probability be based on the power of Parliament to legislate for the "Peace, Order, and Good Government of Canada" in respect to a matter which had come to be of overriding national concern. It is my guess that the courts, and most importantly of course the Supreme Court of Canada, will not overturn the federal law in the absence of significant opposition from the governments of the provinces to it. However, even if the legislation were to be declared *ultra vires* it appears that much the same results could be attained through intergovernmental cooperation by the provinces delegating powers to a federal administrative agency such as the Anti-Inflation Board.

Federal-provincial fiscal relations are likely to be affected by the new circumstances. These relations developed over a period where both levels, most importantly the federal level, were relatively "flush", there was little taxpayer resistance to increasing levies and federal revenues were highly income-elastic — i.e., even at stable rates, federal revenues increased rapidly as a proportion of GNP. These conditions are changing. There are increasing public sentiments that federal expenditures are themselves a major influence toward inflation. The provincial and local governments face similar pressures and in some cases are in situations in which they will be able to borrow in capital markets only at increasingly unfavourable rates. The expenditures restraints announced by the federal government in December 1975 did not involve payments to the provinces or other federal expenditures of direct and immediate importance to these jurisdictions. However, it seems likely that in the period ahead there will be increasing incentives for Ottawa to limit its commitments to such matters as interprovincial fiscal equalization and regional economic development. In a period of increasing fiscal stringency we can expect even more severe tensions than before in federal-provincial relations.

Since the Preface was written I have read and learned much from the study *Divided Loyalties: Canadian Concepts of Federalism* by my friend and former colleague Edwin Black. As I indicate in Chapter 9, I disagree pointedly with Black's prescription of "special status for all" advanced at the end of his book. However, in a masterful way he outlines, disentangles and analyzes the issues which have revolved around the Canadian federal system since its beginnings, and his work is a must for serious students of the subject.

D.V. Smiley
Toronto
January 7, 1976

CHAPTER 1

THE CANADIAN CONSTITUTION AND THE FEDERAL SYSTEM

Among students of law and politics the term "constitution" is used in two different ways. In the first sense we refer to a legal code which within a geographically delineated area overrides all other enactments or acts of government and is usually amendable by a procedure less flexible than that related to other legislation. The second way we use the term constitution involves subject-matter, the laws and settled usages within a state which determine the respective powers and privileges of the various institutions of government and the essential aspects of the relations between citizens and the political community. In many circumstances the procedural and subject-matter definitions of what is constitutional will coincide where the legal document prescribing the basic political relations of a community is both paramount over other political acts and subject to amendment by procedures less flexible than those by which other laws can be changed. On the other hand, jurisdictions with codified constitutions in this sense sometimes include provisions about substantive public policy, as when the United States Constitution was amended in 1919 to prohibit the manufacture or sale of alcoholic beverages. Contrariwise, the United Kingdom does not have a codified constitution at all, and from time to time the most fundamental of political relations are determined by the Crown in Parliament through the same procedures by which enactments relating to the most trivial of public matters come into being. In general, the usual distinction between written and unwritten constitutions is not very helpful, and the most useful classification is between codified and uncodified constitutions and between codified and uncodified elements of the same constitutional system.

There is a codified part of the Canadian constitution, including at a minimum the British North America Act of 1867 and its subsequent amendments and those British and Canadian statutes and Orders-in-Council providing for the entry of the various provinces and territories into Confederation after 1867. Although, as we shall see later in this chapter, the Fulton-Favreau formula was not enacted, this proposed procedure for constitutional amendment agreed upon by the federal and provincial governments in the fall of 1964 included this definition:

> 11. Without limiting the meaning of the expression "Constitution of Canada", in this Part that expression includes the following enactments and any order, rule or regulation thereunder, namely,
> (a) the British North America Acts, 1867 to 1964;
> (b) the Manitoba Act, 1860;

(c) the Parliament of Canada Act, 1875;

(d) the Canadian Speaker (Appointment of Deputy) Act, 1895, Session 2,

(e) the Alberta Act;

(f) the Saskatchewan Act;

(g) the Statute of Westminster, 1931, in so far as it is part of the law of Canada; and

(h) this Act.[1]

There are a number of enactments of the Parliament of Canada which in a strict legal sense are solely at the discretion of that legislature but which are constitutional in their subject-matter. It is, however, unlikely that any group of students of such affairs could be brought to agreement on a list of Canadian constitutional statutes.[2] Certainly there should be included the War Measures Act, the Canadian Bill of Rights and the Supreme Court Act. But should such a categorization include, for example, the Canada Elections Act and the Canadian Citizenship Act? And moving away from enactments of Parliament, what about the minute of the Privy Council of October 25, 1935, which details the powers of the Prime Minister of Canada? Informed observers would differ.

Beyond its codified elements and certain statutes and Orders-in-Council of constitutional significance, the Canadian constitution can reasonably be regarded as including certain settled conventions of governmental structure and practice. The preamble of the British North America Act of 1867 stated that the colonies had expressed a desire to be federally united under the Crown "with a Constitution similar in Principle to that of the United Kingdom". We can suppose that by this phrase the framers of the Act were referring to the conventions of responsible parliamentary government, the independence of the judiciary and, outside Quebec, the common law system. Some of these understandings were enacted in the British North America Act itself, e.g., the provision of Section 54 that a bill for taxation or for the expenditure of public funds must be brought before the House of Commons by the Governor General — in effect, by a Minister of the Crown — and by the provisions of Sections 44-47 related to the Speaker of the Commons. However, some of the most crucial aspects of British parliamentary government were not mentioned explicitly in the Act. To take outstanding examples, there is no reference to the office or powers of the cabinet as such[3] or of the Prime Minister or to the convention that to remain in office a ministry must retain the continuing support of a majority in the House of Commons.

The Federal Division of Legislative Powers

The most characteristic aspect of a federal constitution is its division of law-making powers between the central and regional governments. Contemporary federal systems have variegated institutional characteristics. Most, like Canada, have a unified judicial system; the United

States has parallel structures of federal and state courts. In several federations, like the United States and the Federal Republic of Germany, the regional governments as such have important responsibilities related to the functioning of the central authority; in Canada it is otherwise. The older federations have had separate and autonomous central and regional bureaucracies; in some of the newer ones there has been reliance on a unified civil service. Despite these and other institutional differences, the distinguishing characteristic of a federation is the constitutional distribution of legislative powers between national and state or provincial governments. There are many kinds of such distributions. In Canada and most of the newer federations the national legislature is given the residual powers, i.e. those not explicitly conferred on the provinces or states, while there is a contrary tradition which defines the federal principle in terms of the national government having only those powers explicitly conferred on it by the constitution. Some federations have a large number of concurrent legislative powers which can be exercised by either or both levels of government, but in Canada explicit provisions for concurrency are limited. In some federations, such as Canada and Australia, the distribution of legislative powers is exhaustive or nearly exhaustive in the sense that if one level cannot enact a particular kind of legislation the other has power to do so, while in the United States there are important constitutional restrictions upon what any government can do. Some federations like the United States provide that all the constituents states/provinces have precisely the same law-making powers while in others, like the Republic of India, there is a differentiation among regional governments. Despite these variations, all federal constitutions provide for a distribution of legislative powers which cannot be altered or amended at the unilateral discretion of either level.

Those who framed the British North America Act did not find it difficult to agree on a distribution of law-making powers between Parliament and the provincial legislatures. There have been several explanations of the relative ease with which the matter was resolved. In a study published in 1939, Donald Creighton suggested that so far as economic affairs were concerned the Fathers of Confederation made an implicit distinction between activities associated with land and activities associated with commerce, and on the basis of this distinction allocated powers to the provinces and the Dominion respectively.[4] The Report of the Quebec Royal Commission on Constitutional Problems published in 1956 argued that in general the subjects given to the provinces were those in respect to which the traditions and interests of the English- and French-speaking communities were significantly different, while Dominion matters were believed to have no such cultural incidence.[5] Peter Waite has said that by "the federal principle" the Fathers of Confederation did not mean the distribution of legislative powers at all, but rather the structure of Parliament and in particular the relation between the Senate and the House of Commons.[6]

The formula for the distribution of legislative authority in the

British North America Act assigned the residual powers to the Dominion. Section 92 enumerated fifteen classes of subjects about which the provinces exclusively might make laws, with a sixteenth category, "Generally all Matters of a merely local or private Nature in the Province". Section 93 provided for exclusive provincial jurisdiction over education, with safeguards for the rights of denominational schools as these rights existed by law at the time of union or were subsequently so established. Section 95 enacted that both Parliament and the provinces might make laws in respect to agriculture and immigration with the proviso that those of the Dominion would prevail in the event of a conflict. These were, then, the legislative powers of the provinces. The opening words of Section 91 enacted "It shall be lawful for the Queen, by and with the Advice and Consent of the Senate and House of Commons to make Laws for the Peace, Order, and Good Government of Canada, in relation to all Matters not coming within the Classes of Subjects by this Act assigned exclusively to the Legislatures of the Provinces." If the Act had not gone on to elaborate this general grant of lawmaking power, the subsequent judicial interpretation of the Canadian constitution would have been very different from what it turned out to be. In passing on the validity of an enactment of Parliament the courts would have had no alternative to ascertaining whether or not it encroached on provincial legislation as specified in Sections 92 and 93, and any provincial enactment would have had to be justified as coming within one of these Sections or Section 95. However, Section 91 went on to enact ". . . and for greater Certainty, but not so as to restrict the Generality of the foregoing Terms of this Section, it is hereby declared that . . . the exclusive Legislative Authority of the Parliament of Canada extends to all Matters coming within the Classes of Subjects next herein enumerated. . . ." There were then listed twenty-nine classes of subjects. There has never been a satisfactory explanation of why the framers of the Act resorted to such an enumeration. As we shall see, judicial interpretation from the late nineteenth century onward came to find the peacetime legislative powers of Parliament not in the authority to enact laws for the "Peace, Order, and Good Government of Canada", but rather in the enumerated headings of Section 91.

In terms of substance, most of the powers of the provinces can be subsumed under one or both of these classes of subjects: (1) those matters where the traditions of the English- and French-speaking communities of the former province of Canada differed significantly; (2) those matters which in British North America of the 1860s were usually the responsibility of local governments. Thus were included jurisdiction over education, what we would now call health and welfare matters, the control of provincial Crown lands and natural resources, municipal institutions, the administration of justice in the province, as well as concurrent powers with the Dominion over agriculture and immigration. The provinces were also given exclusive powers to legislate in respect to "Property and Civil Rights in the Province". From the Quebec Act of 1774 onward Quebec had been given the right to carry on the system of private law derived from France, and thus the provinces were given jurisdiction over property and civil rights so that the civil and common law traditions might continue in Quebec and the provinces with English-speaking majorities respectively.[7]

The powers conferred on the Dominion were deemed necessary to secure military defence, the eventual inclusion of all remaining British territories in North America within Canada and the establishment of an integrated national economy. Under the enumerated headings of Section 91 were included powers over trade and commerce; the various aspects of interprovincial transportation and communication; banking, currency, interest, and legal tender; patents and copyrights. As we have seen, Section 95 conferred concurrent powers on the Dominion and the provinces in respect to agriculture and immigration, with the proviso that federal laws should prevail in the event of a clash. Several Sections of the Act provided for the federal authorities taking action to include remaining British possessions in North America in the Dominion, e.g. Newfoundland, and the western territories still under the control of the Hudson's Bay Company. Parliament received the exclusive power to give legislative implementation to British treaties in Canada. The national authorities were to have exclusive powers over defence. Along with these nation-building and nation-maintaining powers, the exclusive authority to legislate in respect to the criminal law and to procedures in criminal matters was conferred on the Dominion, and the central government was given crucial responsibilities in respect to a unified judicial system.

In conferring what were then the most costly functions of government on the Dominion, the framers of the Confederation settlement provided that Parliament might raise moneys by "any Mode or System of Taxation" while the provinces were limited to direct taxes. The effect was to give the Dominion exclusive access to customs and excise duties, the sources of most public revenues at the time, while the provinces would be confined to taxes on real property, proceeds from the sale of Crown lands and the exploitation of natural resources and to incidental fees and revenues. The provinces were also to receive annual subsidies from the Dominion according to a schedule provided for in the British North America Act.

The B.N.A. Act provided for a single judicial system in Canada rather than, as in the United States, a dual system of courts dealing with national and state matters respectively. Although the Act seemed to contemplate that for the most part the Dominion and the provinces would carry on their respective legislative and administrative responsibilities in relative independence of each other, the judicial system was clearly expected to operate through cooperation between the two levels. The provinces were given exclusive jurisdiction over "The Administration of Justice in the province, including the Constitution, Maintenance, and Organization of Provincial Courts, both of Civil and Criminal Jurisdiction, and including Procedure in Civil Matters in these Courts". However, the Governor-General — in effect the federal cabinet — was to appoint the judges of the superior, district and county courts in each province, these judges were to be paid by the Dominion and were to serve during good behaviour, subject to removal by the Governor-General on an address from the Senate and House of Commons. Parliament was given exclusive authority to legislate in respect to the criminal law and to procedures in criminal matters. It was further provided in Section 101 "The Parliament of Canada may . . . provide for the Constitution, Maintenance, and Organization of a General Court of Appeal for Canada, and for the Establishment of any additional Courts for the better Administration of the Laws of Canada."

Beyond the provisions for the dominance of the Dominion in the ways which have already been outlined, the British North America Act went even further in its attempts to secure federal supremacy by making provision for circumstances under which the central authorities might restrict the provinces in the exercise of the latters' legislative powers:

— under Sections 55 and 90 the provinces were put in a position of colonial subordination to the Dominion executive (as was the central government in respect to the United Kingdom). The Lieutenant-Governor of a province, a Dominion officer, had the power to reserve provincial legislation and when this was done the bill did not become law unless the federal cabinet so decided. Whether reserved or not, any provincial law might be disallowed by the federal cabinet within a year of enactment.

— under Section 92 10(c) the Parliament of Canada was given the power to bring "Works" otherwise within provincial jurisdiction under federal control.

— under Section 93 the federal cabinet and Parliament were made the guarantors of the educational rights of denominational minorities against provincial encroachments. If such rights were overridden, the federal cabinet might take action but if this were ineffective, Parliament was given the power to enact remedial legislation to secure execution of the cabinet's orders.

The distribution of legislative powers made by the British North America Act of 1867 has been explicitly changed by constitutional amendment on only three occasions. In each case the effect was to provide for federal responsibility in the field of income-maintenance programs:

— in 1940 Parliament was given the exclusive legislative jurisdiction over unemployment insurance.

— in 1951 Parliament was given concurrent jurisdiction with the provinces in respect to old age pensions, with the proviso that "No law made by the Parliament of Canada in relation to old age pensions shall affect the operation of any law present or future of a Provincial Legislature in relation to old age pensions."

— in 1964 Parliament was given the power to enact legislation in respect to supplementary benefits to old age pensions, including survivors' and disability benefits, with the same provision as that of the 1951 amendment in respect to the paramountcy of provincial laws.

The Amendment of the British North America Act[8]

The amendment of a codified constitution is the most fundamental of political processes. Formal amendment is only one of the procedures of constitutional change, but as William S. Livingston points out, "It differs from the others in that it is superior to them and may be employed to transcend or repudiate any change that may be brought about by other means."[9] The failure of Canadians to agree on an amending procedure is the most obvious failure of their constitutional experience.

The British North America Act of 1867 did not specify an explicit procedure for its own amendment and the matter is mentioned only once in the Confederation Debates. It was undoubtedly taken for granted that the United Kingdom Parliament would be the amending authority but probably also, in the light of Canadian experience under the Act of Union,[10] that no amendment would be enacted without the request or consent of the Dominion. The procedure by which Canadian initiative would take place was not specified, perhaps because the Fathers of Confederation believed it unlikely they could come to agreement on such a procedure.

From Confederation until the period after the First World War the British North America Act was amended on several occasions by the Imperial Parliament at the request of Canada. However, no settled conventions developed to regulate the procedures within the Dominion for making such a request. Serious and protracted debates about a domestic amending procedure began only in the 1920s when Canada along with the other Dominions was on the verge of attaining full legal recognition of its self-governing status. However, when this development culminated in the enactment by the United Kingdom Parliament of the Statute of Westminster in 1931, it was provided at the request of the Canadian government that "Nothing in this Act shall be deemed to apply to the repeal, amendment or alteration of the British North America Acts, 1867 to 1930, or to any order, rule or regulation made thereunder." The federal and provincial governments had been unable to agree on an amending procedure.

A Dominion-Provincial Conference was called in 1935 and a sub-committee appointed to deal with a procedure for constitutional amendment. The Dominion and all the provinces except New Brunswick agreed that Canada should have the power to amend the constitution if a method satisfactory to all parties could be worked out. The desperate circumstances of the Great Depression soon halted even a desultory attempt to reach agreement. When the Royal Commission on Dominion-Provincial Relations was appointed in 1936 its terms of reference were limited to financial matters and did not include recommendations for an amending procedure.

In 1949 at the request of the Parliament of Canada the United Kingdom Parliament amended the British North America Act to provide the following:

1. The amendment from time to time of the Constitution of Canada, except as regards matters coming within the classes of subjects by this Act

assigned exclusively to the Legislatures of the provinces, or as regards rights or privileges by this or any other Constitutional Act granted or secured to the Legislature or the Government of a province, or to any class of persons with respect to schools or as regards the use of the English or the French language or as regards the requirements that there shall be a session of the Parliament of Canada at least once each year, and that no House of Commons shall continue for more than five years from the day of the return of the Writs for choosing the House: provided, however, that a House of Commons may in time of real or apprehended war, invasion or insurrection be continued by the Parliament of Canada if such continuation is not opposed by the votes of more than one-third of the members of such House.

The British North America Act (No. 2) of 1949 was enacted when the federal government dominated the provinces more than at any other peacetime period of Canadian history. In so bringing about this amendment without provincial consultation or consent the federal authorities undoubtedly wished to facilitate, or force, subsequent agreement with the provinces on an amending procedure. A Constitutional Conference took place in 1950.[11] There was unanimous agreement that the constitution should be divided into six categories with a different amending procedure for each. Subsequently in the same year, discussions were held to divide the constitution into these categories but no agreement could be reached and discussions lapsed.

The 1949 amendment was the assertion by the federal government of two principles:

First, it became part of the constitution that the Parliament of Canada might unilaterally determine its own structure, composition and functioning — apart from those restrictions provided for the 1949 amendment related to the two official languages, to annual sessions and to the five-year life of each House of Commons. Quebec had unsuccessfully challenged this principle in protesting a 1943 amendment providing for the postponement of a reapportionment of seats in the House of Commons until after the war and an amendment of 1946 changing the basis of representation in the House. The federal authorities defended the 1949 change on the basis that Parliament's power over its own form and operations was a corollary of Section 92(1) of the British North America Act which gave the provinces exclusive legislative authority to amend their own constitutions "except as regards the Office of Lieutenant-Governor".

Second, it had been established that the federal Parliament might without provincial consultation or consent determine the procedure by which the constitution was to be amended. Constitutional amendment is the most fundamental of political processes, and, of amendments, those which determine how future amendments are made are most crucial. The 1949 amendment was on the whole an embodiment of existing practice, and by exempting the most critical aspects of the constitution from Parliament's amending power it was still left open for future resolution to determine the procedures by which Ottawa and the provinces would be associated in amendments relating to these matters. However, in effecting the 1949 amendment the federal government alone had drawn the distinctions between those matters subject to amendment by the Parliament of Canada and those by the Parliament of the United Kingdom, with the latter category by convention — but by convention only — involving the unanimous consent of the provinces.

From 1960 onward there was a new round of federal-provincial discussions on an amending formula. These discussions culminated in October, 1964, in the agreement of all eleven governments on what was called the Fulton-Favreau Formula in recognition of the successive federal Ministers of Justice who had chaired the proceedings.[12] The proposed amending procedure was very complex and had the following basic elements:

(1) There was a "sign-off" provision by which no future statute of the United Kingdom would apply to Canada.

(2) The most crucial elements of the constitution were to be amendable only with the consent of Parliament and all the provincial legislatures — provincial legislative powers, the use of the English and French languages, denominational rights in education and the provisions of Section 51 A of the B.N.A. Act determining that a province would always have at least as many members of the House of Commons as Senators.

(3) Certain basic aspects of the structure and functioning of the Government of Canada required the concurrence of at least two-thirds of the provinces having together at least half the Canadian population. This category included provisions related to the Crown and its Canadian representative, the five-year limit on the duration of each House of Commons, the number of members from each province in the Senate and representation of the provinces proportionate to their respective populations in the House of Commons. Apart from these exceptions, Parliament had the exclusive authority to amend the constitution in respect to "the executive Government of Canada, and the Senate and House of Commons".

(4) The rigidities of the proposed amending formula as these related to the distribution of legislative powers were somewhat tempered by provision for the delegation of powers between the two levels by mutual consent. Any of the powers of Parliament might be delegated to the provinces providing Parliament and at least four provincial legislatures enacted similar laws in respect to these powers. Provincial powers over prison and reform institutions, local works and undertakings, property and civil rights and "Matters of a merely local or private Nature" might be delegated to Parliament so long as at least four provinces had so consented or all the provinces had been consulted and Parliament had declared that the matter was of concern to fewer than four.

It thus seemed by the mid-1960s that Canada was on the verge of adopting a wholly domestic procedure for constitutional amendment. However, in January, 1966, Premier Lesage of Quebec informed Prime Minister Pearson that, ". . . the government of Quebec has decided to delay indefinitely the proposal for constitutional amendment."[13] He gave as the reasons for this action conflicting interpretations within the province about the meaning and effect of the proposed procedure and the view that its adoption would make impossible the abolition of the Quebec Legislative Council or the curtailment of its powers without the consent of that body. The more important reason for the Quebec action was undoubtedly the political storm the Fulton-Favreau Formula had raised in the province, including the challenge of the opposition Union Nationale to fight an election on the issue. Quebec governments in the past had always insisted on a rigid amending procedure and Premier Lesage and his colleagues had made as their major defence of the proposed procedure that Ottawa and the provinces had never previously been willing to accept unanimous provincial consent for amendments involving the distribution of legislative powers. However, by the mid-1960s the prevailing currents of thought and policy in Quebec had come to reject constitutional conservatism and to assert that the province's interests required radical constitutional changes. From this latter perspective, the rigidities of the proposed amending procedure became for Quebec what the Leader of the Opposition in the province called "*une camisole de force*", a straight-jacket, in the sense that even the smallest of the provinces could frustrate Quebec's aspirations for change.

Up until late 1970 or early 1971 the Federal-Provincial Constitutional Conferences begun in 1968 did not address themselves to a formula for constitutional amendment. The position of the federal government appears to have been that because agreement had proved impossible on this procedural question in the past, it would be more expedient to press forward on reviewing the substantive content of the Canadian constitution. However, under pressure — apparently — from several of the provinces discussion was turned to an amending procedure at the Constitutional Conference of February, 1971, at Victoria, B.C. and the communiqué issued at the end of this meeting put forward a formula which the heads of government agreed was a "feasible approach". This formula in substantially the same form was embodied in the so-called "Charter" issuing from the Conference of June, 1971, and subsequently repudiated by Quebec.

Under the procedure of the Victoria Charter the most important parts of the Canadian constitution were to be amendable by resolution of the Senate and House of Commons and of at least a majority of the provinces which included:

(1) each province with a population at least 25 per cent of the population of Canada;

(2) at least two of the Atlantic provinces;

(3) at least two of the western provinces having together at least half the population of all the western provinces.

It was provided that the Parliament of Canada might unilaterally amend the constitution "in relation to the executive government of Canada and the Senate and House of Commons" and the provinces might as they chose amend their own constitutions. However, these provisions for unilateral action were qualified by a list of exceptions in

respect to which amendments could be made only by the combined action of Parliament and the provincial legislatures as outlined above:
(1) the offices of the Queen, Governor-General and Lieutenant-Governor;
(2) yearly sessions of Parliament and the provincial Legislatures;
(3) the five-year maximum life of Parliament and the provincial legislatures, subject to provisions contained elsewhere in the constitution for extending the life of those bodies under emergency circumstances;
(4) the powers of the Senate and the number of members to which provinces are entitled in the Senate;
(5) the right of each province to at least as many members of the House of Commons as Senators;
(6) the representation of provinces in the House of Commons proportionate to their population as elsewhere detailed in the constitution;
(7) constitutional privileges of the English and French languages.

The procedure issuing from Victoria thus diverged from both existing practice and the Fulton-Favreau Formula by not requiring unanimous provincial consent for the most important of amendments. Unlike the 1964 proposal, however, the proposed amending procedure did not provide for the inter-governmental delegation of legislative powers. As we shall see in the next chapter, the proposed change was part of a constitutional package rejected by Quebec. Thus for the time being Canadians are back to the 1949 amending procedure, with no immediate prospects of change.

Canada's Other Constitution: Emergency Powers [14]

The complex division of legislative powers between two levels of government which characterizes federalism is obviously inappropriate in times of domestic and international crisis. Contemporary federations make constitutional provisions for such emergencies in very different ways. [15] The Constitution of the United States contains very few and relatively specific provisions respecting emergencies and the late Clinton Rossiter has written of the American constitutional tradition in this respect. "The traditional theory of the Constitution is clearly hostile to the establishment of crisis institutions and procedures. It is constitutional dogma that this document foresees any and every emergency, and that no departure from its solemn injunctions could possibly be necessary." [16] At the other end of the spectrum the Constitution of India adopted in 1949 gave the federal executive sweeping powers to override the normal legislative powers of the states in cases of emergency caused by war, internal disturbances, the perceived inability of a state government to carry on its affairs in accordance with the Constitution and financial instability. These powers have been used by the national authorities on several occasions.

To return to the Canadian situation, the War Measures Act was enacted in August, 1914, and has since remained as a federal statute subject to being brought into effect by proclamation of the Governor-in-Council when, in his judgment, there exists "war, invasion, or insurrection, real or apprehended''. The Act gives the federal cabinet discretion not only to declare the coming into being of such an emergency but also its passing. When the Act is proclaimed in force the cabinet is given almost unlimited powers to cope with the situation, to give effect to its will through orders and regulations and to prescribe penalties for violations of such orders and regulations, with the limitation that no such penalty shall exceed a fine of five thousand dollars or imprisonment for five years or both fine and imprisonment. When the Canadian Bill of Rights was enacted in 1960 there were provisions to associate Parliament with the cabinet in respect to War Measures Act powers. Under the 1960 legislation the cabinet is required to lay a proclamation declaring an emergency before Parliament "forthwith" or "if Parliament is then not sitting, within the first fifteen days next thereafter that Parliament is sitting". Further, when a proclamation is laid before Parliament any ten members of either House can force a debate that the proclamation be revoked and if both Houses so decide actions of the cabinet taken under the Act cease to have future effect. Thus under emergency conditions as determined by the federal cabinet Canada becomes what Rossiter has called a "constitutional dictatorship", with the federal cabinet assuming many of the most important functions of Parliament and overriding the normal legislative jurisdiction of the provinces.

As interpreted by the courts, the constitutional justification of emergency powers lies in the general authority of Parliament to legislate for the "Peace, Order, and Good Government of Canada".[17] The national authorities may override provincial powers not only when international hostilities are in progress but also for a time after in dealing with the economic and other dislocations occasioned by the war. Further, "The length of time that an emergency may exist and hence relevant Dominion legislation may be upheld on emergency grounds is uncertain; but the question is essentially a political one and the courts are therefore very loath to question the decision of the Dominion Parliament on the length of the emergency period."[18] Canada was governed under emergency legislation during the First World War and afterward and also from 1939 to 1954 under the War Measures Act and subsequently under various federal emergency enactments of more limited scope.

Although the War Measures Act mentions insurrection, until the Quebec crisis of 1970 Canadians had almost universally regarded the Act within the framework of the country's involvement in international conflict. However, in the early morning hours of October 16 of that year the Act was proclaimed in force and the Public Order Regulations issued under its authority. The Regulations declared to be illegal Le Front de Libération du Québec, any successor organization or any group advocating force or crime as a means of accomplishing governmental change in Canada. There was specified a list of indictable offences for individuals who belonged to unlawful political associations, advocated force or crime to bring about political change or who gave assistance to such unlawful activities. Peace officers, including members of the Armed Forces, were given sweeping powers of search and arrest without warrants and at the discretion of the Attorney-General of a province a person might be detained up to twenty-one days before being charged with a specific offence under the Regulations. Prime Minister Trudeau gave this justification of the action of the federal cabinet:

> The first fact was there there had been kidnappings of two very important people in Canada and that they were being held for ransom under the threat of death. The second was that the government of the province of Quebec and the authorities of the city of Montreal asked the federal government to permit the use of exceptional measures because, in their own words, a state of apprehended insurrection existed. The third reason was our assessment of all the surrounding facts . . . the state of confusion that existed in the province of Quebec in regard to these matters.[19]

The Regulations were replaced by the Public Order Temporary Measures Act on December 3, 1970. The latter enactment shortened the period of detention without charge and required stronger proof of adherence to an unlawful political organization. Despite opposition from the government of Quebec, this Act lapsed on April 30, 1971, and Canada returned to a régime where illegal political activity was defined entirely by the normal processes of law. The War Measures Act remains, however, as a Canadian statute subject to proclamation by the Governor-in-Council.

The 1970 crisis was unique in Canadian constitutional theory and practice. Previously, emergency legislation in Canada had come into existence at the initiative of the federal government alone and had had the effect of overriding the normal legislative jurisdiction of the provinces. However, in 1970 the proclamation of the War Measures Act appears to have resulted from a common perception of the crisis by the federal, Quebec, and Montreal governments, and the Public Order Regulations enhanced the powers of the law enforcement authorities under the immediate control of the Attorney-General of Quebec. During the debates of the House of Commons Prime Minister Trudeau and his colleagues asserted again and again the exclusive responsibility of the Quebec government for the administration of justice in the province and refused to intervene in these matters. However, in its refusal to renew the Public Order Temporary Measures Act when it expired in 1971 the federal authorities in a sense re-asserted their power to determine what legislative powers were necessary for the effective control of subversion in Quebec.

It remains a matter of contention whether the suspension of the normal constitutional processes in the fall of 1970 was justified. Early in 1975 the Leader of the Opposition, Robert Stanfield, said that he "regretted" having supported the action of the government at the time. After a painstaking review of the public record, including the strength of the revolutionary forces in Quebec and the will of the revolutionaries to exploit those resources, John Gellner has concluded that the proclamation of emergency powers and the mobilization of the Armed Forces was unnecessary, "an act of political folly", which contributed to the polarization and radicalization of Quebec politics.[20] Only two convictions were obtained for offences under the Public Order Regulations and Public Order Act and in August 1971 the Attorney General of Quebec stayed proceedings against the thirty-two persons who still faced charges under the Act.[21] Supporters of the federal action assert that this response forestalled a potentially revolutionary situation in Quebec in the fall of 1970 and may have contributed to the subsequent decline of revolutionary violence in the province. Frank Scott put it in these terms: "A shock treatment was needed . . . it was given, and it worked."[22] This case rests on what might be called the need for therapeutic repression.

Human Rights and Canadian Federalism

The protection of human rights in Canada is related directly to federalism because jurisdiction over what are variously regarded as rights is divided by the British North America Act between Parliament and the provincial legislatures. Judicial decision has left several crucial aspects of this division unclear. Further, in the past generation there has been an influential body of thought and policy in Canada which argues that human rights can be effectively protected only by their further constitutional entrenchment.

The British North America Act of 1867 gave explicit protection to human rights only in respect to circumstances where a linguistic or religious group was in a minority position:
(1) Section 93 restricted the rights of provinces to encroach on the privileges of separate Roman Catholic and Protestant schools existing "by Law" at the time of union or subsequently so established.
(2) Section 133 provided that:

> Either the English or the French Language may be used by any Person in the Debates of the Houses of the Parliament of Canada and of the Houses of the Legislature of Quebec; and both those Languages shall be used in the respective Records and Journals of those Houses; and either of those Languages may be used by any Person or in any Pleading or Process in or issuing from any Court of Canada established under this Act, and in or from all or any of the Courts of Quebec.
>
> The Acts of the Parliament of Canada and of the Legislature of Quebec shall be printed and published in both those Languages.

(3) Various Sections protected the representation of the English-speaking minority in Quebec in Parliament and the Legislature of that province.[23]

Beyond these explicit recognitions of minority rights, the British North America Act was based on the principle of legislative supremacy qualified by a constitutional division of legislative powers. The protection of human rights was to rest on the traditional safeguards of the civil and common law systems as these safeguards were from time to time modified by enactments of Parliament and the provincial legislatures. Although there was a restricted entrenchment of human rights as such, there were significant constitutional prescriptions concerning the legislative bodies which would enact laws in respect to human rights and other matters.[24]

Judicial review of the Canadian constitution in respect to human rights has been dominated by what two writers of a recent text on constitutional law have called "the division of powers approach".[25] In this approach, what are variously regarded as human rights do not possess any independent constitutional value and when any federal or provincial enactment allegedly overriding such rights is subjected to judicial review the only relevant question to be decided by the courts is whether Parliament or the provincial legislature has trespassed on the powers of the other level. If it is determined that it did not, the legislation is valid even if it overrides the most fundamental of human rights.

The constitutional division of legislative powers over human rights is a complex and contentious matter whose elements are given here only in summary form.[26] Some of the most important of rights relating to arrest, detention and trial are squarely within Parliament's exclusive jurisdiction over the criminal law and criminal procedure, although in fact some of these rights may be qualified by practices of the provinces and their constituent municipalities in the processes of law enforcement and the administration of justice. Beyond the requirements of Section 133, Parliament and the provinces appear to have unlimited discretion in respect to linguistic rights as these relate to activities within the respective legislature powers of each level. Similarly, the national and provincial authorities are free as they wish to protect egalitarian rights of non-discrimination on the basis of sex, religion, race, national origin or other individual characteristics, as these relate to matters otherwise within these respective legislative powers.[27] The most contentious area relates to what Bora Laskin, now Chief Justice Laskin of the Supreme Court of Canada, calls "political civil liberty", whose substance is "freedom of association, freedom of assembly, freedom of utterance, freedom of the press (or of the use of other media for dissemination of news and opinion) and freedom of conscience and religion".[28] Laskin argues that these freedoms "are embraced by federal power to make laws for the peace, order, and good government of Canada which includes power to legislate in relation to the criminal law".[29] The contrary argument is that in part at least these liberties are within provincial jurisdiction over "property and civil rights".[30] Both the historical circumstances of Confederation and subsequent judicial interpretation of the British North America Act support the Laskin opinion. In 1867 the conferring of jurisdiction on the provinces over property and civil rights was meant to preserve the system of private law based on civil law principles in Quebec, and although Section 92(13) was subsequently interpreted by the courts to give the provinces extensive powers over economic matters, it cannot reasonably be used to justify provincial jurisdiction over political freedoms.[31]

From time to time some Canadian judges have attempted to break out of the seeming rigidities of the division of powers approach and to erect barriers to governments encroaching on human rights other than those of the jurisdiction of Parliament or the provinces as the case may be. The most important attempt in this direction has found in the preamble to the British North America Act an implied bill of rights. In *Reference re Alberta Statutes*[32] in 1938 an Alberta statute encroaching on freedom of the press was invalidated by the Supreme Court of Canada. In their opinions Duff, C. J. and Cannon, J. advanced the wholly unprecedented constitutional principle that because the preamble to the British North America Act stated that the colonies wished to be united with "a Constitution similar in Principle to that of the United Kingdom", provincial restrictions on rights essential to the workings of parliamentary government were invalid. This argument was used in several subsequent Supreme Court decisions striking down provincial legislation and in his *obiter* in the *Switzman*[33] case in 1954, Abbott, J. suggested that the preamble imposed similar restrictions on Parliament. It is significant, however, that in most of the opinions in which judges referred to the preamble of the 1867 Act as a restriction on provincial legislative power they also used more orthodox division-of-powers arguments, often that a province had encroached on Parliament's exclusive jurisdiction to legislate in respect to the criminal law.

Since the end of the Second World War Parliament and all the provinces have enacted legislation for the protection of human rights.[34] The most important of these statutes is the Canadian Bill of Rights of 1960.[35] Throughout his adult life Prime Minister Diefenbaker had been committed to the more effective protection of human rights and would clearly have preferred the entrenchment of such rights by a constitutional amendment binding on all governments in Canada. However, it appears to have been the judgment of the federal government that unanimous provincial consent for such an amendment could not be secured and the 1960 Bill of Rights applies only to matters otherwise within federal jurisdiction and can be altered or repealed by the same procedures as relate to other enactments of Parliament. The Bill of Rights affirms the existence of the traditional rights of religion, speech, assembly and the press; legal rights relating to arrest, trial and detention; and the right not to be discriminated against "by reason of race, national origin, colour, religion or sex". There were two contradictory directions in which the courts, and in particular the Supreme Court of Canada, could move in interpreting the meaning and effect of the Bill of Rights. The first was to regard it as only a guide to the interpretation of federal statutes which would not invalidate any enactment of Parliament unambiguously contrary to its terms. For almost a decade this interpretation appeared to be the authoritative one accepted by the Supreme Court.[36] However, in 1969 the Court by a 6-3 majority invalidated Section 94 (b) of the federal Indian Act which contained a harsher penalty for an Indian being intoxicated in a public place than for other citizens of the Northwest Territories where the particular offence occurred.[37] It was thus established that the Bill of Rights is a constitutional statute by whose provisions other federal legislation is to be measured and, if found wanting, invalidated.

For a generation there has been a strong current of influence pressing for the constitutional entrenchment of human rights in Canada. In the decade immediately after the Second World War this argument was often advanced in terms of Canada's alleged inability to fulfil its international obligations as a member of the United Nations without such entrenchment. This position is now less common. At the first Federal-Provincial Constitutional Conference of February, 1968, the federal government presented a comprehensive proposal for a constitutionally-entrenched Charter of what it classified as political, legal, egalitarian and linguistic rights.[38] In Ottawa's view, such a measure would not only give more effective safeguards but would also remove at one stroke the existing ambiguities of the division of legislative powers related to human rights. Subsequent discussions with the provinces soon made it apparent that no agreement was possible on entrenchment as extensive as that desired by Ottawa, and the Charter issuing from the Constitutional Conference of June, 1971 provided for much more limited safeguards, as we shall see in the next chapter.

Whether or not there is a further entrenchment of rights in the Canadian constitution, the question will remain in contention as to the extent to which courts should substitute their judgment for that of legislatures in the protection of human rights. In American terms, the issue is between judicial activism and judicial self-restraint. The recent textbook of Lyon and Atkey on Canadian constitutional law presents the case for activism in its most extreme form. These writers are impatient with the division-of-powers approach to constitutional review in respect to human rights. Their prescription is this: "If a fundamental rights issue is clearly perceived, a court should attempt to meet the issue head-on, and should be loathe to allow *any* level of government to deny this right through claims that it is merely acting within its proper sphere of legislative jurisdiction."[39] Lyon and Atkey are not very precise as to how courts would rationalize decisions reached on this basis, although it may be conjectured that a heavy reliance would be placed on the implied restrictions on federal and provincial legislative power in the preamble to the British North America Act. The Report of the Ontario Royal Commission of Inquiry into Civil Rights published in 1969 contains the most sophisticated argument that has ever been made in Canada on behalf of legislative supremacy in the determination of human rights.[40] Part of the McRuer Commission's argument is that in terms of democratic theory legislatures have a better claim than courts to make the final and authoritative decisions about rights. Further, the courts of law suffer from certain institutional disabilities and the Report thus states what it believes the appropriate role of the judiciary to be:

> In the judicial process, typical judicial law-making in response to the need for social change is interstitial. Cases are dealt with as they arise, proceeding gradually from precedent to precedent. In the modern world this is a valuable and necessary supplement to the primary legislative

process; but the judicial system being interstitial so far as innovation is concerned, assumes that the main rules have been provided by the customs of the people (in older times) or by ordinary statutes (in modern times). Without these there would be no interstices — no gaps to be filled by sensible judicial adjustment and innovation.[41]

It must be emphasized that the dispute between proponents of judicial activism and judicial restraint in the protection of human rights remains whether or not there is a further entrenchment of rights in the Canadian constitution. The 1960 Bill of Rights preserves the principle of legislative supremacy in that Parliament retains the powers to amend or abolish the Bill as it chooses and to enact laws explicitly overriding such rights as are there specified, and it is also provided that when the War Measures Act is in effect nothing done under its authority shall be deemed an "abrogation, abridgment or infringment of any right or freedom recognized by the Canadian Bill of Rights". However, in causing the Bill to be enacted it was the intention of Prime Minister Diefenbaker and his government that the courts would invalidate federal legislation which in their judgment did not meet with the Bill's prescriptions, and the *Drybones* judgment a decade later established the Bill of Rights as a constitutional statute. Yet *Drybones* posed a clear-cut circumstance where racial discrimination was sanctioned by law. Subsequent cases have involved the clash of priorities which are more plausibly defensible and in most of these cases the majority of the Court has refused to overturn federal legislation or challenge the discretion of officials operating under federal law.[42]

Judicial Review of the Canadian Constitution

The British North America Act of 1867 did not provide explicitly for judicial review, i.e., the procedure by which judicial bodies determine the validity of legislative enactments or executive acts in terms of their compatibility or otherwise with the terms of a codified constitution. The domestic constitutional system of the United Kingdom did not include such a procedure since the Crown in Parliament was sovereign and there could be no legal challenge to its will. From the early days of the British Empire, however, it had been customary to allow appeals to the Crown against enactments of colonial legislatures and the procedures for such appeals had been formalized with the recognition by Imperial statute of the Judicial Committee of the Privy Council in 1833.[43] As Peter Russell has pointed out, the power of the courts to pass on the validity of Canadian legislation in the early years of Confederation "might have been as much a corollary of imperialism as of federalism".[44] The British North America Act was an Imperial statute and according to the Colonial Laws Validity Act of 1865 enactments of colonial legislatures were invalid if they conflicted with those of the United Kingdom. However, as it happened, judicial review of the British North America Act did not evolve as an instrument for securing Imperial influence in Canadian affairs but rather as a practical device for delineating the respective legislative powers of Parliament and the provinces.

Until the abolition of appeals to this body by an act of the Canadian Parliament in 1949, the Judicial Committee of the Privy Council was the final appellate authority in interpreting the Canadian constitution. The Judicial Committee was composed of members of the House of Lords usually named to the Committee because of their distinguished judicial backgrounds.

There is a vast literature of analysis and criticism of the work of the Judicial Committee in reviewing the British North America Act[45] and its general directions in interpreting the Act are here summarized in very brief form. After the mid-1890s the dominant trends of judicial interpretation by the Committee worked in the following directions:

— the general power of Parliament to legislate for the "Peace, Order, and Good Government of Canada" was interpreted restrictively. Thus in most circumstances federal enactments had to be justified as coming within one of the enumerated powers of Section 91.

— the power of Parliament to legislate in respect to "Trade and Commerce" was interpreted restrictively. The United States Supreme Court has found in the power of Congress to regulate interstate commerce a very wide scope for national control over economic matters but the dominant Canadian tradition of interpreting the trade and commerce power has been otherwise.

— the exclusive power of the provinces to legislate in respect to "Property and Civil Rights" was interpreted broadly. In respect to economic matters this became the *de facto* residual power of the constitution.

In *Re Regulation and Control of Aeronautics* in 1932, Lord Sankey speaking for the Judicial Committee thus summarized "four propositions"[46] about the division of legislative powers which had been developed through previous decisions of that body:

(1) The legislation of the Parliament of the Dominion, so long as it strictly relates to subjects of legislation expressly enumerated in Section 91, is of paramount authority, even though it trenches upon matters assigned to the provincial legislatures by Section 92.

(2) The general power of legislation conferred upon the Parliament of the Dominion by Section 91 of the Act in supplement of the power to legislate upon the subjects expressly enumerated must be strictly confined to such matters as are unquestionably of national interest and importance, and must not trench on any of the subjects enumerated in Section 92, as within the scope of provincial legislation, unless these matters have attained such dimensions as to affect the body politic of the Dominion.

(3) It is within the competence of the Dominion Parliament to provide for matters which, though otherwise within the competence of the Provincial Legislature, are necessarily incidental to effective legislation by the Parliament of the Dominion upon a subject of legislation expressly enumerated in Section 91.

(4) There can be a domain in which Provincial and Dominion legislation may overlap, in which neither legislation will be *ultra vires* if the field is clear, but if the field is not clear and the two legislations meet, the Dominion legislation must prevail.

Three decisions by the Judicial Committee in 1937 denied the federal government the powers which many thoughtful Canadians believed necessary to deal with the social and economic circumstances of the Great Depression.

— three enactments of Parliament in 1935 dealing with minimum wages, the limitation of working hours and a weekly day of rest in industrial undertakings were declared invalid. This legislation was declared to be within provincial jurisdiction over property and civil rights.[47] In justifying this legislation the federal authorities had asserted that it was in fulfilment of international obligations accepted by Canada as a member of the International Labour Organization. The Judicial Committee denied this claim, and asserted the important principle that Parliament did not acquire any legislative power it would not otherwise have had by virtue of Canada as such incurring an international obligation.

— the Judicial Committee declared *ultra vires* federal legislation providing for the regulation of the marketing of natural products through a national Board.[48] The Committee found the legislation to be an encroachment on property and civil rights because it dealt in part with intra-provincial trade in natural products.

— the Judicial Committee struck down a national scheme of unemployment insurance.[49] Again the major grounds were that federal legislation encroached on provincial jurisdiction over property and civil rights.

There was what one might call a counter-tradition of interpretation by the Judicial Committee which found in Parliament's power to legislate for the "Peace, Order, and Good Government of Canada" an independent source of legislative authority.[50] Although from the mid-1890s onward this was not the prevailing tradition, from time to time it did allow Dominion legislation to be upheld on the grounds that some matter could be dealt with only by the national government. By reliance on the general power, Parliament and the federal cabinet were permitted to override the legislative jurisdiction of the provinces in the two World Wars and to deal with the economic and other dislocations occasioned by international conflict after hostilities had ended. In other circumstances the Judicial Committee was able to find justification in the general power for federal legislation regulating the sale of alcoholic beverages and broadcasting and for the incorporation of companies with Dominion objects.

Until the past few years at least it has been the conventional wisdom in English Canada to be critical of the work of the Judicial Committee in interpreting the Canadian constitution. There have been two currents of criticism. The first asserts that according to the rules of statutory interpretation accepted in the Anglo-Canadian tradition, the Judicial Committee misinterpreted the clear meaning of the British North America Act. The most exhaustive argument along these lines was made in a Report of the Parliamentary Counsel of the Senate, William F. O'Connor, published in 1939.[51] On the basis of a thorough review of Canadian constitutional experience up to and including the events surrounding Confederation, O'Connor concluded that the framers of the British North America Act had clearly embodied a scheme for the distribution of legislative powers in its terms. However, from 1896 onward this scheme had been repealed by "judicial legislation". O'Connor proposed that this situation be righted by a constitutional amendment which would in effect direct the judicial authorities to interpret the B.N.A. Act by the normal legal rules. The second line of criticism has come from the judicial activists.[52] According to this kind of argument, the normal rules of statutory interpretation are not in themselves adequate guides to courts in reviewing a constitution. Judicial review is inevitably a policy-making role, and in performing it judges should explicitly take into account their own considered views of the basic nature of the polity and its needs, and the social and other contexts of the matters before them. Within this formulation, the tradition of "black letter" statutory interpretation followed by the Judicial Committee was inadequate in resolving some of the basic problems of Canadian life. The criticisms based on technical standards of statutory interpretation and on the perspectives of the judicial activists were in a logical sense contradictory, although some detractors of the Privy Council supported both at once. The two streams of criticism were in agreement, however, in their general conclusion that the powers of the Dominion had been unduly restricted and those of the provinces unduly expanded by the Judicial Committee.[53]

The Judicial Committee has of course had its supporters. Using a highly technical approach, a 1967 book by G. P. Browne has attempted a refutation of the O'Connor argument that the Judicial Committee deviated from the normal rules of statutory interpretation in review of the British North America Act.[54] Among French-speaking scholars it has been argued that the result of the Judicial Committee's work was to recognize in a prudent and basically statesmanlike way the pervasive cultural and other particularisms of Canadian life. In a 1951 article Louis-Phillipe Pigeon, now Mr. Justice Pigeon of the Supreme Court of Canada, defended the way the B.N.A. Act has been interpreted in these terms:

> A great volume of criticism has been heaped upon the Privy Council and the Supreme Court on the ground that their decisions rest on a narrow and technical construction of the B.N.A. Act. This contention is ill-founded. The decisions on the whole proceed from a much higher view. As appears from passages I have quoted, they recognize the implicit fluidity of any constitution by allowing for emergencies and by resting distinctions on matters of degree. At the same time they firmly uphold the fundamental principle of provincial autonomy: they staunchly refuse to let our federal constitution be changed gradually, by one device or another, to a legislative union. In doing so they are preserving the essential condition of the Canadian confederation.[55]

Pierre Elliott Trudeau put the same view pithily in 1964. "It has long been a custom in English Canada to denounce the Privy Council for its provincial bias; but it should perhaps be considered that if the law lords had not moved in this direction, Quebec separatism might not be a threat today: it might be an accomplished fact."[56] A distinguished English Canadian scholar of the constitution, G.F.G. Stanley, assented to the Pigeon-Trudeau viewpoint in 1969:

> The decisions handed down by their Lordships of the Judicial Committee set the pattern of our constitution for over seventy years. Uninfluenced by local sympathies or party affiliations they set out conscientiously to maintain the true federal character of Canada and to resist the encroachments of the Federal Parliament upon the powers of the Provincial Legislature and *vice versa*. The Judicial Committee, by its careful and unprejudiced approach to Canadian problems, lessened the political dangers of excessive centralization and preserved that federalism which is the distinctive feature of our country.[57]

Both critics and supporters of the Judicial Committee appear to have exaggerated its importance in determining the shape of Canadian federalism. By the end of the nineteenth century several important developments other than judicial review had worked toward enhancing the strength and independence of the provinces — the parliamentary enactment of 1873 ending joint membership in Parliament and the provincial legislatures; the emergence of strong provincial leaders and parties able and willing to challenge the dominance of the Dominion; the adverse economic circumstances of 1873 onward which denied the federal government some of the legitimacy it might otherwise have had; the failure of the Dominion authorities to give effective aid to the educational minorities in the provinces when the privileges of these minorities were challenged by provincial action; and the election in 1873 and again in 1896 of federal Liberal governments more sympathetic to provincial sensibilities than the Conservatives they displaced. Thus it can plausibly be argued that the Judicial Committee's decisions in 1896 and soon after did little more than give retroactive recognition to the underlying particularisms of Canadian life which the framers of the Confederation settlement had too sanguinely believed would yield to the integrative thrust of the Dominion power.

The context of the Privy Council decisions of the 1930s restricting federal jurisdiction is perhaps more complex, and the most vigorous line of Canadian criticism of the Judicial Committee appears to date from this decade rather than before. Critics of the Judicial Committee's work during this decade have sometimes argued as if all right-thinking Canadians recognized the need for a significant extension of federal powers to meet the desperate circumstances of the Great Depression. The Canadian electorate, however, seems to have been more divided on the relative powers appropriate to the federal and provincial authorities. The Bennett government, whose major "New Deal" reforms were overturned by the Judicial Committee, sustained one of the most decisive defeats in Canadian history in the general election of 1935, dropping from the 1930 results from 137 to 40 seats in the House of Commons and from 48.8 per cent to 29.6 per cent of the popular vote. The incoming Liberal government was significantly more hesitant than its predecessor in asserting federal power. Also, the 1930s brought into office strong provincial leaders devoted to provincial autonomy —

Aberhart in Alberta, Duplessis in Quebec, Hepburn in Ontario, Macdonald in Nova Scotia and Pattullo in British Columbia. J.R. Mallory argued in a book published in 1954 that throughout the history of judicial review of the Canadian constitution the courts, and of course the Judicial Committee, had stood against the public regulation of economic activity by both the Dominion *and* the provinces.[58] Thus, "The plea of *ultra vires* has become the automatic litigious response to attempts by governments to regulate economic life, just as the due process clause was employed for a similar purpose in the United States."[59] Mallory described the 1920s and 1930s this way: "The paralyzing effect of judicial interpretation on the Canadian constitution in the years between the wars was a reflection of the continuing indecision of the Canadian people. For much as an increase in the activity of the state was demanded by a large section of the population, the same measure was bitterly contested by other groups who stood to gain more by the old equilibrium than by the new. Thus every halting step in the direction of satisfying collective wants was transferred into a debate on constitutional first principles."[60]

As Alan C. Cairns has pointed out, the Judicial Committee had several weaknesses as the final appellate body in Canadian constitutional cases.[61] It was isolated "from the scene in which its judgements applied". There was the absence in Canada of a sophisticated tradition of critical jurisprudence. The Judicial Committee's decisions were expressed as single opinions and the absence of dissents "hindered the development of a dialogue over the quality of its judgements". But its most important weakness in Cairns' view was the legal doctrine which ostensibly guided its decisions. This doctrine directed the judicial authorities "to eschew considerations of policy and to analyze the BNA Act by the standard canons for the technical construction of other statutes". However, ". . . it is self evident that no technical analysis of an increasingly ancient constitutional document can find answers to questions undreamt of by the Fathers."[62] The result was the concealment of the real grounds for many of the Judicial Committee's most important decisions and the masking of the actual policy choices it made "behind the obfuscating language and precedents of statutory interpretation".

Until 1949 the Supreme Court of Canada was very much subordinate to the Privy Council in judicial review of the constitution. A large number of cases from provincial courts went directly on appeal to the latter body and bypassed the Supreme Court: in 1938 such appeals had outnumbered those from the Supreme Court by 329 to 198.[63] The Supreme Court also believed itself rigidly bound by the precedents of the Judicial Committee. As Bora Laskin wrote, "As Privy Council decisions multiplied, the Supreme Court became engrossed in merely expanding the authoritative pronouncements of its superior. The task of the Supreme Court was not to interpret the constitution but rather to interpret what the Privy Council said the constitution meant."[64]

Since it became the final appellate court in Canada, the Supreme Court has shown some disposition to give a more extended scope to federal power than was so in the dominant tradition of constitutional interpretation bequeathed by the Privy Council.[65] In a few cases the Court has resorted to the minor tradition which finds in "Peace, Order, and Good Government" an independent source of Parliament's peacetime legislative power. Also, in a few cases the Court has been willing to give a somewhat more generous interpretation than did the Judicial Committee of Parliament's power to legislate in respect to trade and commerce. There have, however, been relatively few decisions under these two headings mentioned above. The Supreme Court in no case has turned its back explicitly on precedents established by the Judicial Committee. The Court has on occasion, however, shown some tendency to attenuate the positivistic tradition of constitutional interpretation which dominated the Privy Council. W.R. Lederman has lucidly summarized the two different ways in which courts may approach judicial review. ". . . there are principally two types of interpretation — literal or grammatical interpretation emphasizing the words found in statutes and constitutional documents — and, sociological interpretation which insists that constitutional words and statutory words must be carefully linked by judicially noticed knowledge and by evidence to the ongoing life of society."[66] Judicial review of the Canadian constitution has been predominantly in the first tradition, but in a tentative and hesitant way the Supreme Court of Canada since 1949 has come to accept some of the perspectives of the second.

In the post-1945 period judicial review has played a less important part in shaping the Canadian federal system than was the case in the earlier history of Confederation. There have been several factors at work. J.A. Corry suggested in 1958 that the business elites in Canada had come to think in national terms and to find fewer incentives than before to press legal challenges to federal power.[67] F.R. Scott in 1961 pointed out the influence of new kinds of fiscal policies on the way that powers were distributed between Ottawa and the provinces:

> From the time of its economic proposals in 1945, the federal government became committed to a policy of high and stable levels of employment and income. Keynes became kind of a post-natal Father of Confederation. . . The emergence of fiscal and monetary policy as economic regulators has become so important a factor today as almost to make us forget the question of legislative jurisdiction. It seems to have by-passed Sections 91 and 92 of the B.N.A. Act. The lawyers are moving out and the economists are moving in. Since Ottawa has the most money, and exclusive control of banking and currency, the fiscal approach restores federal influence though no new judgements are forthcoming from the courts to enlarge federal jurisdiction.[68]

From Quebec has come a series of direct challenges to the legitimacy of the Supreme Court of Canada as the final appellate tribunal in constitutional matters. The dominant argument here is that because the Court operates entirely under federal law, and because its members are appointed by the federal cabinet, a neutral and objective interpretation of the constitution is impossible. After an exhaustive review of this kind of criticism Peter Russell concluded, ". . . this viewpoint . . . has been sustained, not by any tangible evidence that members of the Supreme Court are biased in favour of the level of government which appointed them, but by an objection in principle to the constitutional arbitration by a tribunal which is organically part of the federal level of government."[69] Other Quebec arguments, usually advanced less urgently, point to the lack of bilingual capacity of the Court and its staff and the alleged dilution of the civil law when cases involving that legal system are decided by a Court composed of a majority of judges from the common law tradition.

In his *Judicial Review of Legislation in Canada*, published in 1968, Barry L. Strayer made a thoughtful and moderate case for an enhanced role for the courts in "the maintenance of the federal system".[70] The judiciary should broaden the grounds of judicial standing so that it is easier for individuals and groups to establish that they have a sufficiently direct interest in a matter to be litigants. The Supreme Court of Canada might without breaking directly with the rule of precedent become more creative in distinguishing amoung precedents as evolving circumstances so require. The courts should in constitutional decisions "take more cognizance of the world of facts" and broaden the grounds of admissible evidence to include an examination of the economic and social contexts of the matters before them. Such directions could be taken without any dramatic breaks with the past in an evolving recognition by the courts that inflexible adherence to the ordinary rules of statutory interpretation is not completely adequate to judicial review of the constitution.

Paul Weiler's *In the Last Resort: A Critical Study of the Supreme Court of Canada* published in 1974[71] presents a highly original argument that the Court has not played and cannot play a useful role as the "umpire of Canadian federalism". In Weiler's view the cases that characteristically come before the courts in this connection are essentially social, economic and political in nature, and he believes that they cannot be dealt with appropriately by the normal processes of statutory interpretation. In federal countries the original compromise as embodied in the constitution is usually a fairly accurate reflection of the common understandings of the time. Yet as these understandings are displaced over time and as new and unforeseen circumstances arise the constitution must somehow be adapted. The courts do not play a very useful part in this and their ongoing elaboration of what is essentially "a new federal scheme" is masked by the mistaken notion that they are interpreting a stable constitutional law. From his examination of the Court's decisions in constitutional cases between 1950 and 1972 Weiler argues that there has been no development of stable and coherent legal principles, that in effect the judicial umpire has made up the rules as the game proceeded. Such matters are better resolved by federal-provincial negotiation and, in using the analogy of industrial relations, the argument is made that genuine bargaining is often frustrated when the parties have final resort to arbitration. Weiler counsels that the judges of the Supreme Court "should be fully aware of the political desirability of judicial restraint in the area of federalism". He also recommends that no private litigant have the right to mount a challenge in the courts on the grounds that a federal or provincial law trespasses on the jurisdiction of the other level of government. There would remain those circumstances, presumably rare, where federal and provincial laws impose contradictory obligations on individuals or groups. However, even in these situations judicial discretion would be removed by resort to the paramountcy rule that federal legislation should prevail.

It is difficult to judge with any assurance whether or not the Supreme Court of Canada will come to have a more important part than in the recent past in umpiring Canadian federalism. Between 1950 and 1972 inclusive the Court rendered 84 decisions on the federal-provincial division of legislative powers and such matters continue to come before the Court at the relatively steady rate of 3 to 4 each year.[72] In a 1974 essay G. Bruce Doern and V. Seymour Wilson suggest that the increasing importance of "regulatory issues and regulatory legislation" in federal-provincial relations as against fiscal matters and "big-spending joint programmes" may "involve the courts relatively more often than we have been accustomed to in the recent past."[73] Legislation enacted by Parliament in late 1974 clearly contemplates a more important role for the Supreme Court of Canada in shaping Canadian law. One of these amendments removed the automatic right to appeal to the Court in civil cases where the amount in issue was more than $10,000. Another gave the Court wide discretion to hear appeals from other courts when in the opinion of the former body important issues of law or of fact were involved. And it may be that as the scope of public regulation is extended, more litigants than in the recent past will be disposed to mount judicial challenges to federal or provincial legislation. It is also at least possible that the courts themselves will remove some of the present limitations on judicial standing and thus make it easier for private persons and groups to establish themselves as litigants in constitutional as well as other cases. However, it seems probable that the federal and provincial governments will continue in most circumstances to deal with their conflicts by negotiation rather than judicial review. In none of the 84 constitutional cases between 1950 and 1972 was a federal law declared invalid, although in 20 cases provincial laws were overturned.[74] This circumstance may in itself dissuade the provinces from looking to the courts in defence of what they regard as their rights.

The Flexible Constitution[75]

In a developed federal system the relation between the constitution as judicially interpreted and the operation of the federal system is extraordinarily complex. As we have seen, the Canadian constitution during the past generation has proved somewhat resistant to change through amendment and evolving patterns of judicial review. However, the constitution has demonstrated flexibility in other directions. It has not unduly frustrated federal-provincial collaboration. It has sustained several areas of de *facto* concurrency where either or both levels can find jurisdiction to act when they desire to do so. Through various devices the national government in the years after the Second World War was able to overcome the apparent constitutional impasse of the 1930s and to dominate the federal system. From the late 1950s onward provincialist trends set in, and Canada has evolved as one of the most decentralized federations now in existence. The influences toward national supremacy and subsequently toward the reassertion of provincial powers were overwhelmingly a result of the joint and unilateral action of the federal and provincial governments. Although this statement is subject to minor qualifications, it can be said that the constitution as judicially interpreted contributed to this development only in a negative way by not erecting insurmountable barriers to what governments wanted to do, either unilaterally or by mutual action.

It is, however, prudent not to underemphasize the influence of the constitution as interpreted by the courts in determining the shape of Canadian federalism. The Confederation settlement as embodied in the B.N.A. Act of 1867 delineated some of the most important features of the continuing federation, and the years in which judicial review was more crucial than more recently in delineating the respective powers of the two levels of government have contributed important influences to our present circumstances. I wrote in 1961, "The federal aspects of the Canadian constitution, using the latter term in its broadest sense, have come to be less what the courts say they are than what the federal and provincial Cabinets and bureaucracies in a continuous series of formal and informal relations have determined them to be."[76] This statement is somewhat of an exaggeration and W.R. Lederman has wisely pointed out:

> . . . the text of the federal constitution as authoritatively interpreted in the courts remains very important. It tells us who can act in any event. In other words, constitutionally it must always be possible in a federal country to ask and answer the question — What happens if the federal and provincial governments do not agree about a particular measure of cooperative action? Then which government and legislative body has power to do what? And even though federal-provincial agreement on some matter may come at the end of difficult negotiations, the question and answer just referred to will have influenced the result because the answer is a primary element in defining the bargaining power of the federal government on the one hand and the provincial governments on the other.[77]

Lederman points out that in the periodic renegotiation of the federal-provincial taxation agreements Ottawa has usually been able to get its way, partly because under the constitution "the federal taxing power is a much more potent instrument than the taxing power of a province", and that in the Canada-Quebec bargaining about contributory retirement pensions in the mid-1960s Quebec's ability to make its will prevail was based on Section 94A of the B.N.A. Act, which provides for the paramountcy of provincial powers in respect to old age pensions.

A federal distribution of legislative power as interpreted by the courts may either facilitate or frustrate cooperation between two levels of government. The 1937 decision of the Judicial Committee in striking down the federal National Products Marketing Act of 1934 provides a dramatic illustration of the obstruction of intergovernmental collaboration by judicial review.[78] The public regulation of the marketing of natural products in Canada has thrown up a difficult constitutional problem, because to be effective the grading must take place at a point in the productive process where it is in practice impossible to tell what part will be channelled into extra-provincial trade, and thus come under federal jurisdiction, and what will be sold and consumed in the provinces where it was produced.[79] The 1934 enactment setting up a national board to deal with all transactions in natural products was the result of a joint attempt by Ottawa and the provinces to overcome this constitutional hurdle. In invalidating this legislation Lord Atkin in delivering the judgment of the Judicial Committee said:

> The Board were given to understand that some of the Provinces attach much importance to the existence of marketing schemes such as might be set up under this legislation: and their attention was called to the existence of Provincial legislation setting up Provincial schemes for various Provincial products. It was said that as the Provinces and the Dominion between them possess a totality of complete legislative authority, it must be possible to combine Dominion and Provincial legislation so that each within its own sphere could in co-operation with the other achieve the complete power of regulation which is desired. Their Lordships appreciate the importance of the desired aim. Unless and until a change is made in the respective legislative functions of Dominion and Province it may well be that satisfactory results for both can only be obtained by co-operation. But the legislation will have to be carefully framed, and will not be achieved by either party leaving its own sphere and encroaching upon that of the other. In the present case their Lordships are unable to support the Dominion legislation as it stands. They will therefore humbly advise His Majesty that this appeal should be dismissed.[80]

Despite Lord Atkin's references to the possibilities of federal-provincial cooperation in the marketing of natural products, it might well have proved impossible with even the most ingenious of legislative drafting to provide for a joint scheme which met the Privy Council's test.

In the past generation the flexibility of the federal system has been enormously enhanced by the exercise of the power of the national government to lend and spend in respect to matters within the legislative jurisdiction of the provinces.[81] Although it is possible — although perhaps not likely — that the courts will in the future impose limitations on the federal spending power, the present constitutional position is that this power is subject only to the following restrictions, none of which is of great practical importance.

(1) So far as a matter within provincial jurisdiction is concerned, the failure of individuals or groups to conform to the conditions of eligibility for federal largesse cannot be made an offence in federal law.

(2) Parliament may not finance a program within provincial jurisdiction partly or wholly from the proceeds of a levy made for that specific purpose.

(3) The national authorities may not under the guise of the spending power set up what is in essence a regulatory scheme encroaching on provincial jurisdiction.[82]

The federal spending power has been used for purposes as diverse as providing a national system of family allowances, collaborating with the provinces in building the Trans-Canada Highway, giving financial assistance to universities and cultural groups and supporting comprehensive provincial plans of hospital and medical insurance.

A second procedure making for flexibility is the inter-delegation of powers between the federal government and the provinces. In 1950 the Supreme Court of Canada denied the constitutionality of a proposed Nova Scotia enactment providing that the province might delegate its legislative powers concerning labour relations under Section 92 to the Parliament of Canada.[83] However, in 1952 the Court decided that it was valid for one level to delegate its powers to administrative bodies created under the legislative authority of the other.[84] As the exercise of the federal spending power provides a measure of constitutional flexibility where large public expenditures are involved, so delegation mitigates the rigidities of the division of legislative powers in respect to public regulation. This device has been employed in the regulation of the marketing of natural products and interprovincial motor transport.

Flexibility in a federal system may be furthered not only by the facilitation of intergovernmental collaboration but also by procedures which permit the level of government which develops more urgency than the other about particular aspects of public policy to take action in such matters. The most explicit of procedures here is for the constitution to vest certain concurrent powers in both levels with provisions determining which is to prevail in the event of a clash. Under the Canadian constitution such concurrency is limited to agriculture, immigration, and old age pensions; and both Parliament and the provinces may levy direct taxes. However, there are now several other areas of jurisdiction which are *de facto* concurrent, in the sense that either or both levels may find jurisdiction to act when this is deemed expedient.[85] The exercise of the spending power can be and has been used not only to facilitate federal-provincial collaboration, but also to provide for unilateral federal action in respect to matters within provincial jurisdiction, as in the case of family allowances and financial assistance for cultural and scientific development. In public regulation either or both levels can find jurisdiction in respect to environmental pollution, credit-granting institutions, insurance, driving offences, the sale of securities and various aspects of consumer protection. The exercise of the criminal law power may yet prove to be the most effective device by which the national authorities can involve themselves in regulatory activities otherwise partly or exclusively within provincial jurisdictions. Under this justification Parliament has already enacted legislation prohibiting the adulteration of food products, measures in restraint of competition, certain labour practices and particular actions which pollute the natural environment. Although the courts have not yet fixed the boundaries of the criminal law power, it is even possible that this power could be used to give constitutional validity to a federal scheme of either comprehensive or selective controls over prices and wages in peacetime.

There are prices to be paid for constitutional flexibility. It weakens the accountability of governments to their respective legislatures and electorates, and gives politicians plausible constitutional justifications for their failure to act when public action is clearly required. Provinces or regions which are, or believe themselves to be, in a permanent minority position in national affairs can be expected to be anxious when in relation to many important matters their actual position is determined not so much by the constitution as judicially interpreted but by their own political bargaining power — and in relative terms the procedures of flexibility give Ottawa more scope for encroaching on provincial responsibilities than the reverse. Before he entered elective politics, Pierre Elliott Trudeau wrote the most trenchant criticism of flexibility in the Canadian federal system that has ever been made.[86] He said in 1961 that "whenever an important segment of the Canadian population needs something badly enough, it is eventually given to them by one level of government or the other, regardless of the constitution."[87] The main drawback of this circumstance according to Trudeau was that "it tends to develop paternalistic instincts in more enterprising governments, at the expense of democratic maturation in others."[88] Thus if one level finds that it cannot discharge its responsibilities the better remedy is to seek an explicit transfer of jurisdiction through constitutional amendment. Although he and Trudeau were fundamentally opposed in their prescriptions for Canadian federalism, the late Daniel Johnson, while Leader of the Opposition in Quebec, also opposed the flexible nature of the Canadian federal system when he wrote in 1965:

> Au lieu d'une véritable constitution, nous avons un régime mouvant, qui est constamment en mutation et qui est le produit des accords formels ou tacites entre Ottawa et la majorité des provinces.[89]

The Canadian constitution has proved a very flexible instrument in the sense that Canadians have been able to effect very great changes within its framework in the absence of any abrupt breaks with the past. Whether it continues to meet contemporary needs is a matter of dispute. Efforts toward constitutional revision and review are the subject of the next chapter.

An Example: Constitutional Flexibility and Education

Constitutional flexibility, as the term was used in this chapter, manifests itself in its most fully developed form in respect to educational activities in Canada. Section 93 of the British North America Act of 1867 gives the provinces exclusive legislative jurisdiction over education, subject to safeguards for the rights of denominational minorities. However, apart from these denominational rights there has been almost no authoritative definition by the courts about what education means, and in particular what activities of a broadly educational kind the federal government may validly undertake. For the most part the provinces with English-speaking majorities have not been much exercised about such involvement and have in most cases been willing to tolerate and even to welcome Ottawa's educational involvements, although in recent years Ontario has held strong views about its control over educational television. However, it is understandable that dominant currents of thought and policy in Quebec have been otherwise inclined.

In a speech made in 1966, when he was Minister without Portfolio in the Pearson government, the Honourable John Turner put forward a restrictive definition of the meaning of education under Section 93, "In the federal view, education means the imparting of knowledge through a standard curriculum during the period of childhood, adolescence and youth".[90] This definition, in the Minister's view, "does not preclude" federal action in respect to occupational training or retraining, cultural activities, research and aid to individuals (for educational purposes) as against aid to institutions.

The Royal Commission of Inquiry on Constitutional Problems which reported to the Quebec government in 1956 gave a formulation of provincial responsibilities for education directly opposed to that of Mr. Turner.[91] The Commission said: "Education, whose object is to improve Man, may be defined as a processus (sic) of cultural access."[92] The Report made a very complex analysis of culture with an emphasis on the preservation of the "national culture" of French Canada as "the totality of the rational and spiritual values forming the collective patrimony of a determined human group: modes of life, morals, customs, traditions, language, laws etc.".[93] This definition, of course, precluded direct federal involvement in educational activities, and the Commission was critical of all such activity even when it was justified by reference to federal powers over defence, agriculture, immigration and Indians.[94] According to this analysis, Ottawa had a legitimate concern with education, but this concern should be manifested by policies which gave the provinces adequate fiscal resources to meet educational needs rather than direct federal intervention.[95]

In justifying its manifold activities of an educational nature the federal government has resorted to several distinctions.
(1) *Between education and culture.* The federal Royal Commission on the Arts, Letters and Sciences made this assertion in its Report published in 1951, "All civilized societies strive for a common good, including not only material but intellectual and moral elements. If the Federal Government is to renounce its rights to associate itself with other social groups, public and private, in the general education of Canadian citizens, it denies its intellectual and moral purpose, the complete conception of the common good is lost, and Canada, as such becomes a materialistic society."[96] If this close association between education and culture were accepted literally, there would be no limits to Ottawa's involvement in the "general education of Canadian citizens". Federal policy has never gone this far, but has been influenced

by the Commission's formulation of the national government as a general repository of cultural values.

(2) *Between general education and occupational training or retraining.* In its policy as enunciated in the fall of 1966 the federal government undertook to pay all the costs of occupational training and retraining.[97] A distinction was made between such training related directly to the labour market and general education, with Ottawa's responsibilities in the former matter arising because of its generalized role in respect to levels of employment and its specific jurisdiction over unemployment insurance.

(3) *Between assistance in the education of specific groups of Canadians and other kinds of educational involvement.* The federal government has asserted its right to direct involvement in the education of specific groups either through provision of these services or through payments directly to these individuals or to institutions providing educational services. Such groups include Indians and Inuit, immigrants, federal employees, members of the Armed Forces and their dependent children and veterans of military service.

(4) *Between universities and other kinds of educational institutions.* In the past two decades successive federal governments have accepted the general viewpoint of the Royal Commission on the Arts, Letters and Sciences that universities as distinct from elementary and high schools were national institutions and thus in some sense partially Ottawa's responsibility.

(5) *Between the advancement of knowledge and the transmission of knowledge.* At least since the establishment of the National Research Council in 1916 successive federal governments have maintained their right to support research — a term almost as elastic in its meaning as education — whether in connection with specific federal responsibilities or otherwise.[98]

(6) *Between "making a gift and making a law".* In F.R. Scott's terms, the federal power to expend funds on matters within provincial legislative jurisdiction, including of course education, rests on the argument that "Making a gift is not the same as making a law."[99] Thus in respect to education Ottawa can and does insist that parents and guardians of children eligible for family allowances observe the school-attendance laws of the respective provinces as a condition of receiving these "gifts", but the federal government cannot make non-attendance a legal offence. The federal spending power as so interpreted leaves the national government free to support education and other activities within provincial jurisdiction by making loans or gifts to individuals, private groups, local governments and provinces and to impose such conditions as it chooses to make potential beneficiaries eligible for federal financial assistance.

(7) *Between education in the majority and minority official language.* Since 1969 there has been a program of federal grants-in-aid of the official language which is in the minority in a province, i.e., English in Quebec and French in the other provinces.

The distinctions outlined above have justified a very considerable amount of federal intervention in matters which are, broadly speaking, education. Apart perhaps from the spending power, these distinctions rest on pragmatic considerations of policy and on general assumptions about the nature of the Canadian policy rather than constitutional law. In a similar way, the contrary Quebec formulation which restricts the federal role in education as a requirement of the cultural survival of French Canada is related only in a tangential way to the constitution as interpreted by the courts.

In the past decade there have been disputes between the federal and provincial governments about education in respect to two kinds of matters where judicial review of the constitution provides partial but not complete guides to a delineation of the respective powers of the two levels.

(1) *Educational broadcasting.*[100] Is educational broadcasting primarily broadcasting or primarily education? In 1932 the Judicial Committee decided that Parliament had exclusive jurisdiction over radio communications, including both the transmission and reception of broadcasting.[101] Under this power the federal authorities have allocated broadcasting licences, controlled the content of broadcasting and operated national radio and television networks. It was not until the 1960s when the potentialities of television as an instrument of formal instruction emerged that the respective responsibilities of the federal and provincial governments in broadcasting became a crucial, and as yet unresolved, issue.

(2) *International conferences on education.* As we have seen, the Judicial Committee in 1937 decided that Parliament did not acquire any legislative powers it would not otherwise have had by virtue of such powers being necessary to the fulfilment of an international obligation incurred by Canada. During the 1960s there was a protracted and bitter dispute between the federal and Quebec authorities centering on the appropriateness or otherwise of the province participating independently of Ottawa in international conferences on education.[102] In summary form, the Quebec position was that it was in law and practice inappropriate to separate the power to conclude international agreements from the power to give legislative implementation to such agreements, and thus the province should be able to participate without federal interference in international conferences on education and other matters where the subject-matter was within provincial legislative jurisdiction.[103] The federal viewpoint was that responsibility for foreign affairs could not be so divided, that Quebec's position if acceded to would project the province into the community of sovereign states and that — where the subject-matter of international relations was within provincial jurisdiction — cooperation between Ottawa and the provinces was essential.[104]

The situation relating to education points up both the advantages and difficulties of constitutional flexibility. The level of government which has shown more urgency than the other about a particular public problem has been able to find the jurisdiction to take action. For example, in the early 1960s the provinces showed little disposition to establish the kinds of vocational training facilities essential to an industrialized country, but Ottawa was able to induce this development by generous if somewhat indiscriminate grants-in-aid. Similarly, the provinces have been for the most part unwilling without federal encouragement to make the necessary contributions to the development of the more specialized kinds of scientific research and the fine arts. Flexibility brings its difficulties. So far as many kinds of educational activities are concerned, Ottawa maintains that its support is in a sense ex gratia and thus may and has in some cases cut back on its involvement, leaving those who are directly affected to seek assistance from provincial or other sources. Flexibility, as we have seen, leads to claims and counter-claims which have no basis, or almost no basis, in constitutional law and to conflicts for which there is no procedure for authoritative resolution. Most importantly perhaps, flexibility dilutes the accountability of governments to their respective legislatures and electorates.

Notes

1The Honourable Guy Favreau, The Amendment of the Constitution of Canada, Queen's Printer, Ottawa, 1965, p. 13.
2See the collection by Maurice Ollivier, The British North America Acts and Selected Statutes, 1867-1962, Queen's Printer, Ottawa, 1962. This collection contains a very large number of items which are of a constitutional nature but unfortunately the compiler gives no statement of the tests he used to include or exclude documents.
3There is reference in Sections 11 and 13 to the Queen's Privy Council for Canada. However, this body consists at any one time of all living persons who have ever taken the Canadian Privy Council oath, generally all incumbent and former members of federal cabinets and other honorific Privy Councillors, and thus is not the cabinet.
4British North America at Confederation, A Study Prepared for the Royal Commission on Dominion-Provincial Relations, King's Printer, Ottawa, Section IX "The Division of Economic Powers at Confederation".
5Queen's Printer, Quebec, Volume I, First Part, Chapter III "The Political Work of the Fathers of Confederation and the Spirit of the Federative Pact".
6The Life and Times of Confederation, 1864-1867, University of Toronto Press, 1962, Chapter VIII, "Confederation and the Federal Principle".
7Section 94 contemplated an early assimilation of the private law of the common law provinces into a single code under Dominion jurisdiction. This Section never became operative.
8For detailed treatments of this subject see Paul Gérin-Lajoie, Constitutional Amendment in Canada, University of Toronto Press, 1950; William S. Livingston, Federalism and Constitutional Change, Oxford University Press, 1956; and Guy Favreau, The Amendment of the Constitution of Canada, Queen's Printer, Ottawa, 1965.
9Livingston, op. cit., p. 13.
10See generally Sir J.G. Bourinot, A Manual of the Constitutional History of Canada, Copp Clark, Toronto, 1901, pp. 24-37.
11Proceedings of the Constitutional Conference of Federal and Provincial

Governments, (Second Session), September 25-28, 1950, King's Printer, Ottawa, 1950.

[12]Favreau, *The Amendment of the Constitution of Canada.*

[13]The correspondence between Premier Lesage and Prime Minister Pearson is contained in *House of Commons Debates,* January 28, 1966, pp. 421-423 and March 24, 1966, p. 3162. This correspondence is reprinted in Paul Fox, Editor, *Politics: Canada,* Second Edition, McGraw-Hill of Canada, Toronto, 1966, pp. 146-149.

[14]For an excellent analysis of the relation between constitutionalism and emergency powers see Clinton Rossiter, *Constitutional Dictatorship: Crisis Government in the Modern Democracies,* Second Edition, New York, 1963. On the constitutional aspects of the Canadian War Measures Act see Walter Surma Tarnopolsky, *The Canadian Bill of Rights,* Second Revised Edition, Carleton Library, McClelland and Stewart, 1975, Chapter IX.

[15]The newer federations in the Commonwealth have provided more explicitly for emergency powers than do the constitutions of the older federations. See R.L. Watts, *New Federations: Experiments in the Commonwealth,* Oxford University Press, 1966, pp. 315-319.

[16]Rossiter, *op. cit.,* p. 212.

[17]The leading case here is *Fort Frances Pulp and Paper Co. v. Manitoba Free Press,* (1923), A.C. 695.

[18]R. MacGregor Dawson, *The Government of Canada,* Fifth Edition, Revised by Norman Ward, University of Toronto Press, 1970, p. 92.

[19]*House of Commons Debates,* Oct. 23, 1970, p. 510.

[20]*Bayonets in the Streets: Urban Guerrillas at Home and Abroad,* Collier-Macmillan, Toronto, 1974, Chapter 4.

[21]*Tarnopolsky, op. cit.,* p. 346.

[22]*C.A.U.T.,* 1971, Vol. 2., No. 4, p. 1.

[23]Section 22 and Section 23(6) (Senate of Canada), Section 40 (House of Commons of Canada), Section 72 (Legislative Council of Quebec), Section 80 (Legislative Assembly of Quebec).

[24]Section 20 (annual sessions of Parliament); Section 39 (no joint membership in Senate and House of Commons); Sections 44-47 (Office of the Speaker of House of Commons); Section 51 (basis of representation in House of Commons); Sections 53-54 (money bills).

[25]Noel Lyon and Ronald G. Atkey, *Canadian Constitutional Law in a Modern Perspective,* University of Toronto Press, 1970, p. 375.

[26]For a comprehensive account of the division of powers over human rights at that time see Bora Laskin, "An Inquiry into the Diefenbaker Bill of Rights", XXXVII *Canadian Bar Review,* March 1959, pp. 77-134.

[27]However, it is possible that Parliament might validly under the criminal law power make discrimination on such grounds offences.

[28]Laskin, "An Inquiry into the Diefenbaker Bill of Rights", p. 80.

[29]*ibid.,* p. 116.

[30]The clearest statement of this position is in the opinions of Justices Cartwright and Fauteux in *Saumur v. City of Quebec and A.-G. Que.,* (1953), 2 S.C.R., 299.

[31]See the exhaustive discussion of the meaning of property and civil rights in *Report Pursuant to Resolution of the Senate to the Honourable the Speaker by the Parliamentary Council Relating to the Enactment of the British North America Act, 1867, and any lack of consonance between its terms and judicial construction of them and cognate matters,* King's Printer, Ottawa, 1939, pp. 109-145. (Hereafter cited as *O'Connor Report*). See also D.A. Schmeiser, *Civil*

Liberties in Canada, Oxford University Press, 1964, pp. 74-78.

[32](1938) S.C.R. 100.

[33]*Switzman v. Elbling and A.-G. Quebec* (1957) 7 D.L.R. (2nd), 337.

[34]See the summary in the Honourable Pierre Elliott Trudeau, *A Canadian Charter of Human Rights*, Queen's Printer, Ottawa, 1968, pp. 171-174.

[35]*Tarnopolsky, op. cit.*

[36]See particularly *Robertson and Rosetanni v. the Queen* (1963) S.C.R. 651.

[37]*The Queen v. Joseph Drybones*, (1970) 71 W.W.R. 161.

[38]*Trudeau, A Canadian Charter of Human Rights*. For a criticism of the proposed Charter see Donald V. Smiley, "The Case against the Canadian Charter of Human Rights", II *Canadian Journal of Political Science*, September, 1969, pp. 277-291. The issue of entrenchment was discussed at the first Constitutional Conference of February, 1968, *Proceedings*, Queen's Printer, Ottawa, 1968, pp. 265-332.

[39]*Lyon and Atkey*, p. 377. Emphasis in original. For a critique of this argument see my review of the book in L *Canadian Bar Review*, March 1972, pp. 139-148.

[40]Queen's Printer, Toronto, Report No. 2, Volume 4, Chapters 106-108.

[41]pp. 1581-1582. See my article dealing with this aspect of the Report, "The McRuer Report: Parliamentary Majoritarian Democracy and Human Rights", V *Journal of Canadian Studies*, (May, 1970) pp. 3-10. For a similar view to that of the Report see R.I. Cheffins, *The Constitutional Process in Canada*, McGraw-Hill Series on Canadian Politics, Toronto, 1969, pp. 161-169.

[42]See *R. v. Wray*, [1971], S.C.R. 272, *R. v. Osborn* [1971], S.C.R., 184 and *Attorney-General of Canada v. Lavell and Bedard*, [1973], 23 C.R.N.S. 197 (Can.). In the latter case a majority of the Court held that a section of the Indian Act which provided that an Indian woman who married a non-Indian would thereby lose her band membership did not contravene the section of the Bill of Rights related to equality before the law. Here were posed the contradictory values of sexual equality and of the rights of Indian bands to sustain their traditional ways based on other principles.

[43]Lord Sankey's short account of the history of the Judicial Committee of the Privy Council in *British Coal Corporation v. The King* (1935) A.C. 500 at pp. 510-512. This is reprinted in *The Courts and the Canadian Constitution*, W.R. Lederman, Editor, Carleton Library No. 16, McClelland and Stewart, Toronto, 1964, pp. 63-65.

[44]"Introduction" in *Leading Constitutional Decisions*, Peter H. Russell, Editor, Carleton Library No. 23, McClelland and Stewart, Toronto, 1965, p. XI.

[45]See particularly the O'Connor Report (Note 29); G.P. Browne, *The Judicial Committee and the British North America Act*, Toronto, 1967; and, more generally, Edward McWhinney, *Judicial Review in the English-Speaking World*, 4th Edition, Toronto, University of Toronto Press, 1969. See also Alan C. Cairns' brilliant article "The Judicial Committee and Its Critics," IV *Canadian Journal of Political Science* (September 1971), pp. 301-345.

[46](1932) A.C., 54 at pp. 71-72. By permission of Information Canada.

[47]*A.-G. Can. v. A.-G. Ont.* (1937) A.C. 326.

[48]*A.-G. B.C. v. A.-G. Can.* (1937) A.C. 377.

[49]*A.-G. Can. v. A.-G. Ont.* (1937) A.C. 355.

[50]For a comprehensive review of the Judicial Committee's treatment of the general power see Bora Laskin, " 'Peace, Order and Good Government' Re-examined" in Lederman, *The Courts and the Canadian Constitution*, pp. 66-104.

[51]*O'Connor Report, op. cit.*

[52]For one of a number of articles on this general line see Vincent C. MacDonald. "The Privy Council and the Canadian Constitution", XXVI *Canadian Bar*

Review, 1948, pp. 1021ff.

53See Cairns' article cited in n. 45.

54*The Judicial Committee and the British North America Act*, Toronto.

55The Meaning of Provincial Autonomy" by Louis-Phillipe Pigeon, Vol. 29 *Canadian Bar Review* (1951). By permission of the author and the *Canadian Bar Review*.

56"Federalism, Nationalism, and Reason" in Pierre Elliott Trudeau, *Federalism and the French Canadians*, Macmillan of Canada, Toronto, 1968, p. 198.

57*A Short History of the Canadian Constitution*, The Ryerson Press, Toronto, 1969, p. 142.

58*Social Credit and the Federal Power in Canada*, University of Toronto Press, Chapters 3 and 4.

59*ibid.* p. 54.

60*ibid.* p. 56.

61Cairns, *op. cit.*, pp. 327-332.

62*ibid.* p. 327.

63Peter H. Russell, *The Supreme Court of Canada as a Bilingual and Bicultural Institution*, Documents of the Royal Commission on Bilingualism and Biculturalism, Queen's Printer, Ottawa, 1969, p. 26.

64"The Supreme Court of Canada: A Final Court of and for Canadians", Lederman, *The Courts and the Canadian Constitution*, p. 143, Laskin's 1951 article at pp. 125-151 is an excellent analysis of the previous status and future prospects of the Court written near to the time when it became the final appellate tribunal for Canadian cases.

65For general reviews see Peter H. Russell, "The Supreme Court's Interpretation of the Canadian Constitution since 1949" in Paul Fox, Editor, *Politics: Canada*, Third Edition, McGraw-Hill Series on Canadian Politics, Toronto, 1970, pp. 439-452; Martha Fletcher, "Judicial Review and the Division of Powers in Canada" in *Canadian Federalism: Myth or Reality*, J. Peter Meekison, Editor, Methuen of Canada, 1968, pp. 140-158; and the Honourable Vincent C. Macdonald, *Legislative Power and the Supreme Court in the Fifties*, Butterworth, Toronto, 1961.

66"Thoughts on Reform of the Supreme Court of Canada", *The Confederation Challenge*, Ontario Advisory Committee on Confederation, Background Papers and Reports, Vol. II, Queen's Printer, Toronto, 1970, p. 295.

67"Constitutional Trends and Federalism", reprinted in Meekison, *Canadian Federalism: Myth or Reality*, pp. 58-60.

68"Our Changing Constitution" in Lederman, *The Courts and the Canadian Constitution*, p. 27. By permission of F.R. Scott.

69Russell, *The Supreme Court as a Bilingual and Bicultural Institution*, p. 37. For an extended argument along these lines in comparative perspective see Jacques Brossard, *La Cour Suprême et La Constitution*, Les Presses de l'Université de Montréal, 1968.

70University of Toronto Press.

71Carswell, Toronto.

72Unpublished mss. by Peter Russell to be published in Paul Fox, Editor, *Politics: Canada*, Fourth Edition, McGraw-Hill Ryerson Series in Canadian Politics.

73"Conclusions and Observations" in G. Bruce Doern and V. Seymour Wilson, Editors, *Issues in Canadian Public Policy*, Macmillan of Canada, Toronto, p. 341.

74Russell, *op. cit.*

75In this section I have been very much influenced by two articles — W.R. Lederman "Some Forms and Limitations of Cooperative Federalism", XLV

Canadian Bar Review, September, 1967, pp. 409-436 and Barry Strayer, "The Flexibility of the BNA Act" in *Agenda: 1970*, Edited by Trevor Lloyd and Jack McLeod, University of Toronto Press, 1968, pp. 197-216.

[76]"The Rowell-Sirois Report, Provincial Autonomy and Post-War Canadian Federalism," in *Meekison, Canadian Federalism*, p. 70.

[77]"Some Forms and Limitations of Cooperative Federalism", XLV *Canadian Bar Review* (September, 1967), p. 410. By permission of W.R. Lederman and the *Canadian Bar Review*.

[78]*A.-G. B.C. v. A.-G. Can.* (1937) A.C. 377.

[79]See J.A. Corry, *Difficulties of Divided Jurisdiction*, A Study prepared for the Royal Commission on Dominion-Provincial Relations, King's Printer, Ottawa, 1939, Chapter II "Marketing of Agricultural Products".

[80]At p. 389. Reproduced by permission of Information Canada.

[81]J.A. Corry, "Constitutional Trends and Federalism" in *Meekison, Canadian Federalism: Myth or Reality*, pp. 62-63 and Lederman, "Some Forms and Limitations of Cooperative Federalism", pp. 428-433.

[82]On this constitutional issue see Gerald V. La Forest, *The Allocation of Taxing Power under the Canadian Constitution*, Canadian Tax Foundation, Canadian Tax Paper No. 46, Toronto, 1967, pp. 36-41 and Donald V. Smiley, *Conditional Grants and Canadian Federalism*, Canadian Tax Foundation, Canadian Tax Paper No. 32, 1963, Chapter II.

[83]*A.-G. N.S. v. A.-G. Can.* (1950) 4 D.L.R. 369.

[84]*P.E.I. Potato Marketing Board v. H.B. Willis Inc. and A.-G. Can.* (1952) 4 D.L.R. 146. Lederman examines and criticizes delegation as a device of federal-provincial cooperation "Some Forms and Limitations of Cooperative Federalism", pp. 418-428.

[85]Strayer, *The Flexibility of the B.N.A. Act*.

[86]"Federal Grants to Universities" in *Federalism and the French Canadians*, pp. 79-102. His argument went much beyond university grants in its implications.

[87]*Federalism and the French Canadians*, p. 138.

[88]*ibid.*, p. 138.

[89]*Égalité ou Indépendance*, Éditions Renaissance, Montréal, p. 73.

[90]*Politics of Purpose: Politique d'Objectifs*, McClelland and Stewart, Toronto/Montreal, 1968, p. 62.

[91]Particularly Volume II, Part Four, Chapter VII "Practices and Theories in the Field of Education".

[92]Vol. II, p. 19.

[93]Vol. II, p. 15.

[94]Vol. II, p. 15.

[95]pp. 234-237.

[96]Report, King's Printer, Ottawa, p. 8.

[97]For the federal proposal see *Federal-Provincial Conference, Ottawa, Oct. 26-28, 1966*, Queen's Printer, 1968, pp. 48-55.

[98]See *The Role of the Federal Government in Support of Research in Canadian Universities*, John B. Macdonald et al., Queen's Printer, Ottawa, 1969. See also the dissenting Report to this document of L.P. Dugal, pp. 357-361 emphasizing the constitutional problem and the special needs of French-language institutions.

[99]"The Constitutional Background of the Taxation Agreements", 2 *McGrill Law Journal*, 1955, p. 6.

[100]For the fullest account of the issues here see Ronald G. Atkey, "The Provincial Interest in Broadcasting under the Canadian Constitution" in *The Confederation Challenge*, Ontario Advisory Committee on Confederation, Background

Papers and Reports, Volume 2, pp. 189-255.

[101]In *Re Regulation and Control of Radio Communication*, (1932), A.C. 304.

[102]For a description and analysis of these conflicts see Edward McWhinney, "Canadian Federalism: Foreign Affairs and Treaty Power" in *The Confederation Challenge, op. cit.*, Vol. 2, pp. 115-152.

[103]Paul Gérin-Lajoie, the Minister of Education in the Lesage government and a distinguished constitutionalist, made the most coherent defences of the province's powers in foreign affairs that are available. See his Address to the Montreal Consular Corps, April 12, 1965 (mimeo), his interview with *Le Devoir* ler Mai, 1965 and his article in the *Montreal Star*, March 19, 1968.

[104]See the two statements of the federal government, the Honourable Paul Martin, *Federalism and International Relations*, Queen's Printer, Ottawa, 1968, and the Honourable Mitchell Sharp, *Federalism and International Conferences on Education*, Queen's Printer, Ottawa, 1968.

CHAPTER 2

CONSTITUTIONAL REFORM AND REVIEW

In the past decade the federal and provincial governments together have made two series of attempts to revise the Canadian constitution. Both attempts have foundered on the refusal of the incumbent political leadership of Quebec to agree to solutions acceptable to Ottawa and the governments of the other provinces. The circumstances surrounding the repudiation of the Fulton-Favreau formula for constitutional amendment have been outlined in the preceding chapter. An attempt at more comprehensive reform was begun with the Confederation for Tomorrow Conference of the provinces sponsored by the government of Ontario in November, 1967 and continued through a series of Federal-Provincial Conferences from February, 1968, to June, 1971. The process of constitutional review is the subject of this chapter.[1]

The Confederation for Tomorrow Conference was an Ontario initiative directed toward commencing — or resuming — a dialogue on the future shape of Canadian federalism and in particular on the place of Quebec in Confederation. From the Ontario perspective the situation, as it had developed when planning for the Conference began early in 1967, must indeed have appeared critical and unsatisfactory. The Quebec general election of June, 1966, had brought to power a government committed to urgent and early reform of the constitution on binational lines. The emerging attitudes in Ottawa toward the provinces, and in particular toward Quebec, had become increasingly less conciliatory and the growing influence of Pierre Elliott Trudeau and the Liberal "new guard" from Quebec over federal policies combined both a personal distrust of the Union Nationale leaders and an inflexibility toward Quebec's continuing demands for an increased scope of autonomy. From the Ontario point of view, the mutual isolation of Ottawa and Quebec posed grave challenges both to national unity and to the role in national reconciliation that the province, and in particular Premier John Robarts, had assumed. A polarization between the federal and Quebec governments would in the long run give Ontario only the unpalatable options of siding with one of these contenders or of standing aside and leaving some of the most critical issues of the Canadian federation to be resolved without significant Ontario influence on the outcome. Further, there seems to have been some anxiety in the Ontario government that during the past few years many important but piecemeal changes had been effected in federal-provincial relations without adequate consideration of the cumulative impact on the federal system.

The 1967 Conference consisted of a frank and general discussion of the views of the provincial leaders on Confederation with of course a focus on the place and demands of Quebec. No formal resolutions were put forward and the crucial matter of federal-provincial financial relations was excluded from the agenda. At the end of the meeting a committee of four Premiers — those of Alberta, Ontario, Quebec and Nova Scotia — was established to analyze the results of the Conference and to "explore the subjects and form of future discussion".[2] The final communique isolated these broad subjects for subsequent consideration — "constitutional change; regional disparities; language practices and rights".

The reaction of the federal government to the Ontario initiative was cool, although four federal officials attended the meetings as observers. Prime Minister Pearson and his colleagues resented such an initiative being taken by a province, despite the assurances that they had been able to secure from Premier Robarts that the conference would not undertake to make decisions or indulge in constitutional drafting but rather would be a forum for free and wide-ranging discussions unfettered by the procedures which had come to be used in federal-provincial meetings. Prime Minister Trudeau in his press conference of July 27, 1971 reconstructed the federal view of late 1967.[3] It was that revising the constitution was not an urgent priority. The comprehensive reform of the constitution was more complex and more difficult to effect than many of the enthusiasts for such reform supposed. The existing constitution had proved itself to be a flexible instrument and under it there had been in recent years a shift in power to the provinces. However, in Ottawa's view, once the provinces had initiated what amounted to a process of constitutional review it would be irresponsible for the federal government to stand aside. Thus late in 1967 it was announced that the terms of reference of a federal-provincial conference called for early 1968 to discuss the more effective protection of human rights, including linguistic rights, would be broadened to include a comprehensive review of the Canadian constitution.

At the first Constitutional Conference of February, 1968, the federal government presented its plan for reviewing the constitution.[4] The process as suggested would proceed in three stages. First there would be discussion of the more effective protection of human rights through their constitutional entrenchment. Then there would be consideration of "the central institutions of Canadian federalism" — specifically, Parliament, the Supreme Court of Canada, the federal public service and the national capital — in order to make these more representative of the "federal character of the country". At the end of the process the federal and provincial governments would turn their attention to the division of powers between the two levels. The rationale for this sequence seems to have been that if individual rights and cultural and provincial particularisms were more effectively protected by constitutional entrenchment and by restructuring certain institutions of the federal government there would be less pressure than otherwise for safeguarding these rights by an extension of provincial powers.[5] It was also decided by Ottawa that constitutional review should be comprehensive rather than piecemeal, in effect that the governments would not commit themselves to particular changes as the review proceeded but rather would await the eventual negotiation of a new constitutional package.

The federal plan was based on the assumption that rationality in the review procedure required the governments first to discuss and, it was hoped, agree on general principles about the nature of the Canadian community and then to embody these principles in concrete constitutional changes.[6] Such general statements would be enacted as a preamble to the new constitution, and the federal emphasis on the entrenchment of human rights seems to have been based partly on the conviction that such individual rights rather than the older and more collectively oriented purpose of "Peace, Order, and Good Government" had become the primary objective of the Canadian political community. For reasons that were never explained, the federal government felt with some urgency that the new constitution would be — as the existing one had never been — a symbolic focus of Canadian political allegiance.[7] The federal approach reflected very directly the views of Pierre Elliott Trudeau, who throughout his adult life had been deeply concerned with constitutional matters.

Most of the first Constitutional Conference of February, 1968 was devoted to a consideration of what most if not all of the participating governments agreed were the two most pressing substantive problems of the Canadian federation — regional economic disparities and language rights.[8] On the second matter there was a prevailing disposition among all the governments that there should be an extension of the recognition of the French language, and the leaders of all the governments except that of Quebec gave an account of what his administration was doing and proposed to do in this respect. At the end of the Conference a "consensus on language rights" was accepted in terms of a recognition that ". . . French-speaking Canadians outside of Quebec should have the same rights as English-speaking Canadians in Quebec."[9] There were, however, deep disagreements among the governments in respect to linguistic matters. The so-called "consensus" had been reached after the Premiers of Alberta and British Columbia had left the meeting, and throughout the previous discussions Alberta, with some support from Saskatchewan and British Columbia, had argued against the "constitutional and legalistic approach to linguistic matters" and in particular against the constitutional entrenchment of linguistic rights. The federal government and those of several of the other provinces were favourably disposed or at least open-minded to such entrenchment as had recently been recommended by a Report of the Royal Commission on Bilingualism and Biculturalism.[10] The Quebec position was that the division of powers rather than linguistic rights was the matter of urgency, and that a more extensive recognition of such rights should be imposed neither by the Conference nor the federal government.

From the beginning, the provinces showed various degrees of commitment to the process of constitutional review. In one of his first policy statements after the 1968 general election Prime Minister Trudeau was critical of some provinces, which he did not name, for their reluctance about the review process.[11] It is broadly accurate to say that apart perhaps from an amending procedure, a matter absent from the 1968 federal plan for constitutional revision, neither Ottawa nor the governments of any of the provinces with English-speaking majorities felt any urgency about substantive change in the constitution except as such changes might provide for some form of "great new act of accommodation" between the English and French communities as foreseen by Prime Minister Pearson in his opening address to the Conference of February 1968.[12] The governments of the western provinces were generally conservative about constitutional matters, although from time to time the Premier of British Columbia indulged his highly developed talents for obstruction by introducing into discussion daring proposals quite impossible for the other governments to take seriously.[13] As a price for their continuing participation in the review process, all the provinces from time to time insisted on raising issues which were only in a tangential way if at all constitutional, particularly matters of financial relations with Ottawa. At the Conference of February, 1970, for example, there was no discussion of constitutional review at all but rather consideration of substantive problems facing the two levels — inflation, western agriculture, environmental pollution and the administration of shared-cost programs.

Between the first of the Conferences in 1968 and the proceedings leading up to those of February and June, 1971, the process of review was rather diffuse. The sequence for discussion suggested by Ottawa in the first meeting was soon put aside, and the governments encouraged to put forward "propositions" related to constitutional reform. The status of such recommendations was thus defined in a federal document of February, 1969: "The propositions submitted by the Government of Canada, like those of other governments, are for discussion purposes only and are in no sense final. Nor are they intended as proposed drafts of constitutional articles. Propositions may be withdrawn, altered or replaced as discussions continue."[14] At this Conference Ottawa presented a series of detailed proposals related to individual rights and the restructuring of several of the institutions of the federal government. Quebec throughout pressed its plans for a radical reform of the constitution on bi-national lines.[15] The other provinces responded to the call for propositions with widely varying degrees of seriousness and urgency. Under these circumstances it was impossible for discussion to be focused, and from about the middle of 1969 onward the emphasis appears to have shifted for a time to a consideration of several federal position papers related to the division of taxing[16] and spending powers and the respective responsibilities of the two levels of government for income security and social services.

By the fall of 1970 it seemed that the process of constitutional review had almost broken down. The Federal-Provincial Conference of

September of that year, like the one held in the preceding February, dealt entirely with inter-governmental problems other than those directly related to the constitution, although in a formal sense both were constitutional conferences. In a position paper published in June, 1970, the Premier of Alberta analyzed the lack of progress that had been made and concluded ". . . the process of constitutional review has not in any meaningful way reduced the inherent conflicts in the federal system, nor has it facilitated changes in the federal bargain."[17] The Alberta position was basically critical of the "holistic" approach to constitutional review and suggested that more progress could be made if problems narrower in scope could be considered. Other governments than that of Alberta were undoubtedly dissatisfied with the way in which reform of the constitution was proceeding, and so far as public expectations of change had been aroused, the process was losing its credibility.

Sometime late in 1970 there was a renewed effort to focus constitutional review and bring it to some kind of conclusion. The hopeful new element in the situation was the election of the Bourassa Liberals in the Quebec general election of April, 1970, on a straightforwardly federalist platform. Unlike its predecessor, the new government was not disposed to advance the Quebec position through nationalist rhetoric or abstract and doctrinaire statements of principle. Perhaps here there appeared the elements of a possible constitutional accommodation in which Quebec would trade its support for a new amending formula, the first priority in constitutional change for most if not all of the other governments, in exchange for extended provincial powers over social policy. The Constitutional Conference of February, 1971, gave its attention to "the questions of an amending formula and an early patriation of the Canadian Constitution" and published a proposed amending procedure which the "First Ministers agreed . . . was a feasible approach." Consideration was also given to the constitutional entrenchment of human rights, Quebec's demands in the field of social policy and other matters which in a refined form finally appeared in the Victoria Charter.

Between the February Conference and the one held in Victoria the succeeding June there were intensive constitutional discussions between Ottawa and the individual provinces. The federal government appears to have been determined to achieve *some* conclusion from the review process, and in particular to focus discussion on constitutional matters exclusively without the previous diversions to other aspects of federal-provincial relations.[18]

The most difficult substantive problem to be dealt with in the constitutional discussions was in respect to social security.[19] The basic elements of the Quebec proposal were these:
(1) Subject to the important qualifications outlined below, the Parliament of Canada would have the power to legislate in respect to the major areas of income-maintenance where it is now active — family allowances, manpower training allowances, guaranteed old-age income supplement, youth and social allowances, unemployment insur-

ance, old age pensions and supplementary benefits to survivors and disabled persons regardless of age.

(2) In respect to family and manpower training allowances and to the old-age income supplement, any province might enact to the effect that federal law would prevail within the province only to the extent the province so decided. When such action was taken, the non-participating province would receive from the federal govenrment the fiscal equivalent of what otherwise would have been disbursed in the province had the federal law applied. The same provision would apply to new federal income-security schemes.

(3) In respect to youth and social allowances, unemployment insurance and old age pensions and survivors' benefits, no federal law would affect the operation of any present or future provincial enactment. These fields would be concurrent with provincial paramountcy.

The Quebec government argued for its proposal largely in terms of rationalization and efficiency in designing and implementing income-maintenance policies and of the benefits of integrating all aspects of social policy under one level of government.

The net effect of the Quebec proposal would have been to place existing and future federal powers in the income-security field at the discretion of the provinces and this contradicted squarely Ottawa's position that the central government could not responsibly give up its role in equalizing incomes among individuals throughout Canada. Prime Minister Trudeau thus summarized the federal position in his opening statement to the Victoria Conference:[20]

> Quebec's proposal that provincial legislatures should have the power to limit the authority of Parliament to make income security payments such as old age pensions and family allowances within their province is one of the important issues before this conference. By the present system of income security, Parliament transfers billions of dollars a year to the old, the poor, the unemployed and families with children, from taxpayers and contributors who have the ability to pay. This federal redistribution is particularly important to poor people in those parts of Canada where opportunities and incomes are less than average — and that includes seven of our ten provinces. If, as the government of Quebec proposes, provincial laws could nullify federal income security laws in a province, and divert the federal revenue through the provincial treasury to be spent as the provincial government decided, then provincial governments would have a strong inducement to have such laws. But in those circumstances Parliament would be less likely to impose taxes on Canadians generally to make payments to provincial governments than it would to make payments directly to the needy old people and families with children. Taxpayers themselves would be less prepared to pay taxes to the federal government for programmes controlled by provincial governments other than their own, than to support programmes of the federal parliament which they themselves elect. Consequently, the constitutional change proposed by Quebec would, over the years, lead to an erosion of federal income security programmes and their replacement by purely provincial plans. In the latter case, the old and the poor in the wealthier provinces might do as well as if the federal government were

making the payments, but in the other provinces including Quebec, the tax base would not support as good income security payments as Parliament could provide.

The so-called "Victoria Charter" emerging from the June Conference in 1971 had the following elements:
(1) There was a formula for the patriation and amendment of the Canadian constitution. This formula was outlined in the previous chapter.
(2) There was to be constitutional entrenchment of certain human rights in three categories:

(a) No federal or provincial law was to abrogate "freedom of thought, conscience and religion; freedom of opinion and expression and freedom of peaceful assembly and association". However there was this qualification:

> Art. 3. Nothing in this Part shall be construed as preventing such limitations on the exercise of the fundamental freedoms as are reasonably justifiable in a democratic society in the interests of public safety, order, health or morals, of national security, or of the rights and freedoms of others, whether imposed by the Parliament of Canada or the Legislature of a Province, within the limits of their respective legislative powers, or by the construction or application of any law.

(b) Universal suffrage and free elections were declared to be fundamental principles of the constitution. There should be no discrimination against citizens voting or holding elective office because of "national origin, colour, religion or sex". Parliament and each provincial legislature had a maximum life of five years, except under emergency conditions as determined by the federal cabinet when such period might be extended if not opposed by more than one-third of the members of such bodies. There were to be annual legislative sessions.

(c) In terms of linguistic rights, both English and French might be used in the Parliament of Canada and all the provincial legislatures except those of Saskatchewan, Alberta and British Columbia. Statutes, records and journals of Parliament were to be published in both languages. The statutes of each province were to be published in English and French. Both languages could be used in the courts established by Parliament and in the courts of Quebec, New Brunswick and Newfoundland. An individual had the right to use either language in communicating with the head offices of any agency of the government of Canada or the governments of Ontario, Quebec, New Brunswick, Prince Edward Island and Newfoundland. If any province subsequently extended the rights of the two languages beyond those contained in the constitution such privileges could be revoked only by an amendment to the constitution of Canada.
(3) Certain changes were to be made in the Supreme Court of Canada. Of the nine judges, three were to be chosen from the Bar of Quebec. The Governor in Council was to continue to appoint judges but there was a complex procedure for consulting with the provinces in making such appointments. When cases involving the Quebec civil law were before the Court, there were safeguards that these would be heard by judges of

whom a majority were trained in the civil tradition of Quebec.

(4) Parliament might make laws in respect to old age pensions and supplementary benefits and to family, youth and occupational allowances, but such legislation was not to "affect the operation of any law present or future of a Provincial Legislature in relation to any such matter." Enactments could be made only after the provinces had been consulted.

(5) There was to be a conference of Prime Ministers and Premiers each year unless a majority of the heads of government decided otherwise.

(6) The existing provisions providing for the reservation and disallowance of provincial legislation were to be repealed.

It is significant that the Victoria Charter did not include several matters which had been the subject of previous discussion between Ottawa and the provinces and others which might have been expected to come to resolution in a review of the constitution which purported to be comprehensive. In terms of the entrenchment of rights, the Charter omitted entirely traditional rights connected with arrest and trial and linguistic rights in education, and in a sense the Charter was a retreat from the protection of denominational minorities in the existing constitution. Apart from the Supreme Court of Canada, there were no changes in the structure and functioning of the institutions of the central government. With the exception of limited fields of social security there was no change or clarification in respect to the division of legislative powers and the relation between the two levels of government in regard to such matters as taxing and spending, external relations, etc. There was here a very small constitutional package.

Before the first Ministers left Victoria it was agreed that within eleven days each would notify the Secretary of the Constitutional Conference whether or not his government was willing to recommend the adoption of the Charter to the respective legislature. This procedure has been the subject of conflicting interpretations. To some observers, it has been viewed as an ultimatum to Quebec, an indication to the province that the Charter was all that the other governments were willing to give. The federal Minister of Justice denied the validity of this interpretation.[21] According to Mr. Turner, the eleven-day waiting period was requested by the provinces. Reports of the Victoria meeting indicate that of all the heads of government Premier Bourassa was alone in being unable or unwilling to commit his administration to a particular solution at the Conference, and among the other leaders there was apparently a good deal of annoyance at this apparent vacillation.

On June 23, five days before the eleven-day limit expired, Premier Bourassa announced that his government would not accept the Charter in the form that had issued from Victoria.[22] The operative part of the public announcement stated:

> This decision arises from the necessity to agree to as great an extent as possible on clear and precise constitutional texts, thus avoiding to transfer to the judiciary (*sic*) authority a responsibility which belongs first and foremost to the political authority, that is to those elected by the people.

>The texts dealing with income security have an uncertainty that meshes
>badly with the objectives inherent in any idea of constitutional revision. If
>this uncertainty were eliminated, our conclusion could be different.

The Premier's statement reiterated the general commitment of the
Quebec government and people to the federal option and suggested by
implication that constitutional review should continue despite
Quebec's rejection of the Charter.

What was behind Premier Bourassa's statement, "If this uncertainty were eliminated, our conclusion could be different"? Was only
textual ambiguity in the way of Prime Minister Pearson's 1968 hope of
a "great new act of accommodation" among Canadians? It is undeni-
able that the meaning and effect of the terms of the Charter relating to
social security were not very clear. The proposal that in the defined
areas of income-security no federal law "shall effect the operation of
any law present or future of a province" comes from the existing provisions of Section 94A of the B.N.A. Act relating to old age pensions and
the courts have never had the occasion to clarify what this provision
means. If, under the terms of the Victoria Charter, a province enacted a
scheme of family allowances, would this action cause the federal family allowance plan to be terminated within the province? In such circumstances would the provincial government or citizens eligible for
benefits establish a valid legal claim for financial compensation by the
federal authorities? The constitutional vesting of concurrent powers in
both Parliament and the provinces with one or the other having priority
in the event of a conflict has a reasonably precise application so far as
regulatory activities are concerned. For example, although this seems
not to have happened, any clash between Ottawa and a province about
those eligible for entry to Canada as immigrants would be resolved in
favour of the federal authorities. The situation is much less clear in
regard to the service-providing activities of government.

It is reasonable to suppose that Quebec's objections to the Charter
were based on more fundamental grounds than its textual ambiguity,
and it is significant to remember that Premier Lesage advanced the
same reason of ambiguity for his repudiation of the Fulton-Favreau
formula in 1966. Various nationalist groups in Quebec mobilized opposition to the Charter very quickly after the end of the Victoria meeting and the Premier was undoubtedly responding to this pressure.[23]
Within Quebec there are continuing objections to any amending formula which would put Quebec's future constitutional position at the
discretion of the other provinces. One can only conjecture whether the
present or any future Quebec government will be able or willing to
support such an amending procedure, regardless of other concessions
it is able to gain for such support. In general, the proposals relating to
income security as these emerged from the Victoria meeting were quite
obviously the reflection of deep and unresolved differences among the
participating governments rather than inexpert legal draftsmanship.

As they began the process of constitutional review none of the
governments seriously contemplated the direct involvement of the

public or of their respective Parliaments or legislative assemblies in this project. However, largely through the pressures of the Progressive Conservative party in the House of Commons there was established in early 1970 a Special Joint Committee of the Senate and House of Commons on the Constitution of Canada. During the next two years the Committee held public meetings throughout Canada at which 1486 persons appeared as witnesses. The Committee's Final Report was issued in 1972.[24] This document supported the amendment formula of the Victoria Charter, recommended that the Senate's power over legislation be restricted to a six-month veto, called for an extension of provincial power over social policy and of federal jurisdiction over economic matters and made several other proposals. However, because parliamentary procedures do not allow for minority reports to be included in such documents it is impossible to tell the extent of agreement reached by the thirty members of the Committee. Two Quebec MPs, Martial Asselin and Pierre de Bané, issued their own minority report calling for the special recognition in the constitution of Quebec's distinctiveness and of the right of Quebec to self-determination;[25] this latter was the most contentious issue within the Committee. In the Senate of Canada, Eugene Forsey, a member of the Committee, made an eloquent defence of the existing constitution on conservative lines which diverged markedly from the spirit and substance of the Report.[26] Two MPs from the NDP, Andrew Brewin and Douglas Rowland, also issued a minority report whose major recommendations were for constitutional provisions for the inter-delegation of legislative powers and for Parliament to define a national economic emergency to give the federal authorities power to control wages, prices, rent and other forms of income.[27]

The failure to secure agreement on the Victoria Charter brought to an end this pretentious and ill-advised exercise on constitutional review, and whatever hopes there may have been either that a major English-French accommodation might emerge from this process or that agreement could be secured on a newer and purportedly better Canadian constitution. Soon after the Victoria Conference ended there began a series of intensive discussions between the federal and Quebec governments about the powers of the two levels in respect to income-maintenance programs. The result was a considerable victory for Quebec in respect to family allowances as embodied in legislation enacted by Parliament in late 1973. Under this legislation there was to be a payment of $20 per month (subject to cost-of-living increases) on behalf of each child under 18 years of age and resident in Canada. However, within the aggregate amount available in any province under these terms, the province might vary these payments according to the age of the child or the number of children in the family, but the average payment in each province must be $20 and the minimum no less than $12 a month. This then allowed for provincial discretion in respect to an income-maintenance program wholly funded and administered by Ottawa and was a considerable retreat from the federal position on social security as stated both before and during the Victoria Conference. As in the past, the government of Quebec had demonstrated success in its piecemeal quest for autonomy outside the framework of a new constitutional settlement.

It seems unlikely that the process of constitutional review will be reactivated in the foreseeable future. In late 1971 the Prime Minister advised that the functions of the Constitutional Secretariat would be curtailed and its personnel reassigned.[28] Premier Lougheed of Alberta asserted in the Legislative Assembly in March 1972 that his province would not participate in future constitutional discussions unless Ottawa spelled out provincial constitutional jurisdiction in advance, and that his government did not consider itself bound by the Victoria Charter as agreed to by its predecessor.[29] The next day Premier Bennett of British Columbia made a somewhat similar announcement, with the difference that the prior commitment would be required from Quebec rather than the federal authorities.[30] Somewhat surprisingly to most observers, Prime Minister Trudeau in the Speech from the Throne debate in the House of Commons on October 2, 1974 devoted most of his address to parliamentary and constitutional reform and suggested that so far as constitutional amendment was concerned "If no better formula can be found, then we will propose the adoption of the formula which received agreement in 1970 (*sic*) in Victoria."[31] So far as I am aware, this suggestion has received no favourable response from any province and, as we shall see, the explicit reactions of Ontario and Quebec make any renewal of constitutional review unlikely.

One of the unfortunate results of the review process and the vast amount of constitutional discussion that took place in the 1960s was the weakening of the legitimacy of the existing constitution, without agreement on a new and allegedly better one. There was widespread denigration of the procedures and institutions which had evolved over a century, and an unthinking disposition that because the Canadian constitution was in a relative sense old it was therefore inadequate. T.C. Douglas stated this kind of view in 1966, "The time has come for Canadians to free themselves from the dead hand of the past and forge a constitution that will enable Canada to keep its rendezvous with destiny. ... I do not think that the dead hand of the past should be allowed to stay the onward march of progress. Human rights are sacred but constitutions are not."[32] In somewhat more restrained terms but to the same general effect, Prime Minister Pearson said in his opening speech to the Federal-Provincial Constitutional Conference of February 1968, "The British North America Act was a great act of statesmanship in its day. ... It has served as the constitutional basis for the growth of the strong and varied Confederation that we know today. But it is hardly to be expected that an act passed more than a hundred years ago should be adequate for all the needs or aspirations of Canadians today, let alone for the future."[33] Perhaps one of the most extreme attacks on the Canadian constitutional system that was made in this period came in a textbook in constitutional law by J. Noel Lyon and Ronald G. Atkey.[34] The Lyon-Atkey argument was for a radical judicial activism, particularly in the field of human rights, and what was to be overcome was the tradition of legislative supremacy as modified by the constitutional division of legislative powers. Here is their judgement of the Canadian constitutional tradition. "There is nothing wrong with the English constitution, and ours is built upon the solid base that had developed by 1867. However, the Canadian nation is sufficiently different from the English that a process of adoption is called for, and if the 'me too' is our dominant response to the challenge of developing a Canadian nation, it could be argued that we would have been better advised to remain a colony."[35] Such criticisms as these along with various kinds of proposals for radical constitutional change emanating from Quebec almost inevitably sapped the legitimacy of the constitution under which Canada had developed.

In a thoughtful article published in 1970, Alan C. Cairns deplored the "assault on the existing constitution".[36] There had not, unfortunately, developed the notion of a living constitution: "A Constitution is not merely a piece of paper. It is a set of relationships between governments and between governments and people which has become embedded in the evolving habits and values of successive generations of Canadians." Cairns was critical not only of the kinds of attacks on the constitution that had been mentioned above but of attempts to resolve constitutional questions by reference to the original settlement of 1867 and the intentions of the Fathers. But the intentions of the Fathers are in many ways irrelevant to our existing circumstances and one might say, although Cairns did not, that these give no more clues to, say, the control over telecommunications or federal-provincial financial responsibilities for health services than a Christian would find in looking in the Scriptures for advice about the indexing of income taxes. What is rather required is an understanding of the "living constitution" and Cairns lists in summary fashion changes made to the constitution of 1867 — judicial changes in the division of legislative powers, formal amendments to the BNA Act, the proliferation of federal-provincial meetings, grant-in-aid arrangements, interprovincial fiscal equalization etc. He concludes ". . . we might consider whether constitutions are not like wine — much better when aged."

The comprehensive nature of the constitutional review process in 1968-1971 also appears to shut off for the foreseeable future deliberate constitutional change of a more piecemeal kind. As we have seen, Prime Minister Trudeau suggested on October 2, 1974 that there be the renewal of constitutional discussions about an amending procedure. Four days later came the response of Premier Bourassa of Quebec.[37] The Quebec government had no objections "in principle" to the renewal of constitutional discussions, although formal discussions should be preceded by an attempt by more informal means to assess the possibility of an agreement. However, Premier Bourassa's major point was that Quebec would not agree to an amendment formula unless this was linked to a new division of powers between Ottawa and the provinces. As Quebec has linked a new amending procedure to a new division of powers, so Ontario has reacted to Prime Minister Trudeau's 1974 suggestion by linking it with changes in federal-provincial fiscal arrangements. The provincial Treasurer put the Ontario response in these terms in his Budget Statement published on April 7, 1975, "The Prime Minister, Mr. Trudeau, has suggested that the federal government and the provinces should renew discussions concerning patriation of the British North America Act. The Ontario Government again pledges its full support and cooperation towards this objective. However, patriation as such does not provide any solution to the more important constitutional issues, such as disentangling and recasting federal-provincial spending responsibilities, and more appropriate intergovernmental financing arrangements."[38] In general then, so far as the provinces are concerned constitutional review has come to be perceived as a comprehensive rather than a piecemeal process, and one in which the most fundamental of each jurisdiction's objectives and policies must be taken under discussion. As the events of 1968-1971 showed, agreement on a new constitution is in the near future very improbable, and this ill-advised exercise militates against constitutional reform of a more limited nature.

Notes

[1]For an able analysis of this process see Richard Simeon, *Federal-Provincial Diplomacy: The Making of Recent Policy in Canada*, University of Toronto Press, 1972, Chapter 5. A highly partisan account is given by Claude Morin, formerly Quebec's Deputy Minister of Intergovernmental Affairs, in his *Le pouvoir Québécois . . . en négociation"*, Les éditions du boréal express, Montréal, 1972, Dossier VIII. A useful collection of information about the review is contained in *The Constitutional Review, 1968-1971*, Secretary's Report, Canadian Intergovernmental Conference Secretariat, Information Canada, 1974.
[2]This committee did not become operative, as the process of constitutional review under Ottawa's leadership made it redundant.
[3]*Transcript (mimeo)* from the Prime Minister's Office.
[4]The Right Honourable Lester B. Pearson, *Federalism for the Future*, Queen's Printer, Ottawa, 1968.
[5]*ibid.*, pp. 34-36.
[6]For a justification of the comprehensive approach see The Right Honourable Pierre Elliott Trudeau, *The Constitution and the People of Canada*, Queen's Printer, Ottawa, 1969, p. 2.
[7]See generally *The Constitution and the People of Canada*, op. cit. pp. 4-22. ". . . the Constitution must express the purpose of Canadians in having become and resolving to remain associated together in a single country, and it must express as far as this is possible in a constitution what kind of country Canadians want, what values they cherish, and what objectives they seek." pp. 4-6.
[8]*Proceedings*, Queen's Printer, Ottawa, 1968.
[9]*Proceedings*, p. 545.
[10]Book I, *The Official Languages*, Queen's Printer, Ottawa, 1967.
[11]To the Canadian Bar Association National Convention, Vancouver, September 5, 1968 (mimeo).
[12]*Proceedings, op. cit.*, p. 5.
[13]Such as those for ousting Ottawa completely from the direct tax fields, creat-

ing five provinces to replace the existing ten and changing the federal role from interprovincial equalization to equalization among individuals wherever they lived in Canada.

[14]*The Constitution and the People of Canada, op. cit.,* p. 46.

[15]See a summary of the positions taken by Quebec under the Union Nationale government in *The Government of Quebec and the Constitution,* L'Office d'information et de publicité du Québec, Québec, 1969.

[16]The Honourable E.J. Benson, *The Taxing Powers and the Constitution of Canada,* Queen's Printer, Ottawa, 1969.

[17]The Honourable Harry E. Strom, *The Process of Constitutional Review: A Position Paper,* Edmonton, p. 15.

[18]In particular, Ottawa resisted the pressures of Ontario and perhaps other provinces that the Victoria meeting should discuss fiscal matters.

[19]*Outline of Quebec's Constitutional Proposals on Social Security,* Cabinet du Premier Ministre, June, 1971 (mimeo).

[20]Prime Minister's Office, (mimeo), pp. 3-4.

[21]Canadian Broadcasting Corporation Interview "Encounter", Transcript mimeo., July 1971.

[22]Communiqué from Premier Bourassa's Office, June 23, 1971, (mimeo).

[23]Prior to the Victoria Conference all three opposition parties in the Quebec National Assembly had expressed their hostility to what had come to be called the Trudeau-Turner formula for amendment. See Assemblée Nationale, *Journal des debats,* Commission permanente de la Constitution, 18 mai 1971, pp. BB16-1335.

[24]Information Canada, Ottawa, 1972.

[25]*Minority Report,* Ottawa, (mimeo.), March 7, 1972.

[26]*Senate Debates,* March 23-29, 1972, pp. 222-225, pp. 263-271 and pp. 278-286.

[27]*Minority Report,* (mimeo.), March 1972.

[28]However at this time the position of the Secretary of the Secretariat was retained. In May 1973 the Secretariat was superseded by the Canadian Intergovernmental Conference Secretariat which is headed by the former Secretary of the Constitutional Conference and services the various federal-provincial meetings.

[29]*Toronto Star,* March 28, 1972.

[30]*Globe and Mail,* March 29, 1972.

[31]*House of Commons Debates,* p. 7.

[32]*Globe and Mail,* April 13, 1966, quoted in Alan C. Cairns "The Living Constitution", LXXVII, *Queen's Quarterly,* No. 4, 1970, p. 4.

[33]*Proceedings,* p. 13.

[34]*Canadian Constitutional Law in a Modern Perspective,* University of Toronto Press, 1970. For my critical review of this book see L *Canadian Bar Review,* March 1972, pp. 139-148. The Lyon-Atkey formulation was not tied specifically to the need for a new constitution.

[35]*ibid.,* p. V.

[36]Cairns, *loc. cit.*

[37]"La Priorité Pour le Moment, C'est L'Inflation", *Communiqué,* Conseil Exécutif du Québec, Oct. 6, 1974 (mimeo.).

[38]*1975 Ontario Budget,* Toronto, 1975, Budget Statement, p. 34.

CHAPTER 3

EXECUTIVE FEDERALISM

Canada like other federations has moved away from "classical federalism" in which each level of government performed the responsibilities assigned to it by the constitution in relative isolation from the other. In the contemporary world, both the citizens and the constituent governments of federations have become so interdependent that if some matter within the sphere of public decision is of concern only to particular state or provincial communities, it is not crucial even to those communities. For example, if some jurisdictions maintain inadequate health or welfare services, some of the people who suffer from such deprivation move elsewhere in the country and create burdens where they go. A province which maintains lax regulations over the sale of securities defeats the objectives of other governments which wish such regulation to be more stringent. Examples of such interdependence could be multiplied, although almost no serious attempts have been made in Canada to assess with any precision the impact of particular federal and provincial policies on the ability of other governments to pursue their purposes. In general, it is unhelpful to talk about a division of powers and functions in terms of the central government being given these related to the nation "as a whole" while conferring on the provinces those of concern only to these smaller communities.

As we saw in Chapter 1, constitutional amendment and evolving patterns of judicial review have been somewhat unresponsive in redelineating the respective powers of the two levels of government as circumstances change. In the next chapter, it will be argued that relations between the federal and provincial wings of the political parties are not very effective in giving authoritative resolution to conflicts between centrifugal and centripetal tendencies in Canada. Thus, in managing the ongoing federal system a very heavy burden is placed on what may be called executive federalism, which may be defined as the relations between elected and appointed officials of the two levels of government.

The Influences Leading to Executive Federalism

There are several interrelated factors at work to make the interaction between federal and provincial governments more frequent:
— the ever-broadening scope of public decision brings into being new circumstances where federal and provincial objectives must somehow

be harmonized if public policy is to be effective. To take an important example, government responsibility for employment opportunities can be effectively discharged only through a plethora of measures relating to economic stabilization, regional economic development, vocational education and occupational retraining for adults etc. Without minimal levels of cooperation federal and provincial governments will increasingly frustrate the policies of each other by inadvertence or even in some cases by deliberate design.

— nationalist and egalitarian sentiments propel the federal government into action directed toward establishing minimum Canada-wide standards in respect to such public services as are from time to time defined to be vital to the welfare of all citizens. These services are for the most part within the constitutional jurisdiction of the provinces. Gunnar Myrdal has argued that "the welfare state is nationalistic", a series of responses to the dislocations suffered by citizens through the progressive disintegration of the international economic order,[1] and at the successive Federal-Provincial Conferences he attended Premier Smallwood used his gifts of vivid exposition to call attention to the unequal opportunities lying ahead of a baby born in a Newfoundland outport compared with those available to one born in the more favoured parts of Canada, and demanded that Ottawa take steps to remedy these inequalities.

— contemporary levels of taxation — along with the deliberate use of fiscal policy by the federal and provincial governments to secure employment, growth and price stability objectives — mean that there is an increasingly intense competition for tax sources and that the expenditure policies of each level have direct and indirect consequences for the other. These matters will be analyzed in Chapter 5.

— there are an increasing number of fields of public policy where both levels of government are active. In fact, there are few areas of important public decision — general elementary and secondary education is one — where only one level is involved. During the period between the end of the Second World War and the early 1960s, Ottawa came increasingly to take action in respect to matters within provincial legislative jurisdiction, mainly through the exercise of the spending power. More recently the federal government has become somewhat more discriminating in the use of this power, and in particular has not since the medicare legislation of 1966-67 established any major grant-in-aid programs. In the past decade, however, there has come to be a significant degree of provincial involvement in matters previously believed to be of exclusive or almost exclusive federal concern — broadcasting, immigration, international economic relations, banking, etc. It is highly unrealistic to hope for a situation in which all or even most of the responsibilities of government are assigned in their entirety to one level or the other. However, a recognition of the inevitability of *some* level of concurrence need not lead to the acceptance of the extent of joint responsibility that exists, and the master-solution of the Special Joint Committee of the Senate and of the House of Commons on the Constitution of Canada suggested a new division of powers in which the federal government would have exclusive or paramount powers in respect to economic matters and the provinces exclusive or paramount powers in social policy.[2] However, even with a more clear-cut delineation of responsibilities along these or other lines there would still be the need of federal-provincial cooperation in those circumstances where the activities of one level impinged on the responsibilities of the other.

In the face of the growing interdependence of the two levels of government, the development of federal-provincial institutions and procedures to manage such interdependence has consistently lagged behind what informed observers of Canadian federalism have believed necessary. Apart from the judicial system, the framers of the Confederation settlement seem not to have foreseen the necessity of consultation and collaboration between Ottawa and the provinces, and in the early years of the federation relations were of a formal, legal nature carried out through communication between the Lieutenant-Governors and the federal Secretary of State for the Provinces. In more recent times, the desperate circumstances of the Great Depression and the dominance of the federal government during the Second World War and for the decade afterward inhibited the development of institutionalized means of federal-provincial collaboration. Although in respect to many matters of a rather specialized kind such collaboration developed after 1945, there was little machinery for dealing with questions of a more comprehensive nature until the 1960s.

It is significant that pressures for more formalized means of federal-provincial interaction have often come from provinces interested in challenging federal power. At the Dominion-Provincial Conference on Reconstruction in 1945-46 Premier Drew of Ontario pressed unsuccessfully for permanent federal-provincial machinery in respect to economic matters.[3] Premier Lesage of Quebec at the November 1963 Federal-Provincial Conference put forward his variant of "cooperative federalism" which involved both a fastidious respect by Ottawa for the constitutional jurisdiction of the provinces and permanent federal-provincial organisations to determine "tariff structures, transportation and even monetary policies",[4] fields which up to the present were considered as exclusively under federal government jurisdiction. In the same direction, Premier Davis of Ontario at the Federal-Provincial Conference of November 1971 made a proposal that the First Ministers constitute themselves as a "Joint Economic Committee" whose purpose would be "to review and determine, on a continuing basis, national economic goals of a strategic order".[5] As was the case with the previous suggestions by Premiers Drew and Lesage, this was a part of a provincial campaign to resist what were alleged to be the centralizing tendencies dominant in Ottawa.

The development in the past decade of increasingly institutionalized machinery for intergovernmental collaboration has been concomitant with the weakening of the federal dominance which was established during the Great Depression and Second World War and perpetuated for more than a decade after the latter ended. Effective intergovernmental cooperation means that governments will give up their unqualified discretion over matters within their constitutional jurisdiction. Such a surrender is unlikely where one level or the other is dominant. What came in the 1960s to be characterized with some inaccuracy as "cooperative federalism" was a response to the weakening of the power of the central government under provincial pressures.

The Machinery of Federal-Provincial Relations

There have been several attempts to enumerate the institutions of federal-provincial relations. K.W. Taylor in 1957 listed 67 federal-provincial committees.[6] In 1965 the federal government distributed a list of 125 federal-provincial conferences and meetings in that year, although using a somewhat different classification Edgar Gallant found 121.[7] Gérard Veilleux discovered that 119 federal-provincial committees had held 159 meetings in 1967[8] while for the same year the Institute of Intergovernmental Relations of Queen's University enumerated 190 federal-provincial *and* interprovincial committees.[9] Using quite different criteria of selection than any of the other counts, the Descriptive Inventory of Federal-Provincial Programs and Activities as of September 30, 1973 runs to more than 400 typed pages,[10] including 98 items under the category of "Conditional Grants and Payments in respect of Shared-Cost Programs and Activities". These various counts do nót proceed from a common basis of classification, and although they convey a broad impression of the increasing incidence of federal-provincial interaction they are not otherwise very useful for analysis. Tabulations made by the Alberta Department of Federal and Intergovernmental Affairs of the involvement of that province in federal-provincial and interprovincial meetings in 1973 give a more meaningful picture of executive federalism.[11] Alberta representatives participated in 118 meetings and conferences; of these, 25 were bilateral (Alberta-federal), 73 multilateral (federal and all provinces) and 20 regional. So far as the levels of representation at multilateral meetings were concerned, 23 were ministerial, 24 deputy ministerial, 14 assistant deputy and 14 at other levels. It appears that most of the Alberta ministers attended a regular annual conference related to the concerns of their respective departments — labour, education, health, mining etc. The Department also reported that on April 30, 1973 the province was involved in 127 agreements with the federal government.

In the period between the end of the Second World War and the establishment of the Continuing Committee on Fiscal and Economic Matters in 1955, institutionalized federal-provincial interaction was for the most part limited to two kinds of matters — the periodic renegotiation of the tax arrangements and cooperation in respect to specific services and facilities, the latter often within the framework of shared-cost programs. There was relatively little integration of these two kinds of matters and the sharing of taxes and revenues was determined by finance and treasury departments in relative isolation from collaboration between officials and agencies of the two levels with concerns limited to specific programs. Neither, as we shall see in Chapter 5, was there institutionalized collaboration in fiscal policy as an instrument of economic stabilization.

The establishment of the Continuing Committee on Fiscal and Economic Matters in 1955 was a break-through in the institutionalization of federal-provincial fiscal relations.[12] The press communiqué issued by the Conference of Prime Ministers and Premiers on October 3 of that year stated:

> By general agreement the Conference established a committee of federal and provincial officials to meet from time to time to exchange information and examine technical problems in the field of federal-provincial fiscal and economic relations. Representation on this committee will be designated by the Prime Minister or Premier of each government respectively and the chairman will be designated by the Prime Minister of Canada. The Committee will not take collective action but each of its members will report to his own government on the subjects discussed.[13]

It should be noted that the Committee was authorized only to share information and discuss technical matters and was to have no collective responsibility for either recommendation or action. It was made up of senior appointed officials. The Committee performed useful work in connection with the tax arrangements which came into effect in 1957 and acted as a Secretariat for several future Federal-Provincial Conferences. However, it was not until seven years later that more important progress was made in institutionalizing financial relations between the two levels.

The Federal-Provincial Conference of March 31-April 1, 1964 provided for the establishment of the Tax Structure Committee.[14] This new and more ambitious attempt to establish a machinery for fiscal cooperation came at one of the most turbulent of Conferences in recent times, at the end of which an angry Premier Lesage of Quebec issued his own dissenting communiqué and threatened to challenge in the courts Ottawa's alleged encroachments on provincial jurisdiction. The Tax Structure Committee was to consist of Ministers of Finance and Treasurers. It was given the collective responsibility to report on several important matters to the Federal-Provincial Conference of heads of government early in 1966 — probable trends of public expenditure in the 1967-72 period, general problems in shared-cost programs in this period, the joint occupancy of tax fields, equalization grants to the provinces and "future intergovernmental liaison on fiscal and economic matters". The Continuing Committee on Fiscal and Economic Matters was in effect to be the staff agency of the Tax Structure Committee. It was also decided in 1964 that the Treasurers and Ministers of Finance should meet toward the end of each calendar year just prior to the time when each government's budget was being formulated to discuss the general economic and financial situation. This procedure was not regularized until nearly the end of the 1960s but is now in effect.

The beginning of constitutional review in 1968 brought into existence a Continuing Committee of Officials to supervise the process and a Federal-Provincial Constitutional Secretariat to serve the Committee and the Constitutional Conferences of First Ministers. With the virtual termination of constitutional discussions in the wake of the Victoria Conference the Secretariat was disbanded in early 1972.

Along with the machinery relating to the most comprehensive concerns of the two levels, there is a vast and complex network of federal-provincial interactions dealing with more specific matters. These range in particularity from meetings related to the national inventory of historic buildings to the annual conferences of ministers of health, labour, the environment and so on. Often, but by no means invariably, these groupings are focused on one or more programs of federal conditional grants to the provinces. As a general rule, the more limited the scope of such interactions the more likely there is to be agreement-agreement based on the professional norms of engineers, foresters, social workers, public health specialists, and so on.[15] However, in their examination of federal-Ontario relations concerning adult occupational training in the late 1960s, J. Stefan Dupré and his colleagues told of the exacerbation of conflict based on the contradictory goals of officials from the two levels, with the federal concerns being related largely to manpower and employment considerations and those of the province to educational objectives.[16] In the past decade there has been a generalized trend toward subsuming federal-provincial relations at the middle and lower levels of the public services where under most circumstances professional and technical considerations are important to machinery where ministers and their deputies are participants. The concerns of these latter officials are of course more directly related to broader policies and to partisan politics.

At the senior levels of decision the federal and provincial governments handle their relations with each other by various kinds of institutional machinery. This machinery is in process of rapid evolution and has never been carefully studied. (It is a measure of the relative isolation of Ottawa and the provinces in earlier years that Premier Manning of Alberta and the Honourable C.D. Howe, the federal Minister of Trade and Commerce, met only in 1952 after both had been influential members of their respective governments since 1935).[17] Prior to the 1960s federal-provincial relations consisted for the most part of the periodic renegotiation of the five-year tax arrangements and the interactions revolving about particular conditional grants. Thus for ministers and most of their senior officials these relations were of only intermittent concern. Now there is in Ottawa a standing committee of cabinet on federal-provincial relations, an advisor to cabinet in federal-provincal relations who was formerly Clerk of the Privy Council, a Federal-Provincal Relations Division in the Privy Council Office, an Assistant Deputy Minister of Finance for whom the major responsibilities of himself and his subordinates are fiscal relations with the provinces and a Federal-Provincial Coordination Division in the Department of External Affairs. The Lesage government in Quebec established a Department of Federal-Provincial Relations in 1961 and this

Department as reorganized in 1967 as the Department of Intergovernmental Affairs was under the direct control of successive Premiers throughout this decade. Ontario conducts its external relations through the Department of Treasury, Economics and Intergovernmental Affairs, which is also responsible for the normal treasury functions as well as relations between the province and its municipal and regional governments.

Alberta in 1972 established a Department of Federal and Intergovernmental Affairs under its own Minister.[18] The Department is broadly responsible for the coordination and review of all Alberta policies and programs involving the province with the federal government and those of the other provinces and with foreign countries and international agencies. It is organized in three sections — Social and Cultural Affairs, Resources and Industrial Development, and Constitutional and Economic Affairs. It also controls Alberta House in London, whose responsibilities have recently been extended to the European continent, and offices in Tokyo and Los Angeles, as well as the activities of the permanent provincial office in Ottawa. Since its establishment the Department's major involvements have been in the Western Economic Opportunities Conference of 1973, the continuing conflict with Ottawa in respect to energy matters and the negotiation of the General Development Agreement with the federal Department of Regional Economic Expansion which came into effect in 1974.

The Federal-Provincial Conference of Prime Ministers and Premiers has come to be one of the most crucial institutions of Canadian federalism. Prior to the beginning of constitutional review in 1968 such Conferences dealt almost exclusively with fiscal and economic matters and, from time to time, with attempts to agree on a formula for constitutional amendment. However, this range of discussions has come to be more extensive and such meetings are held with increasing frequency, at least twice each year.

The Federal-Provincial Conference very much needs detailed study. It is inaccurate to suggest, as some have done, that it has become the third level of government in Canada. Such an assertion ignores the important difference between the actual and potential powers of this emergent institution. In terms of potentiality, the Conference could prevail over even the constitution because the constitution could and would be amended in any direction on which the federal and all the provincial governments could agree. In fact, the capacity to reach agreement is very much circumscribed by the divergent policy and partisan-political interests of its members. In the absence of further research the following generalizations can be made about this emergent institution:

(1) The Conference has come to be a highly visible forum for the discussion of some of the most important issues facing Canada. The proceedings of the Confederation for Tomorrow Conference of November 1967 were nationally televised, as were those of the Constitutional Conferences of February 1968 and December 1969 and the conferences on energy in January 1974 and April 1975. Some if not all of the particip-

ants dislike this degree of openness[19] and certainly none of the decisive processes of negotiation is going to be conducted before the television cameras. However, the increasing frequency of Conferences and their extensive reportage by the media ensure the prominence of this institution in the consciousness of Canadians concerned with public affairs. At any rate, the very size of these gatherings makes any high degree of secrecy impossible — for example, at the Federal-Provincial First Ministers Conference on Energy held in January 1974 there were fifty-seven ministers and one hundred and thirty advisers officially accredited. Parliament and the provincial legislatures spend relatively little of their time with federal-provincial relations as such — there is not in Parliament or it seems in any of the provincial legislatures a committee dealing with these relations conforming to the more structured machinery on the executive side of government — and the publicity given to First Ministers' Conferences contributes to public awareness of these issues.

(2) Although up until the 1970s most of the discussions of the Conferences centred on fiscal and constitutional matters, there has been a tendency to include other aspects of joint concern and to establish sub-committees, sometimes at the ministerial and sometimes at the official level, to report directly to the Conference. In the past five years there have been discussions about environmental pollution, Indian affairs, foreign investment, energy, the control of inflation, winter unemployment and other matters of mutual interest.

(3) During recent years there has been a vast improvement in the staff work of the Conferences. Prior to the 1960s most of the provinces if not the federal government conducted themselves at such meetings in a somewhat amateurish way. This has now changed, although the variations among the provinces remains very great. At the intergovernmental level the improvement of the staff function came largely with the work of the Continuing Committee on Fiscal and Economic Matters, the Tax Structure Committee and the Secretariat of the Constitutional Conference. As we have seen, Ottawa and some of the provinces have developed specialized structures for federal-provincial relations. There is now in Ottawa a Canadian Intergovernmental Conference Secretariat.[20] A strong case can be made that sophistication in staff work is a significant element in the influence of particular governments in federal-provincial relations. At least this was the message received by the government of Ontario in the mid-1960s, when on the basis of the demonstration effects of the Quebec performance there was a radical restructuring of intergovernmental relations machinery. As we have seen, Alberta has recently embarked on the same course and it is probable that in varying degrees other provinces will follow.

(4) Federal-provincial relations at the level of generalized policy have not evolved formalized and agreed-upon procedures, although these relations have become a crucial part of the ongoing political system they have not been constitutionalized. Who has the authority to cause a Conference to be called? How is the agenda determined? Are Conferences to be open or closed? Should final communiqués contain refer-

ences to disagreements among the participating governments? Is it
reasonable to expect that First Ministers commit their administrations
at Conferences or are there circumstances where such commitment can
be withheld? Is it appropriate for governments to introduce new proposals into Conferences without prior consultation with other governments? To what extent, if at all, is an incoming government bound by
its predecessor? What are reasonable conditions of secrecy in federal-
provincial relations? Because of the lack of firm conventions, these
relations have tended to be carried on in a somewhat personalized way
and participants in the intensive interactions of the middle and late
1960s spoke of the "clubby" atmosphere that had developed among
elected and appointed officials. Yet more recently this informality has
been weakened by the rapid turnover of personnel. Of the first ministers who began the process of constitutional review in February 1968
only one — Premier Alex Campbell of Prince Edward Island — is still
the head of his government and between 1969 and 1974 governments
were displaced in eight of the ten provinces. There has been a similar
turnover of senior appointed officials and such important participants
in the 1960s as R.B. Bryce, A.W. Johnson, Edgar Gallant, Simon Reis-
man, H. Ian Macdonald and Claude Morin are no longer involved. Such
changes of personnel subject federal-provincial relations to added
stress when there are few formalized procedures governing these
relations.

(5) The Conferences require the Prime Minister of Canada to assume
roles which may be in conflict. In this context he is at once chairman,
the head of a government with interests to safeguard, and the leader of
a national political party. Lester B. Pearson asserted that in Federal-
Provincial Conferences the Prime Minister of Canada "should often act
more in an diplomatic capacity than in a political negotiating
capacity".[21] In accord with this strategy Mr. Pearson while in office
made it a practice at Conferences to let one or other of his Ministers put
forward and defend the federal government's inevitably contentious
viewpoints while he himself preferred to carry on negotiations in a
more informal setting. The major aim of the Prime Minister was thus to
preside over the formal meetings of Conferences in such a way as to
facilitate harmony and constructive negotiation. Prime Minister
Trudeau's style inclines him towards confrontation and toward discussion through sharpening points of disagreement. He has also more
firmly-held convictions about the shape of Canadian federalism than
did his predecessor and has thus emphasized his role as the defender of
federal interests.

During the past decade federal-provincial relations have become of
increasing importance to all governments and have been generalized in
the sense that particularized policies have come to be dealt with within
a framework of more comprehensive concerns than was so before. To a
very large extent this can be explained by the very severe strains that
successive Quebec governments in the 1960s imposed on the Canadian
Confederation. Quebec's single-minded strategy in sustaining and enhancing its discretion almost inevitably gave rise to comprehensive

counter-strategies on the part of the federal authorities and to varying degrees those of the other provinces. The process of constitutional review almost by its nature encouraged governments to consider particular matters within the framework of more general principles. The weakening of Ottawa's dominance over the Canadian federal system from the late 1950s onward made necessary intergovernmental negotiation about matters which were formerly decided upon by the federal authorities alone. Further, as we shall see later in this chapter, there has been a dissatisfaction with the incrementalism of the governmental process and a thrust toward dealing with particularized matters within a context of wider concerns. Edgar Gallant has summarized these developments in his assertion that whereas in international relations the establishment of diplomatic machinery with generalized concerns preceded for the most part the growth of specialized functional agencies, the recent evolution of Canadian federalism had been in the other direction.[22]

There is fragmentary evidence that relations between Ottawa and individual provinces and groups of provinces are becoming more important. Prior to the Victoria Conference on the Constitution in 1971, the then federal Minister of Justice consulted intensively in the provincial capitals; the incumbent Minister of Energy, Mines and Resources has more recently followed the same pattern of bilateral meetings in respect to energy matters. Thus, as in international relations summit meetings of heads of government have become a part of the ongoing process of consultation. In the wake of the very weak showing of the federal Liberals in western Canada in the general election of October 1972, Prime Minister Trudeau caused to be convened the Western Economic Opportunities Conference in Calgary in July 1973. Following an intensive review of development programs in 1973, the federal Department of Regional Economic Expansion has negotiated comprehensive General Development Agreements with each of the provinces. As we shall see in Chapter 7, the Foreign Investment Review Act enacted by Parliament in 1973 commits the federal authorities in general terms to take provincial objectives and policies into account when decisions relating to foreign investment are being made. New kinds of relations of a bilateral nature may occur in respect to shared-cost programs; agreements have recently been signed with the provinces reimbursing them for a part of the expenses incurred under their varying legal aid schemes in matters related to the criminal law, and this general procedure may be followed in other matters in the future.

Bilateral federal-provincial relations have potentialities both for overcoming the inflexibilities inherent in multilateral negotiations and for creating suspicions of the federal authorities among the provinces. In the 1960s there were some anxieties among the provinces in respect to Ottawa-Quebec relations, and in this decade some of the provinces have surmised that their legitimate interests were compromised by the federal policy of insulating the negotiations leading up to the General Development Agreements with each province. In the Final Report on Economic Nationalism issued by the Select Committee of the Legislative Assembly of Ontario on Economic and Cultural Nationalism in early 1975, it was recommended that there be established by law more formalized procedures for federal-provincial consultation under the Foreign Investment Review Act and that *all* provinces receive notices filed with the Foreign Investment Review Agency under terms of the Act.[23]

In the years immediately ahead it is likely that federal-provincial relations will increasingly be concerned with regulatory matters in such fields as energy, the environment, consumer protection, communications, transportation, and foreign ownership.[24] If there is to be a measure of coherence in public policies of a regulatory nature there will have to be patterns of federal-provincial cooperation established quite different from those which prevail under grant-in-aid arrangements. In these latter programs, bargaining about the respective roles of the two levels revolves about the circumstances that federal financial incentives are used to persuade the provinces to conform to the will of the central government, while provincial strength arises from the fact that the matters of concern are within provincial jurisdiction. The situation is different in public regulation — federal money cannot be used to gain provincial compliance and the constitutional responsibilities are usually divided between the two levels.

Interprovincial and Tri-Level Relations

Since 1960 there has been an increased institutionalization not only of relations between the federal and provincial governments but of relations among the provinces. Further, although the situation is still fluid, there is some development toward associating federal, provincial and local governments together in what have come to be called tri-level relations.

At the Dominion-Provincial Conference of July 25-27, 1960, the newly-elected Premier Lesage of Quebec indicated his intention to invite the heads of the provincial governments to a meeting to discuss common problems,[25] and from that year onward the premiers have had an annual conference in August. In his more extended analysis of cooperative federalism presented at the Federal-Provincial Conference of November, 1963, the Quebec leader put forward the view that federal involvement in provincial matters could and would be lessened if all the provinces or groups of provinces developed institutionalized procedures for formulating economic policies.[26]

The annual Premiers' conferences, held at the invitation of the various provinces, are informal meetings. Unlike the Federal-Provincial Conferences of Prime Ministers and Premiers, each of the heads of government is usually accompanied by not more than two or three advisers. It is usual for the federal government to send observers, usually officials of the Department of Finance and/or of the Federal-Provincial Affairs Secretariat of the Privy Council Office.

During the 1960s relatively little progress was made towards the Lesage goal of interprovincial cooperation, and by the end of the decade the attendance of the premiers at the annual August conferences was beginning to fall away. However, the present decade has seen the resurgence of interprovincialism and of situations in which all or almost all of the provinces take a common stand against Ottawa. In a brief to the first national trilevel conference held in August 1972, all the provinces except Manitoba endorsed the position that the federal government should deal with the municipalities only through the provincial administrations.[27] At the Premiers' conference of August 1974, all the provinces protested the decision of the federal government in its budget of the preceding May not to allow corporations to deduct provincial royalties from their income as taxable for federal purposes. In September 1974 the provincial ministers of health unanimously rejected Ottawa's proposal for a federal block grant-in-aid of health services with such payments increasing annually as the Gross National Product rose.[28] Finally, the provincial ministers of communications were able in early 1975 to agree on a common policy about the respective roles of the two levels of government in respect to broadcasting and telecommunications.[29] Thus the implicit ground-rules of executive federalism appear to be in process of change. During the 1960s it appears to have been the position of some of the provinces, a position based on both principled and pragmatic considerations, that it was inappropriate to deal with matters of federal-provincial concern in an interprovincial setting. These inhibitions seem to have passed. However, as this is written, (July 1975) there is an instance of the limits of interprovincial cooperation having been reached. In his budget of June 23, 1975 the federal Minister of Finance announced that Ottawa would impose limits to its contributions to provincial medical insurance schemes and gave notice that at the end of the five-year period as required by law the federal government would terminate its existing financial responsibilities in respect to hospital insurance. Early in July the Ontario Minister of Health attempted to convene a meeting of his counterparts to protest this action, but the governments of the four western provinces refused to attend. There is every reason to believe that these latter governments are hostile to the federal action, but it may be are not disposed to cooperate in what they see as the attempt of the Ontario government to enlist their aid in a provincial election campaign, which was expected in the fall where Premier Davis and his colleagues appeared determined to fight on an anti-Ottawa program.

In the past decade there has been some development in the regional associations of the maritime and western provinces. The Council of Maritime Premiers was constituted in 1971, partly in response to the Report on Maritime Union (usually called the Deutsch Report) which had recommended the amalgamation of New Brunswick, Nova Scotia and Prince Edward Island into one province. In a legal sense at least, the Council is a much more extensive recognition of interprovincial cooperation than has hitherto occurred in Canada, as each of the three legislatures has enacted a law giving this body the status of an agent in respect to specific administrative operations. Cooperation has been put underway in such projects as establishing an integrated post-secondary education commission for the three provinces; the standardization of legislation and regulations related to trucking, motor vehicle registration and drivers' licences; a Maritime Land Registration and Information Service; and the establishment of an Atlantic Police Academy. The Council also has its own permanent secretariat. Since the mid-1960s the premiers of the three prairie provinces have been constituted as the Prairie Economic Council. The cooperation among the western governments — more recently joined by British Columbia — was facilitated by the convening on Federal initiative of the Western Economic Opportunities Conference in July 1973. The implications of western regionalism will be more fully discussed in Chapter 7.

During the 1960s and beyond there has been some development of interprovincial machinery focused around particular functions of government. The most significant institutional development here is that of the provincial ministers of education established with its own secretariat in 1967, a body which has been the contact with Ottawa in such matters as international conferences on education and federal programs in aid of instruction in one or other of the official languages. Also there are regular meetings of provincial ministers in such fields as labour, health, welfare, telecommunications and agriculture.

During recent years there has been discussion and some limited development in relating the municipal governments with Ottawa and the provinces in the discussion and formulation of social and economic policy, particularly as this policy relates to the comprehensive phenomenon of urbanization. In 1971 was established the Ministry of State for Urban Affairs whose responsibilities according to the Proclamation setting up this organization were to:

> formulate and develop policies for implementation through measures within fields of federal jurisdiction in respect of
> a) the most appropriate means by which the Government of Canada may have a beneficial influence on the process of urbanization in Canada;
> b) the integration of urban policy with other policies and programmes of the Government of Canada;
> c) the fostering of cooperative relationships in respect of urban affairs with the provinces and, through them, their municipalities, and with the public and private organizations.

So far as federal activities in regard to urbanization are concerned, the Ministry is very much handicapped in that, in terms of David M. Cameron's analysis "Its only strength could derive from persuasion, persuasion directed at a cabinet composed primarily of ministers with operating portfolios, or at a bureaucracy consisting primarily of operating agencies."[30] The basic rationale of the new Ministry was the perceived need for new agencies without important operational responsibilities to formulate and coordinate policies in emergent fields of public concern. Whether such responsibilities can in fact be discharged in the absence of power over operating agencies and departments is doubtful.

The first national tri-level, conference was held in Toronto in November, 1972. Apart from Manitoba, which favoured direct contacts

between the federal and municipal governments, all the provinces agreed that contacts between Ottawa and the local authorities should be
through the provinces. At the 1972 conference and subsequently Ontario opposed tri-level consultations on a national basis, arguing that
the provinces alone were responsible for municipal development and
that what was desperately needed was more federal money granted
unconditionally for urban development.[31] There are now tri-level consultations of a formal or informal variety in several of the provinces and
cities and in Ontario each year federal representatives participate in
one of the quarterly meetings between the provinces and the representatives of Ontario municipalities.

In general terms, the aggressiveness of the provinces has inhibited
the kinds of direct federal-municipal relations which are common in
the United States. For several reasons Canadian municipalities have
been relatively ineffectual in influencing federal and provincial governments — perhaps because of the relative weakness, at least in comparison with the United States, of traditions of local democracy; because the Canadian Federation of Mayors and Municipalities has
lacked effective research and staff services and represents the divergent
interests of all kinds of municipalities; because the CFMM in dealing
with Ottawa and the provinces is a pressure group rather than a government. Further, the increasing sophistication of the provinces has led
them to more comprehensive policies in such fields as housing, urban
transportation and metropolitan development and thus to resist more
aggressively than before federal involvements in such fields.

The Provinces and Foreign Affairs[32]

Up until the past half-century international relations consisted for the
most part of matters of peace and war, trade and the negotiation and
implementation of treaties of a general nature. So far as federal nations
were concerned, these were matters recognized of concern to the central governments and legislatures alone, without active involvement of
the states or provinces. Today there is an increasing range of international interactions covering nearly every important aspect of life —
labour conditions, civil aviation, welfare, environmental pollution,
human rights, education, telecommunications, etc. The constitutions
of federal nations deal with those circumstances in varying ways.

Section 132 of the British North America Act of 1867 reads:

> The Parliament and Government of Canada shall have all Powers neces-
> sary or proper for performing the Obligations of Canada or of any Pro-
> vince thereof, as Part of the British Empire, towards Foreign Countries,
> arising under treaties between the Empire and such Foreign Countries.

Thus Canada could be bound to international obligations by the Imperial government and when this happened the authorities of the federal
government had power to give effect to these obligations even if this
meant trespassing on matters otherwise within provincial jurisdiction.
Canada attained full sovereign status by the Statute of Westminster in

1931, and Section 132 is now obsolete so far as international relations since that time are concerned, although its provisions still apply to Canada's continuing obligations undertaken by the British Empire prior to the Statute of Westminster.

So far as federalism and Canadian international relations are concerned, the leading judicial decision is the *Labour Conventions* reference decided by the Judicial Committee of the Privy Council in 1937.[33] At issue was the constitutional validity of three pieces of social legislation enacted by Parliament in 1935 as part of Prime Minister Bennett's "New Deal". The essential argument of the lawyers for the Dominion was that the legislation was enacted in fulfilment of Canada's obligations as part of the British Empire under the Treaty of Versailles and was thus justified under Section 132, although the matters were otherwise within provincial jurisdiction according to Section 92 of the British North America Act. The Judicial Committee denied this claim in stating, "The obligations are not obligations of Canada as part of the British Empire, but of Canada, by virtue of her new status as an international person. . . ." But the most significant part of the decision was its assertion that the Parliament of Canada did not acquire any legislative powers it would not otherwise have by virtue of the Canadian government incurring an international obligation by way of a treaty or otherwise. Thus "For the purposes of ss. 91 and 92 i.e. the distribution of legislative powers between the Dominion and the Provinces, there is no such thing as treaty legislation as such. The distribution is based on classes of subjects; and as a treaty deals with a particular class of subjects so will the legislative power of performing it be ascertained." The Judicial Committee deliberately refused to give an opinion on the executive power to conclude treaties and other international obligations binding Canada, i.e., whether these might be made by the federal government even though Parliament did not have the power to implement such obligations or, alternatively, whether such agreements might be made only by the authority which had legislative jurisdiction to implement them.

The latter part of the 1960s saw a continuing and bitter quarrel between the federal and Quebec governments about the role of the province in international affairs, a quarrel in which neither government demonstrated any significant amount of maturity. As a manifestation of "*épanouissement*" the new Quebec vastly extended its involvement in international affairs, particularly with France and the former French colonies of Africa. In this drive for international status Quebec was assisted by the de Gaulle government and France's African allies of *la Francophonie*. For its part, Ottawa came to believe, with considerable justification, that France was deliberately and mischievously involving itself in domestic Canadian affairs with the eventual objective of breaking up the Canadian federation. Throughout these incidents Quebec officials allowed themselves to be taken in by the flattery of being treated by the French government as representatives of a virtually sovereign state, while Ottawa reacted to these circumstances with an unduly touchy seriousness.

So far as the Quebec-Ottawa struggle was conducted in terms of legal and constitutional argument, the contestants based their cases on conflicting claims to conclude international agreements,[34] a matter which, as we have seen, was left unresolved by the Judicial Committee in the *Labour Conventions* reference. The Quebec assertion was that the prerogative power to conclude such agreements followed the division of legislative powers in the BNA Act. The implication was that so far as matters within provincial legislative jurisdiction were concerned, Quebec might assume any international status that other nations were willing to confer on her. Ottawa's case was that the prerogative power to enter into international arrangements and to conclude agreements binding in public international law resided in the federal executive alone. However, because in many circumstances the subject-matter of international relations was partly or wholly within provincial legislative jurisdiction, the provinces could and should play an important role in international affairs so long as they did not do this independently of the federal government. Thus, in constituting the Canadian delegations to international conferences dealing with provincial matters the federal authorities would normally choose provincial ministers or appointed officials. The federal authorities made much of the point that Canada had a single international personality and that the United Nations and its specialized agencies, as well as other international associations and international law, drew a very sharp line between jurisdictions which were sovereign states and those which were not. The general case was made that "foreign policy is indivisible", although in the Canadian circumstances this did not preclude the provinces in cooperation with the federal government being involved in international affairs.

The death of de Gaulle and the coming to power of the Bourassa government in Quebec made possible a, lessening of tension between Quebec City and Ottawa in respect to the international involvement of the province. In October 1971 the federal and Quebec governments concluded an agreement relating to their conditions of participation in the Agency for Cultural and Technical Cooperation, the major organization for such purposes in the French-speaking world.[35] This agreement provided that a Quebec government official would occupy one of the two positions allotted to Canada on the Board of Directors of the Agency, that in the official conferences of the Agency there would be Quebec ministers or officials and that these would express the Quebec point of view on matters within the constitutional jurisdiction of the provinces and that the Quebec government would pay half the Canadian contribution to the expenses of the Agency's Secretariat. Despite this agreement, two 1974 enactments of the Quebec National Assembly made clear that the provincial government was still determined to assert its position in international affairs. One of these enactments, "An Act respecting diplomatic and consular immunities and privileges", granted to consular officials and their staffs resident in Quebec and to those of the International Civil Aviation Association whose headquarters is in Montreal immunities in judicial and financial matters generally recognized by international custom. At the same Session of the National Assembly was enacted legislation redefining the responsibilities of the Minister and the Department of Intergovernmental Affairs, giving them the power to regulate all activities of Quebec government agencies as well as those of all local governments outside the province.

The provinces other than Quebec have had and continue to have relations outside the territorial boundaries of Canada. Thomas Levy reported in 1972 that only Newfoundland, Prince Edward Island, and Manitoba had no trade offices abroad, and Ontario, with more extensive international involvement in this respect than the other provinces, had offices in Düsseldorf, Brussels, Vienna, Stockholm, London, Tokyo, New York, Boston, Atlanta, Cleveland, Minneapolis and Los Angeles.[36] Provincial premiers and their cabinet colleagues have become indefatigable foreign travellers in search of investment and markets for provincial products, and in his highly-publicized tour of Italy in 1974 there were suggestions, malicious or otherwise, that Premier Davis of Ontario was seeking to enhance his political support among Italian-born immigrants at home. In August 1971, immediately after the government of the United States imposed its drastic solution of American balance-of-payments problems, spokesmen for both Ontario and Alberta suggested that offices in Washington be established for the better protection of provincial interests, although these intentions were not in fact implemented. Despite these involvements, the provinces other than Quebec have not been disposed to carry on their international involvements with challenges to a single Canadian personality in foreign affairs, and this lack of emphasis on the symbolic aspects of external affairs has undoubtedly decreased the possibility of conflict with Ottawa.

The increasing aggressiveness of the provinces, particularly in respect to economic matters, has brought about renewed pressure that Ottawa should establish more effective channels of consultation with the provinces in respect to international economic policies within federal jurisdiction. In particular, the provinces have demanded that they be consulted in Canadian policies toward the reduction of barriers to international trade carried on through the instrumentalities of GATT. Ontario has also insisted on being involved in Canada-US negotiations about the automobile agreement between the two countries.

Executive Federalism: Evaluation and Prospects

Contemporary circumstances have imposed a heavy burden on a relatively small number of elected and senior appointed officials of the federal and provincial governments in adjusting the Canadian federal system to the changing demands made upon it. In evaluating executive federalism only very modest criteria of performance are realistic. In general terms, we might ask how well the existing complex of relations has done in mitigating the disabilities inherent in a situation of autonomous though interdependent levels of government. By these modest standards, the achievements are considerable:

(1) There have been developed both formal and informal channels by which the federal and provincial governments can and do communicate information, perceptions and intentions to one another. This circumstance need not and often does not lead to agreement and in some cases may sharpen disagreement; it is one of the superstitions of the contemporary age that human conflict is overwhelmingly the result of inadequate communication rather than genuinely contradictory aspirations and interests. For example, the Tax Structure Committee in 1964 was directed to make projections of public revenues and expenditures for the 1967-72 period. In the course of this exercise considerable progress was made by the eleven governments in agreeing on more uniform classifications of expenditures and revenues. However, the Committee's report, when made public in 1970, demonstrated rather conclusively the continuing fiscal imbalance between the two levels, in which provincial expenditures were projected to increase more rapidly than revenues while for the federal government the reverse was true. This report was the basis for renewed provincial pressures for fiscal concessions from Ottawa. In reality, all that effective communications in this context can do — and this is sometimes decisive in the resolution or mitigation of conflict — is to ensure that governments which are both autonomous and interdependent proceed from accurate perceptions of facts and of one another's intentions. Executive federalism has achieved some success in this direction.

(2) Largely through the operations of executive federalism the role of the federal government in attempts to narrow regional economic disparities has gained a measure of legitimacy among the people and governments of the more prosperous parts of Canada. In particular, it is heartening that the more prosperous provinces have come to accept, albeit somewhat grudgingly at times, the principle of interprovincial equalization as this is embodied in the tax arrangements in effect from 1957 and the efforts of the federal government in regional economic development now carried on under the Department of Regional Economic Expansion. This acceptance has a measure of ambivalence and at times overt opposition to equalization is expressed. As in the 1930s Premier Hepburn of Ontario spoke of his province as the "milch-cow of Canada", so in the early 1970s Premier Bennett asserted that so far as Ottawa was concerned British Columbia was "a goblet to be drained"[37] and at one point the B.C. Attorney-General threatened an appeal to the courts on the constitutionality of equalization payments. In recent years Ontario's pressures for financial concessions have characteristically been framed not in terms of opposition to equalization as such — the principle of equalization is vehemently and frequently affirmed — but rather of the special fiscal needs of provinces and local jurisdictions undergoing rapid growth. It is impossible to gauge with any accuracy the toleration for interprovincial equalization among the citizens or governments of the more favoured parts of Canada. The incumbent federal government is more fully and explicitly committed to narrowing these disparities than any of its pre-

decessors, without displaying any profound disposition to educate those in the richer areas of the country about the rationale of these policies. It is also possible that the increasing aggressiveness of the provinces in enhancing their autonomy will weaken the will of federal politicians to tax Canadians and to distribute a large part of the proceeds to the provinces without concomitant powers to determine how these funds will be spent. Despite what appear to be setbacks, the legitimacy of Ottawa's role in interprovincial equalization has been established as a part of the operative Canadian constitution.

(3) As we shall see in Chapter 5, Canada has established and sustained important elements of an integrated tax structure in the crucial fields of personal and corporate income taxes. Although such integration is in the process of piecemeal dissolution, this tax-sharing system combined with interprovincial equalization of revenues through unconditional grants is particularly striking in contrast to the United States, where such has not been achieved.

(4) Executive federalism has been crucial to the evolution of the Canadian welfare state. Most of the crucial elements of health and welfare services are within the constitutional jurisdiction of the provinces. It is of course impossible to make any definitive judgements about what the state of these services would have been without the financial and administrative involvement of the federal government but it is reasonable to suppose that this has contributed both to a measure of nation-wide equality in the range and standard of these programs and to a larger total amount being spent on them than would have otherwise occurred. Further, federal action has been able to remove most barriers to the free movement of people within Canada, as these obstructions would otherwise have been occasioned by provincial and local residence requirements for access to public services. Particularly through federal grants-in-aid of hospital and medical insurance plans and of public assistance, residents are able to move throughout Canada without any break in their eligibility to receive these benefits. Similarly, the Canadian Pension Plan and the Quebec Pension Plan have been harmonized to facilitate free movement.

In respect both to fiscal matters and to federal grants-in-aid to the provinces there are developments which lessen the degree of federal-provincial integration which have developed in the past generation, and move Canada in these fields part of the way back toward classical federalism. These developments will be discussed more fully in Chapter 5 but may be noted briefly here:

— from 1966 onward it has been Ottawa's policy to force the provinces to meet rising expenditures from their own sources rather than reductions in the rates of federal income taxes. Under the abatement system in effect from 1957 to 1972, the provinces were from time to time able to influence the federal government to lower its rates of such taxes so that the provincial authorities could increase theirs without raising the total burden on the taxpayer. This abatement system was ended in 1972 and the federal government has also withdrawn from the field of estate taxes. Under agreements with the provinces Ottawa also collects personal income taxes in all parts of Canada except Quebec, and corporate income taxes for all provinces except Quebec and Ontario. These collection agreements in which provincial taxes are levied at the *rates* these jurisdictions determine give the participating provinces a direct interest in the *base* of the federal tax. However, this important measure of integration is in process of partial dissolution as Alberta has given notice that it will begin to collect corporate income taxes within two years, although the province would undoubtedly prefer that Ottawa collect these taxes on a radically revised base as set by Alberta. It seems likely that within the next five years Ontario will begin to collect its own taxes on individual incomes.

— current developments in conditional grants almost inevitably decrease the instances of federal-provincial collaboration in respect to highly particularized matters. During recent years several grant-in-aid arrangements such as those related to forestry and specific activities in the fields of public health have been ended, and the Canada Assistance Plan of 1966 incorporated several conditional grant programs into a coordinated scheme by which Ottawa meets half of all provincial public assistance costs regardless of the circumstances under which recipients were in need. Federal legislation related to medical insurance enacted in 1966 differed from previous grant-in-aid schemes in that it provided that assistance would be given to provincial plans which met certain specified requirements, without subsequent procedures for detailed controls enforced by the federal authorities. Quebec has accepted the alternative of contracting-out of certain established conditional grant schemes, and both Ontario and Alberta have announced their desire to do the same if acceptable financial compensation can be negotiated with Ottawa. It is not altogether unlikely that within the next five years the federal and provincial governments will come to agreement on a block grant scheme in the health field which would incorporate both medical and hospital services. There appear to be no new conditional grant schemes of any great consequence in the offing, and if new programs should be enacted it seems likely that Ottawa will support defined provincial activities without important controls over those activities, as is now the case with post-secondary education, legal aid and various activities supporting the teaching of the official languages.

As in international relations, the autonomous but interdependent governments of Canada and the provinces from time to time bypass the cumbersome processes of consultation and resort to unilateral action. During recent years the pressures for consultation have usually been in a one-way direction — from Ottawa to the provinces — and the provinces characteristically insist on exercising their powers without federal involvement or influence in regard to such matters as, for example, higher education, the development of natural resources and provincial and local borrowing in foreign capital markets, although in these and other circumstances important interests of the central government are directly engaged. On the other hand, prior consultation with the provinces was scanty or non-existent in several important federal decisions of consequence to the provinces in the last decade, including such decisions as those related to medical insurance in 1966, the 1966 plan for the financing of post-secondary education, the 1968 Social Development Tax and the provisions of the 1974 federal budget not to allow corporations to deduct royalties paid to the provinces from their taxable income.

Federal-provincial relations are the despair of those who accept the desirability of rationalty in the devising and implementing of public policy. Yet there has been an explicit commitment to rationality by Prime Minister Trudeau and his most influential cabinet colleagues and advisers[38] and rationality has come to be important in the thought and action in some of the provincial administrations, specifically Ontario and Quebec. There are three interrelated imperatives here. First, the objectives and priorities of public policy should be explicitly formulated. Second, the aims of policy should be stated at a high level of generalization and more specific aims controlled by broader ones. Third, the effectiveness and efficiency of ongoing or projected policies should be measured with as much precision as possible. The characteristic devices of administrative rationalism are cost-benefit analysis, systems analysis, long-term program budgets, the use of social indicators, the employment of econometric models in economic forecasting and Planning, Programming and Budgeting System (PPBS). The key agencies in these ascendant ways of thinking and administering in Ottawa have been the cabinet Committee on Priorities and Planning and the vast extension under Prime Minister Trudeau of the Prime Minister's Office, the Privy Council Office, and the Treasury Board. Rationality is a reaction against what has come to be called incrementalism, the making of public policy through the uncoordinated formulation and implementation of very specific adjustments with a minimum of effective over-head coordination or deliberative priority-setting.

When enthusiasts for administrative rationality encounter the intractabilities of federal-provincial relations there is a characteristic retreat suggesting more effective procedures of consultation and coordination. But consultation is a notoriously imprecise idea and may be regarded at one extreme as no more than jurisdictions giving each other advance notice about their intentions, and at the other a situation where governments have in fact surrendered their independent powers to agencies of joint decision-making. Between these poles, there are various circumstances where continuous patterns of mutual communication result in the interests of one level having an influence on the activities of the other. Coordination is capable of more exact definition. Thus according to the economist Charles E. Lindblom, "A set of decisions is coordinated if adjustments have been made in it such that the adverse consequences of any one decision for other decisions in the set are to a degree and in some frequency avoided, reduced, counterbalanced, or outweighed."[39] Or in budgetary terms, coordination would consist of all levels of government engaging in a joint process of ranking their priorities of expenditure so that the last dollar spent on each service or facility, however categorized, would contribute equally to agreed-upon objectives.

A student of contemporary American government has written what is equally true of Canada, "The quest for coordination is in many respects the twentieth-century equivalent of the medieval search for the philosopher's stone. If only we can find the right formula for coordination, we can reconcile the irreconcilable, harmonize competing and wholly divergent interests, overcome irrationalities in our government structures, and make hard policy choices to which no one will dissent."[40] G. Bruce Doern and V. Seymour Wilson criticize the rationalist revolt against incrementalism in Canada as being excessively managerial and as making an unwarranted separation of politics and administration.[41] "It is . . . unrealistic to speak of political policy co-ordination in terms which are analogous to managerial co-ordination or to co-ordination in any single policy field."[42] In referring to conversations with ministers and senior appointed officials, the authors of the Report on Intergovernmental Liaison in Fiscal and Economic Matters published in 1969 stated:

> Most of those with whom we talked agree with co-operative federalism as an idea. Some were prepared to accept it in the abstract as the logical working government form in Canada, but really with little idea of what this might mean in the long run. But in all too many cases we found an unwillingness, or at least an inability, to relate the principle to the practice and it is perhaps less interesting but nevertheless true that it is in the practice in particular cases that effective cooperation in government will succeed or fail. Part of the trouble may be in the fundamental state of uncertainty as to what kind of country we really want.[43]

The last sentence of this quotation suggests that the failure of federal and provincial governments to agree on particular matters arises from genuine and intractable differences, differences based on the conflicting partisan objectives of governments and their differing kinds of responsibilities. Coordination means almost by definition that there are procedures for giving authoritative resolution to divergent objectives and ranking of priorities. Again almost by definition, such procedures are absent in federal-provincial relations.

The patent unreality of administrative rationality is nowhere better illustrated than in the field of mineral policy. In April 1973 the federal and provincial ministers met together in a continuing association as "a first step . . . towards the formulation and implementation of comprehensive mineral policies for Canada". Out of this meeting came a glossy booklet with coloured pictures and a graphic representation of "proposed mineral objectives for Canada". The master-objective here was to "Obtain Optimum Benefit for Canada from Present and Future Use of Minerals" with twelve sub-objectives like the following: "Relate Mineral Development to Social Needs . . . Improve Mineral Conservation and Use . . . Foster a Viable Mineral Sector." etc."[44] At its second meeting in December 1974 the ministers jointly issued an even glossier compendium of charts, pictures and general intentions.[45] Yet in this latter year Ottawa and the provinces had been locked into one of the most bitter struggles in the history of federal-provincial fiscal relations about the taxation of depletable resources, a struggle with direct and immediate consequences for the future of mineral development in Canada.

A somewhat less dramatic example of the consequences of the intractable and, to a large extent, inevitable conflicts between federal and provincial objectives can be seen in the field of health care. The major federal programs here are carried out under the Hospital Insurance and Diagnostic Services Act of 1957 and the Medical Care Act of 1966-67 which provide that Ottawa will pay roughly half the costs of provincial hospital and medical insurance plans respectively, so long as these conform to federal requirements. Under both schemes the federal contributions are with unimportant exceptions limited to the most expensive kinds of health services, those given in active-treatment hospitals on the one hand and those performed by physicians on the other. These restrictions on federal assistance no doubt reflected Ottawa's priorities in health care when the two arrangements were established as well as the understandable federal desire to impose limits on contributions to the provinces. Yet such arrangements have contributed to Canada having on a per capita basis one of the most costly health care systems in the world by erecting strong disincentives to the provinces to establish custodial institutions with less expensive care than that of active-treatment hospitals and to provide certain medical services rendered by persons other than physicians.

Rationality in the policy process appears to contribute to increasingly intense conflicts between the two levels. There are several reasons for this view:

(1) G. Bruce Doern has recently written of the impact of Planning, Programming and Budgeting procedures on federal-provincial relations:

> There is already a sense of competitiveness between the federal government and the Ontario government regarding the best way to introduce PPB. It does not tax the imagination to see that we have reached a new era of analytical and bureaucratic competitiveness between the federal and provincial bureaucracies, especially between the big provincial bureaucracies of Ontario, Quebec and British Columbia.[46]

After the publication by the federal Minister of Finance of his White Paper on Tax Reform in 1969, there was a vigorous debate with the Ontario authorities. The substantive issue in dispute was whether Ottawa was concealing tax increases under the guise of tax reform. This debate about the validity of the federal projections of the tax yields consequent on its proposals can reasonably be regarded as a trial of bureaucratic competence between experts of the two governments.

(2) The renewed conflicts in respect to conditional grants from 1960 onward can be explained partly in terms of the sharpening of federal and provincial objectives. The earlier grant-in-aid programs were begun in periods of buoyant federal revenues and of limited concern

for the precise measurement of federal objectives. On the provincial side, "fifty-cent dollars" were more attractive than otherwise in the absence of precise program and budgetary goals. With relative financial stringency in Ottawa and with emphasis on rational priority-setting, a growing restiveness has emerged among federal officials about "open-ended" arrangements in which federal expenditures are determined by provinces, local governments and institutions of post-secondary education. In the provinces, administrative rationalization has made grants-in-aid less attractive than before because of their impact on program standards and expenditure-priorities.

(3) The increasing concern of the provinces with fiscal policy as an instrument of economic stabilization may well sharpen federal-provincial conflict. As we shall see in Chapter 5, this has certainly been so in the case of Ontario which has gone much further than any other province in designing and implementing its own independent fiscal policy in terms of the generalized requirements of full employment, price stability and economic growth.

(4) The provinces have come increasingly to view taxation and expenditure by governments as instruments for deliberate policies of income redistribution and to challenge federal policies in terms of these redistributive goals. Not only Ottawa but most of the provinces have sponsored comprehensive fiscal investigations in the past decade, and the work of these groups has contributed greatly to provincial sophistication in fiscal matters. Thus Ontario waged a determined battle against federal proposals for reforming the individual income tax base in 1969, on the grounds that these proposals did not embody certain conditions regarded by the province as equitable. Quebec's persistent and relatively successful pressures toward full provincial control over public welfare have been based on the alleged necessity of rationalizing all income-assistance programs under one jurisdiction. In respect to equity in taxation and public expenditures as in other matters the increasing sophistication of the provinces leads to more coherent policies and these policies to clashes with the federal government.

(5) It appears almost inevitable that those officials and agencies whose exclusive or major concerns are federal-provincial relations as such will emphasize the power of their respective jurisdictions as an important objective. This was surely the case with the Quebec Department of Federal-Provincial Affairs, later the Department of Intergovernmental Affairs. Part of the incentive for setting up such a department was the assertion of provincial autonomy and the judgement that such autonomy was compromised by uncoordinated and particularistic relations between Quebec and federal agencies. In his account of federal-Quebec relations between 1960 and 1970 the former Deputy Minister of the Department, Claude Morin, describes these relations in terms of a zero-sum game in which the province's "losses" and "gains" are viewed solely in terms of the restriction or enhancement of provincial power.[47] While in the federal government and those of the other provinces these objectives are not so explicitly stated, it seems reasonable to suppose that the thrust toward the coordination of policies on a

jurisdiction-wide basis leads the officials so involved to minimize the uncertainties of the external environment by sustaining and enhancing the autonomy of these jurisdictions.

As we have seen, the Ontario government in 1971 proposed a Joint Economic Council of heads of government to "review and determine, on a continuing basis, national economic goals of a strategic order". According to the argument made by Premier Davis in November, 1971, "The present structure of federal-provincial ministerial meetings and technical committees simply does not work effectively to this end." The problems of "immediate concern" for the Committee would be the role of the provinces in economic stabilization, the coordination of winter works programs and the devising of a permanent framework for dealing with winter unemployment. The communiqué issued at the end of the November 1971 Conference indicates that Ontario had not been able to secure the agreements of the other governments to its proposal. In a press conference following the conference, Prime Minister Trudeau criticized the Ontario plan from the traditional view that it was the responsibility of each level to set its objectives.

The Ontario proposal went further than most other recommendations for the increased institutionalization of intergovernmental relations, by its suggestion that the projected Joint Economic Committee should determine national economic objectives. In a lucid commentary on this scheme R.M. Burns objected on several counts.[48] The national government could not responsibly surrender its duties toward the economic welfare of Canada to such a committee. The pressures for joint decision-making come from the provinces and for the most part are directed toward matters within federal responsibility. The role of committees and of consultation is to adjust and reconcile, not to govern. In general, one might say that there is not the slightest evidence that the provinces which are most insistent about new machinery for federal-provincial collaboration have any inclination to give up important elements of what they regard as exclusive provincial powers to joint decision-making agencies.

It is unrealistic to contemplate a committee like that recommended by Ontario operating as a kind of super-cabinet in respect to the most basic of Canadian economic policies.[49] The conflicts between Ottawa and the provinces involve for the most part important political choices and interests, and these conflicts will not yield to highly sophisticated economic analysis or even more elaborate procedures of federal-provincial collaboration than have as yet been developed. The cabinet, working within the framework of the British parliamentary tradition, has several institutional characteristics which facilitate the resolution of political conflict among its members. It is presided over by a leader to whom its other members owe their offices and who can relieve them of these offices. It works within conditions of secrecy. It has a tradition of collective responsibility which dictates that its members abide by its decisions. It is chosen from members of a single party and the partisan interests of its members are in most circumstances either the same or at least not basically incompatible. In devising and implementing policy it relies on a common bureaucracy. The Conference of Prime Ministers and Premiers has none of these institutional characteristics facilitating agreement.

J.A. Corry once remarked that a tidy mind was a liability in dealing with Canadian federalism, and it is presumed that Principal Corry was referring both to observers and practitioners. The current ascendancy of administrative rationality in Ottawa and some of the provinces is a manifestation of such tidiness. The basic assumption here is that agreement on more fundamental matters should precede consideration of more specific ones. However, it is improbable that a modicum of harmony and stability can be furthered in the Canadian federal system if governments act on this assumption. Let us take a somewhat fanciful example. In 1964 and 1965 were published two attempts by private persons to rewrite the Canadian constitution, and in each case the proposed new constitution had a lengthy preamble.[50] One preamble began "All Authority comes from God through Consent of the People. . ."[51] and the other "We the people of Canada, Recognizing that all authority is from God, Supreme Lawgiver, Judge, and Ruler of Heaven and Earth. . ."[52] Now it is of considerable philosophical and theological consequence whether political authority comes directly from God or from God "through the Consent of the People", or has some other source. And on rational premises the Prime Ministers and Premiers would be required to come to some agreement on this vital matter before going on to deal with such concerns as freight-rates and the taxation of natural resources. Yet some at least of those who have promoted themselves to be first ministers seem ill-equipped by intellect and disposition to resolve such philosophic questions, even if for the moment their new theological advisers replaced the usual complement of economists and systems-analysts. The example is fanciful only in part. At the Constitutional Conference of February 1969 Prime Minister Trudeau introduced a document which contained this pretentious nonsense:

> The first element in Canada's Constitution, in the view of the Government of Canada, should be a statement — a preamble — on the objectives of the federation. The basic role of the Constitution is, of course, to define the system of law and government which shall prevail in Canada. But before doing this the Constitution must express the purpose of Canadians in having become and resolving to remain associated together in a single country, and it must express as far as this is possible what kind of country Canadians want, what values they cherish, and what objectives they seek.[53]

In general, the piecemeal consideration of very specific matters has the disadvantages that such agreement as may result conforms to no coherent body of principles, and that the cumulative product of such incremental adjustments is something that no one wanted or intended. On the other hand, when particularized problems are subsumed under more comprehensive concerns, the most fundamental of interests and aspirations are engaged. In respect to these agreement is often impossible. Flexibility, pragmatism and opportunism are essential elements in the effective workings of executive federalism in Canada.

Notes

[1] *Beyond the Welfare State*, Yale University Press, New Haven, 1960, Chapter 10 "Economic Nationalism in the Western World".

[2] *Final Report*, Information Canada, 1972, Parts IV, V and VI.

[3] *Dominion-Provincial Conference (1945), Dominion and Provincial Submissions and Plenary Conference Discussions*, King's Printer, Ottawa, 1946, pp. 15-17.

[4] *Federal-Provincial Conference, 1963*, Queen's Printer, Ottawa, 1964, generally pp. 44-46.

[5] *Questions on Federal-Provincial Economic Co-Operation*, Statement by the Honourable William G. Davis to the Meeting of First Ministers, Ottawa, November 15-16, 1971 (mimeo), p. 3.

[6] "Coordination in Administration", *Proceedings of the Ninth Annual Conference, 1957*, p. 253.

[7] "The Machinery of Federal-Provincial Relations" in *Canadian Federalism: Myth or Reality*, J. Peter Meekison, Editor, Methuen of Canada, 1968, p. 288.

[8] *The Machinery for Intergovernmental Cooperation in Canada*, Unpublished M.P.A. research essay, Carleton University, 1968, p. 100. I am indebted to Mr. Veilleux for a copy of this essay. See also Appendix A to his *Les Relations Intergouvernmentales, op. cit.*

[9] *Report: Intergovernmental Liaison on Fiscal and Economic Matters*, Queen's Printer, Ottawa, 1969, Appendix D.

[10] Privy Council Office, 1974.

[11] *Inventory of Federal-Provincial Programs in Alberta, 1974*, (mimeo).

[12] A.R. Kear, "Cooperative Federalism: A Study of the Federal-Provincial Continuing Committee on Fiscal and Economic Matters" in Meekison, *Canadian Federalism*, First Edition 1968, *op. cit.*, pp. 305-317.

[13] Quoted in Kear, pp. 309-310.

[14] For the terms of reference as given to the Tax Structure Committee in October, 1964, see *Federal-Provincial Conference of Ministers of Finance and Provincial Treasurers*, Ottawa, November 4-5, 1968, Queen's Printer, Ottawa, 1969, Appendix G.

[15] Donald V. Smiley, *Conditional Grants and Canadian Federalism*, Canadian Tax Paper No. 32, Canadian Tax Foundation, Toronto, 1963, pp. 37-42.

[16] *Federalism and Policy Development: The Case of Adult Occupational Training in Ontario*, University of Toronto Press, 1973.

[17] William Kilbourn, *Pipeline: Transcanada and the Great Debate, A History of Business and Politics*, Clarke, Irwin, Toronto/Vancouver, 1970, pp. 29-30.

[18] *First General Report*, Alberta Department of Federal and Intergovernmental Affairs, Edmonton, 1975.

[19] See the responses of the late Lester Pearson in 1970 in "Two Canadian Prime Ministers Discuss the Office" in Thomas A. Hockin, Editor, *Apex of Power, The Prime Minister and Political Leadership in Canada*, Prentice-Hall of Canada, Scarborough, 1971, pp. 191-192.

[20] This Secretariat developed from the Secretariat of the Constitutional Conference.

[21] Hockin, *op. cit.*, pp. 190-191.

[22] *The Machinery of Federal-Provincial Relations, op. cit.*, p. 290.

[23] p. 87.

[24] G. Bruce Doern and V. Seymour Wilson "Conclusions and Observations" in Doern and Wilson, Editors, *Issues in Canadian Public Policy*, Macmillan of Canada, Toronto, 1974, pp. 340-341.

[25]*Report*, Queen's Printer, Ottawa, 1960, pp. 126-127.

[26]*Report*, Queen's Printer, Ottawa, 1964, pp. 44-46.

[27]*The Toronto Star*, November 22, 1972.

[28]*The Toronto Star*, September, 26, 1974.

[29]*Joint Provincial Statement*, delivered by the Honourable John Rhodes of Ontario to the Federal-Provincial Conference on Communications, May 13-14, 1975, (mimeo).

[30]"Urban Policy" in G. Bruce Doern and V. Seymour Wilson, Editors, *Issues in Canadian Public Policy*, Macmillan of Canada, Toronto, 1974, p. 245. This essay, pp. 228-252 is a valuable account of the circumstances leading to the establishment of the Ministry and its subsequent history.

[31]*The Toronto Star*, November 22, 1973. On the day after the trilevel conference Premier Davis unveiled an ambitious plan for a new rapid transit system for Metro Toronto, estimated to cost $1.3 billions, of which the province would pay 75 per cent of the capital costs. (*The Toronto Star*, November 22, 1973.) Ontario has helped to keep its municipalities in line, so to speak, by its 1973 offer that the province would pass on to local governments "the full benefit of any net gains in new unconditional tax sharing by the federal government".

[32]For a useful collection of documents and commentaries see Howard A. Leeson and Wilfried Vanderelst, Editors, *External Affairs and Canadian Federalism: The History of a Dilemma*, Holt, Rinehart and Winston of Canada, Toronto and Montreal, 1973.

[33]*Attorney-General for Canada v. Attorney-General for Ontario and others*, A.C. (1937), 326.

[34]For the Quebec position see *Working Paper on Foreign Relations*, prepared by the Québec delegation for the Continuing Committee of Officials of the Constitutional Conference, Québec, February 5, 1969 (mimeo). The federal position is contained in Honourable Paul Martin, *Federalism and International Relations*, Queen's Printer, Ottawa, 1968. A narrative account of Quebec — Ottawa relations highly critical of the federal government is given by Edward McWhinney "Canadian Federalism; Foreign Affairs and Treaty Power", in *The Confederation Challenge*, Vol. 2, Ontario Advisory Committee on Confederation, Background Papers and Reports, Queen's Printer, Toronto, 1970, pp. 115-152.

[35]*Communiqué*, Department of External Affairs, October 8, 1971.

[36]"The Role of the Provinces in External Affairs: A Study in Canadian Federalism", a paper presented to the Canadian Political Science Association Annual Conference in Montreal, June, 1972, p. 18 (mimeo).

[37]A new figure of speech has been contrived by Premier Davis of Ontario in response to the federal budget of June 23, 1975: "The Government of Ontario cannot stand idly by while the Government of Canada plucks the Ontario taxpayers and consumers to feather its own nest." *The Globe and Mail*, July 8, 1975.

[38]See two valuable articles by Bruce Doern "Recent Changes in the Philosophy of Policy-Making in Canada", IV *Canadian Journal of Political Science*, June, 1971, pp. 243-264 and "The Budgetary and Policy Role of the Federal Bureaucracy" in G. Bruce Doern and Peter Aucoin, Editors, *The Structures of Policy-Making in Canada*, Macmillan of Canada, Toronto, 1971, pp. 79-112.

[39]*The Intelligence of Democracy*, Free Press, New York, 1965, p. 154.

[40]Harold Seidman, *Politics, Position and Power: The Dynamics of Federal Organization*, Oxford University Press, New York, 1970, p. 164.

[41]"Conclusions and Observations" in Doern and Wilson, Editors, *Issues in Canadian Public Policy*, Macmillan of Canada, Toronto, 1974, pp. 337-345. "While many of the criticisms of incrementalism are valid, it is by no means too

early to point out the other possible extreme absurdity of government, namely, that policy actors will become so dazzled by the interrelationship of everything to everything else that government will develop a severe case of intellectual, political and organizational constipation. There are very real irrational consequences to unbridled rational behaviour. . . ." p. 342.

42ibid., p. 344.

43pp. 120-121. Reproduced by permission of Information Canada.

44*Mineral Policy Objectives for Canada: A Statement by Federal and Provincial Ministers Responsible For Mineral Policy*, Ottawa, 1973, p. 159.

45*Towards a Mineral Policy for Canada: Opportunities for Choice.*

46*The Budgetary Process and the Policy Role of the Federal Bureaucracy*, op. cit., pp. 104-105.

47*Le pouvoir québecois . . . en négociation*, les éditions du boréal express, Montréal, 1972.

48Letter to the Editor, *Globe and Mail*, November 19, 1971.

49I am grateful to Paul Tennant for this comparison.

50Peter J.T. O Hearn, *Peace, Order and Good Government*, Macmillan of Canada, Toronto, 1964 and Marcel Faribault and Robert M. Fowler, *Ten to One: The Confederation Wager*, McClelland and Stewart, Toronto/Montreal, 1965.

51O Hearn, op. cit., p. 34.

52Faribault and Fowler, op. cit., p. 119.

53*The Constitution and the People of Canada*, Queen's Printer, Ottawa, 1967, pp. 3-4. Reproduced by permission of Information Canada.

# CHAPTER 4

THE POLITICS OF CANADIAN FEDERALISM

It is only within the past decade that students of federalism have turned their attention to the study of political parties. Successive editions of K.C. Wheare's influential *Federal Government* exclude parties.[1] Neither does W.S. Livingston's perceptive analysis of the sociology of federalism deal with political parties as such.[2] There is a growing literature on political integration which focuses on the economic, cultural and attitudinal aspects of the building and maintenance of political communities but gives parties little or no attention in its analyses of these processes.[3]

Several recent books on comparative federalism by R.L. Watts,[4] Carl Friedrich[5] and Ivo D. Duchacek[6] give some place to party systems, but it is only William H. Riker's *Federalism: Origin, Operation, Significance*, published in 1964[7], which makes political parties the crucial determinant of what form federations take. Riker's political explanation of federalism is in marked contrast both to those students who proceed exclusively or almost exclusively in terms of formal-legal and institutional forms and those who emphasize popular attitudes, degrees of integration and other circumstances outside the political system. There are, he claims, two explanatory foci through which federalism may best be investigated and understood. The first is the original political bargain concluded by the leaders of political jurisdictions who come together to form a federation. Certain of these leaders, if not all, will desire union to increase the diplomatic, military and economic power of themselves and their respective communities. Under modern conditions it is often more expedient to pursue such aggrandizement through negotiation rather than force and imperial expansion.[8] However, other leaders and other political communities are less urgent about the formation of a union and a bargain between centralization and decentralization is struck through the establishment of a federation. But once the original bargain is concluded will it subsequently be sustained in a centralized or "peripheralized" form? Riker's second explanatory factor comes into operation — the degree of centralization in the party system. Thus,

> Whatever the general social conditions, if any, that sustain the federal bargain, there is one institutional condition that controls the nature of the bargain in all the instances here examined and in all others with which I am familiar. This is the structure of the party system, which may be

regarded as the main variable intervening between the background social conditions and the specific nature of the federal bargain.[9]

Riker's political explanation of federalism can be summarized briefly: federations are centralized to the extent that national political parties can and do impose their wills on their respective provincial/state parties. This argument is suggestive in calling attention to the neglected role of the party system in federations. But Riker nowhere presents conclusive evidence for his assertion that parties do in fact "control" the nature of the federal bargain in the eight countries, including Canada, which he examines. In the absence of such evidence it seems plausible to argue that in some if not all of Riker's eight federations important decisions determining, in the short run at least, the degree of centralization or peripheralization are made by other institutions and processes than intraparty relations — by judicial review of the constitution, by what I called in the previous chapter "executive federalism," by legislative committees at the national level drawing members from more than one party. Riker's attribution of primacy to intraparty relations in determining the shape of federal systems remains assertion and is devoid of any analysis of the widely divergent roles that parties do play in different political systems.

This chapter is organized around an answer to three questions about political processes and the Canadian federation:
(1) What are the capabilities of the patterns of relations between national parties and provincial parties of the same designation for resolving differences in favour of one or the other? This question in itself does not involve consideration of how crucial these differences are for controlling the nature of the federal bargain.
(2) What are the capabilities of popular elections and plebiscites for resolving authoritatively differences between the federal government and the governments of provinces? The asking of this question assumes that some important aspects of federal-provincial conflict will not be amenable to resolution through intraparty relations.
(3) What is the relation between the partisan-political dimensions of Canadian federalism [as examined in (1) and (2) above] and other institutions and processes of public decision in shaping the federal system? This question leaves open for investigation, as Riker's analysis does not, whether and to what extent intraparty relations "control" the nature of the continuing federal bargain.

Relation between Federal and Provincial Parties

It may be useful in examining relations between federal and provincial parties to proceed from alternative models of federal party systems which will be called "integrated" and "confederal" respectively.

Integrated	Confederal
1. *Electoral dependence.* National and provincial parties of the same designation draw very largely on common voter allegiances to both. When there are shifts in voter support at one level these are characteristically accompanied by shifts in the same direction at the other in subsequent elections.	1. *Electoral dependence.* National and provincial parties have significantly different bodies of voter allegiance. Changes in electoral support for parties characteristically arise from circumstances prevailing at one level only and are not accompanied by changes in the same direction at the other level.
2. *Party organization* The same party machinery is used to select and elect candidates of both national and provincial parties. There are authoritative processes within the parties to commit both levels to party policy.	2. *Party organization.* The national and provincial parties are autonomous. This autonomy prevails in respect to nomination of party candidates, electoral competition and policy direction.
3. *Party careers.* Those who pursue party careers characteristically move between national and provincial office. The most important careers are those involving popular election.	3. *Party careers.* Party careerists characteristically fulfil their ambitions through serving at only one level. The most crucial of these careers involve office by popular election.
4. *Party finance.* Donors to political parties characteristically contribute to the party as such. Intraparty procedures distribute those funds between the two levels.	4. *Party finance.* Donors to parties characteristically contribute to one level or the other separately. The federal and provincial parties are financially independent of one another.
5. *Ideology.* Federal and provincial parties share a common ideology. This ideology distinguishes them from other parties in the political systems of both levels.	5. *Ideology.* Federal and provincial parties characterisitcally do not share distinctive ideologies. Parties at both levels adjust themselves to the ideological currents prevailing among their respective activists and electorates.
6. *Party symmetry.* The same political parties contest elections at both levels. The major federal parties are major parties at the provincial level.	6. *Party symmetry.* Federal and provincial elections often see different parties as the major contestants. Important parties are often wholly or largely oriented to political competition at one level rather than both.

These models can be applied to the Canadian party system, with particular but not exclusive emphasis on the two major parties.

Federal-Provincial Electoral Dependence

The electoral dependence of federal and provincial parties is an extraordinarily complex phenomenon which has only recently begun to be investigated. Sophisticated and inevitably costly survey research is needed to determine, for example, the extent to which Canadian voters perceive they live in one integrated political system or in two or more relatively discrete ones.[10] It is probable from the fragmentary evidence now available that the degree of dependence varies greatly among parties, regions and smaller areas within particular provinces, and much detailed work needs to be done even in the preliminary step of isolating the relevant variables.

The institutional forms under which Canadian elections take place clearly work toward the mutual independence of federal and provincial parties. With only a very few constitutional limitations, Parliament and the provincial legislatures have unfettered discretion to determine constituency boundaries, who may vote in their respective elections and other circumstances shaping the electoral process. Elections at the two levels take place at different times and under different administrative auspices. It does indeed seem remarkable to a Canadian student of federalism that scholars of American politics give so little attention to the contrary circumstance in which a complex of intraparty dependencies must surely arise when voters make their choices at the same time and on the same ballot for candidates for elective offices at two or more levels. Although the Republic of India has retained most of the British parliamentary forms, R.L. Watts has pointed out: ". . . with only a few exceptions, state elections have generally been called at the same time as Union elections, and . . . in these elections the candidates for state legislatures were finally selected by the All-India Board of the (Congress) Party."[11]

Some students of Canadian politics have propounded what has come to be called the "balance theory" of federal-provincial voting behaviour. Frank Underhill stated in 1955, "By some instinctive subconscious mental process the Canadian people have apparently decided that, since freedom depends upon a balance of power, they will balance the monopolistic power of the Liberal government in Ottawa by setting up the effective countervailing power not in Ottawa but the provincial capitals."[12] The late Robert MacGregor Dawson put it this way, "The records suggest . . . that provincial electorates show a decided tendency to fall away from the party which gains control of the Dominion Parliament. The provinces would appear to feel happier when they are able to assert their independence of the party in control of the Dominion Parliament: and this tendency steadily grows and spreads and is virtually never reversed until a party change in Ottawa gives impetus in the opposite direction."[13]

Recent investigation gives reason for qualifying if not rejecting the balance theory, although Dawson's argument seems to indicate that it had some validity for an earlier period of Canadian politics:

(1) Howard Scarrow investigated patterns of "alternating party choice" in federal and provincial elections between 1930 and 1957,[14] with such choice being defined as "an election victory for a party at one level of government surrounded by election victories for another party at the other level of government." He found that of a total of 104 elections there had been alternating choices in only 16 and concluded ". . . when

a provincial electorate has registered a preference for one party over a number of years and then changes that preference, the change is reflected in both provincial and federal election results . . . In Canada . . . as in other federations, the normal presumption is that a voter will exhibit relatively consistent voting behaviour in both federal and provincial elections."[15]

(2) In an article published in 1970 John Wilson and David Hoffman turned their attention to explaining the continuing weakness of the Liberal party in the provincial politics of Ontario while the Liberals dominated the province in federal elections. In investigating the prevalence of a belief in the balance theory among a sample of Ontario voters they found that 52 per cent of their respondents disagreed with the theory and only a third agreed. However,

> . . . those who voted for the Liberal party in both (1965 federal and 1967 provincial) elections were actually *more* inclined to agree that the same party should not control both levels of government at the same time than were the federal Liberals. Nearly two-fifths of those who supported the Liberal party in 1965 and again in 1967 claimed to be adherents of the balance theory, while only 27 per cent and 17 per cent respectively of those federal Liberals who switched to the provincial Conservatives and to the provincial NDP gave such a response to the question.[16]

Further, ". . . federal supporters of the Conservatives and the New Democrats who counted as consistent supporters of the balance theory — and who might have been expected to vote again for their party at the provincial level because of their opposition to the Liberals winning in Ontario as well — were actually more inclined than the sample as a whole to switch to the Liberal party in 1967."[17] Wilson and Hoffman conclude, ". . . the theory of balance has played little part in shaping the voting behaviour of Ontario citizens in recent years."[18]

(3) Jean Havel examined the voting behaviour of a sample of Sudbury voters in the federal general election of April, 1963, and the Ontario general election of September, 1963. He concluded, "There does not appear to be in Sudbury . . . any desire to balance power in Ottawa with power in Ontario. The interviewers discovered no indication of feeling in that direction."[19]

There has been a significant amount of recent survey research on federal-provincial voting behaviour and attempts to isolate the characteristics of "switchers" and to explain why some voters vote consistently for one party at successive federal and provincial elections and others do not. In reviewing this evidence from other findings and in presenting their own results from the three federal ridings centred around Waterloo, Toivo Miljan and Bruce Macnaughton conclude ". . . the phenomenon of voters switching from one party at one level of jurisdiction to another party at another level of jurisdiction is to be expected, and is not an 'aberration', but is an integral part of the Canadian federal system. . . . The electorate appears to make voting decisions at the two levels without reference to the other level."[20] The results of some of this research may be summarized briefly:

(1) John C. Courtney and David E. Smith investigated the voting behaviour in Saskatoon at a provincial general election in 1964 and a

federal by-election two months later.[21] This constituency was an interesting one because it had a previous record of electing provincial CCF-NDP and federal Conservative candidates and this record held in the 1964 elections. Of the 1075 voters in the sample 875 (81.4 per cent) voted for the same party both provincially and federally while 200 (18.6 per cent) supported different parties. The allocation of support of these 200 voters was as follows:

Party supported in federal by-election				
Party supported in provincial election	CCF-NDP	Lib.	PC	Total
CCF-NDP	—	26	94	120
Lib.	—	—	58	58
PC	2	20	—	22
Total	2	46	152	200[22]

Courtney and Smith examined some of the characteristics of those who split their vote. Women split their vote to a greater extent than men. Voting articulation increased with age, except that splitting was highest in the 65-and-over age group. The occupational groups which split most frequently were the professional, sales and clerical groups and least frequently the service, transportation and managerial groups. Vote splitting increased with length of residence in the constituency. (2) George Perlin and Patti Peppin undertook pilot surveys just before the Ontario provincial election of 1967 in the federal constituencies of Eglinton and Wellington South.[23] The first constituency had elected a Liberal in the federal general election of 1965 and a Conservative in the provincial election of 1963, while Wellington South had chosen a Conservative in 1965 and a Liberal in 1963. The results of the survey were as follows:

Percentages of Party Vote in the First Election of Each Set Remaining Constant and Changing to Another Party in the Second Election

	Provincial-federal 1963-1965		Federal-provincial 1965-1967*		Provincial-Provincial 1963-1967*	
	%	N	%	N	%	N
Percentage remaining constant						
PC	54.1	46	66.3	55	77.6	66
Liberal	60.2	56	44.9	48	66.7	62
NDP	75.0	12	50.0	14	81.3	13
Percentage changing to another party						
PC	42.3	36	25.3	21	13.0	11
Liberal	34.4	32	41.1	44	22.6	21
NDP	25.0	4	39.3	11	18.8	3

*The calculation of 1967 preferences is based upon vote intentions rather than actual votes.[24]

Interestingly, Perlin and Peppin found that the usual demographic classifications (sex, age, income, education, occupation and religion) had no statistically significant relation to vote-switching. There were also suggestive results about the differing perceptions of federal and provincial politics:

> Among the more interesting findings ... is the significantly greater influence attached by changers to leadership affect in federal politics. Personality generally seems to have been rather more important than we might have assumed since the (local) candidate is maintained at the federal level by more than 60 per cent of the changers and at the provincial level by as many as 47 per cent. Another comparison of interest is the greater frequency with which general past record is mentioned at the provincial level. It might be inferred from this that provincial politics is perceived more frequently in terms of generalized images, while in federal politics leader, candidate, policy and party are more frequently treated as independent objects.[25]

(3) Jean Laponce in his 1965 survey of the federal constituency of Vancouver-Burrard caught the provincial election of October 1963 between a series of federal elections in 1962, 1963 and 1965.[26] Between the federal and provincial elections of 1963, 49 per cent of the respondents "migrated" between one party and another, while between the two federal elections of 1962 and 1963 only 29 per cent changed parties. Of these migrants in the provincial election 93 per cent transferred to Social Credit; the NDP lost 8 per cent of its 1963 federal supporters to Social Credit and the Liberals and Conservatives 55 per cent and 62 per cent respectively. In the ensuing 1965 federal election the NDP recovered all its migrants; the Liberal and Conservative recovery rates were 60 and 71 per cent respectively. The federal-provincial switchers did not have significantly different demographic characteristics than the rest of the voting population. Laponce gives ideology a significant effect and he asserts, "The more ideological an electorate, the greater is the degree of perception of the boundaries around it and the less likely is the electorate to change in behaviour when moved from one political system to the other."[27] Thus the NDP neither gains nor loses significantly from federal-provincial migrations, while the Liberals, and to an even greater extent the Conservatives, are vulnerable to defections of their federal supporters to Social Credit in provincial elections in British Columbia.

(4) In the Wilson-Hoffman article to which reference has been made, the authors set out to explain the relative weakness of the Liberal party in recent Ontario politics, a weakness particularly striking because of the Liberal dominance of the province in federal elections. As we have seen, the balance theory was rejected. Aggregate results for the province indicate a close correlation between Liberal weakness and strength in provincial and federal elections respectively and voter-abstention at the provincial level. However, there are important regional variations. Liberal declines from federal to provincial elections accompanied by a corresponding increase in abstentions is most marked in the larger cities and the urbanized areas of the province from the Toronto-Hamilton areas to the Niagara Peninsula. In a number of

rural constituencies of traditional Liberal strength the party's vote holds relatively consistent in both federal and provincial elections. All Ontario parties lose some of their federal supporters because of abstentions in provincial elections, but the Liberals lose more than others; in 1967 the provincial Liberals retained only 49 per cent of their 1965 federal supporters in Toronto and Hamilton. Throughout the province high-status federal Liberals were more prone than other voters to switch to the Conservatives in provincial elections, lower-status Liberals to abstain. Again there were regional variations, with this tendency most marked in the southern area of the province and particularly in Metropolitan Toronto.

(5) In their survey of the federal riding of Waterloo-Cambridge Miljan and Macnaughton tested the demographic characteristics of switchers between the 1971 Ontario and 1972 federal elections in terms of sex, age, occupation, religion, length of residency, education, income, home ownership, union membership, ethnicity and subjective class.[28] "It was found that only the length of residency and the religion variables showed any statistically significant relationships at all between the non-switchers and the switchers." The religion variable was most consistent and showed that Presbyterian, United Church and "Other Protestant" had the greatest propensity to switch, while Roman Catholics, Anglicans and Lutherans tended toward party consistency. In terms of residence, those who had lived in the constituency between 11 and 15 years had the greatest tendency to switch, those with less than 3 years residency to vote for the same party.

(6) Although the investigation involved consistency of voting in the 1965 and 1968 federal elections, Lynn Macdonald's results are suggestive for federal-provincial voting behaviour. It was found that "switchers tend to move to a party more consistent with their social class, religion and ethnic group membership than their old party was."[29]

The spectacular record of the Diefenbaker Conservatives in the federal general election of 1958 provides a convenient way to determine the impact of a dramatic change in the standings of the federal parties on their provincial counterparts. The following table examines the federal swing between 1953 and 1958 — the 1957 election is here regarded as transitional — and the party results in the immediately succeeding provincial elections.

The impact of the Diefenbaker victory on provincial political fortunes is inconclusive. In the three westernmost provinces the Conservatives made significant gains, but still were not established as important political forces after succeeding provincial elections. It is plausible to attribute to the 1958 sweep some importance in the displacement of Liberal by Conservative governments in Prince Edward Island and Manitoba. However, Quebec's spectacular support for the federal Conservatives in 1958 was followed by the Liberal victory in the provincial election of 1960. Perhaps the most decisive permanent result of the Diefenbaker sweep was the destruction of Social Credit as an important political force in Alberta and British Columbia, although in both provinces these parties remained in office for more than a decade and their

	Conservatives		Liberals		CCF		Social Credit	
	1953-58 federal swing	Provincial swing in election after '58 federal	1953-58 federal swing	Provincial swing	1953-58 federal swing	Provincial swing	1953-58 federal swing	Provincial swing
Newfoundland	+17.1	− 6.7	−12.8	− 8.3	− 0.4			
Nova Scotia	+17.8	− 0.3	−14.6	− 5.6	− 2.2			
New Brunswick	+12.2	− 6.0	− 9.3	+ 7.3	− 1.2			
Prince Edward Island	+14.0	+ 5.9	−13.5	− 5.9	− 0.5	+ 5.9		
Quebec	+20.2	− 5.2 (Union Nationale)	−15.3	+ 6.8	+ 0.8			
Ontario	+16.1	− 2.4	−14.0	+ 3.4	− 0.6	+ 0.3		
Manitoba	+29.7	+19.5	−18.6	− 6.0	− 4.0	+ 3.6	− 4.5	−11.5
Saskatchewan	+39.7	+12.0	−18.1	+ 2.4	−15.8	− 4.8	− 4.9	− 9.2
Alberta	+45.4	+14.7	−21.3	−17.2	− 2.5	− 3.9	−19.2	+ 9.9
British Columbia	+35.3	+ 3.6	−14.8	− 0.9	− 2.1	+ 4.4	−16.5	− 7.0

eventual defeat appears due almost entirely to provincial political factors rather than federal ones.

We still know very little about federal-provincial voting behaviour. The balance theory seems not to apply to recent circumstances. Laponce's finding in Vancouver — Burrard that ideological cleavages between parties discourages voter migration is probably true of other areas, although the very weak support for the New Democratic Party in provinces with NDP governments in the federal general election of 1974 might cause some qualifications of this. It is significant that on the basis of the Laponce, Perlin-Peppin and Miljan-Macnaughton studies, switchers appear not to differ from non-switchers on the basis of the usual demographic categories of age, sex, income, education and occupation. Much more evidence would be needed to demonstrate this conclusively, but it is plausible that voters make their decisions without reference to the other level of government although one might suppose, in the absence of empirical evidence, that this is less true of the Atlantic provinces where the parties are more highly integrated on federal-provincial lines than elsewhere in Canada. The Wilson-Hoffman analysis of federal-provincial voting in Ontario shows significant differences in behaviour among voters in particular regions and areas of the province. Such research as this should discourage easy generalizations about this kind of behaviour on a Canada-wide basis.

Despite our ignorance of the complexities of federal-provincial voting behaviour, we do at least know the outer limits of electoral dependence and some parties at one level have been able to dominate particular provinces for long periods of time while remaining relatively weak at the other level. Thus, for example, Social Credit governed British Columbia from 1952 to 1972 while the party showed little disposition to commit its prestige and resources to federal politics, while in Alberta Social Credit remained dominant provincially until 1971, despite the virtual demise of the federal party outside Quebec from the election of 1958 onward. The Conservatives dominate Saskatchewan federally but have not been a strong force in provincial politics. The NDP governments of British Columbia, Saskatchewan and Manitoba have not been able to translate this provincial support into federal seats. In Ontario the dominance of the Conservatives at Queen's Park has been sustained for over a generation, during which the Liberals were able in most federal general elections to capture a majority of Ontario seats. Apart perhaps from the Atlantic provinces where the classic two-party system has been sustained, any federal or provincial party with serious hopes of electoral success must gain the support of voters who either support other parties or abstain in elections at the other level of government.

Party Organization

Party organization in Canada is an almost unexplored field. The analysis below is thus based on fragmentary information.

Do the same local party activists participate at both federal and provincial levels? Or, alternatively, are large numbers of activists oriented exclusively or almost exclusively toward one level or the other? The three major parties appear to promote the idea that federal and provincial wings are members of the same team. To what extent is this mythology and to what extent a fairly accurate description of Canadian political behaviour? One might suppose, in the absence of evidence, that in provinces and constituencies where parties are strong federally and weak provincially, or vice versa, there are tendencies at work to encourage activists to participate at only one level rather than both. But is this the case?

In a study presented in 1970 Henry Jacek, John McDonough, Ronald Shimuzu and Patrick Smith examined the federal-provincial activity of 180 party officials in three Hamilton constituencies.[30]

High Activity	Liberal	PC	NDP	Total
Provincially only	0	8	2	10
Provincially and federally	36	30	38	104
Federally only	30	16	2	48
At neither level	11	4	3	18
Total	77	58	45	180

This study indicated a very great variation among the parties in respect to integration on federal-provincial lines. The Liberal party is least integrated because the inducements to membership and activity are based largely on federal patronage, and the NDP most integrated because of common ideological and policy commitments. The Conservatives are between the two in degree of integration with rather highly personalized patterns of allegiances among upper-status persons.

For whatever reasons, the extra-parliamentary organizations of the two major national parties were slow to develop. In fact, in the Liberal party the national headquarters until the 1960s seemed to have few important functions, with the heavy reliance of the party on provincial organizations in federal campaigns and the responsibilities of other party business being conducted under the direction of cabinet ministers. From the early 1940s onward the Conservatives were more aggressive in developing a national extra-parliamentary organization[31] and this may have contributed in significant degree to the Diefenbaker victory of 1957.

From the appointment of Keith Davey as National Director of the national Liberal Federation in 1961 onwards, that party has established an extra-parliamentary organization directed almost exclusively to success in the federal political arena. Under the arrangements established by Davey and accepted by the party in the 1960s, the party leader appointed a campaign director in each province whose functions would in large measure displace those formerly carried out by provincial party organizations and members of the federal cabinet. The developments under Richard Stanbury as President of the National party in the early years of the Trudeau government were in the direction of encouraging a higher degree of participation in party affairs, particularly as these related to policy matters. What is important in terms of the analysis of this chapter is that this extra-parliamentary machinery is geared almost exclusively to federal politics. This strategy appears in large part to be validated by the relative federal success of the party in provinces like British Columbia and Alberta where it has not been strong in provincial politics.

Beginning in 1919 with the Liberals and 1927 with the Conservatives the major parties have selected their leaders through representative party conventions.[32] 64 per cent of the potential 2472 Liberal delegates in 1968 were allotted to Liberal riding associations and in the 1967 Progressive Conservative Convention 55 per cent of 2411 delegates.[33] The two parties have somewhat different traditions as to representatives from the provincial party organizations. The Liberals have given delegate status to the presidents and other executive officers of these organizations as well as to those of university clubs and womens' and youth associations of the party. The Progressive Conservatives, on the other hand, do not provide for delegate-status to members of provincial organizations, but grant such status to PC members of provincial legislatures. Voting for leadership candidates proceeds through successive secret ballots; with the candidate having fewest votes being eliminated each time, until one has a clear majority.[34] Provincial leaders do not dominate such meetings as has often been true in the past of their state counterparts in national nominating conventions in the United States. The secrecy of the ballot and the expectation in these two recent conventions that more than one ballot would be required to choose a leader means that serious candidates must secure the support of aggregates of individual delegates rather than provincial blocs.

Both the major parties are now committed by their constitutions to hold periodic national conventions dealing with organizational and policy matters. It is still not clear what role such conventions will assume in designing policy-inputs for their respective parties in Parliament or for the Canadian political system as such. Whatever part such gatherings come to play in this as in leadership matters, it is reasonably certain that they will not be dominated by provincial parties or leaders.

The circumstances under which the premiers of provinces commit their own prestige and organizational resources in federal elections are highly variable. Duplessis of Quebec and Frost of Ontario made such commitments to the Diefenbaker Conservatives in 1957 and 1958, although neither had given such support to the federal party in 1953. Robert Stanfield of Nova Scotia supported the Conservatives in 1965 while little help was given to the national party by Duff Roblin of Manitoba or John Robarts of Ontario. The late Ross Thatcher of Saskatchewan committed little of his support or that of his party organization to the federal Liberals when he was in power between 1964 and

1971. Quebec Liberals from 1960 onward appear to have given little assistance to their federal counterparts, particularly since the almost complete separation of the federal and Quebec wings of the party which was effected in 1964. From 1935 onward the national Social Credit movement was to a large extent the extension of the Alberta party. On the other hand, Premier Bennett of British Columbia showed only a marginal and intermittent interest in federal Social Credit politics. Only in the CCF-NDP has there been a close integration of federal and provincial party organizations.

The support of provincial party organizations is undoubtedly of assistance to federal politicians but, as the results of the 1968 general elections demonstrate, it is by no means decisive. More perhaps than in elections of the two decades before, the provincial Conservatives and Liberal parties throughout Canada were mobilized behind their federal counterparts. The Conservatives had healed some of the internecine quarrels of the Diefenbaker years and the Liberals were riding on the wave of Trudeaumania. However, each of the two major national parties did well in those provinces where it was out of office provincially, with the exception of Nova Scotia. The Union Nationale and Ontario Conservatives supported the federal Conservatives but the latter party received 21.3 per cent and 32.0 per cent of the popular vote respectively in these two provinces. On the other hand, with Liberal governments in power in Newfoundland, New Brunswick and Prince Edward Island the federal Conservatives won 52.8 per cent, 49.7 per cent and 51.8 per cent of the popular vote compared with 31.4 per cent nationally. As for the Liberals, their proportion of the popular vote in provinces with Liberal administrations was 42.8 per cent in Newfoundland, 44.4 per cent in New Brunswick, 44.9 per cent in Prince Edward Island and 27.1 per cent in Saskatchewan, compared with 45.5 per cent nationally. Only in Nova Scotia, where the Conservative proportion of the vote was the highest in the country, 55.2 per cent, was a provincial party able to "deliver," and this result was no doubt due largely to the continuing personal popularity of the Conservative leader and former Nova Scotia Premier, Robert Stanfield. In fact, the relatively poor showing of the Liberals in Saskatchewan and Newfoundland — and perhaps that of the Conservatives in Manitoba — may be attributed to the decreasing popularity of provincial governments of those parties.

On the basis of a detailed study of relations between the federal and provincial wings of the Conservative party in British Columbia during the period when George Drew was national leader, Edwin R. Black has made several perceptive generalizations about party organization in Canada. These generalizations summarize most of what we know about this matter:

> 1. Canada's major parties do not fit the model of unified country-wide parties with hierarchically inferior provincial subdivisions; major party supporters do not exhibit the necessary degree of commitment. 2. Both the structure and the internal operation of a major party resemble that of the Canadian system of government. The sovereignty of provincial party units is as real and extensive as that of the provinces with respect to

Ottawa. 3. Just as the virtual independence of a provincial government's policy-making depends upon the local unit's political resources in comparison with those of the central party, such resources are considered to be size and commitment of membership, financial capabilities, quality and appeal of leadership, and, of course, electoral success. 4. Party organizers must deal with three types of active members: those whose political interests are primarily oriented in provincial terms, those whose interests find primary expression in central-government goals, and those whose interests are multifaceted or else are concentrated on some aspect of political life comprehending both spheres of government — such as the attainment of ideological objectives or general governmental power for the party. 5. A party's policy objectives and organizational requirements in the federal and provincial arenas are often quite different, but both sets of leaders must rely in large measure on the same relatively small group of people and on the same resources for their field work. 6. The interests and energies of the party machinery within one province cannot be converted readily and with equal efficiency to both federal and provincial objectives. Attempts to treat the party as if it were readily convertible impose almost intolerable stresses on the organization, stresses which may be expected to become manifest in difficulties between the party leaders. 7. The public or private character of the expression and resolution of internal party differences is a reflection of the leadership skills and institutional machinery with which the groups are endowed, and of the party's electoral morale. 8. Even where a provincial party organization is controlled by relatively ineffectual persons, if they are determined in their leadership, representatives of the central party can undertake "corrective" action only at considerable risk. 9. The provincial party is a highly-charged organism, with many internal stresses and tensions, which must be capable of frequent integration with as many as nine others of similar nature to produce a country-wide mechanism focussing its power on system-wide problems. 10. The pattern of authoritative relationships between central and provincial party groups will depend upon whether public office is held by one, neither, or both of the two party groups. These relationships will also be affected by the nature of any "rehabilitative" process through which an out-of-office party faction may be going and by the degree of ideological and policy solidarity between the central and the provincial units.[35]

To the extent that in both federal and provincial politics the popularity of party leaders is more crucial than organization in determining levels of electoral support, the interdependence of federal and provincial politicians of the same party is weakened. Peter Regenstrief has said of national politics "The personality orientation of Canadian parties is a functional ingredient of a political system in which social referents are weak mediators of political loyalties."[36] Certainly this appears to have been so in the Diefenbaker and Trudeau victories of 1958 and 1968, if not more generally true of the Canadian political system. Yet what leaders have at one level to assist their partisan colleagues at the other is for the most part organizational resources.[37]

Another factor which may weaken federal-provincial electoral dependence is sometimes expressed in terms of the ripe apple theory of governing parties, the theory that parties in power defeat themselves. According to this view every government party has a life-cycle of indeterminate length. As it goes through this cycle it becomes increasingly complacent, arrogant, incapable both of sustaining its earlier basis of support and encompassing new groups in the electorate and so on. If this is in general true, a government party cannot stave off defeat by the support of its counterparts at the other level, nor is an opposition party crucially assisted in its effects by such support. To take a recent example, the upsurge in support for the provincial Liberals in Ontario as shown in public opinion polls in early 1975 could reasonably be attributed almost entirely to the declining popularity of the Davis government rather than to the success of federal Liberals in the general election of six months before.

Party Careers

According to the 1974 *Parliamentary Guide*, 35 Members of the House of Commons had contested one or more provincial elections and 12 had held seats in provincial legislatures. The party breakdown was this:

	Held provincial seats	Unsuccessfully contested provincial elections
Liberal	2	4
Progressive Conservative	5	9
New Democratic Party	5	7
Créditiste	0	3

Thus only 4.9 per cent of the 264 seats in the House of Commons were filled by former members of provincial legislatures, while 13.3 per cent were held by those who had contested provincial elections successfully or unsuccessfully. The party breakdown is interesting — 38.7 per cent of the NDP Members had contested provincial elections while the corresponding percentages for the Progressive Conservatives and Liberals were 13.6 per cent and 5.9 per cent respectively.

Of the 565 members of provincial legislatures about whom the *Parliamentary Guide* gives information, only 30 or 5.3 per cent had contested federal elections, successfully or otherwise, and of these 12 or 2.1 per cent had been MPs.

In terms of recent federal-provincial relations it is significant to examine the membership of cabinets to determine the extent of the experience of their members at the other level. The three cabinets noted below were those constituted in 1957, 1963 and 1968 by incoming prime ministers. (It is interesting to note parenthetically that Laurier's cabinet of 13 members, formed in 1896, contained no fewer than 3 former provincial premiers and was joined soon after by Clifford Sifton, undoubtedly the most powerful figure in prairie politics and formerly Attorney-General of Manitoba.)

The Diefenbaker cabinet of 1957. Of the 21 ministers only 3 (Nowlan, Brooks and Churchill) had sat in provincial legislatures.

The Pearson cabinet of 1963. Only 1 of 24 ministers (Laing) had ever sat in a provincial legislature.

The Trudeau cabinet of 1968. Of the 28 ministers only 2 (Laing, Kierans) had ever held provincial seats.

Thus recent federal cabinets have been constituted almost entirely of ministers without provincial elective experience. In the three ministries mentioned above, only Eric Kierans had held cabinet office at both levels. (The former premier of New Brunswick, Hugh John Flemming, was federal Minister of Fisheries between 1960 and 1963 and the incumbent Minister of Veterans' Affairs, Daniel Macdonald, was formerly Minister of Agriculture of Prince Edward Island.)

Of 186 provincial cabinet ministers listed in the 1974 *Parliamentary Guide*, only 5 had ever sat in the House of Commons while another 5 had unsuccessfully contested one or more federal elections. Three of the premiers (Moores of Newfoundland, Regan of Nova Scotia and Schreyer of Manitoba) have served as MPs.

In general then, careers in elective office are to a large extent separated, apart from the New Democratic Party. So far as federal-provincial relations are concerned, cabinet ministers deal with one another in the absence of either personal experience or ambition at the other level of government.

Party Finance

Long-run trends in party finance in Canada work in the direction of the mutual independence of the federal and provincial wings of the Liberal and Conservative parties. The most astute student of this subject, K.Z. Paltiel, has argued that this development has had a crucial disintegrative effect on Canadian federalism. He wrote of the older system:

> The traditional methods of financing the two old Canadian parties, the Liberals and the Conservatives, helped overcome the splintering effect of the provinces and provincial party organizations. This was accomplished through a highly centralized system of party finance. This system rested on a common basis: the centralized corporate industrial and financial structures located in Montreal and Toronto. It is common knowledge that the two old parties were largely financed from the same sources. These corporate contributors numbered in the hundreds rather than in the thousands. Under this system, provincial and even municipal elections, as well as federal elections, could be and were financed from the central party funds and sources. The traditional system of party finance had important integrative effects which helped overcome the centrifugal forces in Canadian political life. This beneficial result was made possible by the highly concentrated nature of Canadian industry and finance.[38]

In the period since the end of the Second World War the older system has been weakened. The rise of third parties has contributed to this trend. The increasing importance of natural resource development, primarily under provincial jurisdiction, has given corporate donors incentives to contribute directly to provincial parties. Paltiel described the more recent situation:

> ... the British Columbia and Alberta wings of the federal Liberal and Conservative Parties have become largely self-supporting and contribute on occasion to the support of the Saskatchewan wing. Manitoba in the heyday of the Winnipeg Grain Exchange was self-supporting but now is a net importer of election funds. The rest of Canada, as far as the two major parties are concerned, are beneficiaries of transfer payments; they are in part political colonies except when some grass-roots movement has swept a minor party into power or a traditional party can exploit the advantages of incumbency by using office to gain funds by means fair or foul.[39]

The direct or indirect subsidy from the public purse of parties or of individual candidates for election works against the integration of federal and provincial parties by putting into the hands of parties and candidates resources quite independent of party decisions at the other level. Quebec in 1963 and Nova Scotia in 1969 enacted legislation providing for limits to the expenditure of parties and for subsidies to candidates of recognized parties.[40] It is significant that the Quebec law was enacted at the time when the Quebec Liberal Federation was in process of effecting an almost complete organizational separation from the federal Liberal party.[41] A further amendment of 1974 to the Quebec legislation provides for public subsidies to the permanent organizations of recognized parties to enable each to "cover [its] current administration costs, ensure the propagation of its political program and coordinate the political action of its members".

Parliament in 1974 and the Legislature of Ontario in 1975 enacted legislation to regularize, to make more open and to limit certain campaign expenditures as well as to provide public subsidies for campaign activities. There has not yet been a general election held under this legislation in either jurisdiction and it is not necessary to outline the complex provisions in this context. However, it seems almost inevitable that these will frustrate whatever elements of intra-party integration on federal-provincial lines which may have previously developed. The Ontario law is explicit about transfers between the two levels:

> 21. No political party, constituency association or candidate registered under this Act shall accept funds from a federal political party registered under the Election Expenses Act (Canada) except during a campaign period during which a registered party may accept from such a federal political party an amount not exceeding, in the aggregate, $100 for each registered candidate endorsed by that registered party.
> ...

The federal law contains no such provisions related to intra-party transfers. However, there has been some discussion of the interpretation of 1974 amendments to the Income Tax Act which provide for deductions from individual income tax payable of contributions to registered parties and candidates. The position of the government and the Progressive Conservative Opposition is that political funds so collected should be used to support federal activities only, but the New Democratic Party, with a stronger tradition of financial integration between the two levels, has argued that those moneys should be at the discretion of the parties to spend on federal and provincial politics as they choose.

Contrary to past practices, the new legislation provides explicitly for the public recognition and regulation of political parties. Such regulation, to be effective, will make necessary the cooperation of the parties themselves. At the federal level, the Chief Electoral Officer is made responsible for policing the provisions of the new legislation and has already made progress in institutionalizing the relations between his office, the parties and the broadcasting authorities in this connection. The Ontario law provides for a Commission on Election Contributions and Expenses, composed of a chairman appointed by the Lieutenant-Governor in Council, the Chief Electoral Officer, a bencher of the Law Society of Upper Canada appointed by the Lieutenant-Governor in Council, and two appointees of each political party with at least four members of the Legislature Assembly if that party nominated candidates in 50 per cent or more of the electoral districts in the province in the most recent general election. Early in 1975 Premier Bourassa of Quebec promised that, "*Une Commission de controle des finances politiques sera créé.*"[42] It is premature to judge what the effects of these new kinds of institutionalization in the structures of the parties and their external relations will be except to suggest that such influences are almost entirely against intraparty integration on federal-provincial lines.

Ideology

As is well known, the national Liberal and Conservative parties in Canada are both ideologically inclusive, in the sense that each comprehends persons of divergent ideological viewpoints and attempts to appeal to voters of widely varying ideological persuasions. The Conservative cabinet of Prime Minister Diefenbaker included ministers as diverse in their perspectives as Donald Fleming and Alvin Hamilton; within three weeks after the 1965 general election Prime Minister Pearson conferred important portfolios on Jean Marchand and the late Robert Winters. There are diversities at least as extensive as these in the caucuses and extra-parliamentary organizations of the two major parties. However, despite the lack of conformity on ideology the normal workings of cabinet and of caucus solidarity and of the requirements of future electoral success predispose parties at each level toward agreement on particular issues. Such influences are much weaker or exist hardly at all between federal and provincial wings of the same party. Particularly among the Liberals there have been wide variations. In economic matters Saskatchewan and Manitoba Liberals have been on the right of the political spectrum, while the Lesage and Robichaud Liberal governments put into operation in Quebec and New Brunswick respectively more comprehensive programs of reform than those ever

tish Columbia, Saskatchewan and Manitoba but had only sixteen
ts in the House of Commons — only two each from these three
ovinces. The party which dominated federal politics was in power
ly in Nova Scotia, Prince Edward Island and Quebec and was the
ficial opposition in Newfoundland, Saskatchewan, Ontario and New
unswick. In Quebec both the opposition groups in the National As-
mbly were minor parties and in federal politics the Créditistes were
e major opposition to the Liberals. Since they came to power in 1943,
e Ontario Conservatives had proved able to survive the Liberal domi-
ance of federal politics in the province during most of this period.
hus only in the four Atlantic provinces was the classic two-party
ystem of Liberals and Conservatives sustained.

(Although it does not relate directly to this analysis, Maurice
Pinard's suggestive theory of the rise of third parties in Canada may be
mentioned parenthetically here for the light it sheds on party
asymmetry.[45] He presents an impressive array of evidence from federal
and provincial political history leading to the conclusion that where
one party dominates a political system effective opposition to that
party is likely to find an outlet in a new party rather than a resurgence
of strength in the weak opposition party. Thus ". . . the indications are
that whenever the opposition party (or the strongest of many opposition parties) fails to return at least a third of the votes while in opposition, it tends to be replaced by 'third parties'.")[46]

Asymmetry has direct consequences for intraparty relations, most
of these consequences working in the direction of what I have called
the confederal form. The existence in particular provinces of parties
which are oriented exclusively or mainly to competition at one level or
the other, rather than both, means either that large groups of voters
switch allegiances between federal and provincial elections or that
they abstain from voting, and probably encourages citizens to believe
that they live in two relatively discrete political systems rather than an
integrated system. Those seeking party careers will be predisposed by
asymmetry toward service at one level rather than both in succession;
at the extreme, an ambitious British Columbia Liberal is unlikely to be
attracted to provincial politics and a Saskatchewan socialist with the
goal of being a cabinet minister will perforce look toward Regina rather
than Ottawa. If we assume, as is reasonable, that an important determinant of the success of a party in soliciting campaign funds is its
prospects of electoral success, donors will be predisposed toward giving to one wing rather than both under conditions of asymmetry. Parties which are weak at one level sometimes evolve toward ideological
sectarianism and sometimes become little more than groups of those
interested more in patronage than electoral activity, to the embarrassment in both cases of the more serious politicians at the other level.

There is thus a group of pervasive influences at work in the direction of autonomous federal and provincial party systems in Canada,
toward the confederal form. However, several qualifications to this
generalization should be made.

First, in the Atlantic provinces where the two-party system is sus-

undertaken in Canadian provinces.[43] Interestingly, recei
Conservative governments in the provinces have been n
road in social and economic matters. One might thus hyp
ideological diversities among Liberals are most clearly m
the orientations of the federal and provincial wings of th
that the system provides few requirements that these be re
the other hand, such differences among the Conservatives to
place within the national party and from time to time compu
electoral success of that party. In general, a common and
ideology is not an influence toward federal-provincial in
among the major parties and the national and provincial wi
form to the ideological perspectives of their respective party
and the perceived requirements of electoral victory among their
tive electorates.

It seems not unlikely that in the immediate future ideologi
bates within the New Democratic Party will take place along fe
provincial lines, with the national party maintaining a positio
nificantly to the left of that accepted by the provincial organiza
where the party is in power or in Ontario where the NDP has s
hopes of forming the government. Although the "establishment"
didates of the party won the national leadership in both the 1972
1975 conventions, in each case there was strong support for
second-place contestants, James Laxer and Rosemary Brown respe
tively, who had staked out a position on the far left of the ideologic
spectrum.[44]

(The constitutional division of legislative powers between Parlia
ment and the provinces, as well as cultural dualism, appears to have
had a significant influence on the ideological inclusiveness of the two
major parties. Many but by no means all of the subjects giving rise to
left-right divisions among the electorate are within provincial rather
than federal jurisdiction — the predominant aspects of health, social
security and welfare; collective bargaining and industrial standards for
most workers; municipal government; the exploitation of natural resources. Thus *within* particular provinces there are on occasion or
permanently ideological cleavages between the major political contenders in those jurisdictions, cleavages much more clear-cut than those in
national politics.)

Party Symmetry

Party symmetry in a sense is a residual category, as it is inextricably
related to all the other dimensions of intraparty relations which have
been analyzed above. In general terms, if the party system were sym-
metrical, having the same parties the major competitors at both federal
and provincial levels, there would be important influences toward integration. Conversely, asymmetry contains predispositions toward the
confederal form.

In mid-1975 the Canadian party system had many elements of
asymmetry. The New Democratic Party formed the governments of

tained there is a significantly higher degree of federal-provincial party integration than elsewhere in Canada.[47] Throughout the country, asymmetry works toward the confederal form and symmetry toward integration.

Second, the parties differ in their degrees of integration. The Liberals are most confederal, the Conservatives somewhat less so. However, up until the present at least the New Democratic Party has been relatively highly integrated on federal-provincial lines. More than the two major parties, its electoral strength was manifested at both levels in places where the party was strong. Its traditions of party finance provided for regularized transfers of resources between federal and provincial wings.[48] Party activists from the level of the worker in the local constituency to the national leader characteristically participated in both provincial and federal electoral activity. Party careerists often accepted nominations at both levels in the course of their political service. The recent circumstances of the party as revealed in its 1975 convention showed a lessening of federal-provincial integration. Throughout the history of the party and its predecessor, the Cooperative Commonwealth Federation, socialists had often believed that the route to power in Ottawa was by way of capturing power in the provinces. Yet in the federal election of 1974 the party was reduced to 16 seats in the House of Commons, and of those only 6 were from the three provinces where the NDP formed the governments and where a total of 49 seats was at stake. Obviously it was an ineffective electoral strategy for the federal NDP to continue to rely on the efforts of the provincial parties as in the past, and part of the program of the new national leader was to assign each sitting M.P. the responsibility for stimulating party activity in a group of federal constituencies. Further, as I have indicated, it is not impossible that ideological strains will develop between the national NDP and the parties in the provinces where the socialists hold power or have some prospects of doing so.

Third, in waging partisan conflict both federal and provincial parties are opportunistic about using whatever ammunition they can find from the other level. In the broadest terms and subject to many qualifications, parties tend to be hurt by the unpopularity of their partisan colleagues at the other level of government but do not benefit in equal degree from their popularity. Thus the dismal showing of the British Columbia New Democrats in the 1974 federal general election has been attributed by most observers to the ill-favour in which the Barrett government was held. As this is written in July 1975, the Davis government in Ontario seems disposed to wage a fall election campaign on the unpopular federal budget of June 23 and the provincial Liberals are openly embarrassed by this budget. Despite the confederal forces operating in the Canadian party system, politicians will keep the two arenas separate only when it is convenient.

Fourth, partisan-political activity involves complexes of interpersonal relations which can and no doubt do expert important influences on interactions between federal and provincial wings and on government-to-government dealings. Of all important Canadian in-

stitutions, the two major parties are perhaps least subject to authoritative procedures regulating their internal workings. Despite the influences toward the confederal form, party leaders have important channels of access to their partisan counterparts at the other level. Again,
despite the growing independence of federal and provincial party organizations, most active Liberals and Conservatives believe that they
are in some general sense members of respective teams, and in most
parts of the country and under most circumstances the notion is propa-
gated that there is one party rather than semi-autonomous federal and
provincial wings. Partisan activity involves hates and fears, personal
allegiances and policy commitments, and in many circumstances these
personal factors are important in the working of the federal system.

Despite these qualifications, the two major parties have increasingly manifested confederal forms. In doing so, these parties have almost ceased to be instruments of federal-provincial integration where
the authoritative resolution of federal-provincial conflicts has become
increasingly crucial for the stability if not the survival of Canadian
federalism.

Elections and Federal-Provincial Conflict

If intraparty relations have a diminishing integrative capacity in the
Canadian political system, it is conceivable that popular elections
could be effective instruments to resolve disputes between the national
government and dominant influences in particular provinces or regions. Perhaps the best available way to investigate this matter is to
examine briefly four sets of elections in recent Canadian political history where federal-provincial relations have been of great salience.

(1) *Alberta, 1935.* In the Alberta provincial election of August 1935, the
Social Credit party under William Aberhart came to power with 54.2
per cent of the popular vote. The party was elected on a platform of
monetary reform which challenged some of the most crucial elements
of national economic policies. Six weeks later in the federal general
election the Alberta voters gave Social Credit 46.2 per cent of the vote
and all but two of the province's 17 seats in the House of Commons,
while on a country-wide basis the Liberals came to power with 44.8 per
cent of the popular vote and 173 of 245 seats in the Commons. In the
subsequent period the federal government was willing and able to ob-
struct Alberta's policies for monetary reform on a provincial basis.[49]

(2) *Quebec 1939, 1940.* Premier Maurice Duplessis of Quebec unexpectedly called an election for October, 1939, with the alleged justification
that Ottawa was illegitimately using the wartime emergency to encroach on provincial powers. Prime Minister King and Liberal cabinet
ministers from Quebec took this challenge with the utmost seriousness.
Two such ministers — Charles G. Power and Lucien Cardin — assumed
direction of the provincial campaign, including raising funds from
outside[50] and inside the province and participating in the selection of
local candidates. The four Liberal ministers from Quebec campaigned
actively in the province and threatened to resign if the Union Nationale

was sustained. The result was a decisive Liberal victory, with 53.5 per cent of the popular vote and 69 of the 86 seats in the Legislative Assembly. In the federal election of March 1940 the Liberals received 63.3 per cent of the Quebec popular vote and all but four of the province's 65 seats in the House of Commons.

(3) *Ontario 1940, 1943*. On January 18, 1940, Liberal Premier Hepburn of Ontario and George Drew, the leader of the Conservative Opposition in the province, jointly sponsored a resolution in the Provincial Parliament condemning the federal King government for not prosecuting the war effectively. The Prime Minister of Canada responded by requesting a dissolution of Parliament on January 25 and an election was held on March 29. Hepburn had in the recent past collaborated with both the Quebec Union Nationale and the federal and provincial Conservatives in attempting to displace Mackenzie King. In the 1940 election the federal Liberals increased their share of the popular vote in Ontario to 50.8 per cent from 42.4 per cent in 1935 and of seats from 56 to 57. Hepburn resigned as Premier in October 1942 and in August of the next year the Ontario Liberals sustained a disastrous defeat in the Ontario election, emerging with only 14 seats as against 38 for the Conservatives and 34 for the CCF.[51]

(4) *Quebec 1968, 1970*. In the federal general election of June, 1968, Prime Minister Trudeau and the Liberal party campaigned in Quebec and throughout Canada on Trudeau's view of Canadian federalism. The party was sustained in Quebec with 53.6 per cent of the popular vote and 56 of 74 seats in the House of Commons. In the provincial general election of April, 1970 the Liberal party was returned to power in Quebec with 45 per cent of the popular vote and 72 of 108 seats in the National Assembly. The party had campaigned on a federalist platform.

There is an inevitable arbitrariness in interpreting the situations outlined above. In the Alberta and Ontario cases the results were relatively unequivocal. After the federal election of 1935 Ottawa was willing and able to frustrate Alberta's plans for monetary reform and so a national majority imposed its will on a provincial majority. The 1940 national election sustained the wartime policies of Prime Minister Mackenzie King against the challenge posed by Ontario — as well as Quebec — and the subsequent provincial election resulted in the defeat of the Ontario Liberals. The Quebec results of 1939 and 1940 installed in office in the province a government under heavy political obligations to the federal Liberal leadership, and rallied a provincial majority around that leadership and its policies. However, the Union Nationale was returned to power on a nationalist platform in 1944 and for at least 15 years afterward the provincial Liberals were seriously embarrassed by accusations that they were subservient to Ottawa. It is perhaps too early to assess the long-term results of the 1968 and 1970 elections in Quebec.

If general elections were to be a method of resolving federal-provincial conflicts two conditions would have to be met:

First, some crucial aspect of federal-provincial contention would be so central to electoral competition that the voting results could reasonably be interpreted as a mandate for one side or the other in such contention.

Second, in particular provinces the electorate would be consistent in giving its majority support in successive federal and provincial elections to parties whose policies in federal-provincial relations were not inconsistent.

These two conditions are not often fulfilled.

Most general elections at both levels of government centre on personalities and policies not directly connected with federal-provincial relations. The four circumstances described above were atypical.

However, even when federal-provincial relations are highly salient in federal or provincial elections voters often give their support to parties with quite inconsistent policies and objectives. Quebec voters returned the Duplessis nationalists in the provincial elections of 1944, 1948, 1952 and 1956 but gave overwhelming support to the federal Liberals, who were more centralist than any party in peace-time Canadian history, in the elections of 1945, 1949, 1953 and 1957. During this period the Quebec electorate gave little effective support to the federal Conservatives, who were significantly more solicitous of provincial rights. Similarly, in every British Columbia election between 1952 and 1972, W.A.C. Bennett campaigned against federal power and other allegedly alien influences but the same electorate who responded to him gave majority support to other federal parties. Provincial autonomy is to a greater or less degree the electoral stock-in-trade of most provincial politicians seeking office. However, the electoral success of the most autonomist of these leaders has often little or nothing to do with resolving federal-provincial disputes in their favour.

More than any other federal election in Canadian history, that of June 1968 may reasonably be regarded as conferring a mandate for a party and a leader to implement a particular view of Confederation. Pierre Elliott Trudeau ostensibly entered elective politics to make that view prevail. The view was explained with clarity before and during the campaign. The new Liberal leader made no other important election promises. However, despite the salience of the issue and the relative decisiveness of the electoral result, several of the provinces — including all of the larger ones — continued to contest at several fundamental points the view of federalism on which Prime Minister Trudeau and his party were elected. It is improbable that the Prime Minister and his colleagues could have devised any politically practical way to overcome such provincial opposition.

In general then, elections have a very limited capacity to effect the authoritative resolution of federal-provincial conflict.

The Partisan Political System and Executive Federalism

As we saw earlier in this chapter, Riker's attribution of the decisive role to political parties in federalism makes no analysis of the roles that parties actually play in these political systems. In Canada as in other western democracies parties appear to be of diminishing importance.

John Meisel, in an article written in 1965, analyzed this phenomenon.[52] In his analysis, several of the factors at work in Canada are common to western nations. "Voluntary associations, interest groups, and private and semi-public organizations" have increased in numbers and wealth, and rival parties in the processes by which public decisions are made. There has been a "gradual diminution in Europe and North America of the cleavages in attitudes toward social issues" and in such circumstances parties have become "bland" to maximize their electoral support and have thus surrendered their innovative role to groups with more specific concerns. The specialized nature of modern government has led to the partial eclipse of elected legislatures by "independent or quasi-independent boards, agencies, and commissions, by so-called advisory bodies and, to some extent, even by Royal Commissions" as well as by the expert civil service. The merit system in the civil service and more generally the rationalization of public business have diminished the patronage available to politicians. These circumstances have challenged parties in all the western democracies to a greater or lesser extent but, according to Meisel, have been compounded by factors specific to Canada. The Liberal policy of coopting into positions of influence persons with little or no previous political experience has resulted in amateurism and the lack of adequate political skills in high places. Conversely, the Conservatives have failed to recruit able people into political life. The parties have become increasingly regionalized and have done badly in their vitally necessary role in Canadian integration; creating a "national political culture". Most importantly, from the point of view of this study, federalism itself has been significant in the decreasing role of political parties:

> Canada's federal system has imposed a particularly difficult task on the parties. To the extent that many of our major governmental decisions have resulted from intensive consultations between different levels of government, parties have to some measure been locked out of the most important decision-making processes. Dominion-provincial conferences, meetings of premiers, committees of experts representing the civil services of several provinces, and possibly two or three levels of government, working parties of various provincial ministers and experts, have all downgraded the role of parties who still bear considerable responsibility for the consequences of decisions but cannot always participate in their making. Canadian federalism has, therefore, been a major contributor to the decline in importance and effectiveness of political parties.[53]

Meisel is here referring to what in Chapter 3 was called "executive federalism".

Political parties are thus of decreasing importance in the Canadian federal system. Partisan politics have relatively limited capacities for effecting the resolution of federal-provincial conflicts either through intraparty relations or general elections. We have also seen in Chapter 1 the restricted role of constitutional amendment and evolving patterns of judicial review in bringing about successive redelineations of the powers of Ottawa and provinces as circumstances change. Thus very heavy burdens are thrown on intergovernmental relations in managing the federal system, on executive federalism.

The most obvious linkage between the partisan-political system and executive federalism is that the power of those who make the final and authoritative decisions in federal-provincial relations is legitimated by prior electoral success. Conversely, politicians in opposition at both levels are to an overwhelming degree "locked out", in Meisel's words, of effective influence in these matters; federal-provincial relations absorb a relatively small amount of time in the debates of Parliament and the provincial legislatures and under many circumstances these bodies have no real alternatives to ratifying decisions reached in intergovernmental negotiations. How then are electoral standings influenced by executive federalism?

Somewhat like sovereign states, Canadian provinces have fairly durable and persisting interests. Whatever administrations are in power, Ontario is a large and wealthy province and Prince Edward Island a small and poor one. New Brunswick is inevitably more preoccupied with bilingualism than is Alberta. Every Quebec administration since 1944 has put a higher priority on autonomy than have other provinces. It is safe to predict that despite their egalitarian commitments no NDP governments of British Columbia or Ontario would press for higher equalization payments to less favoured provinces. However, as is the case with sovereign states, these persisting interests do not prevent provincial leaders adopting different strategies in dealing with Ottawa, and ideology in some circumstances is of considerable importance in federal-provincial relations. Ideology appears, for example, to have determined the opposition of the CCF-NDP government of Saskatchewan in the early 1960s toward an inflexible formula for constitutional amendment and such opposition was ended by the displacement of that party by the Liberals in the provincial election of 1964. The personalized and erratic style of W.A.C. Bennett was of some consequence for federal-provincial relations. Premier Robarts of Ontario assumed a crucial role in attempting to reconcile conflicts between Quebec and the rest of Canada, but his successor William Davis has up to now given this activity less importance.

Provinces have thus persisting interests and provincial politicians in power have of course a persisting concern to press these interests in such a way as to be re-elected. Future electoral success at the provincial level has come to depend in large part on appropriate federal policies, particularly in respect to fiscal matters. This, rather than the partisan complexion of the government in power in Ottawa, appears to be the crucial determinant of the stances of provincial leaders toward federal politics. For example:

(1) In the 1957 federal election Mr. Diefenbaker and the Conservatives were perceived by several of the provincial administrations as being more sensitive to provincial interests than were the incumbent Liberals. This perception seems to have been important in winning for the new Conservative leader the organizational support of the governing parties in Nova Scotia, New Brunswick, Quebec and Ontario. This sup-

port, particularly of the two central provinces, appears to have been important in the Diefenbaker victory.

(2) In the 1965 election campaign, Premier Robert Stanfield of Nova Scotia threw the support of his organization behind the federal Conservatives; the party unexpectedly increased its share of the popular vote by 1.9 per cent and won three of the province's ten seats from the Liberals. In a perceptive article Murray Beck attributes part of the strong support of the Premier to Robert Stanfield's predispositions as "a strong party man". Beck goes on to describe other influences at work:

> Mr. Stanfield probably felt impelled to intervene all the more because of his recent relations with Ottawa. For most of his premiership up to 1963, he could expect sympathetic consideration from the federal government of the day, especially since he had been an architect of its initial victory. Certainly he had a direct pipe-line to the fountainhead of authority at Ottawa. That happy situation ended in April, 1963. He could not have expected the same solicitous attention from a Liberal government. Yet he had hoped for greater recognition of the fiscal incapacity of his province. The political maladroitness which characterized the Pearson government in this area, as in many others, provided him with more than enough ammunition for electioneering purposes.[54]

(3) In the 1968 federal election the governments of Quebec and Ontario distrusted the policies of the Trudeau Liberals in respect to the provinces. As we have seen, the support of these two provincial organizations was thrown behind the federal Conservatives.

Provincial political parties, and most importantly those in power, have discretion in determining how much, if any, of their prestige and resources they will commit to their federal colleagues in federal elections. The outside limits of this discretion under the normal political rules are that provincial politicians will not do anything which aids the opposing parties. However, even these limits are sometimes exceeded. As we have seen, in the early part of the Second World War, Liberal Premier Hepburn of Ontario openly cooperated with the Conservatives in an attempt to oust the Liberal government of Prime Minister Mackenzie King. Just a few days before the federal general election of April, 1963, Premier Lesage delivered publicly what was widely interpreted as an ultimatum to both federal parties on future fiscal relations with the provinces; because the Liberals were expected to win the election this statement was a considerable embarrassment to Mr. Pearson and his colleagues. In most circumstances, however, provincial parties will be more solicitous of the interests of their federal counterparts.

Within the context of federal-provincial relations as such, the partisan complexion of the governments involved is not crucial and it would indeed be unusual to see a Conference of Prime Ministers and Premiers divide on party lines. Both the permanent and occasional cleavages in this context are on axes other than partisan ones: between "have" and "have-not" provinces; between governments which put an urgent priority on bilingual and bicultural matters and those which do not; between Quebec and the other jurisdictions; between the heartland of Ontario and Quebec and the peripheral provinces. In recent years Ottawa's policies toward the provinces — most crucially in respect to fiscal matters and to regional economic development — have come to be based on rationalized criteria which do not take into account the partisan complexion of provincial governments. For example, in 1969 the Conservatives were displaced by the Liberals in Nova Scotia and in 1970 the Liberals by the Conservatives in New Brunswick, but it is improbable that in its dealings with Ottawa the position of either province has been changed significantly. In broad terms, neither provincial electorates nor provincial parties can expect to enhance their influence to any marked degree by having governments of the same partisan complexion in power in the provincial capital as in Ottawa. From the federal point of view, whatever parties are in power provincially will press provincial interests. So far as policy matters are concerned, provincial administrations are not notably more or less compliant because of their partisan complexion, and federal politicians have no urgent interest in ensuring that their colleagues are in power provincially. This latter generalization must, however, be qualified in the case of Quebec, where there is an emergent polarization within the provincial party system on federalist-separatist lines. The polarization of Quebec politics on the continuance of Confederation means almost inevitably that federal leaders will be oriented differently towards this political arena than toward others where the choices facing provincial electorates are less crucial. Cultural duality is the subject of Chapter 6.

Notes

[1] Oxford University Press, Editions of 1946, 1951, 1953, 1963.

[2] *Federalism and Constitutional Change*, Oxford University Press, 1956, Chapter 1, "The Character of Federalism" and "A Note on the Nature of Federalism," LXVII *Political Science Quarterly*, No. 1, March, 1952, pp. 81-95.

[3] The most influential of the integration theorists is Karl Deutsch. See his *Nationalism and Social Communications*, John Wiley and Sons, New York, 1953; with William J. Foltz (editors) *Nation Building*, New York, Atherton Press, 1966, and *The Nerves of Government*, The Free Press, New York, 1963.

[4] *New Federations: Experiments in the Commonwealth*, Oxford University Press, 1966.

[5] *Trends of Federalism in Theory and Practice*, Praeger, New York, 1968, particularly Chapter 5, "Federalism and Party System".

[6] *Comparative Federalism: The Territorial Dimension of Politics*, Holt, Rinehart and Winston, New York, 1969, pp. 329-341. As well as the book-length treatments of federalism by Watts, Duchacek and Friedrich the book of readings *American Federalism in Perspective*, edited by Aaron Wildavsky, Little, Brown, Boston, 1967, has a long excerpt from Riker's book and of the other twelve articles four are devoted to federalism and the party systems of the United States, Canada and Australia.

[7] Little, Brown, Boston. Particularly Part I, "A Theory of Federalism," and pp. 135-136.

[8] Riker, like C.J. Friedrich, seems to me to make an unduly clear-cut distinction

between federalism and imperialism. See the latter's treatment in *Man and His Government*, McGraw-Hill, New York, 1963, Chapter 31, "Empire: Coercive World Order", and Chapter 32, "Federalism: Consensual World Order". However, in the Canadian case a major impetus to the original federal bargain was the prospect of a vast hinterland to be peopled, developed and exploited by the Canadian heartland of Ontario and Quebec. On the Canadian prairies during the 1930s we were sometimes told that the region was in the most humiliating of all possible circumstances as "a colony of a colony".
[9]Riker, *op. cit.*, p. 136.
[10]In a study of political perceptions, attitudes and behaviour in Vancouver, Burrard Jean Laponce asserted that the electors operate within three political systems, federal, provincial and American. He found "... the greater one's involvement with Canadian politics, the greater is the intellectual involvement with American affairs." *People vs. Politics*, University of Toronto Press, 1969, p. 165.
[11]*New Federations: Experiments in the Commonwealth*, Oxford University Press, 1966, p. 338.
[12]"Canadian Liberal Democracy in 1955", *Press and Party in Canada*, G.V. Ferguson and Frank Underhill, Ryerson Press, Toronto, 1955, pp. 39-40.
[13]*The Government of Canada*, University of Toronto Press, 1946, p. 575.
[14]"Federal-provincial Voting Patterns in Canada", in John C. Courtney, Editor, *Voting in Canada*, Prentice-Hall of Canada, Toronto, 1967, pp. 82-89.
[15]*ibid.*, p. 84.
[16]"The Liberal Party in Contemporary Ontario Politics," III *Canadian Journal of Political Science*, No. 2, June 1970, p. 198. By permission of the authors and the Canadian Political Science Association. Emphasis in text.
[17]*Ibid.*, p. 199.
[18]*Ibid.*, p. 199.
[19]*Politics in Sudbury*, Laurentian University Press, 1966, p. 85.
[20]"Federal-Provincial Party Support: The Case of the Waterloo Ridings", Paper prepared for the Annual Meeting of the Canadian Political Science Association, Edmonton, 1975 (mimeo.).
[21]"Voting in a Provincial General Election and a Federal By-Election: A Constituency Study of Saskatoon City" XXXII *Canadian Journal of Economics and Political Science*, No. 3., August, 1966, pp. 339-353.
[22]*ibid.*, p. 344. By permission of the authors and the Canadian Political Science Association.
[23]"Variations in Party Support in Federal and Provincial Elections: Some Hypotheses" IV *Canadian Journal of Political Science*, No. 2, June 1971, pp. 280-286.
[24]*ibid.*, p. 281. By permission of the authors and the Canadian Political Science Association.
[25]*ibid.*, p. 286. However, the authors suggest that the importance of federal "affect" in Ontario politics is atypical and that provincial affect is relatively more important in the Atlantic provinces. By permission of the authors and the Canadian Political Science Association.
[26]*People vs. Politics*. On federal-provincial switching see pp. 168-176.
[27]*ibid.* p. 17.
[28]Miljan and Macnaughton, *op. cit.* pp. 14-26.
[29]"Party Identification, Stability and Change in Voting Behaviour: A Study of the 1968 Canadian Federal Election in Ontario" in Orest M. Kruhlak, Richard Schultz and Sidney I. Pobihuschy, *The Canadian Political Process: A Reader*, Holt, Rinehart and Winston of Canada, Toronto, 1970, p. 273.

[30]"Federal-Provincial Integration in Ontario Party Organization — The Influence of Recruitment Patterns", Paper presented to the 1970 meeting of the Canadian Political Science Association (mimeo.) p. 102.

[31]For an excellent account of Conservative organization during the Second World War see J.L. Granatstein, *The Politics of Survival, The Conservative Party of Canada 1939-1945*, University of Toronto Press, 1967.

[32]See generally John C. Courtney *The Selection of National Party Leaders in Canada*, Macmillan of Canada, Toronto, 1973.

[33]*ibid.*, p. 117.

[34]For an analysis of the relation between the voting system at conventions and delegate behaviour see Donald V. Smiley "The National Party Leadership Convention in Canada: A Preliminary Analysis" I *Canadian Journal of Political Science*, No. 4, (December 1968), pp. 378-380.

[35]"Federal Strains within a Canadian Party", in Hugh G. Thorburn, Editor, *Party Politics in Canada*, Second Edition, Prentice-Hall of Canada, Toronto, 1967, pp. 139-140. By permission of the author and *The Dalhousie Review*.

[36]*The Diefenbaker Interlude: Parties and Voting in Canada*, Longmans Canada Ltd., Toronto, 1965, p. 24.

[37]For an account of a previous period in which the reliance of a national party leader on provincial organizations was greater see Heath Macquarrie's statement in *Robert Laird Borden: His Memoirs*, Vol. I, Carleton Library Series 1969, p. VIII.

[38]"Federalism and Party Finance: A Preliminary Sounding", in *Studies in Canadian Party Finance*, Committee on Election Expenses, Queen's Printer, Ottawa, 1966, pp. 4-5. Reproduced by permission of Information Canada. This collection of studies is invaluable for the student of Canadian party organization as well as party finance, as is K.Z. Paltiel, *Political Party Financing in Canada*, McGraw-Hill Series on Canadian politics, Toronto, 1970.

[39]"Federalism and Party Finance", p. 13. Reproduced by permission of Information Canada.

[40]See Paltiel, *Political Party Financing*, p. 121 and pp. 124-132.

[41]For an exhaustive account of these intra-party relations see Gérard Bergeron, *Les partis libéraux du Canada et du Québec*, Unpublished Research Document of the Royal Commission on Bilingualism and Biculturalism, 1967(?).

[42]*Le réforme électorale se poursuit*, Communiqué, (mimeo.), 28 janvier 1975, p. 3.

[43]In an article published in 1961 Pierre Elliott Trudeau criticized the democratic socialists in Canada for what he regarded as over-rigid adherence to common policies and a common ideology throughout the country. He advised different policies to meet the varied needs and degrees of political maturity of the individual provinces. "Practice and Theory of Federalism", in *Social Purpose for Canada*, Michael Oliver, Editor, University of Toronto Press, pp. 371-393. One can assume that the Prime Minister finds the desired degree of ideological heterogeneity in the party of which he is now national leader.

[44]For an analysis of the strains between "movement" and "party" in the CCF see generally Walter D. Young *The Anatomy of a Party: The National CCF*, University of Toronto Press, 1969. Perhaps the same movement-party strains have had an impact on Social Credit; in a CBC broadcast on the virtual elimination of Social Credit as a significant political force in Alberta as a result of the provincial election of 1975 Gilles Caouette attributed this defeat to the Alberta party having turned its back on Social Credit principles. Caouette's view has some plausibility in terms of the vulnerability of Alberta Social Credit to a rising opposition party on the right of the ideological spectrum. See generally, John H. Barr *The Dynasty: The Rise and Fall of Social Credit in Alberta*,

McClelland and Stewart, Toronto, 1974, particularly Part III.

[45]*The Rise of a Third Party: A Study in Crisis Politics*, Prentice Hall, Englewood Cliffs, N.J., 1971.

[46]*ibid.*, p. 37.

[47]In Newfoundland, according to S.J.R. Noel, "Federal politics have been in practice an extension of provincial politics — a further test of the premier's popularity." *Politics in Newfoundland*, University of Toronto Press, 1971, p. 282. The present leader of the Newfoundland Conservatives, Frank Moores, resigned his seat in the House of Commons to take that position and was formerly President of the Progressive Conservative Party of Canada. For an anecdotal account of Maritime politics pointing up among other things the complex relations of federal and provincial politicians, see Dalton Camp, *Gentlemen, Players and Politicians*, McClelland and Stewart, Toronto, 1970. An unpublished article by Agar Adamson on the 1970 leadership contest in the Nova Scotia Progressive Conservative party has shown me the close interrelation of federal and provincial Conservative politicians in that party.

[48]The Finances of the Cooperative Commonwealth Federation and the New Democratic Party", Khayyam Z. Paltiel, Howat P. Noble and Reginald A. Whitaker, in *Studies in Canadian Party Finance*, pp. 317-404.

[49]See generally J.R. Mallory, *Social Credit and the Federal Power in Canada*, University of Toronto Press, 1955.

[50]See particularly *A Party Politician: The Memoirs of Chubby Power*, Edited by Norman Ward, Macmillan of Canada, 1966, pp. 120-132 and pp. 344-356.

[51]See Neil McKenty, *Mitch Hepburn*, McClelland and Stewart, Toronto, 1967, Chapters 13, 15 and 16.

[52]"Recent Changes in Canadian Parties" in Thorburn, *Party Politics in Canada*, pp. 33-54.

[53]*ibid.*, p. 37. By permission of the author.

[54]"The Electoral Behaviour of Nova Scotia in 1965", in Courtney, *Voting in Canada*, p. 97. By permission of J.M. Beck and *The Dalhousie Review*.

CHAPTER 5

THE FISCAL AND ECONOMIC SIDE OF CANADIAN FEDERALISM

The fiscal and economic dimension is the most complex aspect of Canadian federalism to understand, particularly for the academic observer, who must rely for the most part on the published statements of governments. In 1947 the late Robert MacGregor Dawson gave his assessment, "This world of Dominion-Provincial finance has, indeed, an air of grotesque unreality, untrammeled by logic and the ordinary restrictions and meanings of words."[1] Since Dawson wrote, these conflicts have continued in increasingly complex forms. Like prostitutes and golfers, those concerned with fiscal relations have developed their own argot, their own specialized vocabulary for communicating among themselves and mystifying outsiders. Thus we have "contracting out" and "tax room" and "fiscal equivalents" and "revenue equalization" and so on. In very recent years two new terms, "indexation" and "deconditionalization", have been added to this ghastly lexicon — certainly travesties of at least one of Canada's official languages if not of sound public policy. Nowhere more than in federal-provincial economic relationships is the threefold classification of falsehoods as "lies, damned lies and statistics" so applicable, and nowhere do Canadian politicians so embellish their pursuit of the crassest of purposes with appeals to the elegancies of economic analysis or what purport to be immutable principles. It is unlikely that in these matters the limits of chicanery have yet been reached. In 1974 W. Blackman, an economist at the University of Calgary, presented a study of the economic costs of Confederation to Alberta and the economic circumstances of a hypothetically independent Alberta under a series of assumptions.[2] Under these assumptions the material burdens of Canadian federalism were very heavy for the province, and the consequences of independence almost entirely favourable. At the end of his investigation Blackman suggested that similar studies be made for each of the provinces to discover whether Confederation was in an economic sense desirable. If this recommendation were followed, one can well imagine a future conference of first ministers being faced with the demand of some or even all of the provinces that Ottawa compensate them for the privilege of including them within the Canadian Confederation at all.

Since Confederation Canadian political leaders have from time to time attempted to forestall conflicts between the federal and provincial governments about financial matters by embodying fiscal settlements in the constitution. Section 118 of the British North America Act of

1867 stipulated that the scale of subsidies to the provinces laid down in the Act "shall be in full Settlement of all future Demands on Canada". Despite what has been called the "finality clause", less than two years after the Dominion was established the threats of Nova Scotia separatism led the federal government to make an upward revision of the original schedule of subsidies.[3] The subsidy question then evolved as a focus of continued federal-provincial conflict, and Section 118 became and remained until the Second World War what J.A. Maxwell called "a flexible portion of the British North America Act".[4] In 1907 Ottawa and all the provinces except British Columbia agreed on a new scale of subsidies which was enacted as an amendment to the B.N.A. Act as a "final and unalterable settlement". This attempt at finality was no more successful than the one of four decades before. Since then, the old impulses have not died. During the process of constitutional review begun in 1968, the Conservative government of Nova Scotia — an administration otherwise characterized by responsibility and good sense in federal-provincial relations — pressed for the entrenchment of an equalization formula in a revised constitution to remove conflicts among Ottawa and the provinces about this matter. In a similar spirit, Prime Minister Trudeau so stated his hopes for constitutional reform in a document introduced into the Conference of February, 1969:

> What is required is a new orientation to intergovernmental cooperation — a clearer definition of the roles of the two orders of government may well help to achieve this — a new orientation which would focus the attention of governments on the whole complex of public services and on the whole of Canada's tax system, *as they affect the citizen.* This new orientation, this focus, is what federal-provincial relations must come to mean to the citizen, instead of the unhappy disputes which have persisted between governments during the postwar period as to the share of certain taxes which each government ought to get."[5]

Apart from embodying fiscal provisions in the constitution, there have been proposals for eliminating or resolving conflicts between Ottawa and the provinces about fiscal matters by establishing executive agencies to adjudicate competing claims. The Royal Commission on Dominion-Provincial Relations, in its Report published in 1940, recommended a Finance Commission to advise the federal government on requests for National Adjustment Grants whose objective, in the Commission's formulation, would be to place every province always in a position to provide services at national average levels without levying taxes at rates above the national average.[6] In his 1964 attempt to rewrite the Canadian constitution, Peter J.T. O Hearn envisaged a federal Council of federal and provincial delegates with the power to make "a binding Allocation between the Government of Canada . . . and the Governments of the Provinces . . . for any period not exceeding Ten Years, of the Powers to tax and borrow and may determine the Limits of Rates or Amounts that shall apply to this Allocation. . ."[7] Similarly, Marcel Faribault and Robert M. Fowler, in their outline of a "possible Canadian constitution" published in 1965, recommended a Fiscal

Commission with members chosen partly by Ottawa and partly by the provinces, with a corporate responsibility for regulating a wide range of fiscal matters.[8] As we saw in Chapter 3, the Ontario government in 1971 suggested that the Conference of Prime Ministers and Premiers constitute itself as a Joint Economic Council "to review and determine, on a continuing basis, national economic goals of a strategic order".

It is wildly improbable that federal-provincial conflict in respect to economic matters will be or can be ended through either a new constitutional settlement or through those governments giving up their freedom of independent action to some kind of joint executive authority. Such conflict is inherent in the Canadian federal system. Those who place a high priority on rationality and coherence in public policy can easily demonstrate that this lack of federal-provincial articulation exacts a high price; in 1969 one of Canada's most influential economists, Jacques Parizeau, after nearly a decade as adviser to successive Quebec governments decided the price was too high and joined the Parti Québécois.[9] Yet the hope persists that Ottawa and the provinces will come to agreement on the most fundamental of economic matters. The federal Royal Commission on Taxation, for example, believed that the demonstrable benefits of effective policies for economic stabilization were so overwhelming that with experience, the federal and provincial governments could progress from more effective consultation about economic matters to the "development of binding commitments and agreements" about stabilization.[10] After the establishment of the Tax Structure Committee in 1964, some of the provinces hoped that this group would be able to evolve federal-provincial agreement on tax-sharing and expenditure-priorities. The reality makes such solutions unlikely.[11] At the most elemental level, federal-provincial fiscal relations are shaped by the desire of provincial politicians to spend public revenues without levying taxes for these purposes and of course by the resistance of Ottawa to such pressures. There are inherent conflicts of interest between "have" and "have not" provinces and between the government with national responsibilities and those with provincial responsibilities. D.G. Hartle has come to this realistic assessment: "... *It is most unlikely that we will ever attain, under a federal system of government, the situation where all governments get together, agree on priorities for expenditures, and then parcel out the revenues among themselves in accordance with these agreed priorities. There are major and unavoidable conflicts of interest between levels of government that can only be resolved through hard bargaining.*"[12]

In respect to economic matters then, Ottawa and the provinces are both interdependent and unwilling to give up their individual freedom of action either to the other level or to any kind of joint decision-making agency. J.A. Corry asserted in 1958, "Dominion-Provincial Conferences, notably those held to negotiate about tax agreements every five years, have become clearing houses for many disputed issues between the Dominion and the provinces. One can almost say that the various stresses and strains of the system are negotiated down to tolerable compromises in the course of hammering out the next tax agreements."[13] Since Corry wrote, the number of economic issues subject to joint federal-provincial action has markedly increased in scope and importance.

The Basis of the Present Fiscal Regime

The current patterns of fiscal and economic relations between the federal and provincial governments can be understood only against the background of a series of interrelated developments during and immediately at the end of the Second World War.

The Rowell-Sirois Report, published in 1940, recommended a very new distribution of tax sources, revenues and responsibilities between the federal and provincial governments.[14] The federal authorities were to be given exclusive responsibility for unemployment insurance and for a proposed system of contributory old age pensions and exclusive access to the taxation of personal and corporate incomes and of estates. The existing system of statutory subsidies to the provinces was to be eliminated and the federal authorities would assume the responsibility for provincial indebtedness. In place of the tangled web of subsidies which had developed without coherent purpose, there was to be a system of unconditional National Adjustment Grants paid so as "to enable each province (including its municipalities) without resort to heavier taxation than the Canadian average to provide adequate social, educational and developmental services."[15] Significantly, the thrust of the Commission's recommendations was toward the financial and administrative independence of the two levels and against the complex of joint arrangements which came to be described, with considerable inaccuracy, as "cooperative" federalism. The preoccupations of the Second World War and the opposition to the Report by the governments of Ontario, Alberta and British Columbia prevented serious negotiation about the new scheme for Canadian federalism recommended by the Commission.

In retrospect, the most significant and lasting contribution of the Rowell-Sirois Commission was its approach to interprovincial fiscal equalization based on a rational evaluation of fiscal need. The Commission investigated, and it must have taken great forebearance to do so, the claims of the individual provinces for upward revision of their respective subsidies. These claims were in most cases based on the most tendentious accounts of the purportedly contractual commitments incurred by Ottawa when the various provinces entered Confederation, and the allegedly adverse effects of national tariff and transportation policies on the western and maritime provinces. The reasons the Commission gave for rejecting federal compensation based on the workings of the national policy were both principled and pragmatic. On the side of principle, it was asserted that so far as national economic policies were concerned the government of the Dominion was responsible to the House of Commons and the people of Canada rather than to the provinces. In practical terms, the burdens and benefits of national policies were so complex and so interrelated that it was impossible to evaluate with any precision their incidence on the various provinces and regions. Thus the Commission in rejecting these claims proposed a subsidy system based on provincial fiscal need. Such need was a great deal less subject to precise measurement than the Commission believed, and in particular the Commission ignored the circumstance that the costs of and needs for provincial and local services could not be evaluated without a great deal of subjectivity. Further, in the light of past and subsequent experience it was patently unrealistic to suggest that the government of Canada would be willing to allow an independent fiscal commission in effect to determine the scale of subsidies to the provinces. On the other hand, the fundamental idea that Ottawa, through unconditional subsidies, should guarantee the revenues of the provinces to a national average has been an influential standard in federal-provincial fiscal relations from the publication of the Rowell-Sirois Report onward.

In 1941 the federal government preempted the income tax and succession duty fields with compensating payments to the provinces. This action projected Canada into a system of tax and revenue sharing whose major elements still exist. The complexities of the various tax agreements from the Second World War onward have been described and analyzed elsewhere. This fiscal coordination has moved in three directions, in each case resulting in the interpenetration of federal and provincial interests and policies:[16]

(1) Federal tax abatements have transferred revenue sources from Ottawa to the provinces. The procedure here is a reduction in the federal rates of direct taxation allowing the provinces to increase their levies at no political risk since the taxpayer's provincial obligation is offset by a reduction in his federal burden. The abatement system, which has now ended, has led to the continual struggle between Ottawa and the provinces about "tax room", that is, pressures for and against decreases in federal rates of direct taxation.

(2) Federal equalization grants transfer funds to some provinces, to be expended as the latter wish. As we shall see, the major part of equalization grants has been related to the actual or imputed yields to the provinces from certain tax sources.

(3) Federal-provincial tax collection agreements have been concluded for the convenience of taxpayers and the coordination of federal and provincial tax policies. Because Ottawa will collect income taxes for the provinces only on the condition that the latter make their levies on the federal tax base, this base becomes a matter of concern to both levels.

There was a significant amount of federal planning for post-war social and economic reconstruction, even during the most critical years of the Second World War, and as hostilities drew to a close this activity was intensified. In April 1945 the government issued its "White Paper" on Employment and Income[17] and in August of the same year announced the "Green Book" proposals to the Dominion-Provincial Conference on Reconstruction.[18] Taken together, these formulations gave a comprehensive focus to national economic policies which perpetuated federal dominance over the provinces throughout the next decade and which contributed both to a smooth transition to peacetime conditions and to prosperity and growth in the postwar world. There were four interrelated elements in those policies:

First, the government of Canada committed itself to maintaining "a high and stable level of income and employment". The chief policy instrument here was fiscal policy, i.e., the adjustment of federal rates of taxation and expenditure in the interests of stabilization. The White Paper put this commitment in these terms:

> The Government of Canada will be prepared, in periods where unemployment threatens, to incur the deficits and increases in the national debt resulting from its income and employment policy, whether that policy in the circumstances is best applied through increased expenditure or reduced taxation. In periods of buoyant employment and income, budget plans will call for surpluses. The Government's policy will be to keep the national debt within manageable proportions and maintain a proper balance in its budget over a period longer than a single year.[19]

This was a decisive break from the older practices by which the federal government attempted to balance its budget each fiscal year, and by which during the Depression declining public revenues were countered by increased rates of taxation.

Second, to make its use of fiscal policy effective the federal government needed exclusive access to the fields of individual and corporate income tax. On the taxation side of fiscal policy, the most effective device was seen as being discretionary changes in the rates of these taxes as the demands of full employment and price stability dictated. Thus there was an offer by the federal government at the last session of the Dominion-Provincial Conference on Reconstruction in May 1946 to "rent" the income tax and succession duty fields from the provinces for an annual compensation of $15 per head of provincial population.

Third, the federal government and the provinces would cooperate in building a developed welfare state in Canada. It was believed at the end of the Second World War that when the economy returned to peace-time conditions there would be a chronic deficiency of aggregate demand in the absence of heavy and continuous public expenditure.[20] Thus it was recommended at the Conference on Reconstruction that Ottawa cooperate with the provinces in establishing a national scheme of health insurance, that the federal government assume total administrative and financial responsibilities for old age pensions to all residents 70 years and over and without a means test and pay half the cost of a $30 pension to all Canadians aged 65 to 69 who qualified through a means test, and that the federal unemployment insurance scheme be quickly extended to cover all employees.

Fourth, in collaboration with other nations Canada would work toward the reconstruction of the international economic order on liberal lines.[21] It was taken for granted that domestic economic objectives could not be effectively pursued without such reconstruction.

The 1945 proposals taken together constituted an ambitious plan for post-war Canadian federalism. However, federal-provincial agreement on the plan proved impossible and the Conference on Reconstruction adjourned *sine die* on May 3, 1946. It was essential to the federal plan for post-war Canada that Ottawa's dominance in fiscal matters be secured. To this, Ontario and Quebec would not assent. Despite this failure, almost from the day the Conference adjourned the federal government proceeded to implement the grand design of 1945 by piecemeal measures and by a decade later most of these objectives had been in large part achieved.

The Passing of Federal Dominance[22]

The Canadian federal system as it emerged from the Second World War and persisted for more than a decade afterward was dominated by the central government. As we have seen, Ottawa at the end of the War had committed the country to a set of objectives which was at the same time precise and comprehensive. In its pursuit of these objectives the political leadership was assisted by a sophisticated and aggressive federal civil service. Although federal dominance in taxation and public expenditures declined from wartime levels, in 1955 federal taxes were 16.9 per cent of Gross National Product compared with 6.9 per cent for provincial and local authorities combined. This structure of federal dominance was buttressed by the predisposition of an overwhelming majority of Canadians, outside Quebec at any rate, to look to Ottawa rather than to their respective provincial capitals for leadership in meeting urgent public needs. The provinces had never fully recovered from the difficulties of Depression and War, and the balance of both political and bureaucratic competence ran strongly in favour of the central government.

The story of Canadian federalism since the late 1950s is the story of the steady attrition of the power of the central government. It is tempting to date this development from the coming to power of the Diefenbaker administration as a result of the general election of June 10, 1957, although its predecessor had already destroyed an important element of the previous system by its decision to divorce tax rental from equalization payments to the provinces in the agreements which came into effect on April 1 of that year. According to John Meisel's analysis of the 1957 election,[23] the longevity in power of the Liberals had made both the political and bureaucratic leadership in Ottawa increasingly insensitive to regional needs and grievances, particularly those which had developed in the Prairie and Atlantic Provinces. The Progressive Conservatives under their new leader were remarkably successful in exploiting these disparate regional grievances without in the process formulating any new and coherent set of national objectives.[24]

If we take the years 1955 to 1965 we can see the very great changes in the fiscal balance between Ottawa and the provinces in this decade:
— in 1955 federal expenditures on goods and services were 8.5 per cent of G.N.P. while provincial and local expenditures combined were 6.0

per cent. In 1965 the corresponding proportions were 5.1 per cent and 7.9 per cent.[25]

— classes of expenditure mainly within provincial and local control increased in importance. Health expenditures were 1.3 per cent of G.N.P. in 1955, 3.1 per cent in 1965; social welfare 3.7 per cent in 1955 and 4.6 per cent in 1965; and education 3.0 per cent in 1955 and 5.3 per cent in 1965. The major direct responsibility of Ottawa, defence and mutual aid, declined during the decade from 6.5 per cent to 3.0 per cent of G.N.P.[26]

— in terms of tax revenues, federal taxes were 74.3 per cent of total levies paid by Canadians in 1955, provincial and municipal taxes combined 25.7 per cent. The corresponding proportions in 1965 were 60.9 per cent and 39.1 per cent. Provincial tax levies in this period increased 5.3 times.[27]

— federal transfer payments to the provinces increased from $440.0 millions in 1955 to $1,569.5 millions in 1965.[28]

The most urgent of public priorities thus came to be within provincial rather than federal jurisdiction. This was reflected not only in the new fiscal balance but in the increasing sophistication and aggressiveness of the provincial administrations and the increasing disposition of Canadians to look to their provinces and local governments rather than to Ottawa for meeting emergent social and economic needs.

The structure of federal dominance coming out of the Second World War could be legitimated only so long as the national government demonstrated its capacity to manage the economy effectively. By the latter 1950s this ability was no longer apparent. In 1957 unemployment as a proportion of the civilian labour force increased from 3.4 per cent in the previous year to 4.9 per cent and to 7.1 per cent in 1958.[29] During these years Canada was experiencing a rate of economic growth lower than that of other industrialized nations, and in 1958 its per capita product at constant prices actually declined.[30] Contrary to the expectations of those who had accepted the Keynesian analysis, high rates of unemployment and inflationary pressures were experienced at the same time. Out of this inadequate record of economic performance came not only an attenuation of the legitimacy of Ottawa's dominance but, in varying degrees, more aggressive and deliberate provincial action to encourage economic development.[31] All of the provinces engaged in efforts to seek markets and developmental capital and most committed themselves to one version or another of economic planning.

The weakening of federal dominance in fiscal and economic matters has been manifested in several developments:

— in the tax agreements which came into effect in 1957 equalization payments were made to the provinces whether or not they rented the direct tax fields to the central government.[32] It was a central presupposition of the 1945 plan that Ottawa could ensure full employment and price stability only if it had exclusive access to taxation on incomes. Thus the federal government was very much constrained in moving toward the interprovincial equalization of revenues by the circumstance that its schedule of unconditional payments had to be designed to induce the provinces to surrender the direct tax fields. However, this unified taxsharing system was shattered in 1954 when Quebec began to levy its own tax on individual incomes. The divorcing of tax rental from equalization in 1957 was a crucial element in the destruction of the centralized fiscal regime. The 1957-62 agreements also began the abatement system. Under this scheme the provinces were to receive the following shares of federal taxation or, at their request, an abatement of federal taxes of the same amount: 10 per cent of federal personal income tax, 9 per cent of corporation profits and 50 per cent of succession duties.

— in the tax arrangements which came into effect in 1962 the tax rental system was ended.[33] The abatement of corporation income tax remained at 9 per cent, that of personal income tax was increased to 16 per cent to increase one percentage point annually to 20 per cent in 1966-67. Thus the provinces were to levy their own taxes of personal and corporate incomes, although the federal government offered at no charge to the provinces to collect these taxes on the condition that the levies were made on the federal tax base.

— in 1965 the Parliament of Canada enacted the Established Programmes (Interim Arrangements) Act which permitted the provinces to contract out of certain established conditional grant programs and receive fiscal equivalents in compensation. This procedure will be discussed later in the chapter.

— in 1965 the Canada Pension Plan was established, giving the provinces access to capital funds built up by contributors to this plan and its Quebec counterpart.[34] The Liberal government when it came to power as the result of the federal general election of April, 1963 was committed to the inauguration of a compulsory plan of contributory retirement pensions with benefits paid from general revenues. Led by Quebec, there was vigorous provincial resistance to the attempt of the federal authorities to establish such a scheme. What finally resulted was the Quebec Pension Plan and, outside that province, the Canada Pension Plan. Under the latter, the funds accumulated are made available to the provinces in proportion to the amounts paid into the funds by the contributors from each participating province. These funds are used to purchase the securities of the government of Canada and of the provinces. Between 1966 and 1969 securities to the amount of $2,023.0 millions had been so purchased.[35]

The Lesage government which came to power as a result of the Quebec general election of June 1960 played a decisive role in attenuating the centralized fiscal and economic regime which had been built up during the War and perpetuated afterward.[36] With singleness of purpose and sophistication the Quebec government on issue after issue challenged both the presuppositions and the structures of federal dominance. However, Quebec's pressures for autonomy were for the most part in harmony with the emergent aspirations of the other provincial governments.

As we shall see later in this chapter, the federal authorities from late 1966 onward have re-asserted the powers of Ottawa in fiscal and economic matters. However, these new directions have been a refusal to accede to the further attenuation of federal power rather than to commit Canada to a new set of national objectives.

Economic Stabilization

The White Paper on Employment and Income committed the federal government to ensuring full employment and price stability in the national economy. The formulation of the White Paper was an application of the analysis of J.M. Keynes in his *General Theory of Employment, Interest and Money*, published in 1936. In the broadest of terms, it can be said that the Keynesian theory demonstrated that the free movement of prices and interest rates could not be depended upon to bring about conditions of price stability with full employment. It was thus the responsibility of national governments to devise policies ensuring appropriate levels of aggregate demand.

As T.N. Brewis has pointed out, "One of the chief attractions of the Keynesian theory was its association with an analytical formula which lent itself to ready administration."[37] Canadian policy-makers, both elected and appointed, found very compelling at the end of the Second World War an analysis which purported to show how under peace-time conditions the federal government might effectively stabilize the national economy without the extension of government ownership, the precise planning of economic objectives or specific controls over wages, prices and profits.[38] However, in retrospect the Keynesian formulation as applied to Canada did not take into account the constraints imposed on the federal government by provinces with a range of autonomous powers in economic matters. These constraints were not very important in the perspectives of Ottawa officialdom as the War ended. In 1945 the central government made 83 per cent of all public expenditures in Canada, and while it was no doubt expected that this proportion would decline with the return to peacetime conditions, it was probably expected that federal spending would remain dominant. On the taxation side, it was an essential element of Ottawa's perspectives that it would retain the exclusive access to levies on individual and corporate income. Thus the 1945 plans contained a very limited recognition of the needs for intergovernmental collaboration in sustaining full employment and price stability. It was, however, suggested that the federal government collaborate with the provinces and municipalities in planning a "shelf" of public works to be undertaken when, in Ottawa's view, general economic conditions made this appropriate,[39] and there should be cooperation with the provinces for the conservation and development of natural resources.

As we have seen, national fiscal and economic policies showed themselves incapable of sustaining full employment, price stability and growth from the late 1950s onward. Out of this inadequate record of performance came two contradictory lines of criticism of national economic policies. According to the first, the federal government had failed to act effectively through the fiscal and monetary instruments available to it to ensure appropriate levels of aggregate demand. In a scathing analysis of post-war federal policy published in 1965,[40] H. Scott Gordon argued that Keynesianism "has made little headway in advancing the analytical work in the bureaucracy that underlies the formulation of employment and other economic policies, and despite some brief periods of favour, it does not appear to have won its way to any appreciable extent as a sound principle of fiscal policy."[41] According to Gordon, federal fiscal policy for most of the time since the White Paper had been based on the "Gladstonian" principle that "the government should keep its expenditures low and always balance its budget or have a small surplus" and on what he called the "Ricardian" view which attributed unemployment ro a "structural mismatching of the demand for labour and the supply of labour" rather than, in Keynesian terms, a deficiency of aggregate demand. The contrary view had been put forward by Jacques Parizeau in 1964. Parizeau saw the problem in terms of the rigidities introduced into the thinking of the federal authorities by the Keynesian theory itself: "The framework of federal action upon the economy had to be quite general, or to put it differently, national in scope. The emphasis was on the variations in the total aggregate demand and on large aggregates. Regional discrepancies in growth and structural bottlenecks were hardly considered and, in fact, at times the federal authorities explicitly refused to consider them."[42] A similar note was struck by Maurice Lamontagne in his analysis of postwar economic policy delivered at the Study Conference on National Goals convened by the federal Liberal party in 1960:

> Stagnation, inflation and unemployment have a very important regional and industrial incidence, especially in Canada. Certain regions or industries grow rapidly while others are depressed. Certain industries may enjoy rising prices while others, at the same time, suffer from relatively low prices. Some industries or regions may experience heavy unemployment while others suffer from a scarcity of labour. Our national aggregates, such as the gross national product, the cost of living index and the national percentage of unemployment, are frequently the result of conflicting tendencies prevailing in different industries and different regions. It is always unrealistic and dangerous to interpret these national aggregates without taking their regional and industrial components into account. It is even more dangerous to attempt to solve such economic problems as unemployment as if they had the same causes and intensity throughout the country and as if they could be effectively met by the same policies in all industries and all regions.[43]

Whatever the respective merits of the aggregate-demand and structural analyses, it has become apparent since the late 1950s that the incidence of both price stability and employment — as well as of federal fiscal and monetary policies — varies greatly among the provinces and regions of Canada. This is particularly striking in terms of unemployment, since whatever the national averages there are consistently higher rates of unemployment in the Atlantic region, Quebec and

British Columbia than in the prairie provinces and Ontario. The Report of the Royal Commission on Taxation published in 1966 recommended that as an objective Canada should adopt a short-term unemployment rate of 3.5 per cent, an objective compatible with what the Commission regarded as acceptable annual increases in the consumer price index of 1.5 to 2 per cent.[44] However, it was estimated that the national average rate of unemployment of 3.5 per cent would be accompanied by the following rates across Canada:

Atlantic Provinces	6.0 per cent
Quebec	4.6 per cent
Ontario	2.6 per cent
Prairie Provinces	2.2 per cent
British Columbia	4.0 per cent[45]

The extent to which it is possible for federal fiscal and monetary policies to be tailored to fit the different economic circumstances of the provinces and regions of Canada remains a matter of debate among specialists. The Economic Council of Canada in its Fifth Annual Review published in September, 1968, saw very restricted possibilities in a "regionally oriented stabilization policy" undertaken by the federal government.[46] One of the difficulties is that there appeared to be almost insurmountable obstacles in measuring the impact of expenditures in particular provinces or regions on other provinces or regions. However, even if this difficulty was in part overcome there were other limitations faced by Ottawa in implementing fiscal policies so as to meet regional needs. Federal expenditures make up a declining proportion of total public spending and ". . . federal expenditures cannot be quickly changed to deal with short-run changes in the national economy. A dominating proportion is devoted to contractual or statutory payments that cannot be easily or quickly raised or cut back in response to short-run changes in the economic situation." On grounds of equity, the Council rejected "regionally discriminating tax changes for stabilization purposes". It was also argued that monetary policy was an inadequate instrument of regional differentiation because of "the essential unity of the capital market", the difficulty of erecting safeguards against funds being re-lent elsewhere than as designated, and the circumstance that access to borrowing was not the chief problem of slow-growth areas.

The Report of the Standing Senate Committee on National Finance on the subject of Growth, Employment and Price Stability published in November 1971 saw somewhat greater possibilities for regional discrimination in national fiscal and monetary policies than had the Economic Council.[47] The Bank of Canada finds it possible to exercise a degree of "moral suasion" to induce the chartered banks "to take a particular (sic) tender view of applications for credit from the slow-growth regions". The federal government should decentralize its own decision-making and should try to persuade private corporations to do the same, although it was not made clear just what the impact of such decentralization would be on private and public policies. Service industries should receive more recognition in policies for regional development. Federal purchasing policies rely too heavily on services in Central Canada. Despite this qualified optimism of the Senate Committee about regionally discriminating economic policies toward stabilization and growth, the general tenor of the Report saw limited possibilities for national policy in this direction.

Whether or not the provinces should design and implement their own fiscal policies oriented towards price stability, full employment and growth is a matter of dispute. A common viewpoint is that in the absence of such policies or federal-provincial collaboration in economic stabilization, provincial and municipal tax and expenditure policies will be "perverse" in the sense that these jurisdictions will raise taxes and/or cut back on spending in times of adversity and lower tax rates and/or increase expenditures in prosperous periods. In its examination of provincial and municipal spending between 1945 and 1961, the Royal Commission on Taxation found that this had not been so and that these expenditures "did not exercise a destabilizing influence on the economy ... The changes in provincial and municipal expenditures are as cyclically stable or more stable than the combined private and federal expenditures they replaced."[48] In the Commission's judgment this "built-in" stability was in large part the result of the provinces and municipalities relying very heavily on revenues from indirect taxes which were "relatively insensitive to short-run fluctuations in the level of economic activity". The increasing reliance of the provinces on direct taxation gave the Commission cause for concern that this stability was being attenuated and it was recommended that the federal government resist pressures to withdraw further from the income tax field.[49]

The Royal Commission on Taxation opposed independent stabilization policies by the provinces.[50] It was argued that because of the effects of such policies outside the borders of the respective provinces "unless each province took into account what all the other provinces and the federal government were doing, and were going to do, the individual provincial efforts could be offsetting, too extreme, or ill timed." The alternative was federal-provincial cooperation in designing and implementing stabilization policies.

In his study prepared for the Ontario Committee on Taxation in 1967 Clarence L. Barber argued for independent provincial fiscal policies directed toward price stability, full employment and economic growth.[51] Barber pointed out that the larger provinces had both populations and incomes comparable to those of several industrialized nations. He examined the constraints on provincial policies which did not exist in the case of sovereign states — provinces cannot control their own monetary policies, exchange rates or immigration policies. These did not, however, make it impractical or undesirable for provinces to have individual fiscal policies. There are of course leakages in provincial expenditures where the effects of changes in spending are partly experienced outside provincial borders and this "does seriously limit the effectiveness of provincial fiscal policy unless all or a number of provinces act in parallel fashion." However, several of the smaller industrial nations have such leakages as great as the larger Canadian provinces, and again this limitation on the provinces is "a difference in degree rather than kind". In Barber's view, the key question was whether provinces had adequate borrowing capacity to sustain counter-cyclical policies. He was relatively optimistic that the provinces had such capacity in meeting cycles of "moderate amplitude". Thus the provinces, and in particular the larger ones, had the ability to carry out independent fiscal policies and Barber was convinced that it was appropriate they should do so. The control of expenditures in many important matters is within provincial rather than federal jurisdiction. There is regional variation in the need for policy measures and the federal government has a limited ability to meet these varying needs through its own policies. The most effective stabilization policies will of course be those carried out in cooperation between all levels of government. However, Barber was willing to regard as appropriate provincial pressure through fiscal policy to change federal policies deemed inadequate to the needs of particular provinces or regions.

There appear to be no published studies on the extent to which the various provinces have designed fiscal policies toward economic stability and growth. The Ontario government has recently directed its fiscal policies in terms of the "full employment budget" defined as "a measure of the government surplus or deficit that would occur if the target of full employment were attained".[52] According to a 1971 Ontario Budget Paper, "The most significant feature of the total public sector's fiscal impact on Ontario is a permanent full-employment surplus, implying a built-in tax drag on the provincial economy. This permanent tax-drag is due wholly to the financial operations of the federal government in Ontario."[53] It was estimated that this permanent federal surplus, more influenced by discretionary changes in tax rates than in expenditure policies, was rapidly increasing — from 2.6 per cent of potential Gross Provincial Product in 1962 to 4.5 per cent of potential GPP in 1969.[54] Thus, according to the Ontario analysis, the net effect of federal policies was permanently "contractionary" in Ontario, and Ottawa's attempts to mitigate interprovincial disparities had frustrated full employment and economic growth in that province. From the Ontario perspective, provincial and municipal fiscal policies were necessary to counter the effect of federal action.

From the mid- and late 1960s onward policies directed toward economic stabilization have become the focus of intense federal-provincial conflict. In terms of taxation, it is generally agreed by specialists in public finance that changes in the rates of taxes levied on personal and corporate income are the most useful stabilization devices available to governments. Yet from 1957 until the new federal policies of late 1966 there was a headlong retreat from these tax fields until under the 1967-72 arrangements the individual income tax abatements in respect to Quebec had reached 50 per cent and in the other provinces which had not accepted contracting out 28 per cent, while corporate taxes were abated at 10 per cent. In its policies enunciated in the fall of 1966, and still in essentials maintained, the federal government announced its intention not to yield to further provincial pressures for tax room. This new firmness can in part be attributed to Ottawa's apprehension that such yielding would impair critically the federal capacity to undertake effective stabilization policies, and at that time and afterward it was a federal rule-of-thumb that the national government required at least 50 per cent of the personal income tax field throughout Canada. In terms of expenditures, those made for services and facilities provided by Ottawa have been a constantly declining proportion of total public spending and it is likely this decline will continue. The provinces, it is true, are heavily dependent on federal transfer payments of both a conditional and unconditional nature. However, apart from certain developmental projects almost all of these transfers are of a contractual or semi-contractual nature and thus cannot be adjusted to short-run economic conditions.

It is not within my purpose or competence to judge the potential effectiveness of the management of aggregate demand by national governments in harmonizing the goals of price stability and full employment. It is, however, obvious in the persistence of "stagflation" in all the western industrialized countries that this is a more complex and difficult responsibility than was believed a generation ago. Writing in *Newsweek* of August 19, 1974, one of the world's most distinguished macroeconomists, Paul Samuelson, said bluntly, "No mixed economy — not the U.S. or the U.K., Sweden or Switzerland, Germany or Japan, France or Italy — knows how to have sustained full employment." However this may be, the potential effectiveness of aggregate-demand policies are in the Canadian context significantly constrained by the circumstances of federalism.

The Equalization of Inter-Regional Disparities

Canada consists of several regional economies, rather weakly integrated with one another and providing widely different levels of economic opportunities and material welfare to their respective residents. Per capita incomes in the poorest province remain just over half those in the most prosperous:

Personal Income Per Capita, 1972 dollars

Newfoundland	2,462
Prince Edward Island	2,443
Nova Scotia	2,991
New Brunswick	2,793
Quebec	3,359
Ontario	4,324
Manitoba	3,580
Saskatchewan	2,968
Alberta	3,757
British Columbia	4,078
Yukon and N.W.T.	3,418
Canada	3,750[55]

As we have seen, the Rowell-Sirois Commission proposed that from time to time National Adjustment Grants be paid to the provinces based on their fiscal need. Douglas H. Clark has more recently defined fiscal need grants as "intergovernmental payments to political units which, on the basis of capacity to raise revenues from their own tax-payers, are determined to be in need of financial assistance to enable them, without having to impose unduly high rates of taxation, to pro-vide reasonable standards of public service in relation to other political units having the same expenditure responsibilities and the same revenue-raising capacity."[56] The determination of grants on such a basis thus involves judgements both about the capacity of jurisdictions to raise revenues and the costs they incur in providing public services.

Despite the claims of fiscal need, federal unconditional grants to the provinces have come to be based on revenue equalization alone and have not taken into account the respective needs of the provinces for public services or the costs of providing these services. Clark has so defined revenue equalization grants as "intergovernmental payments to political units which, on the basis of their capacity to raise revenues from their own taxpayers, are determined to be in need of financial assistance in relation to other units having the same revenue-raising capacity."[57] The revenue equalization principle was given explicit rec-ognition in the tax arrangements which came into effect in 1957; prior to that time the rental system, based on the urgency of exclusive federal occupancy of the income tax fields, meant that compensation to the provinces had to be designed so as to induce the most reluctant of them — in effect Ontario and Quebec — to refrain from levying such taxes.

The tax arrangements which came into effect in 1967 provided for provincial revenue equalization to the national average based on 16 major sources of provincial revenues. With some minor modifications, the 1967-72 arrangements were extended for a second five-year period at the latter date. Equalization is now based on 20 revenue-sources, including from 1973 onward taxes paid to local governments for school purposes. The detailed calculation of such payments is somewhat complex. For a particular revenue source, if a province's proportion of the Canadian population exceeds its proportion of the aggregate re-venues it is entitled to equalization. Thus, if from one source the total provincial levies in a particular year brought in $1 billion, and Quebec with a population (1973-74) of 27.6 per cent of the national average received $200 millions from this source, the province would be entitled to $270M − $200M = $76 millions from that source. The total equaliza-tion payments due to each province are thus computed by aggregating its entitlements, negative and positive, from the 20 revenue sources. Estimates made by the Department of Finance for 1973-74 gave the "have not" provinces the entitlements shown on the next page.

The relative success of the equalization program can be measured by the circumstance that in 1973-74 the per capita provincial expendi-tures of the seven "have not" provinces were $1,234 and of the "have" provinces $1,256, a gap of only about 2 per cent;[59] and even this small discrepancy might yield to the inclusion within the equalization for-

	Equalization (Thousands of dollars)	Per capita equalization (1971 census)
Newfoundland	157,181	$343.26
P.E.I.	35,294	$296.45
Nova Scotia	178,328	$241.93
New Brunswick	151,055	$252.64
Quebec	664,129	$125.52
Manitoba	104,799	$113.70
Saskatchewan	141,622	$153.07[58]
Total	$1,432,408	

mula of local taxes levied for school purposes. However, the energy crisis from 1973 onward and the rapid accrual to the oil-producing provinces, particularly Alberta, of large revenues from this source, have caused Ottawa to retreat from full revenue equalization to the national average. Thus in December 1974 Finance Minister John Turner spelled out Ottawa's position for the remaining period of the tax arrangements which expire on March 31, 1977 by distinguishing between "basic" revenues "which are not attributable to the international oil disturbance" and "additional" revenues which are so attributable. According to the Turner scheme, basic revenues were to be equalized in full and additional revenues to the extent of one-third.[60]

Ottawa and the provinces have begun their negotiations for the equalization arrangements which will come into effect in 1977. With the rapid increase in oil and natural gas revenues accruing to Alberta it was inevitable that the principle of revenue equalization to the national average be abandoned.[61] Whether the new arrangements will include only partial equalization of such revenues as now prevails or whether some wholly new formula comes into force is still in doubt.

Grants to jurisdictions based on fiscal need or on revenue equalization alone do not take into account the levels of economic prosperity or development in those jurisdictions. Thus progress in securing the revenues of provinces can and does co-exist with the persistence of wide inter-provincial and interregional economic disparities. In its Fifth Annual Review published in September, 1968 the Economic Council of Canada concluded:

> Differences in both the levels of economic and social well-being and in economic opportunity among the various regions and provinces of Canada are large, and have persisted with only modest change for over 40 years. This persistence has been remarkable; neither strong national economic growth nor the strains and turbulences of depression and war have had lasting effects on the basic pattern of regional disparities. There is little reason to suppose that the historical mix of market forces and public policy is likely to lead in good time to a significant reduction in those disparities.[62]

From the coming to power of the Diefenbaker government in 1957 there has been a steadily increasing recognition of the special needs of depressed areas in Canada.[63] Special Atlantic Province Adjustment Grants above the regular equalization payments were begun in 1957-58 and at nearly the same time was enacted federal assistance to those provinces for hydro-electric development. In 1961 Parliament enacted the Agricultural Rehabilitation and Rural Development Act, the forerunner of later federal schemes for regional economic development. The aim of the Act was to raise farm income by finding more profitable uses for marginal and sub-marginal agricultural lands, by increasing employment opportunities in agricultural areas and by increasing the productivity of farm lands through soil conservation and the development of water supplies. The Minister of Agriculture was empowered to enter into agreements with the provinces to accomplish these objectives and in most cases the federal government paid half the costs of approved projects.[64] In 1966 a Fund for Rural Economic Development of $50 millions was established. As the ARDA and FRED programs progressed the emphasis shifted from land improvement toward the building of more effective social and economic infrastructures in depressed areas and toward education and training for employment in non-primary industry. The 1960s also saw the creation in 1962 of the Atlantic Development Board and a preliminary attempt to evolve a regional economic stragegy for the easternmost provinces.

In 1963 the recently-elected federal Liberal government sponsored legislation providing for the encouragement of "industrial development in areas of chronic unemployment on a planned basis". This program as it developed provided for both tax relief incentives and cash grants to industry in such areas as were designated by the federal Area Development Authority. According to T.N. Brewis, such designations were made on the basis of the most inadequate statistics, and incentives were given to industry without any effective attempt to specify what objectives were being pursued.[65]

The Regional Incentives Development Act which came into effect on July 1, 1969 has become the federal government's major instrument for encouraging economic development in the less favoured areas of Canada, and between 1966-67 and 1970-71 incentives to industry grew from 2.0 per cent to 39.7 per cent of total federal assistance for regional development. Under the provisions of the legislation, grant and loan guarantees are available to assist in the modernization, location and expansion of manufacturing and processing activities, as well as certain commercial activities, in "designated areas" as defined by the federal government.

The Trudeau government has given a higher priority than did any of its predecessors to the narrowing of regional economic disparities in Canada, and the Prime Minister and his colleagues have often expressed the view that the persistence of these disparties along with the autonomist pressures emanating from Quebec constitute the most critical threats to the stability and even survival of Canada. In 1969 the

Department of Regional Economic Expansion was established under one of the most powerful ministers in the cabinet, Jean Marchand, with the responsibility of coordinating the various federal programs in regional economic development, and despite the relative financial stringency of the past years DREE's budget has continued to increase rapidly. The regional and provincial distribution of the Department's expenditures may be seen from the following table:

Cumulative DREE expenditures — 1969/70 to 1972/73

	% of Canadian total	% of population of Canada
Atlantic Provinces	45.8	9.54
Quebec	26.5	27.76
Ontario	4.9	35.85
Manitoba	5.4	4.54
Saskatchewan	5.1	4.20
Alberta	5.3	7.59
British Columbia	2.1	10.29[66]

During 1972 the Department of Regional Economic Expansion carried out an evaluation of its performance which resulted in a twelve-volume study made public in July 1973. The general thrust of this study was toward more coordinated federal strategies for the development of particular provinces and regions. As a result of this study and other influences toward more coherent federal policies comprehensive General Development Agreements have been signed between DREE and each of the provinces. The Department has also carried out some considerable devolution of its operations and four Assistant Deputy Ministers were appointed in 1973 to head the regional staffs in Moncton, Montreal, Toronto and Saskatoon.

In direct efforts to stimulate economic development, i.e., in efforts other than those related to the management of aggregate demand, governments in Canada have embarked on an almost uncharted sea. Some of these issues and unresolved problems may be mentioned briefly:
(1) *The choice of policy instruments.* There continues to be a debate among specialists in economic development about the relative effectiveness of different policy instruments. For example, experts disagree about the emphasis which should be given to increasing investment expenditures on machinery and equipment as against enhancing the occupational skills of the labour force.
(2) *The appropriateness of direct measures to stimulate growth in depressed regions as against those to enhance the overall productivity of the national economy.* According to the Act establishing the Department, DREE's main responsibility is "to ensure that economic growth is dispersed widely enough across Canada to bring employment and earnings opportunities in the slow-growth regions as close as possible to those in the other parts of the country, without interfering with a

high overall rate of national growth". In a root-and-branch attack on Canadian developmental policies from the early 1960s onward, Alan C. Green has argued that these goals might more effectively be pursued through the operations of the free market.[67] Specifically, Green criticizes federal policies toward regional development for their emphasis on "moving capital into low-income regions" and their weak commitment to "promoting labour emigration." In this view, the goals of national and regional development can and should be made compatible by decisive federal policies towards concentrating economic activity on the basis of the comparative advantages of provinces and regions. Another economist, R. Ian McAllister, is dismayed by the overlapping jurisdictions and intergovernmental friction characteristic of recent developmental policies in Canada and concludes ". . . the question is whether the Canadian federal system of government has reached already a point where substantial dismantling might be in order — and that for greater emphasis might be placed on closer and more systematic planning with, and delegation to, the private sector."[68]

(3) *The extent to which regional development policies can be and should be harmonized with other national objectives and policies.* DREE does not operate programs of its own but rather is responsible for coordinating the developmental activities of the provinces and of other federal departments and agencies. So far as the latter are concerned, economic development is so comprehensive a concept that it might reasonably be applied to all those parts of the central government concerned with social and economic matters. But is it either feasible or desirable that DREE should get its way with, say, the domestic programs of Industry, Trade and Commerce, with the Departments of Transportation and of Communications and National Health and Welfare?[69] Is it legitimate that the activities of such federal crown corporations as Air Canada and the Industrial Development Bank be pressed into the service of regional development objectives? There are almost inherent conflicts in developmental policies between those public agencies like DREE which are specifically oriented to regions, and those oriented to particular sectors of the economy like communications, transportation, agriculture and resource development; it is by no means obvious that in cases of such conflict regional objectives should always prevail.

Despite the vast amount of talk about the need for intergovernmental coordination in economic development, it is almost inevitable that the goals of various jurisdictions will remain to a large extent irreconcilable. As McAllister has pointed out, a municipality will see development almost exclusively in terms of employment and the generation of tax revenues within its boundaries.[70] The poorer provinces have a single-minded concern for the creation of jobs. A larger and more prosperous province like British Columbia or Ontario will have more complex goals related, for example, to the protection of the environment, foreign ownership and the intraprovincial dispersion of economic activity. Federal objectives will almost inevitably be more comprehensive still, and more characterized by aims which are not easily reconcilable with each other. These intergovernmental differences in objectives are compounded by the circumstance that in this policy area perhaps more than in any other there is a very vague constitutional delimitation of the powers and responsibilities of the two levels of government.

Shared-Cost Programs

Shared-cost programs involve financial concessions made available by one level of government to compensate another level for part of the costs incurred in providing particular services or facilities. One form of this device is the conditional grant,[71] in which the recipient government receives funds for performing functions according to standards which are determined either unilaterally by the donor government or by the two levels in collaboration. The other variant provides the recipient jurisdiction either with grants or tax abatements, or a combination of the two, but does not involve any regulation of the standards or procedures imposed by the government which makes these funds available.[72]

In Canada as elsewhere, shared-cost arrangements help governments to meet certain basic circumstances faced by contemporary federations. There are insistent pressures toward the central government ensuring country-wide standards in the range and quality of public services, and taking measures to improve the productive capacities of less prosperous regions. The central authorities have a fiscal capacity superior to that of the provinces or states in responding positively to these pressures. Yet the constitution as judicially interpreted provides a relatively stable and inflexible allocation of responsibilities between the two levels. The shared-cost arrangement is of crucial importance in allowing some reconciliation of stability and change.

The first shared-cost program, and one still in effect, was inaugurated in 1907 as the Railway Grade Crossing Fund now administered by the Canadian Transport Commission. In 1912 Ottawa began a program of assistance to the provinces for agricultural education with expenditures of $10,000,000 over a ten-year period. The first of the major continuing conditional grant arrangements was established in 1927 with federal support for provincial schemes of old age pensions. It was not, however, until after the Second World War that conditional grants became a central element of the federal system and increased from 5.3 per cent of gross provincial revenues in 1953-54 to 19.8 per cent in 1962-63. The general growth of conditional and unconditional assistance can be seen in the table on page 135.

Conditional grant and cost-sharing arrangements prevail in respect to purposes as specific as paying the shipping costs for carlots of livestock sent to the Royal Winter Fair and as comprehensive as supporting hospital insurance plans. The Inventory of Federal-Provincial Programs and Activities issued by the Privy Council office in 1974 lists ninety-eight items under the category "Conditional Grants and Payments in respect of Shared-Cost Programs and Activities".[74] However, four of these arrangements make up the bulk of this conditional assis-

Cumulative figures for all provinces

	Gross general revenues (thousands of dollars)	Conditional Transfers from federal government (thousands of dollars)	Conditional Transfers as percentage of gross revenues	Unconditional Transfers from federal government (thousands of dollars)	Conditional as a percentage of unconditional transfers
1962-63	4,226,692	839,892	19.8	275,450	305.0
1969-70	12,068,753	1,729,410	14.3	952,872	178.4
1972-73 (est.)	16,741,500	3,048,200	17.2	1,275,200	239.1[73]

tance to the provinces, estimated by the Provincial Treasurer of Ontario to be 90 per cent of such assistance paid to this province in the current fiscal year.[75]

Hospital Insurance and Diagnostic Services (1975-76 Estimates: $1,545,969,000)
Under this arrangement the federal government contributes to the provinces approximately half the cost of providing hospital services, excluding the costs of institutions for the treatment of tuberculosis and mental illness and custodial care institutions. The federal contribution to each province for in-patient and insured out-patient services is calculated as 25 per cent of the national average per capita cost of such services plus 25 per cent of the average per capita cost of services in that province multiplied by the number of insured persons in that province.

Medical Insurance (1975-76 Estimates: $862,330,000)
The federal government contributes approximately one-half the costs incurred by each province under its medical insurance plan: The annual federal contribution to each province is calculated as 50 per cent of the national average per capita cost of providing medical care insurance in all the provinces multiplied by the average number of persons insured in that province during the year. Sharable costs cover all services performed by medical practitioners for insured persons except any services an insured person is entitled to under other federal or provincial legislation.

Canada Assistance Plan (1975-76 Estimates: $700,530,000)
Under the CAP the federal government pays the provinces 50 per cent of the sharable costs of financial assistance paid to persons in need. The Plan declares to be sharable direct costs of welfare assistance, salaries and fringe benefits of employers administering the eligible programs and certain training and research costs associated with eligible programs.

Support for Post-Secondary Education (1975-76 Estimates: $511,000,000, not including values of equalized tax points)

The Federal government makes fiscal transfers to the provinces for half the operational costs of post-secondary institutions of education. One part of the transfer is the federal government's action in reducing its revenues in each province by the equivalent of 4.357 "equalized points" of personal income tax and one "equalized point" of corporation income tax. The other part of the transfer is a cash payment to make up the deficiency between the transfer of tax points and half the operating costs of eligible institutions.

Until 1960 there was, apart from Quebec, little principled provincial resistance to conditional grant programs, although from time to time provinces complained that certain costs related to such programs were not reimbursable. The Duplessis administration had opposed grants-in-aid on ideological grounds and, at considerable financial cost to the province and its residents, had remained outside several of these arrangements, although it had participated in others. The other provinces were for the most part content to accept such federal assistance and its accompanying conditions. At the 1960 Dominion-Provincial Conference, however, several of the provincial leaders launched attacks on the principle and operation of conditional grants.[76] The newly elected Premier of Quebec announced that his government would accept on a temporary basis the grants that the province was not then receiving but would engage in a principled opposition to the encroachment on provincial autonomy inherent in the grant-in-aid device. The leaders of the less prosperous provinces complained that the existing programs did not take into account the respective fiscal capacities of the recipient governments. There was a good deal of criticism of the effects of conditional grants in limiting the budgetary and program discretion of the provinces. During the previous periods grants-in-aid had been discussed, apart from Quebec, almost entirely within the perspective of particular services and facilities. From 1960 onward this device became a central element in the evolving relations between Ottawa and the provinces.

In 1965 Parliament enacted the Established Programs (Interim Arrangements) Act as a positive response by the federal Liberal government to Quebec's objections to conditional grants as unwarranted encroachments on provincial autonomy.[77] Under the Act the provinces were given the opportunity of contracting out of five established programs. The federal government in compensating provinces which had accepted this alternative would lower its individual income tax rates up to 20 per cent, with cash transfers between the two levels to make up the differences between the yields of such taxes and the amount the non-participating provinces would have received as conditional grants. The abatements were to be as follows:

Hospital insurance	14 points
Assistance for old age, blind & disabled persons	2 points
Unemployment assistance	2 points
Vocational training	1 point
Health grants	1 point

During varying transitional periods specified in the Act, non-participating provinces were to provide the specified services under the same conditions as had prevailed under the previous arrangements.

Only Quebec has accepted the alternative made available under the 1965 enactment and since that time contracting-out has had a somewhat intricate history. New fiscal policies adopted by the federal government in 1966 were in the direction of a uniform division of responsibilities between Ottawa and the provinces and uniform rates of federal taxation throughout Canada.[78] There was here a judgement that by accepting the contracting-out option Quebec had assumed a *de facto* special status and a desire on the part of Ottawa that this situation be righted by the other provinces following the Quebec lead. However, in the federal White Paper on Taxation of 1969 the Minister announced that the 1966 offer had lapsed and would be revised "after the reform of the income tax is implemented and the relative value of 'tax points' and the cost of the major, continuing joint programs can be better appraised". The federal offer has never been renewed, although both Ontario[79] and Alberta have indicated their desire to accept the contracting-out alternative if adequate conditions for continuing federal assistance can be negotiated.

For the federal government, the four major shared-cost programs — as well as many of the smaller ones — are "open-ended" in the sense that the total amounts of federal financial assistance for costs defined as sharable are determined by the action of the provinces and of institutions of post-secondary education. The expenditures for these purposes have been increasing rapidly. Thus in a period of relative financial stringency Ottawa has assumed a group of heavy commitments over whose size it has little or no effective control. Further, there has been a long-range trend toward giving federal financial assistance for increasingly comprehensive purposes and away from the relative specific purposes for which grants-in-aid were given in earlier years. Some of the developments in this process can be mentioned briefly. First, at the Federal-Provincial Conference of October 1966 the federal authorities announced a very new plan for sharing the financial responsibilities for post-secondary education with the provinces. This scheme replaced the arrangements under which Ottawa had assisted the provinces in meeting the capital and operating costs of technical and vocational education through a system of grants for specific programs and activities, and had paid an annual $5 per capita of provincial population in aid of colleges and universities. Under the new arrangements, the provinces would receive, as each chose, either 50 per cent of the operating costs of post-secondary institutions or $15 per capita annually. This was in effect a block grant for post-secondary education.

Second, from 1948 onward the federal government made payments to the provinces in respect to very specific programs and activities in the field of health care — including at the outset health surveys, hospital construction, professional training, crippled children, mental health, tuberculosis control, public health research, cancer control and general public health. At the Federal-Provincial Conference of

November, 1968 the federal government announced the phasing-out of the health programs over a three-year period except those for professional training and general public health. In 1966 was established a Health Resources Fund of $500 millions for assistance to the provinces up to 1980 in the "planning, acquisition, construction, renovation and equipping of health training and research facilities".

Third, the Canada Assistance Plan which came into effect in 1966 eliminated four previous schemes of federal grants-in-aid for categorical public assistance programs — old age assistance, blind persons' allowances, disabled persons' allowances and unemployment assistance. Again there was in effect a block grant for an important and costly area of provincial activity.

The comprehensiveness of the purposes for which grants-in-aid are now given makes it very difficult if not impossible for the federal authorities to exercise effective controls over the activities for which such moneys are given. This circumstance has no doubt become increasingly intolerable because of the currents of administrative rationality prevailing in Ottawa and described in Chapter 3, according to which there is to be a deliberate ranking of the purposes for which public funds are expended and an ongoing process of evaluating how effectively and efficiently these purposes are being achieved.

During the 1970s Ottawa has attempted to secure the agreement of the provinces for limiting federal financial contributions on behalf of post-secondary education and health services, and because such agreement has proved impossible to secure has moved toward such limitations by unilateral action. In May 1973 proposals were made to the provinces on these lines:

— in respect to post-secondary education, the new formula would be based on the actual federal contribution for 1973-74, escalated by the rate of growth of the population group 18-24 years of age and a further escalation factor of 7 per cent.

— in respect to health services there would be a block grant, whose amount would escalate with the GNP and in respect to which compensation would accrue to the provinces from further tax room (a reduction in the rates of personal income tax of 6 per cent beginning in 1977 and the elimination of federal excise taxes on tobacco and alcoholic beverages) and cash grants.

It has been impossible to get provincial agreement on these and other federal proposals made both before and after the ones outlined above. Under the existing arrangements Ottawa has imposed a 15 per cent limit on annual increases to its contributions for post-secondary education. In the federal budget of June 23, 1975 the federal Minister of Finance made the following announcements:

— the government gave to the provinces the 5-year notice required by the Hospital Insurance and Diagnostic Services Act that the arrangements relating to hospital insurance be terminated and new arrangements undertaken.

— for 1976 and subsequent years increases in the federal per capita contributions to the provinces on behalf of medical insurance would be limited as follows; 1967-'77 — 13 per cent; 1977-'78 — 10 ½ per cent and 8 ½ per cent in 1978-'79 and subsequent years. [80]

To widely varying degrees the provinces have become hostile to the conditional grant device, particularly as this has been applied to the major shared-cost programs. In his Supplementary Budget of July 7 1975, the Treasurer of Ontario presented this bill of particulars against shared-cost programs:

— *Provincial priorities are distorted by the availability of federal dollars.* The classic example of this, discussed below, was Medicare. Massive financial leverage by the federal government forced Ontario to join this program even though the Province already had a perfectly satisfactory system of medical insurance.
— *Capricious changes in policy by the federal government leave the provinces stranded to carry the burden of programs that were often imposed upon them in the first place.* An example of this was the abrupt withdrawal of assistance to technical and vocational education in 1967.
— *Unilateral imposition of arbitrary ceilings on the rate of growth of federal contributions to established programs is unreasonable.* It leaves provinces with an undue financial burden, and also creates great inequities because of the differential levels of service provided in different jurisdictions. Classic examples are the existing ceiling on post-secondary education and the ceilings on Medicare introduced in the recent federal budget.
— *Provincial administrative structures are interfered with.* One famous case concerned the offer of federal funds for the care of juvenile delinquents. In order to take advantage of this proposal, the Province would have had to switch a whole administrative unit from one department to another. Recent discussions have led to a mutually satisfactory arrangement, but potential sharing was lost for many years.
— *Rigidly defined criteria for eligibility result in inequities, feuds and distortions.*
— *Administrative costs are unnecessarily high.* [81]

On this basis, Ontario reiterated its desire to opt out of the major shared-cost programs and was particularly urgent about health services. It is reasonable to suppose that this provincial hostility to shared-cost arrangements arises in large part from the increasing administrative sophistication. The earlier arrangements came into effect when the provinces were on the whole little disposed to budgetary or program planning. Thus "50-cent dollars" were attractive and the restrictions on provincial autonomy in the range and standards of services not very onerous. These circumstances have now changed. Just as administrative rationality has made federal officials anxious that the conditional grant device leads to heavy and unpredictable financial burdens without any guarantees that national purposes are effectively and efficiently pursued, so increasing administrative sophistication in the provinces results in reactions to the uncertainties and controls inherent in federal participation. On the whole it seems unlikely that Ottawa and the provinces can come to agree on new conditions for federal assistance in the major shared-cost programs and in the absence of such agreement the unilateral imposition by the federal government of ceilings on its contributions will lead almost inevitably to increased tensions between the two levels.

The shared-cost device is of course employed for a very large number of purposes other than those in the fields of health, social assistance and post-secondary education. Many of these smaller problems are carried out harmoniously and even those provinces like Ontario and Quebec most solicitous of provincial autonomy manifest little objection to them. Although this statement must be made with some qualifications, the increasing aggressiveness and sophistication of the provinces has resulted in the federal government being less willing than in earlier years to enforce specific conditions on the provinces. Although the situation in respect to training in the official languages may be an extreme example of permissiveness, we have here a situation in which significant amounts of federal grants are being made to the provinces with little or no effective control to ensure that federal purposes are being achieved. The largest of these programs is for "Bilingualism in Education at Pre-University Levels" and in 1972-'73 some $54,383,901 was granted to the provinces for this purpose. Yet the 1973-'74 Report of the Commissioner of Official Languages indicated that in the secondary schools of the provinces other than Quebec the percentage of students enrolled in French as the second language had between 1970-71 and 1974-'75 *decreased* from 55.7 per cent to 41.3 per cent.[82]

Although it is likely that Ottawa will continue to dispense relatively small sums of money to the provinces for relatively specific purposes, the development of the conditional grant device is towards block grants for a broad range of activities as now prevail in respect to post-secondary education. Even though such grants do not impose specific conditions on the provinces, they impose significant constraints on these jurisdictions by the very fact of specifying which costs are sharable and which are not, constraints related both to the provincial function for which assistance is given and to other classes of provincial expenditures. Even more importantly, the provinces are exposed to the continual uncertainties of Ottawa making unilateral decisions about its levels of financial assistance.

The Taxation Aspect of Federal-Provincial Relations

Up to now the discussion of this chapter has been concerned almost exclusively with the expenditure aspect of federal-provincial financial relations. Attention must now be given to the taxation side, with emphasis on the intense competition of the two levels of government for tax sources.

Under the British North America Act the Parliament of Canada may raise moneys by "any Mode or System of Taxation" while the provinces are restricted to "Direct Taxation within the Province in order to the raising of a Revenue for Provincial Purposes". Despite this plenary grant of power, Parliament is precluded by Section 125 from taxing "Lands or Property" belonging to a province. Although there are many legal intricacies surrounding the limitations of provincial taxing powers,[83] the operative restrictions are these:

— the provinces may not levy sales or excise taxes at the manufacturer's or wholesale levels.

— the provinces may not levy taxes on estates or their executors but may tax the beneficiaries of estates.

— although federally-incorporated companies are subject to provincial laws of general application, the provinces cannot use their taxation powers to destroy the status and capacity of such companies.

— the provinces are precluded from erecting barriers to the free movement of goods across provincial boundaries by Section 121 which states: "All Articles of the Growth, Produce, or Manufacture of any one of the Provinces shall, from and after the Union, be admitted free into each of the other Provinces."

— the provinces may not tax "Lands or Property" of the federal government.

From the 1941 action of the federal government in assuming exclusive occupancy of the personal and corporate income tax fields, Canada has sustained important elements of an integrated tax system. However, this integration has been in process of piecemeal elimination over the past generation:

— in 1947 Ontario and Quebec began to levy taxes on corporate income. (Ontario rented the corporate taxes to Ottawa under the 1952-'57 arrangements but reentered the field at the latter date.)

— in 1954 Quebec began to levy individual income taxes.

— in 1957 equalization payments to the provinces were divorced from tax rentals.

— in 1962 the tax rental system was ended in favour of a system of "abatement" of federal tax rates in which the provinces levied taxes on corporate and personal incomes at the rates they chose.

— in 1971 the federal Parliament ceased to levy gift and estate taxes.

— in 1972 the abatement system was ended.

Thus there has been a double movement away from the integration of income taxes and succession duties which came about in the Second World War, a movement away from both uniform national rates and uniform national tax bases. About all that remains of such integration are arrangements under which the federal Department of National Revenue collects, at rates set by the individual provinces, taxes on corporate incomes for all the provinces but Ontario and Quebec and taxes on personal incomes for all but Quebec. The end has not yet arrived. It has for some time been rumoured that Ontario will set up its own system for collecting personal income taxes. In April 1974 the governemnt of Alberta gave notice that it would terminate its agreement with Ottawa in respect to the collection of taxes on corporate income and begin its own collection system.[84]

Tho provinces have developed an intense interest in both the federal tax *base* for individual and corporate incomes, i.e., what elements of income are taxed, and the *rates* at which federal taxes are levied.

The provinces have an interest in the bases on which federal income taxes are levied. So far as those which have tax-collection agreements with Ottawa are concerned, this is the base on which provincial taxes are levied — although beginning in 1972 both Ontario and Manitoba established schemes of property tax credits against personal income tax liability and the federal authorities have cooperated in collecting income taxes for these provinces on their modified bases. However, both these latter arrangements appear relatively simple from an administrative standpoint and it is unlikely that the federal government would participate in more complex schemes. The Alberta government, as we have seen, has given notice that it will begin to levy its own corporate taxes, giving as its reason that the federal tax base could not be accommodated to provincial plans for tax incentives to small business.[85] Beyond this kind of consideration, it is a commonplace that governments pursue other objectives through taxation than the raising of revenues for public purposes, and in the protracted debate on federal tax reform between the publication of the Carter Report in 1966 and the reform legislation enacted by Parliament in 1971, all the provinces participated in blocking various proposals for changing the basis of federal income taxes. In particular, provincial hostility to those parts of the Carter Report which would have eliminated many of the tax privileges conferred on the resource industries was vigorous and on the whole successful.[86] Throughout the debate on tax reform, the government of Ontario waged a sophisticated root-and-branch attack on many of the fundamental recommendations of the Carter Report as these were later presented in a much modified form in the White Paper.[87] The "indexing" of the personal income tax from 1974 onward to compensate for inflation has had implications for the revenues of those provinces which have entered into tax-collection agreements with Ottawa.[88] As we shall see later in this chapter, there has been from the 1974 federal budget onward an intense struggle between Ottawa and the provinces related to whether provincial levies on the resource industries would be deductible for federal tax purposes.

The provincial governments are even more deeply concerned in the rates of federal taxation than the bases on which federal income taxes are levied. The various levels of government are in a very real sense competitors for tax revenues in a period where the proportion of the G.N.P. absorbed by the public sector is growing toward 40 per cent,[89] where for complex reasons governments find it difficult to limit expenditures through internal controls and where the business community and the mass media are vociferous in their demands that governments take the lead in containing inflationary pressures by exercising restraint. There are also a group of somewhat less obvious circumstances leading to tax-competition:

— the remaining elements of the integrated tax system, along with attitudes and policies carried over from an earlier period, lead the provinces in some circumstances to resist increases in federal tax rates and in others to seek decreases in any existing rates. The euphemism here is "tax room", i.e., decreases in federal rates so that the provinces can raise their levies without additional burdens on the taxpayer. Since 1966 these pressures have been resisted by Ottawa on the grounds that Ottawa must retain access to revenues to discharge its expenditure responsibilities and that access to the major portion of the income tax field is necessary for effective fiscal policies toward price stability, full employment and economic growth.

— there is the settled conviction among some of the provinces, specifically Ontario and Quebec, that Ottawa's allegedly favoured position in respect to tax sources leads directly to the federal authorities encroaching on matters within provincial jurisdiction. The issue of "fiscal imbalance" was joined around the Report of the Tax Structure Committee in 1970, whose study showed the revenue position of the federal government relative to its expenditures to be more favourable than that of the other levels.[90] In 1968 there had been vigorous opposition from the provinces to Ottawa levying a temporary 2 per cent surcharge on the taxable income of individuals, designating this as a Social Development Tax and justifying it in terms of the rapidly increasing federal commitments to post-secondary education and hospital insurance. The general provincial argument here is of course that under the existing allocation of tax sources the federal government has a continuing surplus which it inevitably uses to encroach on provincial matters.

— to the extent that provincial fiscal policies are explicitly directed toward the objectives of price stability, full employment and growth, federal tax rates and discretionary changes in these tax rates impinge on the achievement of these objectives. As we saw in chapter 3, Ontario has in recent years oriented its fiscal policy around the "full employment budget". The Ontario government has been persistently critical of federal fiscal policies and its own are designed in large part to compensate for the allegedly adverse effect of the former on the province.[91]

The mid-1970s see conflicts between Ottawa and the provinces about fiscal matters as intense as at any time in the history of Confederation. There are no foreseeable prospects for the lessening of this conflict.

Canadian Federalism and the Energy Crisis

The world energy crisis from 1973 onward has brought about intense conflict in the Canadian federal system. Just as this crisis has resulted in fundamental shifts in geopolitical power between oil-exporting and oil-importing nations and opened up new kinds of cleavages and conflicts between nations, so in Canada new advantages have been realized by provinces with natural endowments of fossil-fuels and new vulnerabilities experienced by provinces and regions deficient in such resources. The prime ministers and premiers and their most influential advisers were in the latter half of the 1960s concerned most urgently with the position of Quebec in Confederation, just half a decade later their preoccupations centred on the price of petroleum and the demands of Alberta and Saskatchewan. In general terms, the energy crisis has directly or indirectly joined a group of crucial issues in public policy, federal-provincial relations and the most fundamental aspects of national life: foreign ownership; the rights of native peoples; the protection and control of the natural environment; the respective roles of government and private enterprise in the economy; interprovincial fiscal equalization and other attempts to reduce regional disparities; patterns of production and consumption based on cheap and what Canadians have believed to be inexhaustible resources of energy.

The basic constitutional aspects of the distribution of powers in respect to fuel and energy matters can be outlined briefly.[92]
(1) Section 109 of the British North America Act of 1867 states:

All Lands, Mines, Minerals, and Royalties belonging to the several Provinces of Canada, Nova Scotia, and New Brunswick at the Union, and all Sums then due or payable for such Lands, Mines, Minerals, or Royalties, shall belong to the several Provinces of Ontario, Quebec, Nova Scotia, and New Brunswick in which the same are situate or arise, subject to any Trusts existing in respect therof, and to any Interest other than that of the Province in the Same.

These provisions were applied to the provinces of British Columbia, Prince Edward Island and Newfoundland when they entered Confederation. When Manitoba in 1870 and Alberta and Saskatchewan in 1905 attained provincial status the federal government retained control over the natural resources within their boundaries, and it was only in 1930 that these provinces attained an equal status with the others.

Apart from those resources alienated to private individuals and groups, the provinces own the resources within their respective boundaries. In general terms, most of the sub-surface rights in the three most westerly provinces have not been so alienated.[93] These powers of ownership give the provincial governments the authority to determine the rate at which resources are developed, the ways such development shall take place and the price of such resources within the province.
(2) Under its exclusive jurisdiction over trade and commerce and over "Lines of Steam or other Ships, Railways, Canals, Telegraphs, and other Works and Undertakings connecting the Province with any other or others of the Province, or extending beyond the Limits of the Province", the federal government is empowered to regulate the conditions under which resources pass into interprovincial and international trade, including the volume and price of these commodities and the facilities by which they are transported.
(3) The federal authorities have exclusive control over natural resources in the Yukon and Northwest Territories. A 1967 advisory opinion of the Supreme Court of Canada gave seabed resources off the west coast to the federal government but there is an unresolved and continu-

ing dispute about ownership of seabed resources between Ottawa and the five easternmost provinces.

(4) The powers of Parliament to raise moneys by "any Mode or System of Taxation" are limited only by the prohibition of Section 125 against the taxation of "Lands or Property" belonging to a province.

The summary account given above indicates only the "parameters of jurisdiction"[94] about resource matters. There are inherent complexities in the circumstance that so far as resources within provincial boundaries are concerned, the rights of ownership are exclusively provincial but legislative jurisdiction over many aspects of resource development is divided between Parliament and the provinces. Two areas of jurisdictional conflict may be mentioned briefly:

— the provinces through their ownership of resources may exercise what A.R. Thompson and Howard R. Eddy call "*de facto* jurisdiction over interprovincial trade in resources".[95] Thompson and Eddy give an example of this in relation to the issuance of licences to develop natural gas which might without violating the law provide that such privileges be terminated if the gas were exported. Also there is little doubt that provinces with resources can validly take measures to ensure that these are available to consumers within the provinces at more favourable prices than to those outside.

— the federal government through its taxation powers may qualify provincial ownership rights over resources. The current tax on oil exports from Canada is a recent and dramatic use of this power, which obviously makes these resources less valuable to the oil-producing provinces than they would otherwise be. The only limitation to the federal taxing power is contained in Section 125 of the British North America Act which provides that no "Lands or Property" belonging to a province are subject to taxation. However, whether he was stating a constitutionally valid position or not, the federal Minister of Justice warned the provinces in November, 1974 that they could not escape federal resources taxes by setting up crown corporations to take over the activities of private companies.[96]

Attention in the Canadian energy crisis has been focused on petroleum and petroleum products, although the rapid escalation in oil prices from 1973 onward has resulted both in increases in the price of natural gas and fundamental changes in the economic circumstances surrounding the development of other sources of energy than the fossil fuels. In 1961 the federal government adopted the National Oil Policy, which ensured western oil the Canadian market from the Ottawa River westward while the rest of Canada would be supplied from cheaper foreign sources, mainly Venezuela and the Middle East.[97] This policy was adopted in the face of a world over-supply of petroleum and an essential element in it was that with the active support of the federal government markets for western Canadian oil would be found in the United States. By 1970 Canada had become self-sufficient in oil, with a domestic production of 1,476,000 barrels per day and a domestic demand of 1,466,000 barrels a day; in this year there were exports of

670,000 barrels a day from the provinces of origin (97.3 per cent from Alberta and Saskatchewan) with imports into Canada of 762,000 barrels per day.[98]

In the past generation, Canada along with other industrialized nations has developed an economic structure and a way of life based upon cheap and abundant energy. Energy costs as a proportion of GNP declined between 1950 and 1970 from 11.5 per cent to 8.9 per cent.[99] In these same two decades oil and natural gas as the sources of primary energy consumption increased from 31.0 per cent to 63.4 per cent while coal decreased from 41.9 per cent to 11.0 per cent.[100] Although these cheap and seemingly inexhaustible supplies of energy made this circumstance of less than crucial concern, Canada during this period became divided into provinces and regions that were high in energy consumption but relatively poor in their endowment of fuels for energy-generation, and provinces with abundant fuels to export outside their boundaries. Most dramatically, the provinces of Ontario and Quebec in 1970 accounted for 61.7 per cent of primary energy consumption in Canada, of which 57.4 per cent was oil and natural gas, but together produced almost none of these fossil fuels.[101] At the other end of the spectrum, Alberta in 1970 produced 76.6 per cent of the total Canadian petroleum and 81.4 per cent of the nation's natural gas, while having only 10.5 per cent of Canada's total energy consumption and using only 8 per cent and 30.8 per cent of the country's oil and natural gas respectively.[102]

Under the National Oil Policy a set of stable, mutually advantageous and harmonious relations developed. That western oil had a secure market west of the Ottawa River with domestic surpluses being exported to the United States was in the interest of the multinational oil companies, who also enjoyed generous tax concessions from both federal and provincial governments. The oil industry had brought unprecedented prosperity to Alberta and a significant degree of economic diversification to Saskatchewan. At the same time, those parts of Canada east of the Ottawa Valley line enjoyed the advantages of offshore oil cheaper than what they could have been supplied with from western Canada. Only those parts of Ontario which could otherwise have been supplied from offshore sources bore the economic burdens of the National Oil Policy, although with the prices prevailing up until 1973 this burden was not a very heavy one.

The energy crisis descended on Canada as on other nations with bewildering rapidity. Some rather hesitant measures were taken to restrict oil exports to the United States in the early months of 1973. A growing awareness of the imminent energy shortage, combined with the rapid escalation of world oil prices by the OPEC nations and the Arab oil embargo, led to more definite responses from the federal government later in the year — the introduction in September of a "voluntary" price freeze to January 31, 1974, the announcement of the extension of a pipeline to Montreal so that eastern markets could be served from western Canadian sources, and the imposition of an export tax on western crude oil. On December 6 1973, Prime Minister Trudeau announced in the House of Commons a new national oil policy whose major elements were the following:

— the abolition of the Ottawa Valley line to give the western provinces a guaranteed outlet for increased production in the eastern provinces and to ensure supplies to these provinces.

— the early completion of a pipeline to Montreal so that eastern markets could be served from western sources.

— the early establishment of a publicly-owned Canadian petroleum company "principally to expedite exploration and development", and aggressive measures to intensify research on oil sands technology.

— the continuance of the export tax on domestic oil equal to the difference between the domestic price and the export price as determined by the National Energy Board.

— a short-term proposal to share the proceeds of the export tax on a 50/50 basis with the producing provinces, subject to a discussion of this and other related matters at a federal-provincial conference to be held in early 1974.

A Federal-Provincial Conference on Energy was held in Ottawa on January 22-23, 1974. The outcome of this Conference was that there would be a single price for oil throughout Canada, modified by transportation costs and differing levels of provincial taxes on that commodity. To attain that end, western oil would be made available to the Canadian market at prices significantly below those prevailing in the world market, while Ottawa would subsidize the costs of foreign oil largely from the proceeds of the export tax.

At the 1974 conference the polar positions were clearly stated by the heads of the governments of Canada and Alberta.

Prime Minister Trudeau's opening statement put the energy crisis and Canadian policies to deal with it within an ideological formulation of Canada as a national community.[103] On the international scene the recent dramatic shifts in power and welfare had come about by "the accidents of geology". However, we in Canada "need not reproduce in miniature the fragmented, sometimes brutal world vision I have just described". Canadians have pursued common purposes in the past through defining the social and economic rights of individuals and through various measures of interprovincial equalization. This concept of "fraternal responsibility" must now be extended to energy matters. Canada must thus move rapidly towards national self-sufficiency in oil both by securing the Canadian market for existing domestic supplies and by moving rapidly towards the development of new supplies of petroleum and other energy sources. In this process it would be necessary for oil prices to increase, both to honour the ownership rights of the producing provinces and to encourage the oil companies, with much more public involvement than in the past, to find and develop new supplies. Despite these provincial rights of ownership, the Prime Minister asked " . . . would it be reasonable for a province to receive continuing revenues which would give it the capacity to spend, in proportion to its population, three or four times as much as other provinces?"

The Alberta position was stated with great forcefulness by Premier Peter Lougheed.[104] When the National Oil Policy was adopted in 1961, and subsequently, Albertans wished to secure the whole Canadian market for western oil but for purely economic reasons this request was refused. Alberta was thus forced to seek export markets in the United States. Why now, when the advantages were reversed, should the rules of the game be changed? The federal export tax on oil was discriminatory, it was not imposed on the export of other natural resources such as lumber or the export, with federal approval, of Ontario electricity to the United States. Provincial ownership of resources is a fundamental element of Confederation and the export tax is "contrary to both the spirit and the intent of Confederation". Further, and most crucially, oil and natural gas are depleting, non-renewable resources and should be sold "only at prices which reflect fair value". Unlike other provinces, the Alberta economy rests on a base of resources which are exhaustible and are being quickly exhausted. In the decade or so immediately ahead it was thus necessary for the province to diversify its economic structure toward becoming less dependent on the sale of unprocessed natural resources, and current federal policies limiting the prices of oil were frustrating this objective.

After the January Conference intensive discussions between the governments continued and on March 27, 1974 the Prime Ministers and Premiers at their meeting agreed that until June 1975 the price of crude oil would be set at $6.50 a barrel. Again, eastern Canadian consumers would be protected against increases in petroleum prices for foreign oil to the extent that such increases were not matched by increases in domestic petroleum prices, and this compensation program would be financed largely through the proceeds of the export tax on oil sent to the United States. Thus "through the combination of the export charge and the oil import compensation program, it was possible for consumers throughout Canada to purchase petroleum products at prices that would have prevailed if pipelines had existed to supply all regions of the country with domestic petroleum."[105]

From the federal budget of May 6, 1974 energy matters in Canada have become entangled with a bitter federal-provincial conflict about the deductibility of provincial royalties and other levies made on the resource industries from corporate income as defined for federal tax purposes. (Earlier in this chapter the impact of higher oil prices on the regime of interprovincial fiscal equalization has been discussed). The non-deductibility of such provincial charges was announced in the federal budget of May, 1974. The government was defeated on this budget in the House of Commons, but subsequent to the election held on July 8 of that year this policy has been maintained by the Trudeau administration. At issue is the distribution of the rapidly escalating revenues derived from the development of non-renewable natural resources among the federal government, the provinces and the private corporations active in such development. Up until the 1970s both Ottawa and the provinces were notoriously generous in extending tax concessions to these industries.[106] The more recent disposition of governments to perceive the returns from resource development in terms of economic rent has led these jurisdictions to impose higher burdens on these corporations and the vast increases in revenues occasioned by the world energy crisis has of course enhanced the possibilities for diverting such revenues to the public purse. All the provinces have in the past three years increased their levies on resource development. Ottawa sees in this an "erosion" of the corporate income tax base and argues that this base must be maintained, so that the federal government can both sustain effective stabilization policies and meet its expenditure responsibilities. The provinces have argued aggressively that the deductibility of royalties is an established principle of taxation, and that federal policy constitutes a direct challenge to the ownership of these resources by the provinces and to provincial management of such resources. This conflict has been particularly bitter in the case of the two oil-producing provinces and the Premier of Alberta claimed that federal policies were in contravention of the agreement on oil prices reached in March 1974.[107] Another set of crucial issues relates to the distribution of revenues between governments and the private corporations in the resource industries and appropriate measures to be taken to ensure that a significant part of industry's share is directed toward the exploration and development of Canadian resources rather than enhanced profits or investment outside Canada.[108]

On April 9-10, 1975 the First Ministers met in Ottawa with the major purpose of discussing the circumstances which would follow the freeze on domestic petroleum prices, which was to expire within the next two months. By this time the federal government was convinced that a significant increase in petroleum prices was necessary. This position seems to have resulted from the pressures of the producing provinces, the decreasing activity in oil exploration by private companies, the increasingly pessimistic estimates of domestic reserves of oil and a recognition of the need for energy conservation. This meeting was one of the least satisfactory ones in the recent history of federal-provincial conferences and adjourned without agreement on domestic oil prices, largely but by no means exclusively because of the refusal of Ontario to accept any price increases. The Ontario position was that in the increase of domestic oil prices from $2.70 per barrel to $6.50 per barrel over the past 18 months, some 90 per cent of the increased revenues had gone to the federal and producing governments and had done very little to enhance the supply of oil and natural gas, and that price increases would contribute to already severe inflationary pressures and to higher levels of unemployment.[109] Because the Conference could not agree the federal government set the domestic price of petroleum at $8.00 a barrel after the former arrangement expired, and in its budget of June 23, 1975 increased the excise tax on gasoline 10¢ per gallon. The Ontario government in its turn imposed a 90-day freeze on the increase from $6.50 to $8.00 per barrel on petroleum sold within the province.

Several rather more general aspects of the workings of Canadian institutions of government during the ongoing energy crisis require consideration:

First, this crisis has forced governments to evolve more comprehensive and coherent policies towards energy, and such policies have led directly to severe intergovernmental conflict. When energy was cheap and in seemingly inexhaustible supply the public authorities did not concern themselves much with alternative energy sources, the impact of energy policies on the economy or energy conservation. These circumstances have now changed. This new coherence has both a conceptual and an organizational dimension. Prior to 1973 responsibility for energy matters was divided in the federal and provincial governments among several agencies which carried on their activities with little relation to one another.[110] The new thrusts have been as clearly as anywhere else reflected in Ontario where there has been created a Ministry of Energy with responsibility for various energy policies, and an Ontario Energy Corporation to develop energy sources. This new degree of coherence has given rise to intergovernmental conflict about energy matters as the various jurisdictions define their interests in respect to energy in a more clear-cut, expert and comprehensive way.

Second, the energy crisis has rapidly extended public involvement in energy matters and has launched the country on experiments in joint public-private ownership. The older mix of public-private involvement in energy development was featured by the dominance of government in the hydroelectric and nuclear fields, private ownership with public subsidies in coal, and a peculiarly unrestrained pattern of private ownership in respect to petroleum and natural gas. This has now changed, particularly in relation to the fossil fuels. Among other developments we have control of petroleum prices in Nova Scotia, at least temporarily in Ontario, and likely soon in the future in other provinces; joint public-private participation in Syncrude and the Pan-Arctic consortium; the formation of a national petroleum company for exploration and development; the Alberta Energy Company and the Ontario Energy Corporation to undertake energy development in those provinces; and the actual setting of domestic petroleum prices by the federal government. In the cases of the Syncrude project for the development of the Alberta tar sands and the Pan-Arctic consortium for development of fossil-fuel resources in Northern Canada, there is a pattern of public-private ownership and control quite new in the Canadian experience. It is possible to foresee complications in such arrangements, not only between their public and private components but also in such circumstances as that of Syncrude (with holdings by the federal, Alberta and Ontario governments) where one or more governments holds equity shares under the jurisdiction of another; this was presumably the kind of consideration which has led Ottawa to block the participation of the government of Quebec in the Pan-Arctic consortium.

Third, in the intense bargaining between the federal and provincial governments during the energy crisis, important and formerly influential interest groups have been rendered relatively ineffectual. Glyn R. Berry, in analyzing the circumstances of 1973 leading up to Prime Minister Trudeau's assertion of a new national petroleum policy on December 6 of that year, states "During these developments the oil industry seemed helpless to prevent measures that, only a year before, the government itself would have rejected as radical and unnecessary."[111] Richard Simeon has said of the more general phenomenon ". . . the operation of the process [of federal-provincial negotiations] itself tends to freeze out interest groups."[112] Berry's analysis states that when decision-making on energy matters was relatively non-controversial the federal and provincial governments were "benevolently responsive" to the interests of the oil industry. This lobby responded very ineffectually to the new circumstances, and the oil companies lost both their former degree of autonomy and their influence over policy, as other interest groups became mobilized against them and as governments began to deal with energy matters at the level of fundamental policy considerations.[113] In general, these close and harmonious relationships between industry and the public authorities were weakened as governments began to respond to one another to the virtual exclusion of other political actors.

Fourth, and perhaps most crucially, the energy crisis has led, in respect to these matters, to a resurgence of power and purpose by the central government. Despite the hostility to nationalism expressed in Pierre Elliott Trudeau's academic writings, the Prime Minister's defence of the new national oil policy on December 6, 1973 and his opening speech to the Federal-Provincial Conferernce on Energy on January 22, 1974 were enunciated in explicitly nationalistic terms. Canada was and must remain, he argued, a "national community" and the new demands of "fraternity" inherent in such a community made necessary national self-sufficiency in energy and decisive action by the national government to protect individual Canadian consumers and the provinces and regions of Canada against dislocations in energy prices, as well as the sharing of revenues accruing from energy development throughout the nation. Significantly, as in the past, the impetus for this reassertion of national power and purpose was a series of events outside the country, a classic example of what Hugh G.J. Aitken has called the "defensive expansionism"[114] which has characterized much of the developmental process in Canada. Significantly too, strong pressures for decisive national action came from Ontario, a province which for a century has led the struggle for provincial autonomy and which in recent years and in other arenas has mounted a determined and sophisticated resistance to federal power.

Conclusions: The Dimensions of Equalization

Despite the recent preoccupations with cultural and linguistic duality, fiscal and economic matters were from the first and remain central to the Canadian federal experience. Presumably both Anglophones and Francophones need health services when they are ill, jobs when they are unemployed and income when they are old, and in the ongoing energy crisis the government of Quebec has acted almost precisely as it might have been expected to do if the majority of its population were English-speaking. If there is a key to these fiscal and economic matters it lies in the increasing scope of equalization in these various dimensions:

— *interprovincial revenue equalization.* The chief device here is of course federal unconditional grants to the provinces. As we saw earlier in this chapter, there has been relative success in this direction as measured by the circumstance that per capita provincial expenditures in the "have" and "have not" provinces are nearly equal. Despite the recent abandonment by Ottawa of full revenue equalization to the national average, it is reasonable to hope that future fiscal arrangements will sustain the progress that has already been made in this dimension.

— *interprovincial equalization in the range and quality of public services.* Progress here has been made through the conditional grant. There are apparently no new major grant-in-aid programs under serious consideration and, as we have seen, federal controls over provincial standards in some of the major existing programs are being eliminated or made less stringent. However, under modern circumstances there would seem to be an increasing degree of uniformity among Canadians in their expectations of an acceptable range and quality of public services. If this is so, this dimension of equalization can be met largely through revenue equalization without the imposition of federal controls on the provinces.

— *interprovincial equalization in tax rates.* Fiscal equity demands not only that provincial governments have the revenues to provide a range and quality of services at national average levels, but that they are able to discharge these responsibilities without subjecting their residents to tax rates above the national average. Although I am not aware of any recent studies of this matter, an impressionistic survey suggest that tax rates are significantly higher in the less prosperous provinces than the more favoured ones.

— *interprovincial equalization in economic opportunities.* Despite the recent efforts in reducing regional economic disparities seemingly intractable inequalities remain, as measured by such obvious indices as personal per capita income and rates of unemployment. Fortunately or otherwise, other national economic policies such as those related to the rationalization of secondary industry and the development of increased supplies of oil and natural gas appear to be working to perpetuate if not to exaggerate these historic disparities.

— *interprovincial equalization in the prices of petroleum.* As we saw in the last section, the federal government has moved toward a single Canadian market for oil. It is hazardous to guess whether the same principle will be applied to other commodities, although Prime Minister Trudeau so spoke at the Federal-Provincial Energy Conference of January 1974: ". . . the dramatic oil crisis of recent months could very well find a parallel in future years with respect to some other resource. But the principles would remain the same: a respect for our common interests, and a sharing of the benefits and burdens of any price or supply change so sudden and so great that it could disrupt the objectives of our Canadian community."[115]

These thrusts toward national equalization in its various dimensions have come about in a piecemeal way and there has never been any comprehensive attempt to harmonize them with each other or with other public policies. For example, it remains a matter of dispute whether conditional grant programs should embody elements of interprovincial fiscal equalization or, alternatively, whether this should be taken care of exclusively through unconditional grants for revenue equalization.[116] It has been charged that some or all of the equalization measures outlined above restrict labour mobility and thus decrease both national productivity and the incomes of individuals and families thus dissuaded from moving to places where they would be more productively employed. It must also be pointed out that apart from petroleum products and wheat,[117] equalization has not come to mean reducing interprovincial disparities in the prices of goods Canadians purchase in the private sector.

Notes

[1]*The Government of Canada*, University of Toronto Press, p. 120.
[2]*The Cost of Confederation, Part I (Economic Activity)*, Calgary, 1974 (mimeo.)
[3]Donald Creighton, *John A. Macdonald: The Old Chieftain*, Macmillan of Canada, Toronto, 1955, Chapter 1 "The Pacification of Nova Scotia".
[4]"A Flexible Portion of the British North America Act, XI *Canadian Bar Review* (1933), pp. 148-157. For a history of the subsidy question see Maxwell's *Federal Subsidies to the Provincial Governments in Canada*, Harvard University Press, 1937.
[5]The Right Honourable Pierre Elliot Trudeau, *The Constitution and the People of Canada*, Queen's Printer, Ottawa, 1969, p. 12. Emphasis Mr. Trudeau's. Reproduced by permission of Information Canada.
[6]Book II, pp. 83-84.
[7]*Peace, Order and Good Government*, Macmillan of Canada, Toronto, p. 45.
[8]*Ten to One: The Confederation Wager*, McClelland and Stewart, Toronto/Montreal, pp. 144-145.
[9]For Parizeau's analysis of federal-provincial financial relations made near the time this political decision was made see "Federal-Provincial Economic Coordination", in *Canadian Economic Problems and Policies*, Lawrence H. Officer and Lawrence B. Smith, Editors, McGraw-Hill of Canada, Toronto, pp. 81-92.
[10]Vol. II, Queen's Printer, Ottawa, p. 104.
[11]The Government of Manitoba pressed persistently for agreement on expenditure priorities. See also the statement of Premier Robarts of Ontario in *Proceedings, Federal-Provincial Tax Structure Committee*, Sept. 14-15, 1966, Queen's Printer, Ottawa, pp. 333-46.
[12]"The Impact of New Tax Policies on National Unity", Institute for the Quantitative Analysis of Social Economic Policy, Research Paper No. 1, 1968, Quoted in *In Search of Balance – Canada's Intergovernmental Experience*,

Advisory Committee on Intergovernmental Relations, Washington, D.C., 1971, p. 103. Hartle's emphasis.

[13]"Constitutional Trends and Federalism", Reprinted in *Canadian Federalism: Myth or Reality*, J. Peter Meekison, Editor, Methuen of Canada, Toronto, 1968, p. 62.

[14]*Report of the Royal Commission on Dominion-Provincial Relations*, King's Printer, Ottawa, *Book II, Recommendations*.

[15]*Ibid.*, p. 126.

[16]*In Search of Balance, op. cit.*, p. 4.

[17]*Employment and Income with Special Reference to the Initial Period of Reconstruction*, King's Printer, Ottawa, 1945. For a fascinating account of the origins of the White Paper by its original author see W.A. Mackintosh, "The White Paper of Employment and Income in its 1945 Setting", in *Canadian Economic Policy Since the War*, S.F. Kaliski, Editor, Canadian Trade Committee, Ottawa, 1966, pp. 9-21.

[18]*Dominion-Provincial Conference (1945), Dominion and Provincial Submissions and Plenary Conference Discussions*, King's Printer, Ottawa, 1946. See particularly the Summary of Dominion proposals as amended, pp. 382-391.

[19]p.21.

[20]For the relation between the full employment and welfare state objectives of the federal government see the statement of the Minister of National Health and Welfare, *Proceedings, op. cit.*, p. 85.

[21]For Keynes' view of the intimate relation between domestic full employment and international objectives see *The General Theory of Employment, Interest and Money*, Macmillan, London, 1936, pp. 381-383. See also *Canadian Foreign Policy 1945-1954, Selected Speeches and Documents*, R.A. Mackay, Editor, Carleton Library, McClelland and Stewart, Toronto/Montreal, 1971, Section III contains documents on Canadian international economic policies.

[22]See Donald V. Smiley, *Constitutional Adaptation and Canadian Federalism since 1945*, Documents of the Royal Commission on Bilingualism and Biculturalism, Queen's Printer, Ottawa, 1970, Chapter III.

[23]"The Formulation of Liberal and Conservative Programmes in the 1957 General Election", XXVI *Canadian Journal of Economics and Political Science*, November 1960, pp. 565-574.

[24]See Peter Newman, *Renegade in Power: The Diefenbaker Years*, McClelland and Stewart, Toronto/Montreal, 1963, for an account which emphasizes this failure.

[25]From Richard M. Bird, *The Growth of Government Spending in Canada*, The Canadian Tax Foundation, Toronto, 1970, p. 246.

[26]*Ibid.*, p. 256.

[27]*Ibid.*, p. 289.

[28]*Ibid.*, p. 281.

[29]Canada: Dominion Bureau of Statistics, *Canada Year Books*, 1962 and 1963-64.

[30]United Nations, Department of Social and Economic Affairs, Statistical Office, *Statistical Year Book*, 1963, New York, 1964, Table 170. In the period 1955-62 Canada's per capita product grew more slowly than that of any of the other industrialized countries compared — Denmark, France, West Germany, the United Kingdom, the United States and Japan.

[31]See Hugh Whalen, "Public Policy and Regional Development: The Experience of the Atlantic Provinces" in *The Prospect of Change: Proposals for Canada's Future*, Abraham Rotstein, Editor, University League for Social Reform, McGraw-Hill of Canada, Toronto, 1965, pp. 133-142 and T.N. Brewis, *Regional Economic Policies in Canada*, Macmillan of Canada, Toronto, 1969,

Chapter 10, "The Role of the Provinces in Regional Development".

[32]For an account of these circumstances see A. Milton Moore, J. Harvey Perry and Donald I. Beach, *The Financing of Canadian Federation: The First Hundred Years*, Canadian Tax Foundation, Toronto, 1966, Chapter III.

[33]*Ibid.*, Chapter IV.

[34]For accounts of these pension negotiations see Peter C. Newman, *The Distemper of Our Times*, McClelland and Stewart, Toronto/Montreal, 1968, Chapter 22, Richard Simeon, *Federal-Provincial Diplomacy*, University of Toronto Press, 1972, Chapter III and Kenneth Bryden, *Old Age Pensions and Policy-Making in Canada*, University of Toronto Press, 1974, Chapter 8.

[35]*The National Finances, 1969-70*, Canadian Tax Foundation, Toronto, 1970, p. 116.

[36]Donald V. Smiley, *The Canadian Political Nationality*, Methuen of Canada, Toronto, 1967, pp. 59-78.

[37]"Employment Policy" in *Canadian Economic Policy*, T.N. Brewis, H.E. English, Anthony Scotland and Pauline Jewett, Macmillan of Canada, Toronto, 1961, pp. 150-151.

[38]John Kenneth Galbraith has declared, "Canada was perhaps the first country to commit itself unequivocally to a Keynesian economic policy," *Economics, Peace and Laughter*, New American Library, New York, 1971, p. 51. See also Mackintosh's account of the White Paper, note 17.

[39]This planning in public works never came about. The late Dr. Mackintosh asserted that in 1945 the idea of grants to the provinces and municipalities for public works was not attractive to Ottawa politicians and bureaucrats as a device for countering cyclical fluctuations in employment. *op. cit.*, p. 20.

[40]H. Scott Gordon, "A Twenty Year Perspective: Some Reflections on the Keynesian Revolution in Canada", in *Canadian Economic Policy Since the War, op. cit.*, pp. 23-46.

[41]*Ibid.*, p. 46

[42]"Federal-Provincial Fiscal Developments", in Canadian Tax Foundation, *Report of the 1964 Conference*, Toronto, 1965, p. 223. There has been an element in political and economic thought in Quebec which sees the roots of centralization in Canada in the acceptance by Ottawa of the Keynesian analysis. See François-Albert Angers, *Essai sur la Centralisation*, Éditions Beauchemin, Montréal, 1960 and *Report of the Royal Commission of Inquiry on Constitutional Problems*, Quebec, 1956, Vol. II, pp. 294-305.

[43]Growth, Price Stability and the Problem of Unemployment", mimeo., p. 5.

[44]Vol. II, p. 29.

[45]*Ibid.*, p. 29.

[46]Queen's Printer, Ottawa, Chapter 7 "Regional Aspects of Federal Economic Policies".

[47]Information Canada, Ottawa, Chapter VIII "National Policy-Making in a Regional Country".

[48]Vol. 2, p. 93. See also Clarence L. Barber, *Theory of Fiscal Policy as Applied to a Province*, A Study Prepared for the Ontario Committee on Taxation, Queen's Printer, Toronto, 1967, Chapter 3 "Fiscal Policy at the Provincial and Municipal Level: the Historical Recrod."

[49]*Ibid.*, pp. 96-99.

[50]*Ibid.*, pp. 102-103.

[51]Barber, *op. cit.*, Chapter 2.

[52]The Honourable W. Darcy McKeough, *1971 Budget Ontario*, Queen's Printer, Toronto, 1971, Budget Paper A, "New Directions in Economic Policy Management in Canada", p. 45.

[53]*Ibid.*, p. 47.

⁵⁴*Ibid.*, p. 49.

⁵⁵*Economic Review, A General Review of Recent Economic Developments*, Presented by the Honourable John Turner, Information Canada, Ottawa, 1974, p. 101.

⁵⁶*Fiscal Need and Revenue Equalization Grants*, Canadian Tax Foundation and Institute of Intergovernmental Relations, Toronto, 1969, p. 3.

⁵⁷*Ibid.*, p. 3.

⁵⁸Information from Department of Finance.

⁵⁹*Statement of the Honourable John Turner to the Federal-Provincial Meeting of Ministers of Finance and Provincial Treasurers, December, 1974*, p. 12 (mimeo.).

⁶⁰*Ibid.*, p. 1.

⁶¹In a yet-unpublished paper Professor Thomas Courchene of the University of Western Ontario has estimated that at $8.00 per barrel oil, total provincial royalties would almost double over the $6.50 per barrel price and that equalization payments to the provinces would be triple their 1973-'74 levels under full equalization to the national average, with Ontario becoming a "have not" province.

⁶²Queen's Printer, Ottawa, p. 141.

⁶³See generally T.N. Brewis, *Regional Economic Policies in Canada*, Macmilland of Canada, Toronto 1969; Alan G. Green "Regional Economic Disparities" in Lawrence H. Officer and Lawrence B. Smith, Editors, *Issues in Canadian Economics*, McGraw-Hill Ryerson, 1974, pp. 354-370 and R.W. Phidd, "Regional Development Policy" in G. Bruce Doern and V. Seymour Wilson, Editors, *Issues in Canadian Public Policy*, Macmillan of Canada, Toronto, 1974, pp.166-202.

⁶⁴For an account of ARDA see Brewis, *op. cit.*, Chapter 6.

⁶⁵*Ibid.*, pp. 162-163.

⁶⁶From *Phidd*, "Regional Development Policy", *op. cit.*, p. 187.

⁶⁷Green "Regional Economic Disparities", *op. cit.*

⁶⁸"Some Economic Problems of a Federal System", in *Officer and Smith, op, cit.*, p. 406.

⁶⁹For the difficulties in this coordinating role see *Phidd*, op. cit.

⁷⁰McAllister, *op. cit.*, p. 401.

⁷¹For accounts of federal conditional grants to the provinces at different periods of time see Luella Gettys, *The Administration of Canadian Conditional Grants*, Chicago, Public Administration Service, 1938; Donald V. Smiley, *Conditional Grants and Canadian Federalism*, Canadian Tax Foundation, Toronto, 1963 and George E. Carter, *Canadian Conditional Grants since World War II*, Canadian Tax Foundation, Toronto, 1971.

⁷²The major instance of this in Canada is the arrangement by which Ottawa pays half the operating costs of institutions of post-secondary education.

⁷³From *Provincial and Municipal Finances*, 1973, The Canadian Tax Foundation, Toronto, p. 35.

⁷⁴Privy Council Office (mimeo.).

⁷⁵The Honourable W. Darcy McKeough, *Supplementary Actions to the 1975 Ontario Budget*, Queen's Printer, Toronto, 1975, "Ontario's Experience under Cost Sharing", p. 1.

⁷⁶Report, Queen's Printer, Ottawa, 1960.

⁷⁷For accounts of the opting-out arrangements see J.S. Dupré "contracting Out: A Funny Thing Happened on the Way to the Centennial", *Report of the Proceedings of the Eighteenth Tax Conference, 1964* and Carter, *Canadian Conditional Grants, op. cit.*, Chapter 5 "The Development of Contracting Out and Tax Abatements".

The Fiscal and Economic Side of Canadian Federalism 157

[78]Federal-Provincial Tax Structure Committee, Ottawa, September 14-15, 1966, Queen's Printer, pp. 13-14.

[79]For a summary of Ontario's statements on contracting out see *Darcy McKeough, op. cit.,* pp. 9-11.

[80]*House of Commons Debates,* June 23, 1975, pp. 7026-7027.

[81]*Ontario Experience under Cost Sharing, op. cit.,* pp. 2-3. Emphasis in text.

[82]Information Canada, Ottawa, 1975, p. 29. The percentage of instructional time devoted to the second language in secondary schools had remained almost stable in this period, increasing from 11.7 to 11.9 per cent. Some improvements were measured in the elementary schools of the provinces other than Quebec with the proportion of students taking the second language increasing from 29.2 to 36.5 per cent. *ibid.,* p. 28.

[83]For an exhaustive account of the constitutional position see Gerard V. La Forest, *The Allocation of Taxing Power under the Canadian Constitution,* Canadian Tax Foundation, Toronto 1967. A less technical treatment is contained in Honourable E.J. Benson, *The Taxing Powers and the Constitution of Canada,* Queen's Printer, Ottawa, 1969.

[84]Honourable Gordon Miniely, *Basic Objectives and Terms of Reference for Alberta Business Taxation and Incentives,* Edomonton.

[85]*Ibid.*

[86]M.W. Bucovetsky, "The Mining Industry and the Great Tax Reform Debate" in A. Paul Pross, Editor, *Pressure Group Behaviour in Canadian Politics,* McGraw-Hill Ryerson, Toronto, 1975, pp. 89-114.

[87]See *Analysis of the Federal Tax Reform Proposals,* Staff Papers, Department of Treasury and Economics, 1970 and Honourable Charles MacNaughton, *Ontario Proposals for Tax Reform in Canada, 1970.*

[88]Ontario Tax Studies, 9, *The Dynamic Impact of Indexing the Personal Income Tax,* Staff Paper, Ontario Ministry of Treasury, Economics and Intergovernmental Affairs, 1974.

[89]See generally Richard M. Bird, *The Growth of Government Spending in Canada, op. cit.*

[90]*Report,* Ottawa, (mimeo.)

[91]For the most recent actions and their justification see *McKeough, op. cit.* The Supplementary Budget of July 7, 1975 was ostensibly designed to offset the impact on Ontario of the federal budget of June 23, specifically the actions of the latter in increasing energy prices and imposing limits on federal assistance for medical insurance. The previous Ontario budget had been brought down on April 7 and was allegedly "undercut" by subsequent federal policies. One of the elements of the Ontario budget was the removal until December 31, 1975, of the 5 per cent sales tax on passenger automobiles built in Canada or the United States, except some classes of luxury cars. This in effect was an Ontario tariff against automobiles made elsewhere than North America. After a considerable resistance from Ottawa and those connected with the importation of automobiles from outside North America, including a legal case challenging the constitutionality of the measure, this concession was extended to all buyers of automobiles.

[92]See Gerald V. La Forest, *Natural Resources and Public Property under the Canadian Constitution,* University of Toronto Press, 1969, and A.R. Thompson and H.R. Eddy "Jurisdictional Problems in Natural Resource Management in Canada" in W.D. Bennett et al., *Essays on Aspects of Resource Policy,* Science Council of Canada, Information Canada, Ottawa, 1973, pp. 67-96.

[93]Thompson and Eddy state that in Alberta "approximately 86 per cent of mines and minerals remain in provincial ownership", pp. 75-76.

[94]The term is used by Thompson and Eddy, p. 74.

[95]*Ibid.*, p. 74.

[96]*Globe and Mail*, Toronto, November 27, 1974. On the federal taxation of provincial organs see Gerald V. La Forest, *The Allocation of Taxing Powers under the Canadian Constitution*, Canadian Tax Foundation, Toronto, 1967, pp. 42-44.

[97]For an account of the background of the National Oil Policy see J.G. Debanné, "Oil and Canadian Policy" in Edward W. Erickson and Leonard Waverman, Editors, *The Energy Question: An International Failure of Policy*, *Volume 2 North America*, University of Toronto Press, 1974, pp. 125-136.

[98]Computed from *An Energy Policy for Canada, Vol. I. – Analysis*, Department of Energy, Mines and Resources, Information Canada, Ottawa, 1973, p. 39.

[99]Advisory Committee on Energy, *Energy in Ontario: The Outlook and Policy Implications, Volume Two*, Queen's Printer, Toronto, 1973, p. 86.

[100]*An Energy Policy for Canada, op. cit.*, p. 32.

[101]*Ibid.*, p. 33.

[102]*Ibid.*

[103]*Opening Statement*, Jan. 22, 1974 (*mimeo.*)

[104]*Statement*, (*mimeo.*)

[105]*Background Paper on the Canadian Energy Situation*, Prepared by the Government of Canada for the Conference of First Ministers, April 9-10, 1975, (*mimeo.*) p. 2.

[106]See M.W. Bucovetsky "The Mining Industry and the Great Tax Reform Debate" in A. Paul Pross, Editor, *Pressure Group Behaviour in Canadian Politics*, McGraw-Hill Ryerson, Toronto, 1975, pp. 89-114.

[107]See the correspondence on these matters between the Prime Minister and Premiers Lougheed and Blakeney between March 22, 1974 and November 22, 1974 as tabled in the House of Commons in late 1974. Available from the Prime Minister's Office.

[108]This was a major issue of the April 1975 conference of First Ministers. The Saskatchewan government here presented a plan, unacceptable to Alberta, according to which all proceeds resulting from increases of the price of domestic oil above $6.50 a barrel be transferred to an Energy Security Fund to make Canada self-sufficient in energy.

[109]Opening Statement of Premier William G. Davis (*mimeo.*).

[110]For an outline of the Ontario situation see *Energy in Ontario, op. cit.*, Chapter 13.

[111]"The Oil Lobby and the Energy Crisis", 17 *Canadian Public Administration*, Winter 1974, p. 603.

[112]*Federal-Provincial Diplomacy: The Making of Recent Policy in Canada*, University of Toronto Press, 1972, p. 282.

[113]Berry's article, *op. cit.*, pp. 630-635 is excellent on this. He states that as the crisis proceeded on the basis of federal-provincial negotiations of a constitutional nature and involving fundamental policy the industry was left "clinging to redundant technical arguments", p. 634.

[114]"Defensive Expansionism: The State and Economic Growth in Canada", in W.T. Easterbrook and M.H. Watkins, Editors, *Approaches to Canadian Economic History*, Carleton Library, McClelland and Stewart, Toronto, 1967, pp. 183-221.

[115]*Opening Statement*, (*mimeo.*), p. 9.

[116]For an analysis of this issue see George E. Carter, *Canadian Conditional Grants since World War II, op. cit.*, Chapter 3.

[117]The Albertans are understandably quick to point out the significance of these two commodities in their provincial economy while, for example, British Columbia lumber and the manufactured goods of Ontario are sold under no such limitations.

CHAPTER 6

CULTURAL DUALITY AND CANA-
DIAN FEDERALISM

Canada was established as a federation in 1867, albeit a federation of a somewhat centralized kind, largely because of cultural and linguistic duality. Most of the English-speaking Fathers of Confederation from the province of Canada and some of those from the Maritimes would have preferred a "legislative union", a constitutional order in which the powers of whatever political authorities there were other than the central government would exist at the discretion of that government. Yet the French-Canadian leaders would not have it this way, as George Brown stated in the Confederation Debates, "We had either to take a Federal union or drop the negotiations."[1]

To understand anything of how cultural duality impinged on Confederation it is necessary to examine briefly the development of French-English relations in the United Province of Canada under the regime provided for by the Act of Union.[2] The Act of Union enacted by the Parliament of the United Kingdom in 1840 was the response of the Imperial authorities to the rebellions of 1837 in each of the Canadas and to the famous Report of Lord Durham, who was sent to British North America to examine and to deal with the circumstances which had climaxed in those rebellions. The Report made two major recommendations. First, it was proposed that Canada be granted responsible government, that the Governor appointed by the Imperial authorities carry out his executive functions — so far as these related to colonial rather than Imperial matters — through ministers who had the continuing support of majorities in the colonial legislature. Second, there should be a legislative union of the two Canadas with the avowed intention of assimilating the French into the English language and culture.

The Imperial government rejected Durham's proposal for responsible government, although this was granted in 1848, but accepted his recommendation for legislative union. The Act of Union provided for a single legislature for Canada, with equal membership from each of the two sections, which from the Constitutional Act of 1791 had had their own legislative assembly, legislative council and executive council. This equality in the 1840 Act was explicitly designed to swamp the French. In 1841 Lower Canada (Quebec) had a population of about 670,000, Upper Canada (Ontario) of about 480,000. It was anticipated that the English Canadians from Upper Canada would join with their counterparts from the other section to render the French a permanent minority. Further, the Act provided that the proceedings of the Legislative Assembly and the Legislative Council be in the English language only.

Both Lord Durham and the Imperial government of the day held highly unrealistic notions about the disappearance of the French language and culture in Canada. It was naïvely and confidently expected that once the government of the United Kingdom took decisive action in rendering the French a permanent political minority, this group, through its leaders, would choose early and easy assimilation into the dominant culture. This was not to be. The French Canadian community again demonstrated its tenacity for survival and no Imperial authority, much less the English Canadian politicians, ever seriously considered the draconian measures that might have led to such assimilation. Throughout the period from 1841 to 1867 the French group in the Canadian legislature manifested a higher degree of cohesion than that of the English Canadians, and were thus in many circumstances able to exercise a decisive influence.

Under the Act of Union régime there developed several quasi-federal devices in response to cultural and linguistic duality:

— from the action of the Governor, Lord Bagot, in bringing the French leader Lafontaine into the executive council in 1842, Canada was governed by ministries with a leader from each of the two sections. There were sixteen such ministries between this date and 1867.

— there was some recognition of the double-majority rule. Under this procedure measures peculiarly applicable to one or the other section were enacted only with the consent of a majority of the legislators from that section.

— apart from the heads of government, there was a considerable bifurcation in the executive council and the departments of government. Such prevailed in education, the departments of the provincial secretaries and attorneys-general, public works, Indian affairs and fisheries.

— prior to Queen Victoria's decision in 1857 to make Ottawa the permanent seat of government, the capital perambulated between the two sections. There was a move from Kingston to Montreal in 1844, and in 1849 it was decided to rotate the seat of government between Quebec City and Toronto every four years.

— in 1848 the United Kingdom Parliament repealed those sections of the Act of Union providing that all records of the legislative assembly and legislative council be in English only. The next year the Governor, Lord Elgin, gave symbolic recognition to bilingualism by reading the Speech from the Throne in both languages.

In broad terms, the Canadian politicians after 1840 very quickly and decisively rejected the assimilationist premises of the Durham Report and the Act of Union, and moved toward a very high degree of what contemporary students of government call "consociationalism".[3] These consociational devices have already been mentioned — legislative groupings confined to English or French members, the double-majority procedure, English-French bifurcation in the political executive and appointed bureaucracy, the official recognition of the two languages. Yet these devices both reflected English-French duality and contributed to English-French conflict. J.M.S. Careless has said of the period between 1841 and 1857 ". . . for all the quasi-federal structure in Canada, there was no effective separation of sectional from common concerns within the single legislature. The cumbersome expedient had frequently confused the two, and so made for angry friction. Certainly Upper or Lower Canadians tended to adopt the view that the province was one or two just as the occasion suited them . . . If quasi-federalism was a response to duality, it aggravated rather than resolved inherent Canadian differences."[4] Most crucially, the province from the mid-1850s onward was brought to political deadlock by insistent demands from important elements in Upper Canada for representation by population. That section grew much more rapidly than the other and was now under-represented in the Legislative Assembly. These demands for "rep by pop" were very easily transmuted, particularly by the Clear Grits, into anti-French and anti-Catholic sentiments. Understandably, the French were steadfastly unwilling to yield to these pressures against a settlement that was originally designed to assimilate them but was now working in their favour. Further, despite the growing cohesion of legislative parties in this period, there was continuing political instability as a succession of dual ministries failed to maintain the continuing support of legislative majorities over extended periods.

Cultural Duality and the Confederation Settlement

The political settlement worked out by the British North American leaders from the late summer of 1864 onward, and in its main outlines enacted by the United Kingdom Parliament as the British North America Act of 1867, was in large part a response to political deadlock in the province of Canada, a deadlock in large degree brought about by cultural polarization. It is, however, a mistake to regard Confederation as exclusively or perhaps even primarily a French-English bargain.[5] The broad outlines of this settlement were worked out in the coalition cabinet of the province of Canada in 1864[6] and then in a sense "sold" to the leaders of New Brunswick and Nova Scotia, and in this second step cultural and linguistic matters were of little importance. Furthermore, over all these negotiations hung the apprehension of American political, economic and military aggression, with the British North American response of establishing a second transcontinental nation under British parliamentary institutions and within the British Empire.

In a negative sense, the Confederation settlement was a decisive rejection of the consociational and dualistic devices that had developed in Canada under the Act of Union. There was to be a single Prime Minister for the Dominion. By implication, the double-majority principle was rejected. There was to be no bifurcation of cabinet posts or administrative departments. In broad terms, a federal division of legislative powers was to be the major constitutional recognition of cultural duality in the new Dominion, with those matters in which the two groups differed most markedly being assigned to the jurisdiction of the provinces. The powerful Liberal leader George Brown spoke of the projected union in these terms: "The questions that used to excite the most hostile feelings among us have been taken away from the General Legislature, and placed under the control of the local bodies. No man need hereafter be debarred from success in public life because his views however popular in his own section are unpopular in the other; — for he will not have to deal with sectional questions."[7] On the French Canadian side, George Étienne Cartier asserted that what was being created was a "new political nationality" and in regard to this nationality the cultural backgrounds and allegiances of citizens were irrelevant.[8] The implication was that those powers necessary to the welfare and survival of the French Canadian community of Quebec were vested in the provinces and that the exercise by the Dominion of its jurisdiction over military and economic affairs was of no direct consequence to the integrity of that community.

It is, however, a mistake to believe that the French Canadian leadership posited any kind of absolute distinction between those matters deemed essential to the interests of this group and those which were not. As we shall see in chapter 8, it was not anticipated that the institutions of the central government would work in an entirely majoritarian way and on this basis French Canadians could realistically expect to exercise a continuing influence in Ottawa. Quebec was to be represented in the cabinet of the Dominion. Legislative parties were less cohesively organized than they subsequently became and this looseness gave cultural and sectional groupings effective power. Quebec was to have equal representation with Ontario and the Maritime provinces, the latter considered as a unit, in the Senate.

Apart from the federal division of legislative powers, the British North America Act contained several other provisions directly related to cultural and linguistic duality:
— Section 133 specified that:

> Either the English or the French language may be used by any Person in the Debates of the Houses of the Parliament of Canada and of the Houses of the Legislature of Quebec; and both those Languages shall be used in the respective Records and Journals of those Houses; and either of those Languages may be used by any Person or in any Pleading or Process in or issuing from any Court of Canada established under this Act, and in or from all or any of the Courts of Quebec.
> The Acts of the Parliament of Canada and of the Legislature of Quebec shall be printed and published in both those languages.

There was here a precise and limited recognition of linguistic duality in the operations of the Dominion and Quebec governments but no constitutional definition of language rights in the other provinces.
— Section 93 conferred on the provinces exclusive jurisdiction over education with the limitation that they could not override the educational rights of Protestant and Roman Catholic minorities existing "by Law" at the time of Union or later so established. If these rights were encroached upon by a province, there could be an appeal to the federal

cabinet and if the cabinet's decision was not executed by the offending province Parliament might enact "remedial Laws" to give effect to this decision. It may be noted that in the pre-Confederation period and for some decades after, the differentiation between French and English was perceived much more in terms of religion than of language.

— Section 94 contemplated the early assimilation of laws related to property and civil rights in the provinces other than Quebec into a uniform code under the Dominion. This section, which was never implemented, did not include Quebec, whose private law was based on the civil code rather than, as in other parts of the Dominion, on the English common law.

— Several provisions of the Act attempted to preserve the rights of the English-speaking community of Quebec rendered by Confederation a minority in the affairs of that province. These provisions guaranteed representation in Parliament and in the Quebec Legislature to areas of the province with English majorities.

French-English Relations: Confederation to 1960

Confederation did not eliminate conflict between the English and French communities. In the period between 1867 and the end of the Second World War the most bitter of these conflicts involved two sets of matters: the position of French and Catholic minorities outside Quebec; and Canadian orientations in external affairs as a member of the British Empire/Commonwealth. When they were mobilized as such, English Canadians in these conflicts got their way. Issues like these — the rights of the French outside Quebec and foreign policy orientations, — rather than the protection of the French Canadian community of Quebec by safeguarding and extending provincial powers constituted the major sources of French-English tension up to the past generation. Quebec from the late 1880s onward emerged as a defender of provincial rights. Yet this was not the major axis of cultural conflict, and in fact Ontario was the more consistent defender of provincial autonomy, perhaps because the latter never had interests in defending the federal power against actions of the other provinces as had Quebec in respect to French and Catholic minorities.

Despite the conflicts mentioned above, there were certain patterns of French-English relations which developed to make Canada prior to the 1960s one of the most stable of the western nations:

(1) *The federal division of legislative powers.* As we have seen, the basic rationale of the division of legislative powers established at Confederation was to vest in the provinces control over those matters where the cultures differed most markedly, while Dominion powers had no such cultural incidence. Up until at least the First World War the major activities of the federal government related to national economic development and in respect to these policies the interests of French and English were not perceived to be in opposition. On the other side, Ottawa for the most part did not involve itself in those matters within provincial jurisdiction believed to be most crucial to the

French language and culture. In general then, the division of legislative powers and governmental responsibilities contributed to harmony between the two groups.

(2) *Institutional self-segregation.* From 1759 there was sustained in Quebec what one might call a counter-culture, with its own justifying system of political, economic and religious thought. Pierre Elliott Trudeau wrote in 1954, ". . . against the English, Protestant, democratic, materialist, commercial and later industrial world, our nationalism worked out a defensive system in which all the opposite forces were stressed: the French language, authoritarianism, idealism, rural life and later the return to the soil"[9] The historian Michel Brunet says the dominant currents of French-Canadian thought were "l'agriculturisme, l'anti-étatisme et le messianisme".[10] These institutions and their justifying values did not in any direct way challenge Anglo-Saxon political and economic power either in Quebec or in Canada as such, and at the individual level most Anglophones and Francophones could pursue their occupational and other objectives without obstruction from members of the other group.

(3) *Mediation "at the summit".* Traditionally, the most important of Anglophone-Francophone political relations have been mediated by leaders of the elites of the two communities. In federal politics Anglophone party leaders have either had their Quebec lieutenants or — as has been the case with the Conservatives for most of the time since the death of Georges-Étienne Cartier in 1873 — have been trying with some urgency to find someone to play this role effectively. Although the Quebec lieutenant was by no means a co-prime minister when the party was in power, he had characteristically a wider scope of discretion in Quebec affairs than did ministers from the other provinces in respect to the areas they represented.[11] In the Quebec cabinet there was usually a cabinet minister from the English-speaking community — often the Minister of Revenue — representing Anglophone business interests.

(4) *The traditional French Canadian distrust of the state.* French Canadians have traditionally distrusted government, even governments in which they themselves have had a numerical dominance. According to Trudeau's analysis, because French Canadians received democratic institutions not through their own efforts but by the will of the English-speaking community, they came to value democracy not for itself but as an instrument of ethnic survival.[12] The Church remained jealous of its privileges and erected a system of social and religious thought which was both authoritarian and anti-statist. Although successive Quebec governments mounted a stubborn defence of provincial autonomy against real or alleged federal encroachments, there was little disposition to use these provincial powers imaginatively. A doctrinaire adherence to anti-statist values became a justification for French Canadian political and religious leaders to cooperate in the economic domination of Quebec by Anglo-Saxon capital.

(5) *The defence of historic, prescriptive rights.* Prior to the 1960s, French Canadian leaders saw the welfare and integrity of their community primarily in terms of an unyielding defence of historic and

prescriptive rights, particularly as these rights were embodied in the Confederation settlement. From the 1880s onward such interests were often defined in terms of the theory of Confederation as a compact either among the provinces or between the English and French communities.[13] The corollary of course was that the terms of Confederation could not legitimately be altered without the consent of the original partners.

These circumstances, taken together, gave a degree of stability to Anglophone-Francophone relations and to Canadian federalism. Institutional differentiation based on contrary value-systems made the individual and group objectives of members of the two communities relatively compatible. The mediation of community relations through the elites provided a regularized procedure for managing the demands of each group on the other. Anti-statism in Quebec facilitated both the domination of the province by English-speaking business interests and, particularly in the period between 1945 and 1960, the extension of federal powers in harmony with the preferences both of Canadians outside Quebec for national leadership and inside Quebec for public action to meet emergent social needs. Adherence by French Canadians to one version or other of the compact theory was an affirmation of the continuing legitimacy within Quebec of the federal system.

Quebec in the 1960s and the Quiet Revolution

Each of the stabilizing elements which has been discussed in the preceding section was abruptly challenged by the so-called Quiet Revolution of Quebec in the 1960s. Despite the speed and the comprehensiveness of change, these developments had their roots in the past. Many years before the death of Maurice Duplessis in 1959, the traditional institutions of Quebec and their justifying ideologies had become progressively less relevant to the circumstances of an industrialized community exposed to a modern and modernizing world. The formulations of the Duplessis era and later Quebec nationalism differed in many important respects but were similar in that they tended to equate Quebec with French Canada, and were for the most part indifferent to the recognition of cultural and linguistic duality in federal institutions or in provinces and areas of Canada outside Quebec where there were significant concentrations of French-speaking people. On the other hand, the older nationalism was primarily defensive and the new currents of thought and policy much less so.[14] In turning from "*survivance*" to "*épanouissement*" the Quebec leadership decisively altered the older patterns of relations between Anglophones and Francophones.

(1) *Conflicts over the federal division of legislative powers.* By the 1960s the original division of legislative powers by which the provinces were given control over those matters directly impinging on culture had broken down. Mainly through the exercise of the spending

power, Ottawa was now directly involved in health, welfare, higher education, vocational training and other such matters wholly or largely within provincial jurisdiction. Further, as we shall see, the Lesage government and its successors defined the survival and integrity of the Francophone community in Quebec largely in terms of the control by the province of its own economic development, and this brought about a challenge to federal powers.

(2) *A breakdown in institutional self-segregation.* What the sociologist Hubert Guindon has called "a new middle class" had developed in Quebec in response to urbanization and industrialization.[15] During the Duplessis period this emergent class had been rendered impotent both by the traditional political and religious leadership and by the Anglophone centres of corporate power. The new groups were committed both by ideology and class interest to the rationalization and modernization of Quebec society. Their frame of reference was secular, materialistic and democratic. Because corporate business was for the most part an Anglo-Saxon preserve, the new middle class turned to public institutions and in the main to the government of Quebec. This kind of development inevitably brought about new conflicts between the French Canadian elites and centres of business and governmental power dominated by English-speaking Canadians.

(3) *An end to anti-statism.* After the election of the Lesage administration in 1960, dominant currents of thought and policy in Quebec turned away from the older suspicion of the state and came to see the provincial government as the major instrument by which Quebec society might be reformed. The interests of the new middle class lay in the expansion of the public sector and in the bureaucratization of public and private institutions. This led inevitably to the displacement of the Church from its dominance in health, education and welfare — as well as to the bureaucratization of the Church itself and the declining political influence of its leaders — and to more intervention than before in the private sector by the provincial authorities.

(4) *Complications in elite accommodation.* From 1960 onward there was overt conflict among the Quebec elites which inhibited the older kinds of elite accommodation between Francophones and Anglophones both within Quebec and outside. During the early 1960s a frequent question asked by English-speaking Canadians was, "What does Quebec want?" The meaning was undoubtedly, "Who speaks for Quebec?" and confusion was made worse because, as one French Canadian scholar pointed out in 1968, "Actually too many individuals among the elite are speaking in the name of the whole French-Canadian population."[16] The overt and vigorous conflicts within Francophone Quebec undoubtedly became more salient for relations between the two communities as an increasing number of Anglophone Canadians came to interest themselves in Quebec affairs. In the federal political parties, the new currents in Quebec were weakly manifested through the Progressive Conservatives[17] and the NDP, and between the retirement of the Right Honourable Louis St. Laurent in 1958 and the period immediately after the general election of 1965, no authoritative

spokesman for Quebec emerged from the federal Liberal caucus. The results of the federal election of 1962 further confused the situation, as the Créditistes displaced the Progressive Conservatives as the major opposition to the Liberals in Quebec federal politics on a program which was at the same time federalist, anti-elitist and based on traditional French-Canadian values.[18] In the redefinition of Quebec's relations with the rest of Canada a number of alternatives from revolutionary separatism to cooperative federalism were proposed and vigorously expounded. By the mid-1960s the older patterns of elite accommodation between the Francophone and Anglophone communities appeared in retrospect to have been relatively tidy and straightforward.

(5) *The turning away from historic, prescriptive rights.* There was little disposition in the 1960s to defend Quebec's rights in terms of the compact theory of Confederation. Pierre Carignan said of prevailing constitutional attitudes in 1966, ". . . il semble que la majorité des Québécois d'expression française sont prêts à rejeter la constitution dans sa forme actuelle. N'ayant pu convaincre leurs compatriotes que la constitution constitue un pacte, ils ont eux-mêmes cessé de la croire: en conséquence, ils ne se sentent plus liés par elle et remettent tout en question."[19] As we saw in Chapter 1 in their acceptance and later rejection of the Fulton-Favreau formula for constitutional amendment, the Lesage Liberals were caught in the crossfire between changing attitudes. Interestingly, the direct challenge to the Fulton-Favreau formula, whose rigidities were a manifestation of constitutional conservatism, was made by the Union Nationale. Writing in 1965 when he was Leader of the Opposition, Daniel Johnson pointed out that Canadians had lived under five constitutions — those of 1763, 1774, 1791, 1841 and 1867 — and said, "Les constitutions sont faites pour les hommes et non les hommes pour les constitutions. *Quant les conditions changent, c'est aux structures juridiques de s'adapter aux circonstances nouvelles . . . Et les conditions ont changé depuis 1867.*"[20] In harmony with the new circumstances Johnson defined Quebec's position not in terms of historically-acquired rights but on the basis of the inherent right of nations to self-determination.

The changes effected by the Lesage government were in the direction of reform of both the private and the public institutions of Quebec. Progress was made in creating a merit civil service, and some of the most able persons in the province were hired either as full-time officials or part-time advisers. Some of the grosser forms of patronage endemic to Quebec politics were eliminated, and in 1963 came legislation which both limited campaign expenditures and provided generous subsidies to candidates of recognized political parties. Through the Societé Générale de Financement private and public funds were channelled into Quebec industry and some attempts were made to rationalize such industry. A provincial Department of Education was established and a comprehensive program of educational reform undertaken from the kindergarten to university levels. Health and welfare systems were rationalized and bureaucratized. Hydro-electric resources were brought under public ownership, significantly increasing the opportunities for French-speaking Quebeckers, particularly in the professional and management categories. There was a new emphasis by the provincial authorities on linguistic and cultural matters, including contacts with the French-speaking world in Europe and Africa. Comprehensive programs of provincial and regional economic planning were devised and some progress was made in their implementation.

Despite the speed and comprehensiveness of reform, the changes being effected by the Lesage government were very much the same as those which had been undertaken in other parts of Canada but over a longer period of time. There were of course some differences. Understandably, these developments in Quebec had repercussions upon the relations between the Francophone and Anglophone communities which were absent from modernizing trends elsewhere in the country. In the eastern part of Quebec the province sponsored the first large-scale program of development through *"animation sociale"* which had ever been undertaken in Canada. The bureaucratization and rationalization of public services involved new relations between the religious and public authorities in Quebec much more than in the other provinces. On the whole, however, the reforms undertaken in Quebec were in the direction of bringing its institutions in harmony with those of other western democracies. This circumstance created an essential sympathy for the province and its new leadership within the federal government and among Canadians throughout the country. For the first time in the history of Canada the source of change was coming from Quebec.

The Lesage government postulated the interests of Quebec largely in terms of an extension of the autonomy of the province as the precondition of cultural integrity. The Premier said this at the Federal-Provincial Conference of November 1963:

> . . . we must exercise constant vigilance. Nobody in Quebec believes that a given measure, — aid to municipalities, the contributory pension programme, or federal assistance to technical education, for example — can, in itself, lead French Canada to assimilation by the English-speaking majority. Nor does anyone believe that any one of these measures, taken simply, is of a nature to threaten our entire cultural heritage. However, we must be systematically opposed to any federal move, whatever it may be, that reduces, in fact, or attacks the field of provincial jurisdiction. We absolutely cannot, even if it concerns a question which appears to be only a secondary one, remain passive in the face of federal initiative which are judged to be detrimental to the exercise of powers entrusted to the provinces. In fact, it is the whole of these measures that must be considered, and it is against each of the items comprising the whole that we must be opposed, because each of them is a threat to the autonomy of the provinces, a threat which constitutes a precedent which is later invoked to justify threats of increasingly detrimental effect.
>
> In short, we are not defending the autonomy of the provinces because it is a question of principle, but rather because autonomy is to us the basic condition, not of our survival which is assured from now on, but of our assertion as a people. . . .[21]

In terms of the general formulation quoted above, the Lesage administration made very specific demands on Ottawa, and pressed these demands in an effective way through the elected leadership and their extraordinarily sophisticated senior advisers. I have said elsewhere of these developments, "Such pressures [toward enhanced provincial discretion] arose as much from the requirements of particular Quebec policies as from a generalized disposition toward autonomy on ideological grounds. . . . The provincial administration was motivated to increase its range of effective discretion because it had very ambitious plans for reform and, to a greater or lesser degree, specific activities of the federal government stood in its path."[22] There were three classes of demands on the federal government:

(1) *For financial autonomy and financial resources.* The reforms undertaken by the Lesage administration were expensive and the Quebec authorities, with of course support from other provinces, pressed for both higher unconditional subsidies from Ottawa and decreases in federal income tax rates so that the province could increase its revenues without at the same time increasing the burdens on its taxpayers.

(2) *For a withdrawal of federal involvement from matters within provincial legislative jurisdiction.* Particularly in the period between 1945 and 1960 the federal government had involved itself in a very large number of matters within provincial jurisdiction, largely through the exercise of the spending power. The Lesage government demanded such encroachments cease, on the double grounds that they threatened the integrity of the French Canadian community and interfered with provincial objectives and priorities. In particular, Quebec demanded that in respect to existing and future shared-cost programs the province be allowed to contract out without either itself or Quebec residents being thereby subjected to financial penalties. Also, the province demanded that the Canada Pension Plan be not applied within Quebec, which would have instead its own scheme of contributory retirement pensions.

(3) *For more institutionalized procedures of intergovernmental collaboration.* In its quest for autonomy the Lesage administration showed a basic distrust of the informal and segmented pattern of relations between the provinces and the federal government. As we saw in Chapter 3, the Quebec government centralized the control of its relations with outside jurisdiction in a Department created for that purpose and under the direct supervision of the Premier. One of the basic elements of Quebec's formulation of cooperative federalism was a fastidious respect by Ottawa for matters within provincial jurisdiction. However, because most federal economic policies had direct and immediate implications for the provinces, Quebec demanded that there be established regularized patterns of federal-provincial consultation in respect to these policies.[23] There was also the desire to institutionalize procedures of interprovincial cooperation.

Throughout its six years in office the Lesage government failed to evolve a coherent constitutional policy, and in particular failed to formulate an unequivocal answer to the question of whether Quebec required explicit constitutional changes to give it a wider jurisdiction than that wanted or needed by the other provinces. In his last year in power Premier Lesage and his chief constitutional advisor, Paul Gérin-Lajoie, the Minister of Education, came to speak in a specific way about a *statut particulier* for Quebec.[24] However, these statements could be read either as a rationalization of the existing contracting-out arrangements, and their future application to other federal-provincial activities, or a rather generalized demand for explicit constitutional change. The specific demands of Quebec for autonomy had been spectacularly successful and because of this — and perhaps because of conflicting pressures operating within and on the government — the Premier and his colleagues chose to proceed in a piecemeal way rather than directing their activities toward comprehensive constitutional reform.

As a result of the general election of June 1966 the Union Nationale under the leadership of Daniel Johnson succeeded to power in Quebec. The anomalies of the electoral system allowed the UN to win a narrow majority in the Legislative Assembly, with 40.8 per cent of the popular vote as against 47.4 per cent for the Liberals. The Liberals had failed when in office to effect a comprehensive electoral redistribution because, so Mr. Lesage claimed after the 1966 election, Section 80 of the BNA Act precluded the legislature from altering the boundaries of twelve electoral districts which in 1867 had English-speaking majorities, without the consent of a majority of the sitting members of the Assembly from those districts.[25]

With the coming to power of the Union Nationale, the focus of Quebec pressures shifted somewhat from the specific demands for provincial autonomy which had characterized the Lesage period to broader and more symbolic matters of constitutional reform and of the role of the province in international affairs. By reason of ideology and the basis of its electoral support the Union Nationale was less interventionist than its predecessor and thus felt less urgency about effecting specific changes which would have brought it into conflict with federal policies. Further, a continuation of reform at the pace set by the Lesage government was impossible without imposing intolerable burdens on the Quebec taxpayer.

While in opposition, the Union Nationale had been persistently critical of what it claimed to be the pragmatism and opportunism of the Lesage government in constitutional affairs. The party was instrumental in having the Legislative Assembly establish a committee on the constitution in 1963 to hear interested and expert opinion and to stimulate debate on these matters. The UN led the struggle against the Fulton-Favreau formula for constitutional amendment and challenged the Lesage government to fight the forthcoming general election on its acceptance of this proposal. Daniel Johnson in 1965 had published his *Egalité ou Indépendance*[26] which called for a radical reform of the Canadian constitution on binational lines. After coming to power the Union Nationale continued to place a high priority on comprehensive constitutional change. In retrospect, this may be explained as an attempt to reconcile conflicts within the cabinet and the party — as well as the wider Quebec society — on the place of Quebec in Confederation. There were undoubtedly many traditional UN politicians whose basic commitment was to the continuation of federalism in a revised form. Other and younger members of the party espoused even the more thoroughgoing variants of Quebec nationalism. All could be brought to at least transient agreement on the desirability of constitutional change on binational lines, but the successive premiers, Johnson and Bertrand, resorted to exquisite equivocation on the urgency of change. On some occasions, such changes were pressed stridently in terms that suggested their almost immediate acceptance was necessary if separation was to be avoided. At other times, the tone if not the substance of Quebec's position was moderate.

The major policy issue on which the federal and Quebec governments came into conflict in the 1966-70 period involved the province's role in international affairs.[27] Under the Lesage administration Quebec had extended its economic and cultural contacts abroad with the opening of several quasi-diplomatic offices in Europe and the United States. The government had asserted its right to participate independently in international relations in respect to matters within provincial legislative jurisdiction, but a major conflict with Ottawa over this issue had been avoided. After the Union Nationale came to power there was a series of incidents involving Quebec's participation in international affairs and both federal and provincial governments were disposed to carry on this struggle in doctrinaire and symbolic terms. Ottawa came to believe that France, with the connivance of its African allies, was engaged in a deliberate policy of encouraging Quebec's international pretensions in an attempt to destroy the Canadian federation, or at the very least to challenge its stability by involving themselves in domestic Canadian affairs. In waging this conflict Ottawa put great emphasis on the abstract principle that foreign policy was indivisible and that in both law and practice there was a vast gulf between sovereign states and other governments.[28] The Quebec authorities on their part were disposed to assert in a symbolic way their right to independent participation in external affairs within the broad but indeterminate limits set by France and the French-speaking nations of Africa.

The Responses to the New Quebec

During the 1960s there were three sets of responses from the federal government, and to a more limited extent from the governments of the other provinces, to the changing circumstances in Quebec.

(1) *Accession to Quebec's demands for fiscal and administrative autonomy.* Particularly after the coming to power of the Pearson administration in Ottawa in April 1963, the federal government was relatively acquiescent in yielding to Quebec pressures for an enhanced range of fiscal and administrative autonomy. On several occasions prior to 1966 the federal authorities extended the range of provincial "tax room" and increased the scale of unconditional subsidies to the

provinces. Parliament in 1965 enacted the Established Programs (Interim Arrangements) Act permitting the provinces to contract out of several established grant-in-aid programs with full fiscal compensation. After a lengthy series of negotiations between the federal and Quebec governments it was agreed that the Canadian Pension Plan should not apply within Quebec.[29] Two other programs, student loans and youth allowances, which elsewhere in the country were funded and administered by the federal authorities, were in Quebec undertaken by the province with unconditional fiscal compensation from Ottawa.

By the time the Lesage government left office in 1966 Quebec had attained significant elements of a *de facto* special status in the Canadian federal system. Alone of the provinces, Quebec had chosen to contract out of several of the established shared-cost programs, thereby both ending federal control in these matters and increasing its own share of personal and corporate income taxes. Alone of the provinces, Quebec had its own machinery for collecting taxes on individual incomes. As we have seen, Quebec established programs in the field of social policy which elsewhere in Canada were carried out by the federal authorities. In all of these situations, each of the provinces had the same options to go its own way but only Quebec used these options.

(2) *Constitutional Review and Reform.* The second response to the new Quebec was the process of constitutional review begun in the Confederation for Tomorrow Conference of 1967 and ended by the Victoria Conference of 1971. These circumstances were described and analyzed in Chapter 2.

(3) *The bilingual and bicultural alternative.* What will here be designated as the bilingual and bicultural alternative was based on the assumption that under the new circumstances in Quebec the demands of the survival of Canada dictated a much enhanced recognition of linguistic and cultural duality in the Canadian community as such. Specifically, the federal government and the provinces must take action to strengthen the position of the French Canadian minorities outside Quebec and the national government must accept a much more explicit and extended commitment to cultural and linguistic dualism. If these measures were taken, it was asserted, or hoped, that the pressures for autonomism from within Quebec could be contained within limits compatible with the continuing survival of the Canadian federation.

So far as the institutions of the federal government are concerned, the most explicit embodiments of the bilingual and bicultural alternative are the Official Languages Act enacted by Parliament in 1969 and the measures taken from 1966 to increase bilingualism in the federal public service.

Article 2 of the Official Languages Act declared: "The English and French languages are the official languages of Canada for all purposes of the Parliament and the Government of Canada, and possess and enjoy equality of status and equal rights and privileges as to their use in all the institutions of the Parliament and Government of Canada." The major objective of this legislation was to ensure that citizens could deal with the government of Canada in whichever of the official languages they chose, at least in places and situations where there was a sufficient demand for English or French to make this practical. In order to delineate these rights more closely, the cabinet was authorized in collaboration with the respective provinces to delineate "federal bilingual districts" which had official-language minorities of 10 per cent or more of the local population.[30] There was also to be a Commissioner of Official Languages appointed during "good behaviour" for a seven-year term, a linguistic ombudsman with wide powers of investigation and publicity to ensure adherence to the Act.

A new linguistic regime in the federal public service was announced by Prime Minister Pearson in April 1966.[31] From a 1938 amendment to the Civil Service Act onward, there was a requirement that in recruitment to local positions the Civil Service Commission should ensure that a successful candidate had a knowledge of either English or French if this was the language "of the majority of the persons with whom he is required to do business". However, the working language of the federal public service remained almost exclusively English, most significantly in the Ottawa-based institutions of the government. The Prime Minister's statement so enunciated the new policy:

> The government hopes and expects that, within a reasonable period of years, a state of affairs will be reached in the public service whereby
> (a) it will be a normal practice for oral or written communications within the service to be made in either official language at the option of the person making them, in the knowledge that they will be understood by those directly concerned;
> (b) communications with the public will normally be in either official language having regard to the person being served;
> (c) the linguistic and cultural values of both English-speaking and French-speaking Canadians will be reflected through civil service recruitment and training.

Other principles were laid down in the policy statement that bilingual requirements should relate to positions and not individuals, and that those in the public service who needed language training should have this at public expense and during working hours. In June 1973 Parliament confirmed those general principles by a Resolution which directed the government to identify the official-language requirements of all positions in the public service and to ensure a greater use of French at all levels in the service.

On November 21, 1974 the President of the Treasury Board tabled a statement in the House of Commons announcing that language requirements had been established for 281,664 positions in the public service.[32]

— 60 per cent of positions were defined as those in which English was essential, 13 per cent French essential, 19 per cent bilingual, and in 8 per cent either language might qualify.

— in the National Capital Region 45 per cent of 79,939 positions required bilingual capacities.

— the bilingual positions were so described by occupational category:

Category	Number of Positions	% of Category Bilingual
Executive	963	93
Administrative and Foreign Service	16,805	37
Scientific and Professional	7,002	27
Technical	4,137	15
Administrative/Support	19,482	25
Operational	4,835	5

Apart from the institutions of the national government, there were also several moves to strengthen the position of the French language and culture outside Quebec. In 1969 New Brunswick enacted its own Official Languages Act, prior to and similar to the federal law, although these provisions have not been proclaimed as fully as have those of the federal enactment. Ontario in the 1960s significantly extended opportunities for education in French by the establishment of two public bilingual universities and a French-language high school system in areas where there were concentrations of Franco-Ontarians.[33] There were also federal efforts in the same direction through such measures as the vast extension outside Quebec of the French-language services of the Canadian Broadcasting Corporation and a system of grants-in-aid to the provinces to assist in financing instruction in their minority official languages.

As a scholar and publicist and later as Minister of Justice and Prime Minister of Canada, Pierre Elliott Trudeau has forcefully supported the bilingual and bicultural alternative as an integral part of his general formulation of Canadian federalism. This formulation can be summarized in five propositions:[34]

(1) *The distribution of legislative powers between Ottawa and the provinces under the British North America Act corresponds to the needs of the French Canadian community in Quebec.* During the Duplessis period Trudeau had supported the secularization and democratization of Quebec society. According to his view then and subsequently, the powers conferred on the provinces by the constitution are those necessary to the integrity and survival of French Canadian society in Quebec.

(2) *The federal authorities must respect provincial jurisdiction.* In American terms, Trudeau was and is a "strict constructionist". During the 1950s he broke with other liberals and socialists in Quebec by supporting Duplessis' defence of provincial autonomy. For Trudeau, Quebec's interests rest not only on the effective and imaginative exercise of provincial powers but also on a fastidious respect by Ottawa for provincial jurisdiction.

(3) *A special status for Quebec is unacceptable.* In Trudeau's view,

Quebec is well served by the existing distribution of legislative powers. If Quebec had more extensive powers than the other provinces, Quebeckers would not be able to participate as influentially in the affairs of the federal government as did other Canadians.

(4) *There must be an enhanced recognition of the French fact in Canada as such.* From 1964 onward Trudeau has supported the further constitutional entrenchment of the rights of the French language in Canada. So far as individuals are concerned, he has argued that French Canadians have failed to play as influential a role as they should have in Canadian affairs largely through choice rather than the resistance of the Anglophone community. Canadian society and government must be reformed so that Francophones feel that the whole of Canada is their country and be ready to assume their rightful place in participating in this wider framework rather than in Quebec alone.

(5) *Liberal and nationalist values are diametrically opposed and the latter are incompatible with Canadian federalism.* The major philosophical axis of Trudeau's political views is the clash between liberalism and nationalism. The enemy is the nationalist state, i.e., the sovereign political community embodying the interests and values of only one cultural and linguistic group. In Canada, according to Trudeau, nationalism can only result in the destruction of the federal system — as well as liberal and humane values — in the clash between Quebec and Canadian nationalisms.

Pierre Elliott Trudeau has thus formulated a coherent view of Canadian federalism, and as Prime Minister he has lost no opportunity to try to polarize politics within Quebec and throughout Canada on this issue. In pressing this polarization Trudeau has defined as unacceptable the views of some of those whose allegiances are basically federalist. For example, during the 1968 election campaign the Prime Minister attacked the Progressive Conservative party as supporting the "two nations" solution, because of the views of the Quebec Conservative leader, Marcel Faribault, although Faribault had spoken and written extensively in support of federalism. Within his own party Trudeau had previously taken a very strong position against the very cautious special status position elaborated by Maurice Lamontagne in 1966, although Lamontagne was like Trudeau both a federalist Liberal and a distinguished student of Canadian federalism.

Quebec and Canadian Federalism under the Bourassa Regime

In 1969 Robert Bourassa succeeded Jean Lesage as leader of the Quebec Liberal party. The Quebec general election of April 29, 1970 returned the Liberals to power with 45 per cent of the popular votes and 72 of the 108 seats in the National Assembly.[35] In the next election of October 30, 1973 the Bourassa government won a massive victory with 102 of 110 seats in the National Assembly and 54 per cent of the popular votes.

This latter election returned Quebec to its two-party tradition with the virtual elimination of the Union Nationale and Créditiste parties as significant political forces in the province, and polarized the province on separatist-federalist lines, since the Parti Québécois increased its proportion of the popular vote from 1970 from 23 to 30 per cent and won 6 legislative seats.

The Bourassa government is less disposed than its predecessors of the 1960s to advance the province's interests by rhetorical and symbolic appeals to Quebec nationalism. In formulating the general rationale of its policies, it talks of the cultural sovereignty of the province within the framework of Canadian federalism as a set of economic devices which are profitable to Quebec.[36] On the side of what it has defined as culture the province has been very aggressive. Its linguistic legislation, enacted as Bill 22, will be discussed in the next section. In collaboration with other provinces it has worked to restrict federal jurisdiction in the field of telecommunications and has expanded the facilities of Radio-Québec. It has extended Quebec activity in the field of immigration. In the negotiations succeeding the breakdown of the Victoria Conference on the Constitution in 1971, Quebec was successful in achieving arrangements whereby the provinces would have a significant range of discretion over the allocation of federal family allowance payments. Less immediate goals appear to be to challenge the activities of such federal cultural agencies as the Canada Council and the National Film Board.

In pursuing its quest for power and autonomy in a piecemeal and pragmatic way the Bourassa government claims a high degree of success. Its achievements in respect to family allowances have already been mentioned. In 1971 an agreement was signed with Ottawa providing for Quebec participation with the federal government in the international Agency for Cultural and Technical Co-Operation.[37] Also in 1971 an arrangement was concluded by which "orientation officers" of the Department of Immigration of Quebec might work in federal immigration officers outside Canada.[38] However, perhaps the most significant successes have been in the field of interprovincial cooperation. Premier Lesage convened the first of the annual interprovincial conferences of premiers in 1960, and he frequently expressed the view that cooperation among the provinces should be developed as a substitute for federal initiatives in some cases and as a prelude to federal-provincial negotiations in others.[39] Yet relatively little was achieved in this direction in the 1960s. In reviewing the events of 1973 Premier Bourassa said this:

> The most striking aspect of recent developments in Canadian federalism is the fact that the provincial governments have been adopting increasingly similar attitudes towards most problems. The provinces have in fact arrived at an identity of views on how to approach and solve most of Canada's economic and social problems. This identity of views finds expression in joint efforts to bring about a greater decentralization of the federal system, particularly in the following areas:
>
> 1. Federal finances: it is hoped to obtain a distribution of the resources

that is more in keeping with the constitutional responsibilities of the federal government and the provincial governments.

2. Economic development, particularly respecting the problems of regional disparities and unemployment;
3. Social development, with special emphasis on social security programs.
4. Cultural identity.[40]

Quebec appears to have been particularly successful in forging an interprovincial united front against Ottawa in the field of communications policy. The rationale for provincial control here as in the field of welfare policy is stated in terms of both cultural sovereignty and administrative rationalization.[41] At the federal-provincial conference on communications in May 1975 the provinces were able to agree on a proposal which would in its more important elements transfer to them jurisdiction over private and educational broadcasting, cable television and telecommunications within provincial borders.

The Bourassa government is thus committed to *"fédéralisme rentable"*, profitable federalism, with the corollary that for Quebec separation from Canada as proposed by the Parti Québécois would be economically disastrous. In the statement at the end of 1973 which has already been quoted, the Premier said this:

> The Canadian federal system is a powerful instrument for developing national [Quebec] resources, as may be seen from some recent examples:
> — Québec will be receiving an additional $78 million annually following changes in equalization payments announced in Mr. Turner's last budget speech,
> — Quebeckers will be getting $315 millions in family allowances following the successful conclusion of negotiations between Mr. Lalonde and Mr. Castonguay.
> — Québec received over half — $93 million of $167 million — of the federal funds allocated to the bilingualism program between September 1970 and March 1973,
> — Over the next three years, Québec will be getting one billion dollars, payable at the rate of $300 million annually, for housing and wastewater (sic) treatment,
> — Québec takes in over half — $66.5 million out of $128.6 million — of the federal funds distributed by the Department of Regional Economic Expansion in the form of regional expansion grants.[42]

Bill 22 and the New Linguistic Regime in Quebec

In the Official Language Act, popularly called Bill 22, which came into effect on July 31, 1974 the government of Quebec demonstrated its determination to effect a new linguistic regime in the province. Section 1 declares that "French is the official language of the province of Québec" and subsequent sections give the executive sweeping powers to establish and sustain the primacy of French in public education, private business and government. Some of the most contentious parts of the Act relate to education. It is the intent that children whose mother tongue is neither English nor French receive their education in the latter language, and the Minister of Education is given sweeping powers to determine the linguistic competence of pupils which will determine the language of instruction of their education. French is to be the language of private business, including relations with the public and labour relations, and the Lieutenant-Governor in Council is empowered to issue certificates to firms who have "adopted and are applying a francization program". With specified exceptions, members of professions to be so certified are required to have a working knowledge of French. Again with specified exceptions, French is the sole language of the government of Quebec and the public authorities and local authorities operating under the jurisdiction of the province.

Bill 22 has been subjected to very heavy criticism both from within Quebec and elsewhere in Canada.[43] The federal cabinet has refused either to disallow the legislation or to submit it to the Supreme Court of Canada for an advisory opinion as to its constitutionality,[44] although it seems likely that within the next two or three years the Act will find its way before the courts by way of private litigation. Both those who wish to enhance the position of French in Quebec and those who do not criticize the sweeping executive discretion conferred by the legislation, the first group suggesting that this will be an excuse for government inaction and the second fearing arbitrariness. Those residents of Quebec whose mother tongue is neither English nor French are alarmed that Bill 22 challenges their tradition of having their children educated in English, and raise the cry of parental rights. Lastly, Bill 22 is criticized as a retrograde movement away from cultural and linguistic duality when what I have called the bilingual and bicultural alternative has been accepted by the federal government and, to widely varying degrees, by the other provinces.

To the extent that the far-reaching provisions of Bill 22 are embodied in action, a very new pattern of relations will be effected between the English and French communities in Quebec. As Michel Brunet has asserted, the French in the province are for the first time since the Conquest beginning to act as a majority. For the time being at least, Bill 22 has decisively shifted the focus of French-English conflict in Canada away from the political and constitutional relations between Quebec and the rest of the country to the respective positions of the two groups within Quebec itself. The consequence of this shift, and in particular the relation between the bilingual and bicultural alternative which Bill 22 challenges and the continuing survival of the Canadian federation, will be discussed in Chapter 7.

The Separatist Option

The formation of the Parti Québécois in 1969 and the voting strength displayed by the PQ in the 1970 and 1973 general elections means that henceforth each Quebec provincial election is in a sense a plebiscite on the continuance of Confederation. It is not for a writer unfamiliar with the intricacies of domestic Quebec politics to hazard speculations about the prospect of the Parti Québécois acceding to power. Maurice

Pinard's research of the 1970 Quebec election indicated a two-party system (Liberal–PQ) in Montreal and a four-party system (Liberal–PQ–Union Nationale–Créditiste) elsewhere in the province.[45] However, the virtual demise of the Union Nationale and the Créditistes as serious political forces in the 1973 election brought about a more uniform alignment throughout the province — in all the 31 seats on Montreal Island the Liberals and the PQ were either first or second in popular votes and this circumstance prevailed in 53 of the 79 ridings elsewhere in Quebec.[46] Vincent Lemieux has asserted that since Confederation "the most constant characteristic of provincial party politics in Quebec has been the two-party system"[47] and in the most recent election Quebec returned to this pattern.

Pinard asserted in his 1973 article that the several opinion polls in Quebec during the last decade showed "the proportion favourable to separatism, in all of French-speaking Quebec, has always been below 20% and, in fact, around 15%."[48] Presumably in response to this kind of circumstance the Parti Québécois has moved to reassure the electorate in two ways:

First, from its beginning the PQ has postulated that national independence would be succeeded by a continuing economic union with the rest of Canada. The 1973-'74 program committed a Parti Québécois government to

1. Reconnaître le degré actuel d'intégration des économies québécoise et canadienne (surtout ontarienne) et l'avantage réciproque de conserver le principe de la libre circulation des marchandises entre ces deux marchés; à cet fin, renoncer, avec la réciprocité de l'autre partie, à l'établissement de tarifs douaniers entre les deux, tout en prévoyant un régime particulier touchant les denrées agricoles.
2. Discuter et conclure, si telle est la volonté des parties, un traité d'union douanière formalisant cette renonciation réciproque et prévoyant, si possible, l'harmonisation et la coordination d'un nombre plus grand de politiques économiques de même que la mise en commun d'un certain nombre de services incluant les mécanismes monétaires.[49]

The clear implication here is that the separation of Quebec from Canada would not decrease in any marked way the existing levels of economic integration, particularly of course between the Ontario and Quebec economies. In an interview published in late 1971 the chief economic spokesman of the PQ, Jacques Parizeau, asserted that he would prefer a customs union with Canada, in which Canada and Quebec would have no tariff barriers against each other and would establish identical tariffs with other nations, rather than a common market which would involve agreement on various other kinds of economic policies as these relate to transportation, agriculture, etc.[50] Parizeau also favoured a common currency, although each of the nations would have its own financial institutions, presumably including a central bank. The major business interests of what is now the central Canadian heartland would oppose any measures to weaken the economic links that prevailed before independence and Parizeau thus stated his views:

After all, what are we speaking of when we speak of a negotiation within Canada to form two separate countries? We're speaking of Ontario and Quebec. I don't mean that our commercial links with the Maritimes and the West have no importance, but no part of Canada is interwoven with us like Ontario. Toronto and Montreal are economic suburbs of each other.

Second, in 1974 the Conseil National of the PQ committed the Party to the policy that a Parti Québécois government would begin to exercise the powers of a sovereign state only after receiving the support of the Quebec population in a referendum on this issue. This means presumably that the PQ is prepared to govern Quebec within Confederation if the result of such a vote should be negative. Because the electoral strength of the Parti Québécois is significantly greater than support for separatism, such a result is not totally unlikely.

Race, Language and Culture: The Multicultural Diversion

The terms of Reference of the Royal Commission on Bilingualism and Biculturalism appointed in 1963 directed this body to ". . . inquire into and report upon the existing state of bilingualism and biculturalism in Canada and to recommend what steps should be taken to develop the Canadian Confederation on the basis of an equal partnership between the two founding races, taking into account the contribution made by the other ethnic groups to the cultural enrichment of Canada and the measures that should be taken to safeguard that contribution." In its membership the "other ethnic groups" were represented on the Commission by a French-speaking professor of Polish origin and an English-speaking professor of Ukrainian descent, in addition to four Anglophones and four Francophones. The last of the Commission's four Reports was entitled "The Cultural Contributions of the Other Ethnic Groups" and contained a series of recommendations for improving the circumstances of members of these ethnic minorities.[51]

The charter of Canadian multiculturalism is contained in a speech made by Prime Minister Trudeau in the House of Commons on October 8, 1971. In announcing, among other policies related to these matters, a program of federal grants to ethnic groups the Prime Minister asserted, "For although there are two official languages [in Canada] there is no official culture, nor does any ethnic group take precedence over any other." Mr. Trudeau later appointed to his cabinet a Toronto physician of Polish descent as Minister of State Responsible for Multiculturalism.[52]

Although as yet the multicultural formulation and policies based on it have not caused much overt conflict between the French and English communities in Canada, a new irritant has been introduced into these relations. Outside Quebec, particularly in the western provinces, multiculturalism can be and is used as a denial of the cultural duality of Canada by its implicit assertion that the French are no more than one of several ethnic groups. Within Quebec, the provincial authorities are intent not on preserving non-English non-French languages and cultures but rather of working toward the assimilation of citizens with these origins into the majority community.

Notes

[1]p.108.

[2]The Act of Union period has been intensively studied by several contemporary scholars. See particularly in relation to this discussion J.M.S. Careless, *The Union of the Canadas: The Growth of Canadian Institutions*, McClelland and Stewart, Toronto, 1967 and J.E. Hodgetts, *Pioneer Public Service – An Administrative History of the United Canadas 1841-1867*, University of Toronto Press, 1955. For the roots of federalism in this period see W. G. Ormsby, *The Emergence of The Federal Concept in Canada, 1839-1845*, University of Toronto Press, 1969.

[3]See the collection of essays edited by Kenneth McRae, *Consociational Democracy, Political Accommodation in Segmented Societies*, Carleton Library Series, McClelland and Steart, Toronto, 1974.

[4]From *Union of the Canadas* by J.M.S. Careless (p. 210) reprinted by permission of The Canadian Publishers, McClelland and Stewart Limited, Toronto.

[5]For a cogent criticism of recent attempts to see Confederation in these terms see Donald Creighton's essay "The Use and Abuse of History" in *Creighton, Towards the Discovery of Canada*, Macmillan of Canada, Toronto, 1972, pp. 65-83.

[6]Because of the traditions of cabinet secrecy — and the casual way in which cabinets of that day carried on their internal business — we know very little about these negotiations except for references by participants in the Confederation Debates, particularly Macdonald and Brown.

[7]*Confederation Debates*, p.96.

[8]*ibid.* pp. 53-61.

[9](trans) In Pierre Elliott Trudeau (editeur) *La grève de l'amiante*, Université Laval Presse, 1954, p. 12. See also Trudeau's essay "Some Obstacles to Democracy in Quebec", in Pierre Elliott Trudeau, *Federalism and the French Canadians*, Macmillan of Canada, Toronto, 1968, pp. 103-123.

[10]"Trois dominantes de la pensée canadienne-française; l'agriculturisme, l'anti-étatisme et le messianisme", in *La présence anglaise et les canadiens*, Montréal, 1958, pp. 113-166.

[11]See generally *Cabinet Formation and Bicultural Relations: Seven Case Studies*, Frederick W. Gibson, Editor, Studies of the Royal Commission on Bilingualism and Biculturalism, Queen's Printer, Ottawa, 1970, and more particularly Gibson's conclusions "Co-Prime Minister, Chief Lieutenant or Provincial Spokesman", pp. 155-159 and ff.

[12]Trudeau, *Some Obstacles to Democracy in Quebec*, "Regardless of how liberal were the conqueror's political institutions, they had no intrinsic value in the minds of the people who had not desired them, never learned to use them and finally only accepted them as a means of loosening the conqueror's grip." p.106.

[13]For a history of the compact theories see Ramsay Cook, *Provincial Autonomy, Minority Rights and the Compact Theory, 1867-1921*, Studies of the Royal Commission on Bilingualism and Biculturalism, Queen's Printer, Ottawa, 1969. See also R. Arès S.J., *Dossier sur le pacte fédératif de 1867*, Les Éditions Bellarmin, Montréal, 1967.

[14]See Leon Dion, "The Origin and Character of the Nationalism of Growth",

Canadian Forum, Vol. XIII, No. 516, January 1964, pp. 229-233, and H. Guindon, "Social Unrest, Social Class and Quebec's Bureaucratic Revolution", *Queen's Quarterly* LXXXI (Summer 1964), pp. 150-162.

[15]"Two Cultures: An Essay on Nationalism, Class and Ethnic Tension" in *The Canadian Political Process*, Orest Kruhlak, Richard Schulz and Sidney Pobihuschy, Editors, Holt, Rinehart and Winston of Canada, Toronto, 1970, pp. 75-93.

[16]Fernand Ouellett in *Quebec: Year Eight*, Glendon College Forum, C.B.C. Publications, Toronto, 1968, p. 80.

[17]For accounts of the failure of Prime Minister Diefenbaker in respect to Quebec by two former Conservative MPs from that province, see Pierre Sevigny, *This Game of Politics*, McClelland and Stewart, Toronto, 1965 and Vincent Brassard, *Les insolences d'un exdeputé*, Montréal, n.d. (1963?)

[18]Maurice Pinard, *The Rise of a Third Party: A Study in Crisis Politics*, Prentice-Hall, Inc., Englewood Cliffs, N.J., 1971.

[19]*Le Devoir*, 29 Octobre, 1966.

[20]*Égalité ou Indépendance*, Éditions Renaissance, Montréal, p. 35. Emphasis in text.

[21]*Federal-Provincial Conference 1963*, Queen's Printer, Ottawa, 1964, p. 40.

[22]*The Canadian Political Nationality*, Methuen of Canada, Toronto, 1967, pp. 66-67.

[23]*Federal-Provincial Conference, 1963, op. cit.*, pp. 44-46.

[24]For the Premier's statement see his Ste. Foy speech reprinted in *Le Devoir*, 23 et 24 décembre 1965. M. Gérin-Lajoie spoke along similar lines to the 1965 Couchiching Conference, Gordon Hawkins, Editor, *Concepts of Federalism*, Canadian Institute on Public Affairs, Toronto, 1965, pp. 62-68.

[25]The provisions of Section 80 were nullified by the National Assembly after the 1970 election.

[26]Johnson, *op. cit.*

[27]For an account of those incidents see Edward McWhinney, "Canadian Federalism' Foreign Affairs and Treaty Power" in *The Confederation Challenge*, Ontario Advisory Committee on Confederation, *Background Papers and Reports*, Volume 2, Queen's Printer, Toronto, 1970, pp. 115-152.

[28]For the federal position see the Honourable Paul Martin, *Federalism and International Relations*, Queen's Printer, Ottawa, 1968; and the Honourable Mitchell Sharp, *Federalism and International Conferences on Education*, Queen's Printer, Ottawa, 1968. The best analysis of the Quebec position came from Paul Gérin-Lajoie, Chapter I, n. 91. See also Jacques Brossard, André Patry et Elisabeth Weiser, *Les pouvoirs extérieurs du Québec*, les Presses de l'Université de Montréal, 1967.

[29]For accounts of the pension issue see Kenneth Bryden, *Old Age Pensions and Policy-Making in Canada*, McGill-Queen's University Press, Montreal and London, 1974, Chapter 8; Richard Simeon, *Federal-Provincial Diplomacy*, University of Toronto Press, 1972, Chapter 3 and Peter C. Newman, *The Distemper of Our Times*, McClelland and Stewart, Toronto, 1968, Chapter 22.

[30]As this is written the Bilingual Districts Advisory Board under the chairmanship of Professor Paul Fox has been at work for several years, but the government has not proclaimed such districts.

[31]See the analysis in the essay by V. Seymour Wilson, "Language Policy" in G. Bruce Doern and V. Seymour Wilson, Editors, *Issues in Canadian Public Policy*, Macmillan of Canada, Toronto, 1974, pp. 253-285.

[32]*Official Languages in the Public Service of Canada*, A Report by the Honourable Jean Chrétien, President of the Treasury Board, November 21, 1974.

[33]For the recent recognition of bilingualism and biculturalism in Ontario see

T.H.B. Symons "Ontario's Quiet Revolution" in R.M. Burns, Editor, *One Country or Two?*, McGill-Queen's University Press, Montreal and London, 1971, pp. 169-204.

[34]See *Federalism and the French Canadians, op. cit.*

[35]For an analysis of this election see Vincent Lemieux, Marcel Gilbert et André Blais, *Une élection de réalignment: l'élection générale du 29 avril 1970 au Québec,* Cahiers de Cité Libre, Montréal, 1970.

[36]". . . la souveraineté culturelle du Québec dans un fédéralisme économique." *Discours* in the National Assembly, 21 March 1973, Gouvernement du Québec, Conseil Exécutif, Information (mineo), p. 9.

[37]*Communiqué,* Department of External Affairs, Ottawa, October 8, 1971.

[38]See the text of this agreement reprinted as Appendix "D" to 2 *The Immigration Program; A Report of the Canadian Immigration and Population Study,* Information Canada, Ottawa, 1974.

[39]For two of these statements see *Dominion-Provincial Conference 1960,* Queen's Printer, Ottawa, 1960, pp. 126-127 and *Federal-Provincial Conference 1963, op. cit.* pp. 44-46.

[40]*Communiqué* of December 22, 1973, Gouvernement du Québec, Conseil Exécutif, Information, *mimeo,* pp. 10-11.

[41]"The [Quebec] plan is based on the assumption that it is preferable for communications to be handled by a single authority in view of Quebec's requirements with respect to culture, education and language." *Communiqué, op. cit.* p. 13.

[42]*ibid.,* pp. 11-12.

[43]For a criticism of this legislation in more moderate terms than most, see the speech of Senator Eugene Forsey, *Senate Debates,* October 8, 1974, pp. 54-58.

[44]Premier Hatfield of New Brunswick requested that the federal government seek such an advisory opinion.

[45]"The Ongoing Political Realignments in Quebec", in Dale C. Thomson, Editor, *Quebec Society and Politics: Views from the Inside,* McClelland and Stewart, Toronto, 1973, pp. 119-139.

[46]Calculations from the election results as published in *The Toronto Star,* Oct. 30, 1973.

[47]"Quebec: Heaven is Blue and Hell is Red" in Martin Robin, Editor, *Canadian Provincial Politics,* Prentice-Hall of Canada, Scarborough, 1972, p. 262.

[48]Pinard, *op. cit.,* p. 136.

[49]Parti Québécois, *Le programme, l'action politique, les status et réglements,* Edition 1973, p. 16.

[50]"Ontario Big Business Would Support an Independent Quebec", Robert McKenzie, *Toronto Star,* November 10, 1971.

[51]Queen's Printer, Ottawa, 1969.

[52]Dr. Haidasz was dropped from the cabinet after the general election of 1974 and these responsibilities re-assigned to the Minister of Labour, although most of the actual activity in supporting multicultural activity is within the Department of the Secretary of State.

CHAPTER 7

THE THREE AXES OF CANADIAN FEDERALISM

The study thus far has dealt almost exclusively with the structures and processes of Canadian federalism. This chapter shifts emphasis by a somewhat more speculative analysis of the relations between these structures and processes and a complex of substantive matters crucial to Canadian nationhood.

For purposes of analysis, the challenges confronting the Canadian political community might be divided into those common to western democracies and those specific to Canadian circumstances. Everyone might contrive his own list in the first category, but mine would include; the protection and prudent development of the natural environment; in the working of political institutions some reconciliation of the values of effectiveness, accountability and responsiveness; measures of control over inflation and substitutes for economic growth as a source of social and political legitimacy; the elimination of poverty; the creation of consensus and the minimization of coercion in the face of the progressive erosion of shared values; intelligent responses to the demands of hitherto relatively quiescent groups, in some cases for equality within the existing system and in others for radical change; sophistication in recognizing and courage in supporting those elements of decency and stability which persist in a violent world. Canadians must deal with these and other matters of crucial public concern through the intricacies of federal institutions and processes. However, Canada like other nations is confronted with problems specific to its geographical environment and historical experience. Wryly but perceptively Marcel Rioux has said, "We might briefly define Canada as a collection of North American territories whose major problem is not the Black problem."[1] To Rioux as to others the Canadian problem is the relation of English and French.[2]

As I see it, there are three particular and continuing problems of Canadian nationhood, each with a jurisdictional-territorial dimension: (a) the relation between Canada and the United States; (b) the relation between the English and French communities of Canada; (c) the relations between the central heartland of Ontario and Quebec and those Canadian regions to the east and west of this heartland. In one or other form, these sets of relations are at or near the top of the agenda of Pierre Trudeau's government in the fall of 1975, as they preoccupied the first government of John A. Macdonald in 1867. At different times in Canadian history public concern has been focused almost exclusively on one set of relations to the relative neglect of the others. To take a recent example, the 1960s were characterized by a preoccupation with cultural duality which gave way by the mid-1970s to concern with American power and western regionalism. Not only does one of these sets of concerns have the tendency to displace one or both of the others as a focus of public concern, but the political cleavages formed in relation to whichever is at the centre of attention characteristically complicates divisions relevant to the other issues. Thus, for example, Canadian economic nationalists on the left of the political spectrum have recently been sympathetic to Quebec nationalism, thereby espousing the contradictory solutions of a higher degree of Canadian independence from the United States and the destruction of Confederation.[3]

Canadian Federalism and American Power

Events of the first half of the 1970s ushered in a new era in Canadian–American relations, particularly in the crucial economic dimension of these relations. What has been demonstrated in the short run at least is that the existence of two sovereign states north of the Rio Grande imposes very important limitations to continental economic integration. In part, these limitations arise from a growing awareness in Canada that the public authorities cannot effectively discharge the scope of responsibilities they have assumed if crucial economic decisions affecting Canadians are made outside the country, either by multinational corporations or foreign governments. Even more crucially, the American government itself is imposing barriers to continental integration.

The drastic action taken in August 1971 by the government of the United States to deal with its balance-of-payments difficulties was a profound shock to Canadian policy-makers.[4] The immediate response from Ottawa was an attempt to gain exemption from the American policy on the apparent assumption that Washington had inadvertently failed to take into account the extent of the economic integration of the two countries and the consequent effect of the new measures in Canada. Such exemptions had been secured in 1963 and 1968 in relation to the Interest Equalization Tax and American restrictions on capital outflows respectively, but in 1971 the United States government was adamant in its refusal. Because of the manifest ineffectiveness and confusion of the federal government in the face of the new circumstances, the provincial administrations of Alberta and Ontario declared themselves in favour of establishing Washington offices for the more adequate protection of provincial interests.[5] Most if not all of the provinces attempted to cushion their economies from the effects of the American policies by winter-works programs before Ottawa belatedly announced to them its plans in mid-October, in the same month the Premier of Ontario announced he would recommend to the provincial Parliament a 3 per cent reduction in the provincial income tax following a similar move in the recent federal budget.

The events of late 1971 and subsequently have demonstrated that the government of the United States is now determined to treat Canada as a foreign country and to refuse to exempt Canadians from American international economic policies. In his speech to the House of Commons in April 1972 President Nixon spoke of the new American approach to foreign relations "based on the premise that mature partners must have autonomous, independent policies" and John Holmes suggested that the President "was not so much recognizing the Canadian right to independence as proclaiming an American independence of special obligations [to Canada]."[6] So far as trade matters were concerned, a Report issued in February 1972 by the Subcommittee on Foreign Economic Policy of the House of Representatives Committee on Foreign Affairs indicated the new American directions. This Report attributed the beginning of the "new era in United States-Canadian relations" not to the events of the previous August but rather to a developing Canadian nationalism coinciding with the centennial celebration of 1967 and the coming to power of the Trudeau government in 1968. The document went on to say:

> In general, U.S. trade relations with Canada are governed by the same principles and rules which govern our relations with other industrialized non-Communist countries. From time to time in the past there has been interest in both the United States and Canada in exploring the feasibility of setting up a United States-Canada Free Trade Area either generally or for particular economic sectors. At present, such an arrangement seems an ulikely possibility; and it would appear more constructive for our two countries to join in a multilateral approach to establish a non-discriminatory international economic system. By resolving bilateral questions through multilateral rather than direct bilateral negotiations, both the United States and Canada could minimize the stresses that bilateral confrontation may arouse.[7]

In the wake of the energy crisis in the fall of 1973 President Nixon proclaimed national self-sufficiency in energy — "Project Independence", linked symbolically by Nixon and his successor with the bicentennial of the Declaration of Independence — in these terms: "The United States is a great nation. No great nation must ever be in a position where it is dependent on any other nation, friend or foe, for its energy." The exact implications of "Project Independence" are not yet apparent, but what it does mean is an increasing disposition of the Americans to discount price considerations in ensuring security of supplies from domestic sources and to drive hard bargains to insulate the conditions under which energy and energy fuels are available to them from future changes in the policies of Canada and other foreign nations.

In general then, the policies of the government of the United States impose significant limits to continental economic integration. Robert Gilpin has pointed out that within the United States in recent years there has been a shift of "industrial, financial and political power" to the south and southwest, "and that this has weakened the economic ties between eastern Canada and the American industrial-financial cores located along the eastern seaboard and the Great Lakes" which constituted the essence of the "special relationship" between the two countries.[8] Further, it is at least possible that Washington itself will increasingly perceive divergences between the interests of the political sector and those of multinational business enterprises.[9]

But if we take a particular set of limits imposed by the United States to continental integration as given, what is the relation between such integration and the workings of the Canadian federal system? There are persuasive strains of argument which assert that provincialism equals continentalism, that only a strong and purposeful national government can resist these influences. Donald Creighton has put this case in its most uncompromising form. In an article "Watching the Sun Quietly Set on Canada" published in 1971[10], he described the two persistent dangers to Canadian survival as "internationalism" and "provincialism and localism". Creighton saw internationalism in its Canadian variant as a cover for American imperialism, and provincialism — particularly as this manifested itself in a special status for Quebec — as a formula for national disintegration. There was here a Confederation fundamentalism, an argument that Canada could survive only if the elements of the 1867 settlement were preserved in all their essentials. Another line of analysis, relating provincialism to continental economic integration, proceeds by way of emphasizing the breakdown of the "Macdonald-Laurier National policy" of national economic integration on east-west lines through the trilogy of policies encouraging industrial development through tariffs, settlement through immigration and the building of railways through various forms of public assistance.[11] This policy made an independent nation possible because the north-south pulls were counterbalanced by the integration of the economies of Canada and the United Kingdom. However, with the "end of the Atlantic triangle" the integration of the provinces and regions of Canada with contiguous areas of the United States proceeds without impediment. This integration is based largely on the export of Canadian natural resources in a raw or semi-finished form. The ownership of these resources by the provinces, along with the concern of the provincial governments for rapid economic growth and their aggressiveness in seeking foreign investment, results in a reinforcement of other pressures toward continental integration.

The relation between provincialism and continentalism appears, however, to be more complex than the analyses outlined above suggest. In 1973 Garth Stevenson mailed a questionnaire concerning foreign investment to the members of all provincial legislatures.[12] His results "do not suggest a particularly strong degree of hostility towards economic nationalism on the part of provincial politicians as a group." Also ". . . the data seem to suggest that federal initiatives in the direction of economic nationalism would have the support of legislators in several provinces, provided that these were taken in close consultation and collaboration with the governments of those provinces. Provincial legislators in Ontario and the western provinces would seem generally quite supportive while at the same time they seem quite jealously protective of provincial autonomy. Nevertheless constitutional uncertainties and the fear of losing industry to other provinces would almost certainly impose restraints on unilateral action by a province."[13]

There is also the prospect that what one might call provincial economic nationalisms will impose obstructions to continental integration. In his analysis of resource development policies in Ontario in the last decade of the nineteenth century and the early years of the twentieth H.V. Nelles has given an account of such influences oriented around what he called the "manufacturing condition" which demanded that "Ontario's natural resources be manufactured into finished products within the boundaries of the province."[14] Those organized interests supporting the "manufacturing condition" were successful in securing provincial legislation prohibiting the export of uncut logs and pulpwood from crown lands and these measures appear to have been decisive to the establishment of strong lumbering and pulp and paper industries in Ontario. Increasingly the provinces are designing their own industrial strategies and there is no reason to believe that these strategies will always favour continental economic integration. For example, current Alberta policies to establish a petrochemical industry and to favour Alberta investors in provincial resource development impose barriers to both continental and national integration.

It has increasingly come to be recognized that foreign direct investment is crucial to continental economic integration. The provinces have very different attitudes to the restriction of such investment, as a consequence of their very different levels of economic development and the ideological commitments of their incumbent governments. The NDP governments of British Columbia, Saskatchewan and Manitoba are on the whole ideologically hostile to foreign investment, particularly in the field of resource development. Alberta policy is disposed to favour such investment, although there are attempts to mobilize capital within the province for the exploitation of natural resources and the province has a relatively coherent industrial strategy favouring provincial development. There is a considerable support in Ontario, both in public opinion and provincial policy, for the further restriction of foreign investment.[15] In Quebec and the Atlantic provinces the needs for economic development are perceived as being so urgent that the incumbent governments are hostile to measures restricting direct investment from the United States or other foreign countries. Also in these provinces there is no profound disposition to favour Canadian as against foreign capital, and actual or projected policies supporting the former are often seen as strengthening Ontario's domination of the Canadian economy.[16]

The Foreign Investment Review Act was enacted by Parliament in late 1973 and its provisions for screening the takeovers of existing Canadian businesses came into effect on April 9, 1974.[17] As this is written (June 1975), those provisions of the Act related to the screening of new foreign businesses proposed to be established has not been proclaimed by the federal cabinet and this delay has been attributed in part by observers to opposition from some of the provincial governments. Section 2(2) of the Act provides that the criteria in determining whether an investment is of significant benefit to Canada should include the compatibility of this investment with "national industrial and economic policies, taking into consideration industrial and economic policy objectives enunciated by the legislature or government of any province likely to be significantly affected." Beyond this general provision, the legislation does not provide for consultation with the provinces or what weight provincial wishes should be given in the federal screening process. However, the incumbent federal government appears to be sensitive to the provinces in these matters and so far as I am aware there has been no objection by a provincial government to any decision from Ottawa preventing a foreign takeover.[18] It may be guessed that federal-provincial relations in respect to these matters will become more complex when and if the provisions of the Act respecting the establishment of new foreign businesses are proclaimed in effect. In general, however, it seems unlikely that Ottawa will frustrate foreign investment in those provinces and areas where the needs of development are most urgent.

Canadian attitudes and policies toward American power and continental economic integration are in a process of rapid flux. For example, the cleavage between the New Democratic Party and other parties are sharper on this than on any other major issue and the defeat of any one of the three NDP governments would be a considerable victory for continentalism. The energy crisis from late 1973 onward has given impetus to economic nationalism in Ottawa and several of the provinces, largely but by no means exclusively as defensive responses to American policies towards self-sufficiency in energy. It is reasonable to suppose that Quebec attitudes and policies towards American economic power will become less relaxed, and as Daniel Latouche has pointed out, even the Parti Québécois has failed to give careful or systematic attention to U.S.-Quebec relations.[19] Yet if people of influence in the province come to see a threat to Quebec in American economic power it is almost certain that the response will be Quebec economic nationalism rather than pan-Canadian nationalism.

In general terms, the working of the Canadian federal system even when the currents of provincialism are dominant do not lead in any direct and straightforward way to continental economic integration. The larger provinces have themselves developed industrial strategies whose implications in some cases at least appear to be a decreasing integration both with the rest of Canada and with contiguous areas of the United States. While the relation between provincialism and continentalism is complex, there is reason to believe that these two influences contain important elements of contradiction.

French-English Relations in Canada

As we saw in the last chapter, the focus on French-English relations in Canada has decisively shifted from a preoccupation with the place of Quebec in Confederation to the respective position of the two historic communities within Quebec itself. The collapse of constitutional negotiations in mid-1971 demonstrated the impossibility of a reconciliation between Quebec and the rest of Canada by way of thoroughgoing constitutional reform. More significantly perhaps, the linguistic policies of the Quebec government cast doubt on the bilingual and bicultural alternative — or at least on the rationale for this alternative made by its supporters — as an effective response to Quebec nationalism.

As it was formulated by Pierre Elliott Trudeau and by the Royal Commission on Bilingualism and Biculturalism, the bilingual and bicultural alternative proceeded on three assumptions: (a) the historically-acquired rights of the English Canadian community in Quebec provided a bench-mark for the treatment of French Canadian minorities outside Quebec; (b) the linguistic and cultural regime within Quebec was relatively stable; and (c) the enhanced recognition of cultural and linguistic duality outside Quebec would dampen autonomist influences within the province. These assumptions have proved to be largely invalid. The respective position of the two communities within Quebec is in process of change as the French begin to act as a majority. Since the coming to power of Maurice Duplessis in 1936 successive Quebec governments appear not to have been much concerned with Francophone minorities outside the province, and since 1960 have responded to the bilingual and bicultural alternative as either a matter of secondary importance or as an irrelevant diversion from the more crucial question of a new distribution of powers between Quebec and Ottawa. In general, the relation between Quebec nationalism and the enhanced recognition of duality outside Quebec is much more complex than supporters of the bilingual and bicultural alternative have alleged, although Prime Minister Trudeau has recently begun to speak of federal policies toward bilingualism as a "contract" with the French Canadian community whereby the latter would give up separatism.

The new linguistic regime in Quebec and the emergent pattern of French-English relations in that province does not in my view challenge the essentials of Confederation. The government of Quebec is the most effective instrument for the survival of the French language and culture in North America and will no doubt by itself find the practical limits to these majoritarian policies. Neither need such changes as those embodied in Bill 22 cause any retreat from the bilingual and bicultural alternative as this relates to the institutions of the federal government rather than the French Canadian minorities outside Quebec. What is, however, needed is more realism from supporters of this alternative, a realism which dissociates dualism within the shared institutions of the government of Canada from dualism within Quebec or the other provinces and which recognizes that the strength of Quebec nationalism is decisively determined by other factors than the degree of recognition of cultural and linguistic duality outside that province.

The one aspect of the bilingual and bicultural alternative which is least often discussed is more crucial than the others to the survival of

Canada. This is the presence of French Canadians in crucial decision-making roles of federal political institutions, what Prime Minister Trudeau has inelegantly described as "French power". Trudeau wrote in 1962 ". . . with the sole exception of Laurier, I fail to see a single French Canadian in more than three-quarters of a century whose presence in the federal cabinet might be considered indispensable to the history of Canada as written — except at election time. . . . Similarly, in the ranks of senior civil servants, there is probably not one who can be said to have decisively and beneficially influenced the development of our administration. . . ."[20] As Prime Minister, Trudeau has done much to remedy the situation he so described and to provide an Ottawa focus for the ambitions of a significant number of able French Canadians. This counter-attraction for the French Canadian elites to the institutions of the province of Quebec and to Quebec nationalism would appear to be a prerequisite to the survival of Confederation.

With the emergence of the Parti Québécois as a significant electoral force each Quebec election becomes in a sense a verdict on the continuance of Confederation. However, as we saw in the last chapter the PQ has attempted to reassure Quebec voters, first, by the pledge that if it became the government it would not exercise the full powers of a sovereign state until after an affirmative result to this effect in a popular referendum, and second, by the projection that serious economic dislocations as a result of separation would be avoided through common market arrangements between Quebec and Canada. This latter seems unlikely. Any estimate of the economic consequences of the dismemberment of Canada must be based on inevitably arbitrary assumptions.[21] However, Canada as an economic unit was established through a complex of deliberate national policies and it is most improbable that the political ties of Confederation could be broken without some disruption of the economic links. Furthermore, sovereign nations do not enter into common-market relations indiscriminately and it has nowhere been demonstrated that such an arrangement would be to Canada's material advantage, and in particular to the advantage of western Canada, which would be after separation relatively more influential than before in Canadian affairs and therefore more capable of challenging the economic dominance of the central heartland. Economic nationalism has been central to the Canadian experience[22] and it is likely that after separation such impulses would be directed against Quebec. In general, it is most unlikely that Canada would be willing to confer on a sovereign Quebec a veto over the former's most vital economic policies.

The polarization of Quebec society on the national issue — either as this involves the relations between Quebec and the rest of Canada or French-English relations within Quebec itself — constitutes dangers for the Canadian federation. So long as Quebec elections are in effect plebiscites on the continuance of Confederation, there will be incentives for external political actors to involve themselves; these are absent in the case of the other provinces. Even more critically, the rapid changes in Quebec since 1960 appear to have resulted in the weakening of legitimacy in the province's political institutions to the extent that it may be possible to govern it if at all only by the use of measures which are by Canadian standards repressive. Vincent Lemieux has argued that in the past the legitimacy of the Quebec system of government had been based on charisma but that with the recent decline in the prestige of political leaders this legitimacy has been weakened without new supports based on rational-legal foundations in a Weberian sense being established.[23] Raymond Breton in his analysis of the October crisis of 1970 outlines a situation whose basic circumstances may well recur.[24] According to Breton, during the 1960s there had been a "redistribution of power and influence" in Quebec which had reached into almost every aspect of institutional life. This redistribution brought with it dislocations and confrontations between various groups which challenged both the legitimacy and the effectiveness of the public authorities. As the events of the fall of 1970 unfolded, there was created an arena for group confrontation in which under conditions of great uncertainty all the actors had incentives to escalate the intensity of the struggle. Furthermore, the public authorities controlling the régime's major instruments of physical coercion were of course participants on one side of the conflict.

As happened to some extent and for a relatively brief period in the fall of 1970, it is almost inevitable that if the ongoing polarization in Quebec leads to repression there will be a greater or lesser degree of polarization outside Quebec around these cleavages. Those who attempt to project the future often posit a situation in which the separatist option is accepted with virtual unanimity in Quebec, thus giving other Canadians — and of course the government of Canada — the clear-cut alternatives of either acquiescing or mobilizing the means of physical force at their disposal in an attempt to preserve Confederation. The circumstances as they are likely to develop may well be more complex than this.

The Central Heartland and the Peripheries

From the first the Canadian federal system has had to manage a persistent conflict between the interests of the central heartland provinces of Ontario and Quebec and those of the regions to the east and west of this heartland. Confederation was itself a Canadian initiative, i.e., an initiative of the political leadership of the United Province of Canada. Its proximate objective was to integrate into one national economy the formerly separate economies of Canada and the maritime colonies. But inherent also in the Confederation settlement were plans for the acquisition and subsequent development of the remaining British territories of North America west of the Great Lakes.[25]

So far as the Atlantic provinces are concerned, successive federal governments under Diefenbaker, Pearson and Trudeau have committed themselves in an increasingly explicit and increasingly comprehensive way to the narrowing of regional economic disparities. In this process the four most easterly provinces have come in large part to be clients of Ottawa. At the extreme, Prince Edward Island has ceased to be a province in other than in the narrowly juristic sense and in Edwin R.

Black's terms, "The economic development agreements of the sixties virtually turned the entire province into a federal receivership."[26]

It is the four western provinces rather than those bordering on the Atlantic which have come to impose significant strains on the Canadian Confederation. Beyond the specific grievances of the western provinces in economic matters, residents of that region came in the 1960s to feel themselves outside the mainstream of national life by the acceptance in Ottawa and among the elites of the central heartland of an orthodox formulation of Canada and the Canadian experience which had little relevance to western circumstances and traditions. Donald Creighton in an essay published in 1966 criticized this emergent orthodoxy which asserted the primacy of cultural values in these terms, "It grotesquely exaggerated the importance of language and culture: it absurdly minimized the importance of everything else."[27] This new way of looking at Canada was most fully embodied in the Reports of the Royal Commission on Bilingualism and Biculturalism and the views of Pierre Elliott Trudeau. This formulation involved relatively few changes for the West as such.[28] However in its general perspectives — as well as those which came to prevail within the federal government and the universities and media of central Canada — there was the assertion that cultural duality was *the* central element of Canadian life and that all responsible Canadians must put aside other concerns to deal with English-French relations. Western Canada never accepted this dualist view of Confederation.

Western Canada was from the first, and to a considerable extent remains, an economic colony of the country's central heartland. Chester Martin asserted of the transfer of Rupert's Land and the "North-Western Territory" to Canada in 1870, "It transformed the original Dominion from a federation of equal provinces each by a fundamental section (109 of the British North America Act) vested with control of its own lands, into a veritable empire in its own right, with a domain of public lands five times the area of the original Dominion, under direct federal administration."[29] Despite the conferring of the jurisdiction over natural resources on the prairie provinces in 1930, the relations between the central heartland of Canada and its western hinterland have continued to be regulated by the classic devices and principles of mercantilism:

— metropolitan policies confined the hinterland to the production of staple products exported from the hinterland in a raw or semi-finished state;

— metropolitan policies required the hinterland to buy the manufactured goods of the heartland;

— capital development in the hinterland was carried out by institutions controlled in the heartland;

— in external economic relations, the interests of the hinterland were characteristically sacrificed to those of the heartland;

— the hinterland and the heartland were physically linked by transportation facilities controlled by and operated for the benefit of the heartland;

— many of the crucial aspects of hinterland-heartland relations were carried out through the instrumentalities of large business organizations protected by the heartland authorities from both foreign and hinterland competition;

— there was a continuing pattern controlling the political authorities of the hinterland in the interests of the heartland.

From the challenge raised by Manitoba against the monopoly clause of the CPR charter in the 1880s onwards, there have been western Canadian revolts against that region's place in Confederation — revolts expressed through the various farmers' movements, Progressivism, the Social Credit and CCF parties, and some influential elements of Diefenbaker Conservatism. These pressures have from time to time had a considerable success as manifested in the cancellation of the C.P.R. monopoly clause in 1888, the Crow's Nest Pass differential, Liberal tariff reforms in the 1920s, the establishment of the Prairie Farm Rehabilation Administration in the Great Depression, the National Oil Policy of 1961 and the recent commitment of the federal Liberal government to freight-rate structures based on the costs of service and the removing of some of the restrictions on the provincial governments owning equity stock in chartered banks.

After the relatively weak showing of the federal Liberals in the general election of 1972, Prime Minister Trudeau caused to be convened a Western Economic Opportunities Conference in Calgary in July 1973 among leaders of the four western provinces and the central government. The provincial premiers were able to eliminate from the agenda of the Calgary meeting such matters as energy and resource development matters and fiscal equalization on which the interests of the individual western provinces diverged from one another, and thus to evolve a group of common recommendations on such matters as agriculture, transportation and economic development.[30] In his opening statement to the Conference the Prime Minister showed a shrewd realization of the basic issues at stake by contrasting the "old national policy" based on a "central Canadian 'metropole' with an agricultural and resource hinterland" with current needs for a "new national policy" of "more balanced and diversified regional growth throughout the country."[31] However, as the Conference proceeded the western Premiers were able to demonstrate that certain elements of Ottawa's industrial strategy — specifically measures to strengthen research and development and the established secondary manufacturing sector — were working to perpetuate or even to exaggerate the economic dominance of Central Canada.

The western revolt is multidimensional and involves challenges to eastern dominance in secondary manufacturing, publishing and broadcasting, banking, graduate education and research in the universities, the processing of certain western raw materials, and other matters.[32] In its essential elements, however, the western demand is for a more important role in the secondary manufacturing sector now concentrated in the Quebec City-to-Windsor complex and for the processing in the west of the region's natural resources to their finished state. This demand is a fundamental challenge to the industrial and commercial structure created by the older national policy.

Within the general context of western regionalism Alberta has emerged as a province *"pas comme les autres"*, largely but by no means exclusively because of its ownership of most of the Canadian supply of fossil fuels. The Alberta situation in terms of the general pattern of Canadian development is an intriguing one, since one of its economic sectors is based on the older agricultural staples and the other on the new staples of petroleum and natural gas. The distinctive position of Alberta within the Canadian federation may be outlined briefly:

— Alberta is Canada's newest province in terms of development. It was the last part of North America to come under agricultural settlement. Even more importantly for current circumstances, the discovery of petroleum at Leduc in 1947 decisively altered the structure of the economy in a way not experienced by any other province.[33]

— Alberta is a politically aberrant province.[34] Not since 1911 has Alberta had a provincial administration of the same political complexion as that in power federally. Since the attainment of provincial status in 1905 Alberta has had only three changes of government (1921, 1935, 1971) and there has been a pattern of one-party dominance in contrast with the vigorous inter-party competition of neighbouring Saskatchewan and British Columbia. Between 1921 and 1971 Alberta was governed by minor parties, and although the incumbent Lougheed government bears the Progressive Conservative label it is largely indigenous to the province and its revival owes little to the national party. With the possible exception of Douglas Harkness as Minister of Agriculture and later Minister of National Defence in the Diefenbaker government, Alberta has not produced an important national politician since R.B. Bennett and in the past generation not a major figure in the appointed federal bureaucracy. Thus attitudes and interests which are specifically Albertan have been channelled almost exclusively through the provincial government.

— prevailing political attitudes in Alberta are considerably to the "right" of those which dominate the federal government and the governments of the other provinces. Alberta is closer in time than other parts of Canada to the individualism of the agricultural frontier and the "new Alberta" has been developed through a free-wheeling variant of private enterprise.

— Alberta is much more dependent proportionately than other provinces on the exploitation of non-renewable natural resources. This makes the province less dependent than other Canadian jurisdictions on revenues levied on individual taxpayers. However, it is believed that the supplies of these resources, specifically conventional reserves of oil and natural gas, are depleting more rapidly than new resources will be discovered.

On the basis of its circumstances Alberta has developed a relatively coherent industrial strategy. This strategy involves the preservation of provincial autonomy in resource matters against federal influence and the sale of petroleum and natural gas at prices as near to those of the world market as possible. Efforts are being made to establish a strong petrochemical industry within the province. There are also provincial policies by which Albertans are given preferential treatment in terms of employment and investment opportunities in the development of the province's resources. Attempts are being made to disperse provincial economic development outside the Edmonton and Calgary metropolitan areas. With these policies directed rather specifically toward Alberta, the province cooperates with other jurisdictions of the region to secure changes in federal transportation and tariff policies.

One of the crucial differences between current western regionalism and that of earlier periods is that western interests and aspirations are now pressed almost exclusively through the provincial governments and have little effective outlet in Ottawa. Under Laurier and King the Liberal party was successful in coopting powerful provincial leaders from the prairies into the federal cabinet — witness such figures as Clifford Sifton, Charles Stewart, W.R. Motherwell, T.A. Crerar, Charles Dunning and James G. Gardiner. The last of such appointments was Stuart Garson, former Premier of Manitoba, as Minister of Justice in the St. Laurent cabinet in 1948. During the period from 1921 to 1935 the western Progressives gave able expression to western interests in the House of Commons and so far as Alberta was concerned the "Ginger Group", mainly from that province, gave a consistently effective expression to western views, particularly after the absorption of most of the Progressives from other provinces into the Liberals after the election of 1926; the recent Conservative MPs from Alberta have been on the whole ineffectual as spokesmen of Alberta interests. Although the Social Credit and CCF parties as they originated during the Depression were manifestations of western revolt, both movements were explicitly committed to effecting a Canada-wide political realignment.[35] The new circumstances were most dramatically illustrated at the Western Economic Opportunities Conference of 1973. None of the federal ministers directly involved with the central concerns of the Conference was a westerner, and this circumstance conferred on the provincial political leaders the exclusive franchise to represent western interests. While Otto Lang, Minister of Justice and Minister responsible for the Wheat Board, has recently emerged as a western leader of some influence in Ottawa, it is significant that unlike such predecessors as Sifton and Dunning and Gardiner, Lang did not begin from a base in provincial politics.

The consequences for Canadian federalism of the current western challenge to the dominance of the Ontario-Quebec heartland are hard to assess. The Pearson-Trudeau Liberals have governed Canada without providing an effective outlet in the party for attitudes and interests which are specifically western. This circumstance confers on the provincial political leaders the almost exclusive franchise to represent these interests and contributes powerfully to other provincialist influences. The success of the western provinces may well be decisively determined by the extent of their cooperation. The circumstances of these provinces are very different and their interests not totally compatible — viz: British Columbia's unique resource base; the divergent interests between "have" and "have not" provinces; the conflicting interests between petroleum-producing and petroleum-consuming provinces, etc. However, the relative insensitivity of the Trudeau government to the West and its lack of sophistication in dealing with western grievances appear to provide a firm foundation for regional unity and a powerful challenge to Central Canadian dominance of the Canadian economy.

Conclusions

Circumstances since 1960 have resulted in important changes in the three sets of relations crucial to Canadian nationhood — relations between Canada and the United States, between English and French, and between central Canada and its eastern and western peripheries. The complex of developments in this period have been manifested in a strengthening of the provinces relative to the national government. This provincialism has led to a more effective expression of regional and cultural demands in the west and Quebec respectively. As we have seen, the relation between provincialism and continentalism are equivocal but there is reason to believe that the first does not lead as directly to the second as is often supposed.

Notes

[1]*Quebec in Question*, translated by James Doake, James Lewis and Samuel, Toronto, 1971, p. 123.

[2]"Canada and the French-Canadian Question is really the Canadian question", Ramsay Cook in the Introduction to his book *Canada and the French-Canadian Question*, Macmillan of Canada, Toronto, 1966, p. 2.

[3]See for example Kari Levitt, *Silent Surrender: The Multinational Corporation in Canada*, Macmillan of Canada, Toronto, 1970 and Abraham Rotstein, *The Precarious Homestead*, new press, Toronto, 1973.

[4]For a journalistic account of these events see Walter Stewart "The Week of the Great Ultimatum", *Maclean's*, March 1972.

[5]Neither of these intentions was carried out.

[6]"Impact of Domestic Political Factors on Canadian-American Relations: Canada", 28 *International Organization*, Number 4, Autumn 1974, p. 612.

[7]U.S.I.S., Ottawa, March 16, 1972, (mimeo), p. 2.

[8]"Integration and Disintegration on the North American Continent", 28 *International Organization*, Number 4, Fall 1974, p. 873.

[9]See for example Part II of Richard J. Barnet's *Roots of War*, Penguin Books Inc., Baltimore, 1972. The economist Ronald Müller argues that the "globalization" of world business had made American macroeconomic policies increasingly ineffective. "A Qualifying and Dissenting View of the Multinational Corporation" in George W. Ball, Editor, *Global Companies: The Political Economy of World Business*, The American Assembly, Prentice-Hall, Englewood Cliffs N.J., 1974, pp. 21-41.

[10]Reprinted as "Canadian Nationalism and its Opponents" in Donald Creighton, *Towards the Discovery of Canada*, Macmillan of Canada, Toronto, 1972, pp. 271-285.

[11]See for example Hugh C.J. Aitken, *American Capital and Canadian Resources*, Harvard University Press, Cambridge, Mass., 1961, particularly pp. 135-137; Kari Levitt *Silent Surrender, op. cit.*, pp. 142-146; Albert Dubuc "The Decline of Confederation and the New Nationalism" in Peter Russell, Editor, *Nationalism in Canada*, McGraw-Hill of Canada, Toronto, 1966, pp. 112-132 and Garth Stevenson, "Continental Integration and Canadian Unity" in Andrew Axline *et al.*, Editors, *Continental Community: Independence and Integration in North America*, McClelland and Stewart, Toronto, 1974, pp. 194-217.

[12]"Foreign Direct Investment and the Provinces: A Study of Elite Attitudes", VII *Canadian Journal of Political Science*, No. 4, December 1974, pp. 630-647.

[13]*ibid.*, pp. 646-647.

[14]"Empire Ontario: The Problems of Resource Development" in Donald Swainson, Editor, *Oliver Mowat's Ontario*, Macmillan of Canada, Toronto, 1972, pp. 189-210. For Nelles' more comprehensive account see his book *The Politics of Development: Forest, Mines and Hydro-Electric Power in Ontario 1849-1941*, Macmillan of Canada, Toronto, 1974.

[15]See the various Reports of the Select Committee of the Ontario Legislative Assembly on Economic and Cultural Nationalism between 1972 and 1975 inclusive, particularly *Final Report on Cultural Nationalism*, 1975 and *Final Report on Economic Nationalism*, 1975.

[16]In an interview given to John Porteous of the *Financial Post* Premier Gerald Regan of Nova Scotia asserted a general preference for foreign as against Canadian investment in the province. His argument was that Canadian companies were primarily interested in the Canadian and inland American markets while foreigners were oriented to wider markets. *The Financial Post*, January 11, 1975, p. 4.

[17]For an analysis from the Ontario viewpoint see *Final Report on Economic Nationalism* of the Ontario Select Committee on Cultural and Economic Nationalism, *op. cit.*, Chapter 4.

[18]Early in 1975 the federal cabinet overruled a decision of the Foreign Investment Review Board prohibiting the takeover by an American company of a Quebec-based assembler of school bus bodies. The Minister of Industry, Trade and Commerce attributed the cabinet's decision to a change in views on the takeover by the Quebec government. *The Globe and Mail*, January 3, 1975.

[19]"Quebec: One Possible Scenario" in 28 *International Organization, op. cit.* pp. 943-948 and pp. 959-960. Latouche concludes ". . . this absence of a United States policy is a symptom of a widespread belief among the P.Q. leadership that [after independence] it should be easier to work out mutually satisfactory arrangements with Americans than with Canadians", p. 960.

[20]*Federalism and the French Canadians*, Macmillan of Canada, Toronto, 1968, p. 166.

[21]For some of the many such accounts see Latouche's article *op. cit.*; Antal Deutsch "The Political Economy of Québec Libre" in Lawrence H. Officer and Lawrence B. Smith, Editors, *Issues in Canadian Economics*, McGraw-Hill Ryerson, 1974, pp. 407-418 and Richard Simeon,, "Scenarios for Separation" in R.M. Burns, Editor, *One Country or Two?*, McGill-Queen's University Press, Montreal and London, 1971, pp. 73-94.

[22]See Donald V. Smiley "Canada and the Quest for a National Policy", VIII *Canadian Journal of Political Science*, March 1975, pp. 40-62.

[23]"The Political Party System in Quebec" in Dale C. Thomson, Editor, *Quebec*

Society and Politics: Views from the Inside, McClelland and Stewart, Toronto, 1973, p. 113.

[24]"The Socio-Political Dynamics of the October Events", in *Quebec Society and Politics, op. cit.*, pp. 213-238.

[25]For an account of the relation between the maritime and western objectives of Confederation as these were discussed in the *Confederation Debates* see Vernon C. Fowke, *The National Policy and the Wheat Economy*, University of Toronto Press, 1957, pp. 33-39.

[26]*Divided Loyalties: Canadian Concepts of Federalism*, McGill-Queen's University Press, Montreal and London, 1975, p. 233.

[27]"The Myth of Biculturalism" in *Towards the Discovery of Canada, op. cit.*, p. 257.

[28]The Report of the Royal Commission on Bilingualism and Biculturalism on Official Languages published in 1967 showed that according to the 1961 census of the 54 census divisions in Canada which had official-language minorities of 10 per cent or more only 6 were in the western provinces, and of these 4 were in Manitoba, one each in Saskatchewan and Alberta and none in British Columbia. While the Commission's recommendation was that public services be provided in both official languages not in these districts but in bilingual districts drawn up otherwise where the minority was more than 10 per cent, it is apparent that little was to be changed in the three most westerly provinces.

[29]*Dominion Lands Policy*, Edited and with an Introduction by Lewis H. Thomas, Carleton Library Series, McClelland and Stewart, Toronto, 1973, p. 9.

[30]See the documents jointly submitted by the Western premiers on Agriculture, Transportation and Economic and Industrial Development Opportunities.

[31]*Opening Speech*, July 24, 1973, mimeo.

[32]Perhaps the most coherent account of the western case from a public official was Premier Harry Strom's speech to the Federal-Provincial Constitutional Conference of February 1969, *Proceedings*, Queen's Printer, Ottawa, 1969, pp. 121-136. For a statement of western views from a group of young Albertans see John Barr and Owen Anderson, Editors, *The Unfinished Revolt: Some Views on Western Independence*, McClelland and Stewart, Toronto, 1971.

[33]For an account of these changes to 1857 see Eric J. Hanson, *Dynamic Decade: The Evolution and Effects of the Oil Industry in Alberta*, McClelland and Stewart, Toronto, 1958.

[34]See generally J.A. Long and F.Q. Quo, "Alberta: One Party Dominance" in Martin Robin, Editor, *Canadian Provincial Politics: The Party Systems of the Ten Provinces*, Prentice-Hall of Canada, Scarborough, 1972, pp. 1-26.

[35]Denis Smith "Prairie Revolt, Federalism and the Party System" in Hugh G. Thorburn, Editor, *Party Politics in Canada*, Third Edition, Prentice-Hall of Canada, Scarborough, 1972, p. 204.

# CHAPTER 8

CANADA: A FEDERAL COUNTRY

F.J.C. Vile began his book-length study of American federalism with this assertion, "The United States is a federal country in spirit, in its way of life, and in its Constitution".[1] Certainly the same judgement could be made of Canada. A federal country is one in which a large number of important human diversities are territorially grouped. In W.S. Livingston's terms, "Federalism is a function not of constitutions but of societies".[2] Yet in accepting such a formulation we should not slip into a determinism which regards federal government as no more than a reflection of underlying social, economic, cultural or other geographically-located differences. There is a complex set of reciprocal relations here in which the structures and processes of government sustain as well as are sustained by the particularisms outside the political system.

The analysis of Canada as a federal country attempts to relate the territorial diversities of Canadian life to the political institutions of federalism. This analysis will proceed by way of an elaboration of four assertions:

(1) There are significant differences in the political cultures of Canada's provinces and regions.

(2) Most private groups in Canada whose main or exclusive functions are to influence public policy are federal in their structures and processes.

(3) Most of the crucial public issues in Canada are raised, debated and resolved within the context of federal-provincial or federal-regional interactions and this circumstance frustrates the development of cleavages on nation-wide lines.

(4) The institutions of the federal government are not effectively representative of provincial and regional attitudes and interests and largely because of this these particularisms have come to be channelled exclusively or almost exclusively through the provinces, with a consequent decline in the relative power of the national authorities.

Provincial Political Cultures/Systems

The term political culture as used by contemporary scholars refers to the cognitive and affective orientations of citizens to the political systems in which they live.[3] Despite a considerable amount of study on Canadian voting behaviour[4], it is only very recently that there have been systematic attempts to investigate the provincial and regional political cultures and the results of these investigations, both published in 1974, are from data gathered as long ago as 1965-1968. The conclusions of Mildred A. Schwartz in her book-length analysis *Politics and Territory: The Sociology of Regional Persistence in Canada*[5] are too complex to be summarized here. Richard Simeon and David Elkins in their article on "Regional Political Cultures in Canada"[6] have a more precise focus on political efficacy and political trust. In respect to these crucial dimensions of political culture they conclude, "The polar regions are Ontario, British Columbia, and Manitoba, where we find high levels of trust and efficacy, and the Atlantic provinces, characterized by a pervasive disaffection from the political process. The other English-speaking groups fall close to the Ontario-BC-Manitoba pattern, though there are some differences between them. French-speaking Canadians fall nearer to the Maritime pattern. These variations are not a function of demographic or socioeconomic differences between the populations of provinces or language groups, even though such factors do independently affect the kinds of orientation we have analyzed".[7]

We know almost nothing about how the workings of the Canadian political system affect and are affected by the differences among provincial political cultures. (Although the measurement of political attitudes by survey research is designated as "behavioral", the "behaviour" that is being investigated is the politically inconsequential act of citizens in responding to the questions of political scientists.) Yet the linkage between attitudes and political behaviour, and in particular the behaviour of the more influential political actors, awaits investigation of the responsiveness of the Canadian political system, or systems, to popular attitudes and popular demands. In their textbook on Canadian government and politics, written within the conceptual framework of systems analysis, Richard J. Van Loon and Michael S. Whittington express some puzzlement that in spite of "rather weak input processes which should keep decision makers only marginally in touch with the environment", most citizens support the political system and its outputs are on the whole "satisfactory".[8] They explain this rather weakly by suggesting that, ". . . decision makers make 'right' decisions for the majority of Canadians because they are socialized to a set of values which are congruent with or similar to those held by the majority."[9] Yet this judgement ignores the crucial circumstance that the Canadian political elites, federal and provincial, are profoundly unrepresentative of their fellow citizens in those characteristics such as age, education, and socioeconomic status which are usually believed to be decisive in determining political attitudes. A more plausible, although admittedly purely speculative, explanation than that given by Van Loon and Whittington is that these elites are somewhat unresponsive to popular attitudes and that the citizenry for whatever reasons has a considerable tolerance for this unresponsiveness. Simeon and Elkins found that interprovincial differences in attitudes toward the political system were smaller at upper-status levels than at lower ones.[10] One might thus speculate that there are elements of a common political culture among the Canadian elite, including most importantly of course the senior decision-makers of the federal and provincial governments. It may also be guessed that the complexities of the federal system discourage political participation and the responsiveness of governments to popular demands: divided and disputed jurisdictional lines weaken accountability and the very intricacies of federalism give large advantages to those who understand or who can command the understanding of these processes.

In his pioneering essay on "The Canadian Political Cultures" published in 1974, John Wilson focuses his attention on the "dominant economic and social relationships" prevailing in each of the ten provinces rather than the affective orientations of citizens to their political systems.[11] These basic relationships (which are categorized in terms of pre-industrial society, industrializing society and advanced industrial society) sustain different kinds of party systems, the latter defined in terms both of the nature of party competition and of the ideological cleavages between parties. Specifically, Wilson argues that because of the different stages of economic and social development of the provinces, class politics in Canada cannot be developed as a unifying force on nation-wide lines.

Canadian Federalism and Interest Groups

To the extent that interest groups are successful in influencing public policies they must accommodate themselves to the structures by which power is organized within the political system. Yet is is almost inevitable that these influences will be to a greater or lesser degree mutual, and that governmental institutions will be shaped by, as well as shape, the structures and activities of these groups. Three essays in a recent collection, *Pressure Group Behaviour in Canadian Politics*,[12] vastly enhance our understanding of these relations:

— Helen Jones Dawson has discussed the profound impact of Canadian federalism among those interest groups concerned with matters where jurisdiction is divided among the federal and provincial governments (agriculture, labour, fisheries) or where jurisdictional lines are not clear (consumer protection, control of the environment).[13] Most of these organizations have federal structures in which the provincial federations dominate national headquarters; in fact many of these as described by Dawson appear to be in the strict sense of the terms confederal rather than federal, with individual members being able to participate nationally only through the provincial associations, national executives consisting of *ex officio* and other members of the provincial groups and the national associations being totally dependent for funds on the provincial bodies. In many cases the provincial groups tailor their policies to the provincial administrations and thus handicap themselves and their national headquarters in articulating national policies. Provincial associations are characteristically jealous of their national headquarters and resist locating these headquarters in Ottawa where they could be most effective or providing them with enough resources to develop professional expertise. Dawson concludes ". . . few national pressure groups have broken out of the vicious circle involving financing, membership and effectiveness, and as a result they are unable to offer services to their clientele which would demonstrate their effectiveness. It seems as if the centrifugal forces of federalism may have been more important to Canadian [pressure] groups than to similar American ones. . . ."

— in his essay "The Mining Industry and the Great Tax Reform Debate" M.W. Bucovetsky presents an intriguing case study of federalism and government — industry relations.[14] Historically, federal income tax legislation has been extraordinarily generous to the extractive industries. In its Report published in 1967 the Royal Commission on Taxation recommended that some of the most important of these privileges be eliminated within the framework of the Commission's proposals for a more rationalized and coherent system of federal taxation. Yet by the time tax reform was embodied in law in 1971 the mining industry had been able to retain most of the elements of its preferred position. The provincial governments were the most effective opponents of the Carter Commission's proposals as later modified in the federal White Paper on Taxation of August 1970. Bucovetsky explains the "potency" of the extractive industries in defending their tax privileges in terms of their "geographic localization". Thus "The mining and petroleum industries can bring intense political pressure to bear because mining shapes so many regionally distinct communities. Where mining exists, it tends to dominate. At the same time, the federal character of the constitution, the national diffusion of the industry, and its common viewpoint on federal tax policy increase the number of political pressure points on which local influences can be brought to bear".[15] It is argued that the major consequence of tax reform was to confirm the extractive industries more strongly than before as "the clients of the provinces". Subsequent to Bucovetsky's essay the vulnerability of these industries to the provincial governments has been manifested by radically higher provincial levies on these industries.

— David Kwavnick formulates and tests two significant hypotheses about the relationship between Canadian federalism and interest groups.[16] "First, it is hypothesized that the distribution of power between the central and regional governments influences the structure, cohesion and even the existence of interest groups; that is, that the strength and cohesion of interest groups will tend to mirror the strength, in their particular area of concern, of the government to which they enjoy access".[17] The validity of this proposition is confirmed by the history of the movements of university students in Canada during the 1950s and 1960s. The establishment of direct federal grants to universities in 1951 and the Canada Student Loan Plan of 1964 created the basis for a strong national movement of university students. However, Ottawa's 1966 action in withdrawing from direct support of the universities was crucial in the subsequent disintegration of the Canadian Union of Students. Prior to this event, the major

French-language universities had withdrawn from the CUS and the strength and aggressiveness of the Union Générale des Étudiants du Québec resulted largely from the purposeful policies of the Quebec government in respect to higher education and the determination of the province to oust Ottawa from direct influence in these matters. Second, "It may be hypothesized that if the federal distribution of powers does have consequences for the strength and cohesion of the interest groups enjoying access to the different levels of government, these groups may attempt to influence the distribution of powers between those governments. That is, the struggle for status, recognition and power between a national organization and a provincial organization may cause the leaders of these organizations to attempt to influence the distribution of powers between the federal and provincial governments".[18] Kwavnick shows the workings of these influences in the relations between the Canadian Labour Congress and the Quebec-based Confederation of National Trade Unions. The main thrust of CLC policy has been to strengthen the power of the central government, that of the CNTU to strengthen the powers of the Quebec authorities and these conflicting policies have reflected the access of the two labour groups to the two levels of government.[19]

The importance of interest groups in sustaining the federal system should not be underestimated. John Meisel has pointed out that in Canada and other western nations interest groups and other private organizations have come to perform many of the functions in interest-articulation and interest-aggregation formerly performed by political parties.[20] Peter Aucoin argues that recent changes in the policy process described in Chapter 3 as administrative rationality have the effect of bringing about "a more public role for pressure groups" in which, more than in the past, these groups must extend their activities from private contacts with departments to central agencies like the Prime Minister's Office and Treasury Board, formulate their demands in the context of competing demands and government priorities and engage in public discussion.[21] As the scope of public activity expends, more and more matters formerly of private concern are brought within the sphere of public decision and new groups are formed to promote and defend such interests, some of these financed largely or wholly by government itself. Yet because most of these interest groups have a greater or lesser amount of business to do with both levels of government, their structures and processes will inevitably be federal if action in influencing public policies is to be effective. Thus the boundaries of province and nation are crucial in delineating the territorial areas of action not only of governmental institutions but of private groups as well.

Federalism and the Resolution of Public Issues

As we have seen throughout this book, most of the major public issues in Canada are raised, debated and resolved within the context of federal–provincial relations. In relation to, for example, environmental pollution, health and welfare services, international economic relations and fiscal policies the major and decisive actors are the elected and appointed officials of the federal and provincial governments.

The structures and processes of political power are influential not only in determining *how* issues are resolved but also *what* issues come onto the political agenda for resolution and what kinds of cleavages and alliances develop in respect to issue-resolution. In the latter connection, Canada has been more resistant than other nations to the development of political cleavages on left-right lines.[22] Within the individual provinces such cleavages are frustrated to the extent that provincial politicians are able to rally their constituents against the real or alleged challenges of federal power. In the national political arena the system works to polarize Canadians on the basis of province or region rather than class.

Those on the left of the Canadian political spectrum have adopted various stances toward federalism and the persistence of territorial rather than class cleavages. With Marxist circles in Quebec there has been some debate as to whether Quebec Francophones constitute a "class".[23] Within the democratic left there have been several contradictory formulations of the relation between Canadian federalism and socialism:

— *an impatience with federalism.* The main thrust of the democratic socialist tradition in Canada from the 1930s to the 1960s was an impatience with federalism and a disposition to effect change through national economic planning.[24] The kind of analysis is most explicitly formulated in John Porter's *Vertical Mosaic*.[25] Porter argued that Canadian federalism contributed to the entrenchment and consolidation of private economic power. The system encouraged immobilism and frustrated "the emergence of that social power which lies in the creative energies of the whole society". The scope of political action was limited because of the real or alleged importance of cultural and regional interests and this makes it difficult "for a professional political career to develop" and results in "avocational politics with a conservative tone".

— *the two-nations formulation.* The NDP has been more sympathetic than the other national parties in Canada to recent Quebec nationalism.[26] Gad Horowitz more clearly than anyone formulated an attempted reconciliation between Canadian socialism and the two-nations view of Canada. He wrote: "Urbanization, by creating similar social conditions in every region nationalizes politics. Conflict among classes which are equally distributed among all regions replaces conflicts among regions with differing class structures. But it must be recognized that urbanization may be laying a foundation for *two* arenas of class politics — an English arena and a French arena — rather than one Canadian arena."[27] The general solution is a unitary or quasi-unitary English Canada with a special status for Quebec "We must have the courage to combine *accommodation* of the French particularism with *resistance* to intra-English particularisms."[28]

— *socialism where it may be practical.* In an article published in 1961 Pierre Elliott Trudeau argued that "other things being equal, radicalism can more easily be introduced in a federal society than a unitary one".[29] Trudeau's argument was a criticism of the general disposition of the democratic left in Canada to assert the power of the central government: "But the true socialist will also be a humanist and a democrat and he will be quick to realize that Canada is very much a federal society from the sociological point of view; people from various parts of Canada do hang together on a regional basis which very often supersedes the class basis."[30] Thus the "different stages of political maturity" in Canada can best be exploited in the cause of reform by a strict regard for the constitutional powers of the provinces. In his 1974 article which has already been quoted in this chapter John Wilson has come to conclusions very similar to those of Trudeau. Essentially Wilson's argument is that because of the different levels of economic development of the provinces a national political realignment on left-right lines and strong national policies toward reform are impossible.

— *egalitarianism as the reduction of regional economic disparities.* In recent policy statements the NDP government of Saskatchewan has argued that the most critical dimension of inequality in Canada is regional. Premier Allan Blakeney asked at the Federal-Provincial First Minister's Conference on Energy in January 1974, "Are we all prepared to give more than lip service to the concept of an equal Canada, a Canada of equal wealth and equal opportunity from sea to sea?"[31] At this Conference the Saskatchewan government presented a comprehensive plan for the reduction of regional economic disparities.

Those who have wished or have prophesied a national political realignment in Canada on left-right lines have characteristically been on the left of the political spectrum. However, in 1967 there appeared a short book, *Political Realignment* by Ernest C. Manning,[32] then nearing the end of his long career as Premier of Alberta. Manning defended the idea of bringing together in a new national party all those Canadians who believed in what he called "Social Conservatism", and called on the Progressive Conservative party to organize itself on these lines. This proposal seems not to have been seriously debated by the party, although in his paper to the Progressive Conservative caucus in November 1974 Robert Stanfield explicitly rejected "the Manning thesis which urges polarization of political viewpoints in this country".[33] The Leader of the Opposition went on to say, "In Canada, a party such as ours has a harmonizing role to play, both horizontally in terms of resolving conflicts between regions, and vertically in terms of resolving conflicts between Canadians in different walks of life."[34]

In general then, Canada is in such an essential way a federal country that national political realignment on left-right lines appears impossible. Within individual provinces of course elements of such a polarization can and do occur.[35] Yet in their external relations the leaders of provincial governments will almost inevitably subordinate ideological consistency to longstanding provincial interests.

Federal Society: Federal Institutions of Government

Canadian institutions of government shape and are shaped by the underlying territorial particularisms of Canadian society. However, these provincial and regional interests may to varying degrees find an effective outlet either through the provinces or the institutions of the national government. Karl Loewenstein has made a useful distinction between "interstate federalism" and "intrastate federalism".[36] Under the first alternative the primary device for coming to terms with regional interests is a division of governmental powers between central and provincial/state authorities, with the latter responsible for most or all of those matters about which people in these jurisdictions differ most markedly. Intrastate federalism sees many of the most important territorial particularisms channelled through the operations of the national government. It is the argument of this section that the Confederation settlement of 1864-67 contained very large elements of intrastate federalism, that over the decades these have given way to interstate federalism and that the narrowing of the range of matters in respect to which Ottawa can decide authoritatively and without provincial consultation or consent is the major "structural defect of Canadian federalism".[37]

The Confederation settlement contemplated a centralized federal system. Most of what were then regarded as the major functions of government were vested in the Dominion. But although this settlement provided for the dominance of the central government, it seems to have been taken for granted that provincial and regional interests would find an effective outlet through these institutions centred in Ottawa. P.B. Waite has asserted that, "Cartier, like Sir Etienne Taché, was confident, perhaps too confident, that French-Canadian privileges could be defended better by French-Canadian ministers in a central government than by a local [provincial] legislature."[38] Waite's general argument is that those who designed the Confederation settlement did not think of the "federal principle" as being embodied in the coordinate jurisdictions of the Dominion and provincial governments, but rather in the composition of the central legislature, and in particular "in the balance between the House of Commons on the one hand and the Senate on the other". In Loewenstein's terminology, there was a preference for intrastate over interstate federalism.

To trace the decreasing sensitivity of the national government to influences which are specifically provincial or regional would be to write the history of Canadian political institutions over more than a century. Yet it may be useful to look in a summary fashion at this dimension of national institutions in terms of how these emerged at Confederation and where we have arrived in the mid-1970s:

The Senate

(a) At Confederation. The composition of the upper legislative chamber was by far the most contentious issue resolved by the Fathers of Con-

federation. It was from the first agreed that the House of Commons
would be formed on the basis of representation in proportion to the
population of the provinces and, as Waite has argued, the federal principle was in large measure embodied in the relations between the
House and the Senate, with the latter body formed of equal numbers of
members from Quebec, Ontario and the two Maritime provinces.

(b) *Today.* Whatever the usefulness of the Senate, it has never been an
effective outlet for provincial attitudes and interests. In his authoritative study of that institution Robert A. Mackay concluded: "The Senate
... has rarely been appealed to as the champion of provincial or sectional rights and, even when appealed to, has not consistently supported claims to such rights."[39] For example, no sophisticated observer
would look to the Senate as a primary channel for contemporary
Quebec nationalism or western regionalism.

The Parties in the House of Commons

(a) *At Confederation.* It was not until the end of the nineteenth century
that two cohesive parties in the House of Commons came into being.[40]
As in the pre-Confederation period, legislative parties during the early
years of the Dominion were coalitions, often of a relatively loose nature,
around several political leaders and characteristically these leaders had
a base of support that was exclusively provincial or regional.

(b) *Today.* It is unnecessary to emphasize the relative cohesiveness of
political parties in the contemporary House of Commons, particularly
in the case of the government party. Although there are countervailing
influences at work to enhance the independence of private Members,
the long-term trends have been in the other direction. So far as the
government party is concerned, the dominance of the prime minister is
strengthened by the circumstance that many MPs owe their election
largely to his popularity, his powers of bringing about a dissolution
and his control over many preferments which Members desire.

The Prime Minister and his Cabinet

(a) *At Confederation.* An historian has said of the first government of
the Dominion:

> It would have been wrong to suppose that Macdonald was leading a
> centralized party. He was rather the chief of a coalition of groups in
> which each obeyed a regional leader, rather than Macdonald himself. To
> keep the confidence of the majority, Macdonald knew he must negotiate
> with these leaders. In this spirit the cabinet was to be, in a certain sense, a
> chamber of political compensation, where the provincial spokesmen
> traded their support in return for concessions to their regions.[41]

(b) *Today.* Canadian Prime Ministers have come increasingly to dominate their cabinets on the basis of their continuing personal popularity
with the mass electorate.[42] There are many reasons for this dominance.
The procedures of the national party conventions by which leaders are

chosen provide for voting by secret ballot and do not encourage convention strategies directed toward forming or coming to terms with provincial or regional blocs. The prime minister has easy and immediate access to the mass media when he wants it. The size of contemporary cabinets and the complexity of issues coming before them decrease the possibilities of genuinely collegial decisions. Particularly under Prime Minister Trudeau, the staff services available to the head of government in the Prime Minister's Office and Privy Council Office have increased enormously.[43] Although recent Prime Ministers have not neglected entirely the principles of regional and provincial balance in constituting their cabinets, they have tailored these requirements to their personal predispositions. More than any of his predecessors, Louis St. Laurent emphasized competence rather than regional representation. John Diefenbaker, after the election of 1958 in which Quebec returned 50 of 75 Progressive Conservative MPs, refused French Canadians important portfolios outside Transport. Since 1968 Pierre Elliott Trudeau has vastly strengthened French Canadian influence, particularly by conferring on Francophones portfolios usually monopolized exclusively or almost exclusively by the other group. A crucial aspect of prime ministerial dominance is the relative decline of the position of cabinet ministers as representatives of particular provinces or regions, and since the departure of the late James G. Gardiner and of Jack Pickersgill it is difficult to think of any minister who has had a base of provincial or regional support independent of the head of government. Further, as the late Donald Gow pointed out, ministers have virtually no staffs involved with the regions or provinces they purportedly represent, and the departments under their control are "oriented to stress values associated with industrial and social structures and aggregates" rather particular cultures and regions.[44]

The Federal Bureaucracy.

(a) At Confederation. At the time of Confederation and for some decades after, the departments of government had a very high degree of autonomy in the recruitment of federal civil servants and positions were characteristically filled by political patronage.[45] Thus to the extent that the cabinet included members of the various provinces and regions — and the early bureaucracy was in a relative sense geographically dispersed — there were strong influences at work to keep the federal civil service broadly representative of regions and provinces.

(b) Today. The establishment of the merit system in the Canadian civil service, particularly with the reform measures of 1918, has had the effect of decreasing the representativity of the federal public service on provincial or cultural lines. This impact has been abundantly demonstrated in terms of the declining proportion of Francophones, particularly in the professional and executive categories, from the end of the First World War[46] until recent efforts were undertaken by the Pearson and Trudeau governments to remedy this imbalance.

The relative incapacity of national political institutions to represent interests and attitudes which are specifically provincial or regional is decisively influenced by the workings of the Canadian electoral system. In a classic article published in 1968 Alan C. Cairns demonstrated both that the federal electoral system contributed to regional cleavages in national politics and made the issues so raised extraordinarily divisive and difficult to resolve.[47] One of Cairns' basic points was that this system grossly distorts the size of party representation in the House of Commons in terms of the popular votes that parties have won in particular provinces or regions; to take a crucial example, in general elections from 1921 to 1965 inclusive there had been 5.6 times as many Liberal as Conservative MPs elected from Quebec, although in terms of the proportion of the popular the ratio was 1.9 to 1. Since Cairns wrote, Alterta has succeeded Quebec as the major dissident province and in the last two (1972, 1974) general elections has not sent a government MP to the House of Commons, although in each case roughly one Albertan in four has voted Liberal. More generally, the electoral system reinforces the Liberals as an Ontario/Quebec party and the Progressive Conservatives as the party of what Peter Newman has called "Outer Canada". In the 1974 general election the Liberals received 49.7 per cent of the popular votes and 71.0 of the seats in the two provinces of the Canadian heartland, and the Conservatives 44.2 per cent of the votes and 65.0 per cent of the seats from the rest of Canada.

To the extent that the workings of the electoral system deny particular provinces or regions effective and continuing representation on the government side of the House of Commons, these areas will understandably come to believe they are left out of crucial decisions in national affairs. There is reason to believe this alienation is cumulative, if only because the parties which are weak in particular parts of the country will have difficulties there in gaining the services as candidates or otherwise of able and ambitious people. The dominance over provinces and regions by particular parties encourages national politicians in some cases to neglect particular areas and in others to seek their support through unduly generous promises or policies. Most importantly from the viewpoint of Canadian federalism, the lack of adequate provincial representation on the government side of the House of Commons confers on the provincial administrations of such areas the almost exclusive privilege of speaking for these sentiments and interests.[48]

It would be inaccurate to attribute the strength of the provinces in the Canadian federal system exclusively to the unrepresentativity of the institutions of the central government, to the dominance of interstate over intrastate federalism. As we have seen throughout this book, other influences have been working in the same direction — the relative failure of national economic policies from the mid 1950s onward to secure adequate conditions of employment, price stability and growth; the sophisticated aggressiveness of the "new Quebec" in pressing provincial interests and the demonstration effect of such efforts on the other provinces; the continuing circumstance that many of the most important public policies and public concerns are exclusively or mainly within provincial rather than federal jurisdiction. However, the relative incapacity of national institutions to reflect interests and attitudes which are explicitly provincial or regional would seem to be an important element in the federal balance. If we compare Canada with the United States, the American national government has a significantly wider range of powers than its Canadian counterpart. Yet — largely perhaps because of the separation of executive and legislative powers, the relative lack of integration in the executive branch and the absence of party cohesion in Congress — state and local interests find a more effective outlet in Washington than do territorial particularisms in Ottawa.[49]

Contemporary provincialism in Canada has two major thrusts. The first is to safeguard provincial autonomy from federal control, though not in most cases from federal financial assistance, in respect to matters which are, or which are alleged to be, within provincial jurisdiction. The second is to extend provincial influence over federal policies which have, or which are alleged to have, a direct impact on the provinces. The most explicit rationale for this variant of Canadian federalism was contained in Premier Jean Lesage's presentation to the Federal-Provincial Conference of November 1963.[50] According to the Quebec leader's prescription for "cooperative federalism" Ottawa would show a fastidious respect for provincial jurisdiction. But because almost all federal economic policies influenced the provinces in the carrying out of their responsibilities, these policies should be formulated by "joint Federal-Provincial organisms" related to "tariff structures, transportation and even monetary policies".[51] There was here a classic statement of the view that what's mine is my own and what's yours is ours. A more recent Ontario formulation of essentially the same view proposes a tripartite division of governmental functions as: (a) federal, in respect to which federal responsibility is exclusive; (b) national, which are to be regulated by joint federal-provincial action, even though those are mainly or exclusively within the constitutional jurisdiction of the national government; (c) provincial, which are to be free of federal influence or control.

The current drive of the provinces to involve themselves in matters within federal jurisdiction is defended on plausible grounds. Obviously, for example, federal policies in respect to international air routes and tariffs have a direct and immediate impact on important provincial responsibilities. Obviously too, interprovincial telecommunications are of concern to the provinces. The federal regulation of banking and federal efforts to reduce regional economic disparities help or hinder the individual provinces over important ranges of provincial responsibilities. Similarly, federal policies towards research in the many forms this activity takes are of vital provincial concern. Federal policies in immigration and federal controls over foreign investment cannot be matters of indifference to provincial administrations. Examples could be multiplied almost without end. Yet there is a noticeable lack of the spirit of reciprocity in current manifestations of provincialism. The borrowing on foreign capital markets by the provincial governments and their crown agencies and local governments has direct implications for Canada's balance of payments, yet provincial reactions to the request of the then Minister of Finance in June 1973 that some cooperation be effected here appears to have been hostile.[52] At the Federal-Provincial Conference of First Ministers in April 1975 Ontario introduced a paper, "Suggestions for the Federal Mini-Budget", lecturing the federal Minister of Finance in a very specific way as to how he should act — less than forty-eight hours after the province's own budget had been brought down, presumably without Ottawa's involvement. The provinces characteristically regulate such matters within their own jurisdiction as higher education and natural resources without seeking federal advice, while becoming mightily agitated when the federal authorities carry out *their* constitutional responsibilities by resorting to unilateral action.

Canada cannot effectively be governed unless *both* levels retain an important range of jurisdiction where they can act decisively and be held accountable to their respective electorates. The current excesses of provincialism are narrowing this range of federal power to a dangerous degree. Federal powers are justified on two distinct but intricately related grounds:

— to deal with what economists call "interjurisdictional externalities",[53] in the Canadian setting the impact of provincial policies on persons and governments outside the boundaries of these respective provinces. We have little specific economic knowledge of these externalities. What impact, for example, do Ontario fiscal policies have for other Canadians? What are the consequences for other Canadian provinces of those provincial governments who maintain relatively low standards of health and education services? What is the incidence on the Quebec economy of Ontario policies to narrow material disparities within the latter province? How and in what ways is the discretion of the provinces in respect to taxation and various kinds of public regulation constrained by what other provinces do in these matters? The current situation in respect to energy demonstrates in an extraordinarily dramatic way the necessity of decisive federal action to temper the control of some provinces by others. From the early days of the Dominion onward, Ontario has been the most persistent and consistent defender of provincial autonomy. Yet recent events have clearly revealed Ontario's vulnerability to the actions of the two provinces who supply her with fossil fuels and Ontario has emerged as a defender of coherent federal policies toward energy.

— to narrow interprovincial disparities in respect to economic opportunities, public services and rates of taxation. The government of Canada has a continuing responsibility for interprovincial equalization in its various dimensions. The incumbent federal administration has accepted this responsibility in more explicit and more comprehensive forms than any of its predecessors. Yet it may be speculated that over the long run federal politicians will have a declining enthusiasm for acting as paymaster to the provinces, for taxing Canadians and dispensing funds to the provincial administrations with decreasing influence over how these moneys are spent and few political rewards to compensate for the pain inflicted on the voters through taxation.

The current situation has been crisply summarized in an article in the February 1973 issue of *Maclean's:*

> There's a basic difference between power and image. Image is going on television a lot. Power is doing things. Federal politics is image. Provincial politics is power. For the last 10 years we're all been looking in the wrong place. We thought Ottawa ran the country. [The provincial premiers] . . . know better. Ottawa runs itself. They run the country.

For most Canadians outside Quebec perhaps, federal politics is a preferred spectator sport to provincial. Yet in a 1968 election survey when a sample of Canadians responded to the qeustion "As far as you are concerned personally which government is most important in affecting how you and your family get on?", 31 per cent indicated federal, 40 per cent provincial and 15 per cent local, and only in Nova Scotia did respondents assert the primacy of the federal over the provincial (in Newfoundland 38 per cent favoured each of those levels).[54] Ottawa's declining effectiveness is in part masked by the increasing numbers of employees in the civil service — an increase between 1961 and 1971 of from 20.9 to 25.1 per 1,000 employees in the Canadian labour force while in the same period the provincial civil services grew from 15.4 to 23.4 per 1,000.[55] However, in a qualitative sense much of the activity in the federal government has shifted away from public regulation and the provision of services to individuals. Confused and indecisive officials have developed insatiable appetites for information as a soporific substitute for action and these appetites are fed by veritable mountains of costly research, much of it of an indifferent quality. Pseudo-social scientists with only the shakiest knowledge of the past or the present are employed in pretentious attempts to design "alternative futures". There is much futile search for consensus where none exists. The work of those officials and agencies with operational responsibilities is distracted and obstructed by elaborate procedures whose alleged aim is to rationalize the governmental process. Highly trained professionals busy themselves in designing increasingly elaborate indicators of social progress in the naïve belief that mankind has never heretofore attempted to evaluate how he was doing. The inspirational and propaganda apparatus of the federal government grows — at its most presumptuous, employed in fabricating value systems purportedly better than those to which we have become accustomed, and in more specific ways lecturing Canadians as to how they might improve their attitudes and behaviour in respect to sexual equality, exercise, nutrition and the conservation of energy. Truly "Ottawa runs itself" — but just barely.

In summary, Canada is in the most elemental way a federal country and can be governed if at all only by institutions and processes which reflect these underlying territorial particularisms. Canadians in the past and today have exhibited considerable qualities of ingenuity and mutual forebearance and support in the design and operation of the complex political apparatus made necessary by such diversities. The fulfillment of the Canadian political experience can be nothing more and must be nothing less than realizing the historic promise of "Peace, Order, and Good Government".

Notes

[1]*The Structure of American Federalism*, Oxford University Press, 1961, p. 1.
[2]*Federalism and Constitutional Change*, Oxford, at the Clarendon Press, 1956, p. 4. See generally Chapter 1 "The Character of Federalism".
[3]See the classic study by Gabriel A. Almond and Sidney Verba, *The Civic Culture*, Princeton, Princeton University Press, 1963.
[4]See John C. Courtney, Editor, *Voting in Canada*, Prentice-Hall of Canada, Scarborough, 1967 and issues of the *Canadian Journal of Political Science* since it began in 1968.
[5]McGill-Queen's University Press, Montreal and London, 1974.
[6]7 *Canadian Journal of Political Science*, September 1974, pp. 397-437.
[7]*ibid.*, pp. 432-433. Reprinted by permission of the author.
[8]*The Canadian Political System: Environment, Structure and Process*, McGraw-Hill of Canada, Toronto, 1971, p. 495.
[9]*ibid.*
[10]p. 431.
[11]"The Canadian Political Cultures: Towards a Redefinition of the Nature of the Canadian Political System" 7 *Canadian Journal of Political Science*, September 1974, pp. 438-483.
[12]Edited by A. Paul Pross, McGraw-Hill Ryerson Series in Canadian Politics, Toronto, 1975.
[13]"National Pressure Groups and the Federal Government", pp. 27-58. See particularly pp. 30-35.
[14]pp. 87-114.
[15]p. 105.
[16]"Interest Group Demands and the Federal Political System: Two Canadian Case Studies", pp. 69-86.
[17]*ibid.*, p. 72.
[18]*ibid.*
[19]*ibid.*, pp. 77-82.
[20]"Recent Changes in Canadian Politics", in Hugh G. Thorburn, Editor, *Party Politics in Canada*, Second Edition, Prentice-Hall of Canada, Scarborough, 1967, pp. 35-36.
[21]"Pressure Group and Recent Changes in the Policy Process" in Pross, *op. cit.*, pp. 182-187.
[22]See generally R.R. Alford, *Party and Society: The Anglo-American Democracies*, Rand-McNally, Chicago, 1963.
[23]For the affirmation of this thesis see Jacques Dofny and Marcel Rioux, "Social Class in French Canada", in Marcel Rioux and Yves Martin, Editors, *French-Canadian Society*, Vol. 1, Carleton Library, McClelland and Stewart, Toronto, 1964, pp. 307-318. For a challenge to the Rioux-Dofny argument see Gilles Bourque and Nicole Laurin-Frenette "Social Classes and Nationalist Ideologies in Quebec, 1760-1970" in Gary Teeple, Editor, *Capitalism and the National Question in Canada*, University of Toronto Press, 1972, pp. 186-210.
[24]On the intellectual origins of the CCF see Michiel Horn "The League for Social Reconstruction, 1932-36" in VII *Journal of Canadian Studies*, November

1972, pp. 3-17. Horn concludes of Canada's variant of the Fabian Society; "Centralism was intended to destroy the privileges of Big Business ... It was typically an LSR conviction ... that the most basic differences in Canada related not to section, language, creed or race, but to social class." p. 4.

[25]University of Toronto Press, 1965, Chapter XII "The Canadian Political System", particularly pp. 379-385.

[26]See David H. Sherwood, *The N.D.P. and French Canada*, Unpublished research document of the Royal Commission on Bilingualism and Biculturalism, Ottawa, n.d. (1966?).

[27]"The Canadian Identity: 3 Articles by Gad Horowitz", *Canadian Dimension Reprint*, Winnipeg, n.d. (1966?), p. 6. Emphasis the author's.

[28]*ibid.*, p. 8. Emphasis the author's.

[29]"The Theory and Practice of Federalism" in Michael Oliver, Editor, *Social Purpose for Canada*, University of Toronto Press, 1961, pp. 371-393.

[30]*ibid.*, p. 378.

[31]Statement to Conference, mimeo, p. 2. For the Saskatchewan design see *Towards a New Canada* submitted to the Conference.

[32]McClelland and Stewart, Toronto.

[33]Quoted in "There is more to life than raising the gross national product", *The Toronto Star*, Nov. 30, 1974.

[34]*ibid.*

[35]On British Columbia for example see Walter D. Young "The NDP, British Columbia's Labour Party", in John Meisel, Editor, *Papers on the 1962 Election*, University of Toronto Press, 1964, pp. 181-200 and Martin Robin "British Columbia: The Politics of Class Conflict", in Martin Robin, Editor, *Canadian Provincial Politics*, Prentice-Hall of Canada, Scarborough, 1972, pp. 27-68.

[36]*Political Power and the Governmental Process*, University of Chicago Press, 1965, pp. 405-407. R.L. Watts has made a similar distinction between "pluralist" and "parliamentary" federal systems. "The basic axiom of the pluralist federations has bene the notion that political authority should be dispersed among multiple centres of power: not simply between central and state institutions, but also among a variety of central institutions." The examples of this are Switzerland and the United States. Parliamentary federations are characterized by "the concentration of central power in a cabinet continuously responsible to a majority in the popularly elected chamber" as of course in Canada and the other federations of the Commonwealth. "Second Chambers in Federal Political Systems" in *The Confederation Challenge*, Ontario Advisory Committee on Confederation, Background Papers and Reports, Vol. II, Queen's Printer, Toronto, 1970, p. 327-328.

[37]See my article of this title in 14 *Canadian Public Administration*, Fall 1971, pp. 326-343.

[38]*The Life and Times of Confederation 1864-1867*, University of Toronto Press, 1962, p. 110. I am very much in debt to Waite's original analysis in Chapter 8 "Confederation and the Federal Principle".

[39]*The Unreformed Senate of Canada*, Revised Edition, Carleton Library, McClelland and Stewart, Toronto, 1963, p. 113.

[40]For the early parties see the excellent article by Escott Reid "The Rise of National Parties in Canada" in Hugh G. Thorburn, Editor, *Party Politics in Canada*, Second Edition, Prentice-Hall of Canada, Scarborough, 1967, pp. 15-22.

[41]Jean Hamelin, *The First Years of Confederation*, Centennial Historical Booklet, No. 3, Centennial Commission, Ottawa, 1967, pp. 3-4. Reproduced by permission of Information Canada.

[42]Denis Smith, "President and Parliament: The Transformation of Parliamen-

tary Government in Canada" in Thomas A. Hockin, Editor, *Apex of Power: The Prime Minister and Political Leadership in Canada*, Prentice-Hall of Canada, Scarborough, 1971, pp. 224-241. For a critique of Smith's prime minister-as-president thesis see Joseph Wearing, "President or Prime Minister", *op. cit.* pp. 242-260.

[43]See generally the two valuable articles by G. Bruce Doern "Recent Changes in the Philosophy of Policy-Making in Canada" 4 *Canadian Journal of Political Science*, June 1971, pp. 243-264 and "The Development of Policy Organizations in the Executive Arena" in G. Bruce Doern and Peter Aucoin, Editors, *The Structures of Policy-Making in Canada*, Macmillan of Canada, Toronto, 1971, pp. 39-78.

[44]*Canadian Federal Administrative and Political Institutions: A Role Analysis*, Unpublished Ph.D. dissertation, Queen's University, 1967, p. 114.

[45]See Robert MacGregor Dawson, *The Civil Service of Canada*, Oxford University Press, 1929, Chapter II "The Spoils System and Proposals for Reform 1867-80".

[46]For the relation between the working of the merit principle and Francophone representation in the federal public service see *Report of the Royal Commission on Bilingualism and Biculturalism*, Book 3A, *The Work World*, Ottawa, Queen's Printer, 1969, Chapter VI.

[47]"The Electoral System and the Party System in Canada 1921-1965", 1 *Canadian Journal of Political Science*, March 1968, pp. 55-80.

[48]At the Western Economic Opportunities Conference held in Calgary in July 1973 Prime Minister Trudeau in effect conferred this franchise on the western premiers, as none of his own cabinet ministers dealing with matters of central concern to the conference was a westerner. Mackenzie King handled western grievances in a much more sensitive way, primarily through the cooption of influential western leaders into his cabinet. See H. Blair Neatby, *William Lyon Mackenzie King, Volume II 1924-1932, The Lonely Heights*, University of Toronto Press, 1963, particularly Chapter 2.

[49]For an elaboration of this point see my article *The Structural Problem of Canadian Federalism*, *op. cit.* pp. 339-340.

[50]*Proceedings*, Queen's Printer, Ottawa, 1964, pp. 44-46.

[51]*ibid.*, p. 46.

[52]*The Toronto Star*, July 14, 1972.

[53]Wallace E. Oates, *Fiscal Federalism*, Harcourt Brace Jovanovich, 1972, pp. 46-47.

[54]John Wilson, *The Canadian Political Cultures*, *op. cit.* p. 444.

[55]J.E. Hodgetts and O.P. Dwivedi, *Provincial Governments as Employers*, McGill-Queen's University Press, Montreal and London, 1974, p. 190.

CHAPTER 9

IS CANADA A NATIONAL COMMUNITY?

Is Canada a national community? Much contemporary thought emphasizes the affective orientations of citizens to their country, including their response to national symbols, as the decisive element of nationhood. We are all familiar with Renan's assertion that a nation is "un plébiscite tous les jours" and the definition of the respected student of contemporary nationalism Rupert Emerson is of the same order, "The nation is a community of people who feel that they belong together in the double sense that they share deeply significant elements of a common heritage and that they have a common destiny for the future."[1]

By what one might call the "feeling criterion" proposed by Renan and Emerson, Canada hardly qualifies as a nation. The results of survey research as presented by Mildred Schwartz indicate the persistence of local and regional sentiments and the weakness of national loyalties.[2] Unlike the United States and most of the less viable principalities of the Third World, our constitution does not include a grandiloquent statement of purportedly transcendent national principles, nor do we have a charter-myth. We are permissive in allowing our fellow citizens, provincial governments and business establishments the flags they prefer as allegiance or anticipated commercial advantage dictate. July 1 is a statutory holiday — although we cannot agree on a name for it — but some Canadians get more emotional satisfaction out of celebrating St. Jean Baptiste or Christopher Columbus, and no doubt a few here and there Queen Victoria, Joey Smallwood or Idi Amin. And when a gracious and forebearing lady visits one of the countries under whose constitution she continues to be head of state she is met by some Canadians with adulation, others with indifference and a few with overt discourtesy.

But if nationhood is sharing and Canadians share few common sentiments, what then are the bonds of Canadian association? It is meaningless to say that we share a common territory — citizens of, say, Windsor share a common territory with their fellow citizens of Halifax or Yellowknife but not with their neighbours in Detroit only because the national boundaries are drawn that way. And it is not very helpful to say that Canadians share a common citizenship without some account of the obligations and privileges of that citizenship. There is perhaps an alternative definition of nationhood along lines such as these:

A national community is based on a sharing of claims, both individual and collective. These claims are made against individual citizens, private groups and public authorities within the nation and against individuals and public and private collectivities outside the nation. These claims are honoured by a structure of political relationships which acknowledges no superior legal authority.

If we accept this definition of national community in terms of shared claims we can find the reality of Canadian nationhood in such places as the Statutes of Canada and the Public Accounts of the Government of Canada. Here are some of the things Canadians share.

(1) A national Criminal Code and code of criminal procedure. In these are embodied some of the most important mutual claims of citizens and the Canadian community. (Canadians also share a common system of penitentiaries for the incarceration of those guilty of the graver offences against these laws.)

(2) A national commitment to the Canadian welfare state to be implemented through joint action of the federal, provincial and local authorities. The most important elements of this national welfare state are the various programs of income-maintenance and the removal of financial barriers between citizens and their access to medical, hospital and educational services. Also, and this is usually given less prominence than it deserves, various actions of the federal government have contributed to the end that Canadians can move freely throughout the nation without thereby suffering a termination of health and income-security benefits.

(3) A national commitment to the alleviation of regional economic disparities.

(4) A national commitment to interprovincial fiscal equalization.

(5) A national commitment to the public support of the arts, letters and sciences, along with other creative activities in broadcasting, film-making, etc.

(6) A national commitment that, wherever practical, Canadians will have access to the government of Canada and its departments and agencies in the official language the citizen chooses.

(7) A recent national commitment to a single price for petroleum in Canada, and, through Ottawa's recent action in refusing to allow the resources industries to deduct provincial levies from their income as determined for federal tax purposes, a national assertion that Canadian resources and the revenues accruing from their development are to be shared on a nation-wide basis.

The list given above is by no means exhaustive and other items might be added in terms of environmental pollution, public legal aid, foreign ownership, the extension of broadcasting services to remote areas, leisure and recreation etc. For example, only in terms of national community is it possible to explain or defend the magnitude of the budget of Indian Affairs compared with the absence of Canadian assistance to other traditional peoples undergoing the strains of modernization elsewhere in the world. Or again, only national community justifies Ottawa's help for Newfoundland fishermen and its lack of help for people in similar circumstances living on nearby St. Pierre and Miquelon.

It is unnecessary to apologize for emphasizing these mundane activities of government as crucial to Canadian nationhood. The piecemeal and hesitant quest of the Canadian community for justice and the alleviation of avoidable suffering proceeds somewhat in terms of the old hymn, "For not with swords loud clashing/Nor roll of stirring drums/But deeds of love and mercy/The heavenly Kingdom comes." We are still some steps away from "the heavenly Kingdom" in Canada, and the seemingly incorrigible disposition of our politicians — who are surely no worse than the rest of us — towards chicanery, insensitivity, stupidity and sometimes corruption continues to block our advance. It is also perhaps sentimental to describe the delivery of promises made by these politicians in election-heat as "deeds of love and mercy". But progress has been made, and I would argue that in those ways where the quality of life is better in Canada than in the United States our advantages can be attributed almost entirely to this country being more effectively and humanely governed.

There are considerable dangers that the government of Canada will retreat from some of our national commitments, particularly those of a costly nature. As we saw in Chapter 5, Ottawa has recently breached the principle of the full equalization of provincial revenues to the national average and has limited its contributions to provincial medical insurance schemes and to post-secondary education. The motives for these actions are understandable. But similar and further retreats by federal governments under great pressures to control their expenditures may challenge Canadian nationhood in its most essential elements. In a crucial dimension I would expect much heightened pressures for autonomy or even separation in Quebec if Ottawa's determination in respect to regional disparities and/or interprovincial fiscal equalization is weakened. Québécois are, I think, too astute and too aware of their individual and collective interests to be bought off in such circumstances by any psycho-therapeutic gimmickry like Abraham Rotstein's notion of conferring on them "the *symbolic* right to independence".[3]

But is national community as I have defined it compatible with Canadian federalism and with the territorial particularisms which undergird our federal institutions of government? Certainly, if it is recognized that the claims of Canadians do not need to be precisely the same or met in precisely the same way in all parts of the country. There *is* a national interest in all children having access to education but this does not mean that Ottawa should dictate the curricula of elementary and secondary schools. There *is* a crucial national commitment to removing the financial barriers between Canadians and access to physicians' and hospital services but this should not frustrate provincial and local experimentation in these matters. Justice dictates that those charged with criminal offences should have access to legal services, but it is probably on the whole better that the federal government gives financial support to varying kinds of provincial legal aid schemes rather than attempt to prescribe uniform nation-wide arrangements. On the basis of past Canadian experience, I would guess that the range of national commitments will be extended more rapidly than otherwise if provincial and local jurisdictions are strong and aggressive, and it is reasonable to suppose that we would not have advanced as quickly as we have towards nation-wide hospital insurance and medicare if socialist governments of Saskatchewan had not pioneered in both programs. In similar terms, recent newspaper reports tell of the callousness of physicians and hospitals to the dying but when we advance here it is more likely than not that chanes will begin at the local level and spread through larger jurisdictions.

I should define progress in meeting human claims as the extension of the geographical limits within which such claims are honoured.[4] It was, I think, Gunnar Myrdal who said that we shall have attained a real international community when some world authority levies an international income tax, however nominal the rate of this tax at its inception — and presumably expends the proceeds of this levy at its discretion. The institutional restrictions of the international order and the limited capacity of contemporary humans for compassion makes this some distance away. But in the meantime we should not casually accept retreats from the progress which has been made by particular national communities. In the Canadian situation, such progress has involved not only national action but also that of the provinces in the equalization of the range and quality of services among their constituent local governments. This latter kind of equalization has been achieved in significant part because provincial revenues were themselves secured by Ottawa.

National Community and Canadian Scholarship

The ideas outlined above express what is perhaps a minority position among Canadian scholars. The last part of this book is a critique of the views of some of these scholars on the national question, specifically the views of political scientists in the English-speaking universities of Canada. For better or worse, Canadian social scientists — with the possible exception of economists — have little direct influence in national affairs, and it is tempting to write off their debates as having no consequence except to the participants. Yet the often quoted words of Keynes in the last paragraph of *The General Theory of Employment, Interest and Money* have relevance to contemporary Canadian circumstances:

> . . . the ideas of economists and political philosophers, both when they are right and when they are wrong, are more powerful than is commonly understood. Indeed the world is ruled by little else. Practical men, who believe themselves to be quite exempt from any intellectual influences, are usually the slaves of some defunct economist. Madmen in authority, who hear voices in the air, are distilling their frenzy from some academic scribbler of a few years back. . . .[5]

The ideas and attitudes which I criticize have found, or are likely to find, acceptance well beyond the limits of the academy and thus are of some significance for the conduct of our national life. There have been, I think, three errors: (1) among English-speaking Canadian intellectuals, an indiscriminate support for Quebec nationalism — and in some cases for the more extreme forms of this nationalism; (2) a two-nations formulation of Canada and the Canadian experience which almost totally neglects non-cultural factors; and (3) a more recent disposition to affirm that Canada is no more than a loose collection of provinces. Each of these formulations denies that Canada is, can be or should be in any genuine sense a national community.

The Support for Quebec Nationalism

The circumstances of the new Quebec from 1960 onward found the intellectual community of English Canada ill-prepared. Traditionally, it had neglected the French-English dimension of the Canadian experience.[6] Just as importantly, modern social science as it had developed in the United States suggested that the ongoing processes of modernization throughout the world would diminish eth-nonationalisms if not eliminate their influence entirely.

Under the new circumstances of Quebec, to whom or to what should English Canadian scholars respond? We might have applied two alternative tests. The first was the cogency of the analyses made by those who claimed to be spokesmen for Quebec and the justice of their demands. But we might have decided to be more hard-boiled and listen to those whom we judged to be the most *powerful* representatives of the new Quebec. Unfortunately, some of us were unwilling to apply either of these tests, but rather proceeded on the basis of what Harry S. Crowe has called the "feeling myth", the contention that "feeling is superior to thinking." Crowe says, "Look down any university corridor today and there is a good chance you will see an academic walking with his hands up in the air, hoping that a student will poke a rolled up man-ifesto into the small of his back. No matter how outrageous a proposal, it will have its defenders whose single point will be that it must have merit because those advancing it feel so strongly about it."[7]

The feeling myth has nowhere been more fully demonstrated than in the seriousness with which Pierre Vallières has been taken by some members of the English Canadian academic community. Vallières' emotional and incoherent book of 1968, *Nègres blancs d'Amérique*, translated in 1971 as *White Niggers of America*[8], was thought fit to be reviewed in such a solemn academic publication as the *Canadian Journal of Political Science* and found its way onto the reading lists of many university courses on the apparent assumption that this was an expression of the violence done to a sensitive *Québécois* psyche by the very existence of the Canadian Confederation. (An otherwise discriminating scholar, David Cameron, describes *White Niggers of America* as an "extraordinary autobiographical and intellectual statement by a preternaturally sensitive Québécois intelligence"[9].) Then in 1972 was published in English translation Vallières' new book

Choose![10], a recantation of his previous revolutionary position and a defence of his membership in the bourgeois Parti Québécois. Another event to be celebrated by English Canadian scholars! Now there is a full-length biography of this equivocal figure whom some of my academic colleagues have elevated almost to the revolutionary stature of a Lenin, a Castro or a Ho Chi Minh. In similar spirit, some university teachers have accepted with undue solemnity Léandre Bergeron's revolutionary caricature of Quebec history to the relative neglect of the serious Marxist scholarship during a long career of Stanley Ryerson. And on the other side of the ideological fence, Gilles Lalande's cogent defence of Canadian federalism published in 1972[11] appears to have been ignored almost completely.

In their sympathy for the peaceful variant of Quebec nationalism, some English Canadian scholars have been willing to involve themselves in domestic Quebec affairs. Even those who have never heretofore shown much support for electoral reform in Canada are mightily exercised about the impact of the Quebec electoral system on the fortunes of the Parti Québécois. Every student of politics knows, or should, that under a system where legislators are elected by pluralities from single-member districts there is a greater or lesser degree of incongruence between the proportion of popular votes that parties receive in particular political communities and the proportion of seats they win in the legislature. It has nowhere been demonstrated that such a system is more inappropriate to Quebec than to other jurisdictions which have accepted it. David Cameron asserts that the working of these procedures in the Quebec provincial election of 1973 ". . . inevitably calls into question the adequacy and fairness of the political institutions which must be the major instruments in resolving the relations between the two national communities [in Canada] humanely and with justice."[12] But under the Canadian constitutional system the legislature of Quebec has full powers to design the provincial electoral system to meet Quebec needs, presumably without the advice and consent of those who live elsewhere. Significantly, the PQ itself has not laid on the Quebec electoral system the kinds of strictures made by Cameron and others. This system in the 1973 election conferred on the party the benefit of the virtual elimination of the Union Nationale and Créditiste parties — who between them received nearly one-sixth of the popular votes but only two Créditiste seats in the National Assembly. One might have expected those latter parties and their supporters to have established a claim for better treatment in the views of Cameron and other critics of the Quebec electoral regime.

One of the most presumptuous judgements about contemporary Quebec made by an English Canadian scholar is contained in the last chapter of Denis Smith's *Bleeding Hearts . . . Bleeding Country*.[13]. Smith's book is an analysis of the Quebec crisis of 1970. He raises the question, "Who among the prophets speaks for the genuine interests of the Quebec public?" Smith considers three candidates — Pierre Elliott Trudeau, Pierre Vallières and René Levésque. In the context of some discussion of the credentials of each of these men he dismisses the first two on these grounds, "In the end Pierre Vallières is as complacent and myopic about the benevolence of technical progress as Pierre Trudeau: because they are both, finally (as are we all), children of the liberal dream." Smith does not say straightforwardly, "I prefer René Lévesque and the Parti Québécois for these and these reasons and I hope they come to power and destroy Canada." By what oracle does he distinguish "the genuine interests of the Quebec public" from other interests which are not to be taken into account? That of Hegel? of Marx? of Toynbee? of Mel Watkins? And if the objective is self-determination for Quebec does it not follow that those of us who live outside the province should let this decision be made without stentorian pronouncements on what we have defined as domestic Quebec affairs?

Smith and Cameron are very much exercised that the separation of Quebec will be resisted by violence from the outside. Smith's analysis in fact asserts that this was what the October crisis of 1970 was all about. However, in my view the measures taken by the governments of Canada, Quebec and Montreal were grotesque over-reactions by insecure and frightened men in the face of what is now known to be a minuscule revolutionary movement.[14] These measures were rightly condemned as gross violations of the civil liberties *of Canadian citizens.* The hoax that has been perpetrated on both the supporters and opponents of such actions was that those governments — and in particular the government of Canada — acted in a purposeful and decisive way. Certainly the repression was short lived and so far as I know no one has yet discovered a settled plan to smash the separatist movement. (If there was as much support for the revolutionaries as has been claimed, there would have inevitably been more resistance to the measures that were taken.) Further, there is common agreement that in the short run at least the most powerful threat to the survival of Canada is the Parti Québécois rather than the revolutionary movements, and certainly neither the Quebec nor the federal governments has shown any recent disposition to combat the PQ with other than the normal means of political competition.[15]

Cameron argues for a great Canadian debate on actions to be taken in the event that Quebec opts for separation, with the preferred outcome of this debate being a national decision not to use violence to frustrate such a result. He would hope such an assurance to be embodied in the constitution. Significantly, no Canadian politician has so far as I know suggested that violence be so employed, and to Cameron's dismay most of these people as well as the rest of us have refused to debate what should be done under hypothetical contingencies.

Eugene Forsey said in 1964, ". . . if Quebec really wants independence, we have neither the right nor the means to stop her. All we can do is to sit down and do some very hard bargaining on the terms. . . ."[16] It would, I think, be unwise to be any more specific than this or to embody in fixed Canadian policy, or even more regrettably in the constitution, what the government of Canada could or should do in the event of a separatist government coming to power in Quebec. Those who argue otherwise have written a very bland scenario in which the verdict of the Quebec people has been manifested in a peaceful and unequivocally democratic way. There are other possibilities and we should not bind in advance the hands of a future Canadian government which may have to respond to them. Unless one takes a pacifist stance of a somewhat extreme nature, that under no circumstances is it permissible to use physical coercion — even by the constituted political authorities — it is a matter of prudential political judgement whether and to what extent force should be employed in the defence of particular values in particular circumstances. Because the future cannot be foreseen, the debate Cameron suggests would be most unfortunate.

The Two-Nations Canada

Those who have sympathized with Quebec nationalism have posited a two-nations Canada with each of its elements being united internally and separated from the other by language and culture. The major difficulty of this formulation was not the positing of Quebec as a nation but rather the premise that cleavages within the rest of Canada are of no significant consequence.

Michael Stein's article "Federal Political Systems and Federal Societies", published in 1968,[17] was an able expression of the two-nations view. The article proceeds on the basis of W.S. Livingston's analysis, which informs this book, that federal political systems must be sustained by federal societies and are an articulation of the geographically-based diversities of such societies. But Stein gives this analysis a new twist in his statement, "It seems to me that the concept of 'federal society' can be most usefully applied *if it is confined to* a society which is conterminously both 'polyethnic' and mutilingual in makeup."[18] However, he nowhere provides evidence of the primary of ethnic/linguistic factors and there is nothing to support this contention in the literature of federalism he cites.

There is no way to demonstrate analytically the overriding importance of cultural/ethnic/linguistic differentation in federal systems or more generally to determine the intensity of human conflict by reference to the source of such conflict. So far as federations are concerned, about all one can say is that when ethnic/linguistic cleavages are reinforced by other territorial particularisms, centripetal forces will be stronger than otherwise.[19] Obviously, the primary of language and ethnicity does not explain the American Civil War, the secessionist movement in Western Australia in the 1930s, the break-up of the West Indies Federation or the strains that the provinces other than Quebec have imposed from time to time on the Canadian Confederation.

Stein's definition of federal society is ideological. If one can define away non-cultural differences it is possible to proceed directly to a two-nations view of Canada. By the early 1970s Canadians had almost ceased to debate the national question in these terms. In an article published in 1973 Hugh Thorburn attempted to revive this debate.[20] He had two worries. The first was "the disaffection of French Canada, which . . . is solidifying into a general preference for special status." Second, the economy was performing badly in terms of increases in foreign control, the rapid depletion of natural resources, persisting regional disparities, high rates of unemployment and the absence of opportunities for innovators, entrepreneurs and scientists. The primary cause of these difficulties, argued the article, "are the present constitutional arrangements".

Thorburn's solution was a straightforward one, the constitutional embodiment of the two Canadian nations in a system where Quebec had most of the powers of a sovereign state but was associated with the rest of Canada organized on quasi-unitary lines. The central government would need to retain jurisdiction over "the defence forces, the currency, the postal service, customs and excise, control of navigation and shipping". Quebec would have all the other powers of government. Thorburn realized that the provinces other than Quebec might oppose "their own demise into one large whole" and so, "To make it politically feasible it might be necessary to retain the provincial governments in, of course, a reduced form. They would perform useful work as an intermediary level of government, performing more local responsibilities than their present ones."

How can a political scientist of Thorburn's demonstrated sophistication in the working of the Canadian political system believe that the country outside Quebec can be organized on unitary lines? At the time he was writing, as at many times in the past, Ontario was in fact waging a more determined and effective struggle against federal power than was Quebec. If Canada outside Quebec could be so organized would our economic difficulties — and Thorburn is particularly concerned about regional disparities — be significantly relieved? Surely in such unitary countries as the United Kingdom, France and Italy regional disparities persist. Would the "have not" provinces be able to make their claims as effectively as now if Quebec were removed from their number? And if the narrowing of regional disparities requires some redistribution from Ontario to these provinces it is a question as to whether Ontario with, say, 45 per cent of the population of "rump-Canada"[21] would be more influential in a unitary system than in one in which it was one of nine provinces.

Thorburn's facile constitutional solution is defensible only on the premise that cleavages of other than a linguistic/ethnic nature are politically inconsequential.[22] This assumption is invalidated by the Canadian political experience and by the operative influences in the Canadian political community. The *second* Canadian nation, English Canada, cannot be created by scholarly fiat.

Canada as a Loose Union of Provinces

The passing of the two-nations debate appears to be leading to a new orthodoxy that Canada is no nation at all but rather a loose union of provinces. In a broad sense, these views parallel and to an extent justify the general trends towards provincialism which have been analyzed elsewhere in this book.

John Wilson's 1974 article "The Canadian Political Cultures", to which several references have been made in earlier chapters, comes to this conclusion, ". . . There does not seem to be any compelling reason for not accepting the proposition that Canada is in reality a loose collection of 10 distinct political systems. By definition, therefore, we have at least 10 political cultures."[23] Wilson thus defines away the eleventh political system — that of Canada. There are after all national elections, national parties, a national legislature, executive and judiciary. How and why then is this political system/culture put by?

Wilson's general analysis is based on the alleged powerlessness of the federal government in relation to the provinces from which he posits the latter as independent political systems:

First, ". . . the transfer payments which the intervention of the federal government effects between the richer and the poorer provinces may be seen as entirely analogous to a system of foreign aid between independent political entities where Canada is a sort of Canadian UNESCO." The analogy, however, breaks down when we compare the dimensions of Ottawa's redistribution within Canada and outside the nation. It is true, according to the 1975-'76 Estimates, that the budgets of the Canadian International Development Agency and the Department of Regional Economic Expansion are of roughly the same magnitude — $553.5 millions to $460.4 millions, eliminating loans in each case. But beyond that Ottawa expected to dispense $2,399.6 millions to the "have not" provinces in equalization payments. Wilson mentions UNESCO to which the Canadian contribution was to be $2.1 millions compared with $511.0 millions in cash payments to the provinces for post-secondary education, apart from the proceeds of tax-points transferred. Such comparisons might be multiplied — $3.3 millions from Ottawa to the World Health Organization but $2,408.3 millions to the provinces for hospital and medical insurance alone. And Wilson ignores the very large sums of money transferred by Ottawa to individual Canadians for which there is no analogy on the international scene.

Second, the provinces are free to spend the moneys from Ottawa as they see fit, "since the practice of giving conditional grants has been largely abandoned". But this is untrue.

Third, "Nor can Ottawa's unlimited taxing power be regarded as a serious inhibition to the provinces' freedom of action." This would be great news for provincial treasury departments! It is just not so.

As in Stein's article, Wilson's analytical definition turns out to be ideological. Both are distortions of the Canadian reality.

At the end of his recent book *Divided Loyalties: Canadian Concepts of Federalism*, Edwin R. Black propounds a new constitutional solution for Canada which he designates as "Special Status for All".[24] Black's primary value is flexibility, by which he means the complete freedom of Ottawa and each of the provinces to conclude any bargain they can agree on about their respective powers and responsibilities.

The restrictions on such flexibility have been imposed by politicians who have sold the English-speaking voter "a gold brick labelled 'equal status for every province' ". Despite such restrictions, the federal system has in fact been responsive in some cases to the special needs of particular provinces and regions and "The whole course of federal-provincial relations throughout this century demonstrates that every province has wanted special status for itself." According to Black, they should have it. The device would be the inter-delegation of powers between the two levels and he would apply to this the amendment formula of the Victoria Charter, although his logic is to go further than the Charter and allow *any* province the right of delegation.[25]

Black is quite explicit in asserting that his version of flexibility may result in the destruction of Canada. If Quebec by such procedures, and with the consent of a majority of its people, negotiates its way out of Confederation this is permissible. But even more questionably in my view, flexibility is to be applied to the continuing federal system. For example, "If the Western provinces can persuade the federal government to take over university education in exchange for a freer hand in natural resources, why not?" There are pretty compelling reasons "Why not". Under the existing constitutional arrangements a "freer hand" for the western or other provinces in respect to resources could mean only one or both of two things: (1) limitations on federal powers to control the quantity and price of such resources, most crucially petroleum and natural gas, as these pass into interprovincial or international trade; (2) limitations on Parliament's unlimited powers to tax the resource industries. Alberta would no doubt be willing to let Ottawa run its universities — although why the federal authorities would agree to do so is obscure — and much else in the province besides, in exchange for such concessions. But has Black realistically considered the results for the rest of Canada of such a bargain?

Not surprisingly, Black's prescription is based on the explicit denial of a national interest. He says of possible objections to his proposal, "In the absence of an agreed and explicit set of national values, any national interest objection is impossible to sustain because of its basic definition in situational expediency." However, the provincial interest rings through loud and clear. But what is the evidence for an "agreed and explicit" set of *provincial* values? I have argued earlier in this chapter that there *are* national commitments and national values — for example, the commitment to remove the financial barriers between individual citizens and their access to health services. Black nowhere makes a case for the primacy of provincial over national values or interests.

Conclusion

Those who have the disposition to resist the disintegration of the Canadian community from within or its absorption into the maw of continentalism from without have for too long been on the defensive. We have been too slow in formulating the credentials of this community, too bemused by our academic colleagues who would define it out of existence, too preoccupied with the emotional, symbolic and cultural dimensions of nationhood. So far as the political order is concerned, there is only one Canadian question and that is how the nearly twenty-three million people who live within our national boundaries can establish and sustain governmental institutions which are at once humane, effective and responsive. As I have tried to show, such national values and national commitments as Canadians have are concretely embodied in particular measures for honouring the mutual claims of citizens and governments on each other. If the present claims can be sustained and new claims from time to time added, Canadian nationhood may need nothing more.

Notes

1 *From Empire to Nation: The Rise to Self-Assertion of Asian And African Peoples*, Beacon Press, Boston, 1960, p. 95.

2 See her *Public Opinion and Canadian Identity*, Fitzhenry and Whiteside, Scarborough, Ontario, 1967 and *Politics and Territory: The Sociology of Regional Persistence in Canada*, McGill-Queen's University Press, Montreal and London, 1974.

3 "Postscript" in Abraham Rotstein, Editor, *Power Corrupted: The October Crisis and the Repression of Quebec*, new press, Toronto, 1971.

4 I am indebted for this general idea to a recent discussion with A. Milton Moore of the University of British Columbia.

5 Macmillan, London, 1949 Edition, p. 383.

6 To take an obvious but important example, in the late Robert MacGregor Dawson's influential textbook on Canadian government.

7 "Liberals, New Democrats and Labour", in Laurier Lapierre, Jack McLeod, Charles Taylor and Walter Young, Editors, *Essays on the Left*, McClelland and Stewart, Toronto/Montreal, 1971, p. 214.

8 McClelland and Stewart, Toronto.

9 *Nationalism, Self-Determination and the Quebec Question*, Macmillan of Canada, Toronto, 1974, p. 170.

10 Translated by Penelope Williams, new press, Toronto.

11 *Pourquoi le fédéralisme*, Hurtubuise/H.M.H. Montréal.

12 *Nationalism, Self-Determination and the Quebec Question, op. cit.*, p. 138.

13 M.G. Hurtig, Edmonton, 1971.

14 My views on the October crisis have been very much influenced by John Gellner's *Bayonets in the Streets: Urban Guerillas at Home and Abroad*, Collier-Macmillan, Don Mills, Ontario, Chapter 4, although I do not wish my conclusions to be attributed to this author. For Gellner's analysis of the revolutionary capabilities in Quebec in 1970 see pp. 92-98.

15 An exception, unfortunate but not very crucial perhaps, is the recent denial to the separatist daily *Le Jour* of certain federal government advertising.

16 In Gordon Hawkins, Editor, *Concepts of Federalism*, Canadian Institute on Public Affairs, Toronto, 1965, p. 26.

17 Reprinted in J. Peter Meekison, Editor, *Canadian Federalism: Myth or Reality*, Methuen of Canada, Toronto, 1968, pp. 37-48.

18 *Ibid.*, p. 40. Emphasis mine.

[19]See the sensitive discussion of other than cultural factors making for provincial autonomy in multicultural federations in Ronald L. Watts, *Multicultural Societies and Federalism*, Studies of the Royal Commission on Bilingualism and Biculturalism, Information Canada, Ottawa, 1970, pp. 70-76. Watts lists these as: "(1) regional economic interests; (2) variations in the size and wealth of regional groups within a society; (3) clashes between the radical and conservative outlooks of different regional groups; (4) regional differences in degrees of modernization." p. 21. He concludes "It appears then that in many of these [multicultural] federations local economic interests and the desire to legitimatize a number of local spoils systems have contributed to the overtly linguistic, racial or cultural demands for provincial autonomy." p. 23.

[20]"Needed! A New Look at the Two-Nations Theory", LXXX *Queen's Quarterly*, Summer 1973, pp. 268-273. For a critique of this analysis on grounds I find largely unacceptable see David Kwavnick, "Quebec and the Two Nations-Theory: A Re-examination", LXXXI, *Queen's Quarterly*, Autumn 1974, pp. 351-376.

[21]The phrase is that of Antal Deutsch. See his article "The Political Economy of Québec Libre" in Lawrence H. Officer and Lawrence B. Smith, Editors, *Issues in Canadian Economics*, McGraw-Hill Ryerson, Toronto, 1974, pp. 407-418.

[22]Even Eugene Forsey, who during the 1960s waged a steadfast battle against various proposals for reforming the constitution on bi-national lines came close to this view in a speech to the 1964 Couchiching Conference. "The problems of Canadian federalism, in my opinion, are not, for the most part problems of federalism at all, but of Canadian dualism. If the whole country were solidly English-speaking, or solidly French-speaking, we should probably be able to settle questions of distribution of power between the Dominion and the provinces as we settle questions of public and private ownership, by asking simply 'Which can do the better job in this particular field at this particular time'?" Gordon Hawkins, Editor, *Concepts of Federalism*, Canadian Institute on Public Affairs, Toronto, 1965, p. 22.

[23]VII *Canadian Journal of Political Science*, September 1974, p. 444.

[24]McGill-Queen's University Press, Montreal/London, 1975, pp. 232-234.

[25]It will be remembered from Chapter I that the Victoria Charter would have allowed the constitution to be amended insofar as the division of legislative powers was concerned by a proclamation of Parliament and a majority of the provinces, of which the latter must include:

(1) every Province that at any time before the issue of such proclamation had, according to any previous general census, a population of at least twenty-five per cent of the population of Canada;

(2) at least two of the Atlantic Provinces;

(3) at least two of the Western Provinces that have, according to the then latest general census, combined populations of at least fifty per cent of the population of all the Western Provinces.

SELECTED BIBLIOGRAPHY

Students may find these bibliographical references helpful:

1. *Federalism and Intergovernmental Relations in Australia, Canada, the United States and other Countries: A Bibliography*, Institute of Intergovernmental Relations, Queens' University, 1967, (mimeo.).
2. *Canadian Public Administration Bibliography*, Compiled by W.E. Grasham, and Germain Julien, The Institute of Public Administration of Canada, Toronto, 1972 and Supplement 1, 1974.
3. J. Peter Meekison, Editor, *Canadian Federalism: Myth or Reality*, Second Edition, Methuen of Canada, Toronto, 1971, pp. 467-486.

Students of Canadian federalism will find useful whatever daily newspaper(s) they read as primary sources. *Le Devoir* is invaluable for events in Quebec and the daily business section of the Toronto *Globe and Mail* useful for fiscal and economic matters, as is the weekly *Financial Post*. Those particularly interested in fiscal affairs will also find useful the publications of the Canadian Tax Foundation, including the annual publication *The Public Finances*. At the academic level almost every issue of these quarterly publications contains one or more articles directly or indirectly related to Canadian federalism: *Canadian Journal of Political Science*, *Canadian Public Policy*, *Journal of Canadian Studies*, *Canadian Public Administration*. Also useful is *Publius: The Journal of Federalism*, published by the Center for the Study of Federalism at Temple University in Philadelphia; *Publius* has had its major focus on American federalism but is now broadening this to include a more prominent comparative dimension.

General and Comparative References on Federalism

Birch, A.H., *Federalism, Finance and Social Legislation in Canada, Australia and the United States*, Oxford, Clarendon Press, 1955.

Bowie, R.R. and Friedrich, C.J., Editors, *Studies in Federalism*, Little, Brown, Boston, 1954.

Brady, Alexander, *Democracy in the Dominions*, University of Toronto Press, 1948.

Duchacek, Ivo D., *Comparative Federalism: The Territorial Dimension of Politics*, Holt, Rinehart and Winston, New York, 1970.

Earle, Valerie, Editor, *Federalism: Infinite Variety in Theory and Practice*, F.E. Peacock, Ithaca, Illinois, 1968.

Franck, Thomas M. et al., *Why Federations Fail*, New York University Press, 1968.

Friedrich, Carl J., *Trends of Federalism in Theory and Practice*, Frederick A. Praeger, New York, 1968.

Livingston, W.S., *Federalism and Constitutional Change*, Oxford, Clarendon Press, 1956.

Macmahon, A.W., Editor, *Federalism, Mature and Emergent*, Doubleday, New York, 1955.

McWhinney, E., *Comparative Federalism*, University of Toronto Press, 1962.

McWhinney, E., *Judicial Review in the English-Speaking World*, Third Edition, University of Toronto Press, 1960.

May, R.J., *Federalism and Fiscal Adjustment*, Oxford, Clarendon Press, 1969.

Oates, Wallace E., *Fiscal Federalism*, Harcourt Brace Jovanovich, New York, 1972.

Riker, William H., *Federalism: Origin, Operation, Significance*, Little, Brown, Boston, 1964.

Sawer, G.F., *Modern Federalism*, C.A. Watts, London, 1969.

Watts, R.L., *New Federations: Experiments in the Commonwealth*, Clarendon Press, Oxford, 1966.

Watts, R.L., *Multicultural Societies and Federalism*, Studies of the Royal Commission on Bilingualism and Biculturalism, Information Canada, Ottawa, 1970.

Wheare, K.C., *Federal Government*, Fourth Edition, Oxford University Press, New York, 1963.

Wildavsky, Aaron, Editor, *American Federalism in Perspective*, Little, Brown, Boston, 1967.

General References on Canadian Federalism

Beck, J.M., Editor, *The Shaping of Canadian Federalism: Central Authority or Provincial Right?*, Copp, Clark, Toronto, 1971.

Black, Edwin R., *Divided Loyalties: Canadian Concepts of Federalism*, McGill-Queen's University Press, Montreal/London, 1975.

Cheffins, R.I., *The Constitutional Process in Canada*, McGraw-Hill of Canada, Toronto, 1969.

Creighton, Donald, *Towards the Discovery of Canada*, Macmillan of Canada, Toronto, 1972.

Crepeau, P.-A. and Macpherson C.B., Editors, *The Future of Canadian Federalism*.

Hawkins, Gordon, *Concepts of Federalism*, Canadian Institute on Public Affairs, Toronto, 1965.

Lower, A.R.M. and Scott, Frank, et al., Editors, *Evolving Canadian Federalism*, Duke University Press, Durham, N.C., 1958.

Mallory, J.M., *Social Credit and the Federal Power in Canada*, University of Toronto Press, 1954.

Ormsby, W.G., *The Emergence of the Federal Concept in Canada, 1839-1845*, University of Toronto Press, 1969.

Porter, John, *The Vertical Mosaic*, University of Toronto Press, 1965.

Ryerson, Stanley, *Unequal Union*, Progress Books, Toronto, 1968. Ontario Advisory Committee on Confederation, *Background Papers and Reports*, Queen's Printer, Toronto, Volume I, 1967, Volume II, 1970.

Smiley, Donald, *The Canadian Political Nationality*, Methuen of Canada, Toronto, 1967.

Smiley, Donald, *Constitutional Adaptation and Canadian Federalism since 1945*, Documents of the Royal Commission on Bilingualism and Biculturalism, Queen's Printer, Ottawa, 1970.

Waite, Peter, *The Life and Times of Confederation, 1864-1867*, University of Toronto Press, 1962.

Chapter I. The Canadian Constitution and the Federal System.

Bissonnette, Bernard, *Essai sur la constitution du Canada*, Les éditions du jour, Montréal, 1963.

Browne, G.P., *The Judicial Committee and the British North America Act*, University of Toronto Press, 1967.

Cairns, Alan C., "The Judicial Committee and its Critics", IV *Canadian Journal of Political Science*, September, 1971, pp. 301-345.

Cheffins, R.I., *The Constitutional Process in Canada*, McGraw-Hill of Canada, Toronto, 1969.

Favreau, The Honourable Guy, *The Amendment of the Constitution of Canada*, Queen's Printer, Ottawa, 1965.

Forsey, Eugene, Three essays in Ontario Advisory Committee on Confederation, *Background Papers, op. cit.*, Vol. I, pp. 159-192.

Forsey, Eugene, "Disallowance of Provincial Acts, Reservation of Provincial Bills and Refusal of Assent by Lieutenant-Governors since 1867," IV *Canadian Journal of Economics and Political Science*, February 1938, pp. 47-59.

Gérin-Lajoie, Paul, *Constitutional Amendment in Canada*, University of Toronto Press, 1950.

La Forest, Gerald V., *Disallowance and Reservation of Provincial Legislation*, Department of Justice, Ottawa, 1955.

La Forest, Gerald V., *The Allocation of Taxing Power Under the Canadian Constitution*, Canadian Tax Foundation, Toronto, 1967.

Laskin, Bora, "Peace, Order, and Good Government Re-examined", XXV *Canadian Bar Review*, December, 1947, pp. 1054-1087.

Laskin, Bora, *Canadian Constitutional Law: Cases, Text and Notes on the Distribution of Legislative Power Third Edition*, Carswell, Toronto, 1966.

Laskin, Bora, "The Supreme Court of Canada: A Final Court of Appeal of and for Canadians" XXIX *Canadian Bar Review*, December, 1951, pp. 1038-1079.

Lederman, W.R., Editor, *The Courts and the Canadian Constitution*, Carleton Library, McClelland and Stewart, Toronto, 1964.

Lederman, W.R., "Some Forms and Limitations of Cooperative Federalism" XLV *Canadian Bar Review*, September 1967, pp. 409-436.

Lyon, J. Noel and Atkey, Ronald G., Editors, *Canadian Constitutional Law in a Modern Perspective*, University of Toronto Press, 1970.

Russell, Peter H. *The Supreme Court of Canada as a Bilingual and Bicultural Institution*, Documents of the Royal Commission on Bilingualism and Biculturalism, Queen's Printer, Ottawa, 1969.

Russell, Peter H. Editor, *Leading Constitutional Decisions*, Carleton Library, McClelland and Stewart, Toronto, 1965.

Saywell, J.T., *The Office of Lieutenant-Governor, A Study in Canadian Government and Politics*, University of Toronto Press, 1957.

Senate of Canada, Session of 1939, *Report Pursuant to the Resolution of the Senate to the Honourable Speaker relating to the Enactment of the British North America Act, 1867, any lack of congruence between its terms and judicial construction of them and cognate matters*, King's Printer, Ottawa, 1940.

Stanley, G.F.G., *A Short History of the Canadian Constitution*, Ryerson Press, Toronto, 1969.

Strayer, B.L., *Judicial Review of Legislation in Canada*, University of Toronto Press, 1968.

Tarnopolsky, W.S., *The Canadian Bill of Rights*, Second Revised Edition, Carleton Library, McClelland and Stewart, Toronto, 1975.

Varcoe, F.P., *The Distribution of Legislative Power in Canada*, Carswell, Toronto, 1954.

Weiler, Paul, *In the Last Resort: A Critical Study of the Supreme Court of Canada*, Carswell, Toronto, 1974.

Chapter 2. Constitutional Reform and Review

Benson, the Honourable E.J., *The Taxing Powers and the Constitution of Canada*, Queen's Printer, Ottawa, 1969.

Burns, R.M. and Smiley, D.V., "Canadian Federalism and the Spending Power: Is Constitutional Restriction Necessary?" XVII *Canadian Tax Journal*, November-December 1969, pp. 467-482.

Canada, published verbatim records of Constitutional Conferences of February, 1968; February 1969 and December, 1969, Queen's Printer Ottawa, 1968, 1969 and 1970 respectively.

Canada, *The Constitutional Review, 1968-1971*, Secretary's Report, Information Canada, 1974.

Faribault, Marcel and Fowler, Robert M., *Ten to One: The Confederation Wager*, McClelland and Stewart, Toronto/Montreal, 1965.

Martin, The Honourable Paul, *Federalism and International Relations*, Queen's Printer, Ottawa, 1968.

O'Hearn, Peter J.T., *Peace, Order and Good Government: A New Constitution for Canada*, Macmillan of Canada, Toronto, 1964.

Ontario, *Proceedings of the Confederation for Tomorrow Conference, 1967*, (mimeo.).

Pearson, The Right Honourable L.B., *Federalism for the Future*, Queen's Printer, Ottawa, 1968.

Quebec, *The Government of Québec and the Constitution*, L'Office d'information et de publicité du Quebéc, n.d. (1969?).

Smiley, Donald V., "The Case against the Canadian Charter of Human Rights," II *Canadian Journal of Political Science*, September, 1969, pp. 277-291.

Trudeau, the Right Honourable Pierre Elliott, *The Constitution and the People of Canada*, Queen's Printer, Ottawa, 1969.

Trudeau, the Right Honourable Pierre Elliott, *Federal-Provincial Grants and the Spending Power of Parliament*, Queen's Printer, Ottawa, 1969.

Chapter 3. Executive Federalism

Aitchison, J.H., "Interprovincial Cooperation in Canada", in J.H. Aitchison, Editor, *The Political Process in Canada*, University of Toronto Press, 1963.

Aucoin, Peter and French, Richard, *Knowledge Power and Public Policy*, Science Council of Canada, Information Canada, 1974.

Black, E.R., "Federal-Provincial Conferences and Constitutional Change", LX-XVIII *Queen's Quarterly*, Summer, 1971, pp. 298-303.

Burns, R.M., "Intergovernmental Relations in Canada, XXXIII *Public Administration Review*, 1973, pp. 14-22.

Cameron, David, "Urban Policy" in G. Bruce Doern and V. Seymour Wilson, *Issues in Canadian Public Policy*, Macmillan of Canada, Toronto, 1974, pp. 228-252.

Caplan, Neil, "Some Factors Affecting the Resolution of a Federal-Provincial Conflict", 2 *Canadian Journal of Political Science*, June 1969, pp. 173-186.

Claxton, Brooke and Gouin, L.M., *Legislative Expedients and Devices Adopted* by the Dominion and the Provinces, King's Printer, Ottawa, 1939.

Corry, J.A., *Difficulties of Divided Jurisdiction*, King's Printer, Ottawa, 1939.

Corry, J.A., "Constitutional Trends and Federalism" in A.R.M. Lower, F.R. Scott *et al.*, *Evolving Canadian Federalism*, Duke University Press, Durham, N.C., 1958, pp. 95-125.

Doern, G. Bruce and Wilson, V. Seymour, "Conclusions and Observations" in Doern and Wilson, Editors, *Issues in Canadian Public Policy*, Macmillan of Canada, 1974, pp. 337-345.

Dupré, J. Stefan *et al.*, *Federalism and Policy Development: The Case of Adult Occupational Training in Ontario*, University of Toronto Press, 1973.

Institute of Intergovernmental Relations, Queen's University, *Report: Intergovernmental Liasion on Fiscal and Economic Matters, 1968.*

Johnson, A.W., "The Dynamics of Federalism in Canada", I *Canadian Journal of Political Science*, March 1968, pp. 18-39.

Leach, Richard, "Interprovincial Cooperation: Neglected Aspect of Canadian Federalism", II *Canadian Public Administration*, June, 1959, pp. 83-99.

Phidd, R.W., "Regional Development Policy" in Doern and Wilson, *op. cit.*, pp. 166-202.

Sharp, The Honourable Mitchell, *Federalism and International Conferences on Education*, Queen's Printer, Ottawa, 1968.

Simeon, Richard, *Federal-Provincial Diplomacy*, University of Toronto Press, 1972.

Smiley, Donald V., "Federal-Provincial Conflict in Canada," 4 *Publius*, Summer, 1974, pp. 7-24.

Smiley, Donald V., "The Structural Problem of Canadian Federalism," XIV *Canadian Public Administration*, Fall, 1971, pp. 326-343.

Smiley, Donald V., "Canadian Federalism and the Resolution of Federal-Provincial Conflict" in Vaughan, Frederick/Kyba, Patrick and Dwivedi, O.P., Editors, *Contemporary Issues in Canadian Politics*, Prentice-Hall of Canada, Scarborough, 1970, pp. 48-66.

Veilleux, Gérard, *Les relations intergouvernmentales au Canada 1867-1967*, Les presses de l'université du Québec, Montréal, 1971.

Westmacott, Martin, "The National Transportation Act and Western Canada: A Study in Cooperative Federalism", XVII *Canadian Public Administration*, Fall, 1973, pp. 447-468.

Chapter 4. Political Parties and Canadian Federalism.

Black, E.R., "Federal Strains within a Canadian Party", XLV *Dalhousie Review*, 1965, pp. 307-323.

Cairns, Alan C., "The Electoral System and the Party System in Canada, 1921-1965", I *Canadian Journal of Political Science*, March 1968, pp. 55-80.

Courtney, John C., *The Selection of National Party Leaders in Canada*, Macmillan of Canada, Toronto, 1973.

Courtney, John C., Editor, *Voting in Canada*, Prentice-Hall of Canada, Scarborough, 1967.

Engelmann, F.C., and Schwartz, M.A., *Political Parties and the Canadian Social Structure*, Second Edition, Prentice-Hall of Canada, Scarborough, 1975.

Granatstein, J.L., *The Politics of Survival: The Conservative Party of Canada, 1939-1945*, University of Toronto Press, 1967.

Latouche, Daniel, "The Independence Option: Ideological and Empirical Elements" in Dale C. Thomson, Editor, *Quebec Society and Politics: Views from the Inside*, McClelland and Stewart, Toronto, 1973, pp. 179-186.

Lemieux, Vincent, "The Political Party System in Quebec" in *Quebec Society and Politics, op. cit.*, pp. 99-118.

Macpherson, C.B., *Democracy in Alberta: Social Credit and the Party System*, Second Edition, University of Toronto Press, 1962.

Meisel, John, *Working Papers on Canadian Politics*, Second Edition, McGill-Queen's University Press, Montreal/London, 1974.

Meisel, John, "Canadian Parties and Politics" in Richard H. Leach, Editor, *Contemporary Canada*, Unviersity of Toronto Press, 1968.

Morton, W.L., *The Progressive Party in Canada*, University of Toronto Press, 1950.

Muller, Steven, "Federalism and the Party System in Canada", in J. Peter Meekison, Editor, *Canadian Federalism: Myth or Reality*, Methuen of Canada, Toronto, 1968, pp. 119-132.

Paltiel, K.Z., "Federalism and Party Finance: A Preliminary Sounding" in Committee on Election Expenses, *Studies in Canadian Party Finance*, Queen's Printer, Ottawa, 1966, pp. 1-21. (See also other essays in this collection for analyses of the finances of the individual parties).

Paltiel, K.Z., *Political Party Financing in Canada*, McGraw-Hill of Canada, Toronto, 1970.

Pinard, Maurice, *The Rise of a Third Party*, Prentice-Hall, Englewood Cliffs, N.J., 1971.

Quinn, H.P., *The Union Nationale: A Study in Quebec Nationalism*, University of Toronto Press, 1963.

Robin, Martin, Editor, *Canadian Provincial Politics*, Prentice-Hall of Canada, Scarborough, 1972.

Simeon, Richard and Elkins, David J., "Regional Political Cultures in Canada," VII *The Canadian Journal of Political Science*, September, 1974, pp. 397-437.

Smiley, Donald V., "The National Party Leadership Convention: A Preliminary Analysis," I *Canadian Journal of Political Science*, December, 1968, pp. 373-397.

Smith, David, *Prairie Liberalism: The Liberal Party of Saskatchewan, 1905-1971*, University of Toronto Press, 1975.

Wilson, John, "The Canadian Political Cultures: Towards a Redefinition of the Nature of the Canadian Political System", VII *Canadian Journal of Political Science*, September, 1974, pp. 438-483.

Chapter 5. The Fiscal and Economic Side of Canadian Federalism.

Angers, François-Albert, *Essai sur la centralisation*, Les presses de l'école des hautes études commerciales, Montréal, 1960.

Bird, Richard M., *The Growth of Government Spending in Canada*, Canadian Tax Foundation, Toronto, 1970.

Brewis, T.N., *Regional Economic Policies in Canada*, Macmillan of Canada, Toronto, 1969.

Bryden, M.H., *Occupancy of Tax Fields in Canada*, Canadian Tax Foundation, Toronto, 1965.

Burns, R.M., "The Operation of Fiscal and Economic Policy," in Doern, G. Bruce, David Wilson, V., Seymour, Editors, *Issues in Canadian Public Policy*, Macmillan of Canada, Toronto, 1974, pp. 286-309.

Canada, *Report of the Royal Commission on Dominion-Provincial Relations*, King's Printer, Ottawa, 1940.

Canada, *Report of the Royal Commission on Taxation*, Queen's Printer, Ottawa, 1966. Particularly Vol. 2, Chapter 3.

Canada, *Federal-Provincial Tax Structure Committee*, Queen's Printer, Ottawa, 1966.

Carter, Geoge E., *Canadian Conditional Grants since World War II*, Canadian Tax Foundation, Toronto, 1971.

Clark, Douglas H., *Fiscal Need and Revenue Equalization Grants*, Canadian Tax Foundation, Toronto, 1969.

Debanné, J.G., "Oil and Canadian Policy" in Erickson, Edward W. and Waverman, Leonard, Editors, *The Energy Question: An International Failure of Policy, Volume 2: North America*, University of Toronto Press, 1974, pp. 125-148.

Dupré, J. Stefan, "Contracting Out: A Funny Thing Happened on the Way to the Centennial," *Report of the Proceedings of the Eighteenth Annual Tax Conference, 1964*, Canadian Tax Foundation, Toronto, 1965, pp. 208-218.

Dupré, J. Stefan, "Tax Powers vs. Spending Responsibilities: An Historical Analysis of Federal-Provincial Finance" in Rotstein, Abraham, Editor, *The Prospect of Change: Proposals for Canada's Future*, McGraw-Hill of Canada, Toronto, 1965, pp. 83-101.

Graham, John F., *Fiscal Adjustment and Economic Development: A Case Study of Nova Socṫia*, University of Toronto Press, 1963.

Graham, John F., Johnson, A.W. and Andrews, J.M., *Inter-Government Fiscal Relationships*, Canadian Tax Foundation, Toronto, 1964.

Green, Alan, G., "Regional Economic Disparities" in Officer, L.H. and Smith, L.B., Editors, *Issues in Canadian Economics*, McGraw-Hill Ryerson, Toronto, 1974, pp. 354-370.

Green, Alan, G., *Regional Aspects of Canada's Economic Growth*, University of Toronto Press, 1970.

Hanson, E.J., *Fiscal Needs of the Canadian Provinces*, Canadian Tax Foundation, Toronto, 1961.

Hood, William C., "Economic Policy in Our Federal State" in Crepeau, P.-A., and Macpherson, C.B., Editors, *The Future of Canadian Federalism*, University of Toronto Press/Les presses de l'Université de Montréal, Toronto/Montreal, 1965, pp. 58-76.

Lynn, James, *Federal-Provincial Fiscal Relations*, Studies of the Royal Commission on Taxation, No. 23, Queen's Printer, Ottawa, 1967.

Mackintosh, W.A., *The Economic Background of Dominion-Provincial Relations*, Carleton Library, McClelland and Stewart, Toronto, 1964.

Mathews, Philip, *Forced Growth: Five Studies of Government Involvement in the Development of Canada*, James Lewis and Samuel, Toronto, 1971.

Maxwell, J.A., *Federal Subsidies to the Provincial Governments in Canada*, Harvard University Press, Cambridge, 1937.

McAllister, R. Ian, "Some Economic Problems of a Federal System", in *Officer and Smith, op. cit.*, pp. 396-406.

Moore, A. Milton, Perry, J. Harvey and Beach, Donald I., *The Financing of Canadian Federation: The First Hundred Years*, The Canadian Tax Foundation, Toronto, 1966.

Nowlan, David M., "Centrifugally Speaking: Some Economics of Canadian Federalism" in Lloyd, Trevor and McLeod, Jack, Editors, *Agenda 1970: Proposals for a Creative Politics*, University of Toronto Press, 1968, pp. 177-196.

Ontario, Ontario Studies in Tax Reform, *Analysis of the Federal Tax Reform*

Proposals, Department of Treasury and Economics, 1968.

Perry, J. Harvey, *Taxes, Tariffs and Subsidies*, 2 Volumes, University of Toronto Press, 1955.

Quebec, *Report of the Royal Commission of Inquiry on Constitutional Problems*, Quebec, 1954.

Queen's University, Institute of Intergovernmental Relations, *Report: Intergovernmental Liaison on Fiscal and Economic Matters*, Queen's Printer, Ottawa, 1969.

Scott, F.R., "Social Planning and Canadian Federalism" in Oliver, Michael, Editor, *Social Purpose for Canada*, University of Toronto Press, 1961, pp. 394-407.

Smiley, Donald V., *Conditional Grants and Canadian Federalism*, Canadian Tax Foundation, Toronto, 1963.

Smiley, Donald V. and Burns, R.M., "Canadian Federalism and the Spending Power: Is Constitutional Restriction Necessary, XVII *Canadian Tax Journal*, November-December 1969, pp. 467-482.

Trudeau, the Right Honourable Pierre Elliott, *Federal-Provincial Grants and the Spending Power of Parliament*, Queen's Printer, Ottawa, 1969.

United States, *In Search of Balance: Canada's Intergovernmental Experience*, Advisory Committee on Intergovernmental Relations, Government Printing Office, Washington, 1971.

Whalen, Hugh, "Public Policy and Regional Development: The Experience of the Atlantic Provinces" in Rotstein, Abraham, Editor, *The Prospect of Change: Proposals for Canada's Future*, McGraw-Hill of Canada, Toronto, 1965, pp. 102-148.

Chapter 6. Cultural Duality and Canadian Federalism.

Arès, R., S.J., *Dossier sur le pacte fédératif de 1867*, Les Éditions Bellarmin, Montréal, 1967.

Brunet, Michel, *Canadians et Canadiens*, Fides, Montréal, 1954.

Brunet, Michel, *Québec-Canada Anglais: Deux itineraires un affrontement*, Éditions H.M.H. Montréal, 1968.

Burns, R.M., Editor, *One Country or Two?* McGill-Queen's University Press, Montreal and London, 1971.

Cameron, David, *Nationalism, Self-Determination and the Quebec Question*, Macmillan of Canada, Toronto, 1974.

Commissioner of Official Languages, *Annual Reports*, 1970-71 and onward, Information Canada, Ottawa.

Cook, Ramsay, *Canada and the French-Canadian Question*, Macmillan of Canada, Toronto, 1966.

Cook, Ramsay, Editor, *French-Canadian Nationalism: An Anthology*, Macmillan of Canada, Toronto, 1969.

Creighton, Donald, "The Use and Abuse of History" and "The Myth of Biculturalism" in Donald Creighton, *Towards the Discovery of Canada*, Macmillan of Canada, Toronto, 1972, pp. 65-83 and pp. 256-270.

Gibson, Frederick W., Editor, *Cabinet Formation and Bicultural Relations*, Studies of the Royal Commission on Bilingualism and Biculturalism, Queen's Printer, Ottawa, 1970.

Forsey, Eugene, *Our Present Discontents*, The George C. Nowlan Lectures at Acadian University, 1967, Published by Acadia University, Wolfville, N.S.

Forsey, Eugene, "Concepts of Federalism: Some Canadian Aspects," in Gordon

Hawkins, Editor, *Concepts of Federalism*, Canadian Institute of Public Affairs, Toronto, 1965, pp. 22-28.

Guindon, Hubert, "Social Unrest, Social Class and Quebec's Bureaucratic Revolution", 71 *Queen's Quarterly*, Summer 1964, pp. 150-162.

Hoffman, David and Ward, Norman, *Bilingualism and Biculturalism in the Canadian House of Commons*, Documents of the Royal Commission on Bilingualism and Biculturalism, Queen's Printer, Ottawa, 1970.

Jones, Richard, *Community in Crisis: French-Canadian Nationalism in Perspective*, McClelland and Stewart, Toronto/Montreal, 1967.

Joy, Richard J., *Languages in Conflict: The Canadian Experience*, Published by the author, Ottawa, 1967.

Lalande, Gilles, *Pourquoi le fédéralisme*, Hurtubise/H.M.H., Montréal, 1972.

Lamontagne, Maurice, *Le fédéralisme canadien*, Les presse universitaires Laval, 1954.

Latouche, Daniel, "Quebec and the North American Subsystem: One Possible Scenario", 28 *International Organization*, Autumn, 1974, pp. 931-960.

Lemieux, Vincent, Gilbert, Marcel et Blair, André, *Une élection de réalignement: l'élection générale du 29 avril 1970 au Québec*, Éditions du jour, Montréal 1970.

Lemieux, Vincent, "Heaven is Blue and Hell is Red" in Martin Robin, Editor, *Canadian Provincial Politics*, Prentice-Hall of Canada, Scarborough, 1972, pp. 262-289.

Lévesque, René, *Option Quebec*, McClelland and Stewart, Toronto, 1968.

Morin, Claude, *Le pouvoir Québécois . . . en négociation*, Les editions du boréal express, Montréal, 1972.

Morin, Claude, *Le combat Québécois*, Les éditions du boréal express, Montréal, 1973.

Morton, W.L., *The Canadian Identity*, Second Edition, University of Toronto Press, 1972, Chapter 5.

Oliver, Michael, "Quebec and Canadian Democracy", 23 *Canadian Journal of Economic and Political Science*, November, 1957, pp. 504-515.

Oliver, Michael and Scott, F.R., Editors, *Quebec States Her Case*, Macmillan of Canada, Toronto, 1964.

Parti Québécois, *Quand nous sommes vraiment chez nous*, Montréal, 1972.

Quebec, Report of the Royal Commission of Inquiry on Constitutional Problems, Four Volumes, Quebec, 1956 (For an abridgement see *The Tremblay Report*, Edited and with an Introduction by David Kwavnick, Carleton Library Series, McClelland and Stewart, Toronto, 1973).

Quebec, *The Government of Québec and the Constitution*, L'Office d'information et de publicité du Quèbec, n.d. (1969?).

Rioux, Marcel, *Quebec in Question*, Translated by James Doake, James Lewis and Samuel, Toronto, 1971.

Rioux, Marcel and Martin, Yves, Editors, *French-Canadian Society*, Vol. I, Carleton Library, McClelland and Stewart, Toronto, 1964.

Royal Commission on Bilingualism and Biculturalism, Reports, Queen's Printer, Ottawa.
Preliminary Report, 1965.
Book I, *The Official Languages*, 1967.
Book II, *Education*, 1968.
Book III, *The Work World*, 1969.
Book IV, *The Cultural Contributions of other Ethnic Groups*, 1969.

Ryerson, Stanley, B., *Unequal Union: Confederation and the Roots of Conflict in the Canadas, 1815-1873*, Progress Books, Toronto, 1968.

Smiley, Donald V., *The Canadian Political Nationality*, Methuen of Canada,

Toronto, 1967, Chapter 3.

Smith, Denis, *Bleeding Hearts . . . Bleeding Country; Canada and the Quebec Crisis*, M.G. Hurtig, Edmonton, 1971.

Stanley, George F., "Act or Pact? Another Look at Confederation", *Report*, Canadian Historical Association, 1956, pp. 1-25.

Thomson, Dale C. Editor, *Quebec Society and Politics: Views from the Inside*, McClelland and Stewart, Toronto, 1973.

Trudeau, Pierre Elliott, *Federalism and the French Canadians*, Macmillan of Canada, Toronto, 1968.

Wade, Mason, *The French-Canadian Outlook*, Carleton Library, McClelland and Stewart, Toronto, 1964.

Wade, Mason, *The French Canadians, 1760-1945*, Macmillan of Canada, Toronto, 1955.

Chapter 7. The Three Axes of Canadian Federalism.

(References related to cultural duality are found under those for Chapter 6.)
1. *Central Canada-periphery relations.*

Barr, John and Anderson, Owen, Editors, *The Unfinished Revolt: Some Views on Western Independence*, McClelland and Stewart, Toronto, 1971.

Black, E.R., "British Columbia: The Politics of Exploitation" in R. Shearer, Editor, *Exploiting our Economic Potential: Public Policy and the British Columbia Economy*, Holt, Rinehart and Winston, Toronto/Montreal, 1968, pp. 23-41.

Blackman, W., *The Cost of Confederation: An Analysis of the Costs to Alberta*, Part I, Economic Activity, Calgary, 1974 (mimeo.).

Clark, S.D., *The Developing Canadian Community*, University of Toronto Press, 1962.

Clark, S.D., *Movements of Political Protest in Canada 1640-1840*, University of Toronto Press, 1957.

Conway, John, "Geo-Politics and the Canadian Union", in *The Confederation Challenge*, Vol. 2., Ontario Advisory Committee on Confederation, Queen's Printer, Toronto, 1970, pp. 28-49.

Fowke, Vernon, *The National Policy and the Wheat Economy*, University of Toronto Press, 1957.

Graham, John F., *Fiscal Adjustment and Canadian Development: A Case Study of Nova Scotia*, University of Toronto Press, 1963.

Hodgetts, J.E., "Regional Interests and Policy in a Federal Structure", XXXII *Canadian Journal of Economics and Political Science*, February, 1966, pp. 3-14.

Innis, Harold A., *Essays in Canadian Economic History*, Edited by Mary Q. Innis, University of Toronto Press, 1956.

Irving, John A., *The Social Credit Movement in Alberta*, University of Toronto Press, 1959.

Lipset, Martin, *Agrarian Socialism: The Cooperative Commonwealth Federation in Saskatchewan*, Revised and Expanded Edition, University of California Press, Berkeley, 1971.

Macpherson, C.B., *Democracy in Alberta: Social Credit and the Party System*, University of Toronto Press, 1953.

Mallory, J.R., *Social Credit and the Federal Power in Canada*, University of Toronto Press, 1954.

Morton, W.L., *The Progressive Party in Canada*, University of Toronto Press, 1950.

Morton, W.L., "The Bias of Prairie Politics" *Transactions of the Royal Society of Canada*, 1955, pp. 57-66. Reprinted in Donald Swainson, Editor, *Historical Essays on the Prairie Provinces*, Carleton Library, McClelland and Stewart, Toronto, 1970, pp. 289-300.

Morton, W.L., "Clio in Canada: The Interpretation of Canadian History" in Cook, Ramsay/Brown, Craig and Berger, Carl, Editors, *Approaches to Canadian History*, University of Toronto Press, 1967, pp. 42-49.

Sanford, Thomas, *The Politics of Protest: The Cooperative Commonwealth Federation and the Social Credit League in British Columbia*, Ph.D. Thesis, University of California, Berkeley, 1961.

Smiley, Donald V., "Canada's Poujadists: A New Look at Social Credit", *Canadian Forum*, September, 1962, reprinted in *Canadian Life and Letters: 1920-1970 Selections from the Canadian Forum*, J.L. Granatstein and Peter Stevens, Editors, University of Toronto Press, 1972, pp. 348-351.

Smith, David E., *Prairie Liberalism: The Liberal Party of Saskatchewan, 1905-1971*, University of Toronto Press, 1975.

Smith, Denis, "Prairie Revolt, Federalism and the Party System" in Hugh G. Thorburn, Editor, *Party Politics in Canada*, Third Edition, Prentice-Hall of Canada, Scarborough, 1972, pp. 204-215.

Strom, the Honourable Harry E., "A Case for the West", in J. Peter Meekison, Editor, *Canadian Federalism: Myth or Reality*, Second Edition, Methuen of Canada, Toronto, 1971, pp. 363-373.

2. *Canadian Federalism and Canadian-American Relations.*

Aitken, H.G.J., *American Capital and Canadian Resources*, Harvard University Press, 1961.

Aitken, H.G.J., "Defensive Expansionism: The State and Economic Growth in Canada", in W.T. Easterbrook and M.H. Watkins, Editors, *Approaches to Canadian Economic History*, Carleton Library, McClelland and Stewart, Toronto, 1967, pp. 183-221.

Canada, *Foreign Direct Investment in Canada*, Information Canada, 1972. (Gray Report).

Canada, *Foreign Ownership and the Structure of Canada Industry*, Information Canada, 1970 (Watkins Report).

Dubuc, Alfred, "The Decline of Confederation and the New Nationalism" in Peter Russell, Editor, *Nationalism in Canada*, McGraw-Hill of Canada, Toronto, 1966, pp. 112-132.

Fowke, Vernon, "The National Policy — Old and New" in *Easterbrook and Watkins, op. cit.*, pp. 237-258.

Gilpin, Robert, "American Direct Investment and Canada's Two Nationalisms", in Richard A. Preston, Editor, *The Influence of the United States on Canadian Development: Eleven Case Studies*, Duke University Press, Durham, N.C., 1972, pp. 124-143.

Gilpin, Robert, "Integration and Disintegration on the North American Continent", 28 *International Organization*, Autumn 1974, pp. 851-874.

Levy, Thomas and Holsti, Kal J., "Bilateral Institutions and Transgovernmental Relations between Canada and the United States", 28 *International Organization, op. cit.*, pp. 875-902.

Levy, Thomas with H. Leach and Donald E. Walker, "Province-State Trans-Border Relations: A Preliminary Assessment" 16 *Canadian Public Administration*, Fall, 1973, pp. 469-482.

Levitt, Kari, *Silent Surrender: The Multinational Corporation in Canada*, Macmillan of Canada, Toronto, 1970.

Latouche, Daniel, "Quebec and the North American Continent: One Possible Scenario", 28 *International Organization, op. cit.*, pp. 931-960.

Masson, Claude, "Economic Relations between Quebec, Canada and the United States" in Andrew Axline *et al.*, Editors, *Continental Community: Independence and Integration in North America*, McClelland and Stewart, Toronto, 1974, pp. 240-249.

Nelles, H.V., "Empire Ontario: The Problems of Resource Development", in Donald Swainson, Editor, *Oliver Mowat's Ontario*, Macmillan of Canada, Toronto, 1972, pp. 189-210.

Ontario, Legislative Assembly, *Final Report on Economic Nationalism of the Select Committee on Economic and Cultural Nationalism*, 1975.

Smiley, Donald V., "The Federal Dimension of Canadian Economic Nationalism" 1 *Dalhousie Law Journal*, October 1974, pp. 541-579.

Smiley, Donald V., "Canada and the Quest for a National Policy," VIII *Canadian Journal of Political Science*, March 1975, pp. 40-62.

Stevenson, Garth, "Foreign Direct Investment and the Provinces", VII *Canadian Journal of Political Science*, December 1974, pp. 630-647.

Stevenson, Garth, "Continental Integration and Canadian Unity" in *Continental Community, op. cit.*, pp. 194-217.

Chapter 8. Canada: A Federal Country

Bucovetsky, M.W., "The Mining Industry and the Great Tax Reform Debate" in A. Paul Pross, Editor, *Pressure Group Behaviour in Canadian Politics*, McGraw-Hill Ryerson, Toronto, 1975, pp. 87-114.

Dawson, Helen Jones, "National Pressure Groups and the Federal Government" in *Pressure Group Behaviour, op. cit.*, pp. 27-58.

Elkins, David J., and Simeon, Richard, "Regional Political Cultures in Canada", VII *Canadian Journal of Political Science*, September 1974, pp. 397-437.

Kwavnick, David, "Interest Group Demands and the Federal Political System: Two Canadian Case Studies", in *Pressure Group Behaviour, op. cit.*, pp. 69-86. Livingston, William S., "A Note on the Nature of Federalism," LXVII *Political Science Quarterly*, March 1952, pp. 81-95.

McRae, Kenneth, Editor, *Consociational Democracy: Political Accommodation in Segmented Societies*, Carleton Library, McClelland and Stewart, Toronto, 1974.

Smiley, Donald V., "The Structural Problem of Canadian Federalism" XIV *Canadian Public Administration*, Fall, 1971, pp. 326-343.

Stein, Michael, "Federal Political Systems and Federal Societies" in J. Peter Meekison, Editor, *Canadian Federalism: Myth or Reality*, Second Edition, Methuen of Canada, Toronto, 1971, pp. 30-42.

Wilson, John, "The Canadian Political Cultures: Towards a Redefinition of the Nature of the Canadian Political System", VII *Canadian Journal of Political Science*, September 1974, pp. 438-483.

INDEX

Abbott, J., 16
Act of Union, the, 1840, 159
Adult occupational training, as area
  of federal-provincial conflict, 59
*Aeronautics, Re Regulation and
  Control of,* 1932, 19
Agricultural Rehabilitation and Rural
  Development Act, (ARDA), 1961,
  131
Alberta, regional feelings discussed,
  195-196, 201
Alberta, Statutes, Reference re, 16
Amendment, of B.N.A. Act, 7-11
ARDA, 131
Area Development Authority, 131
Arts, Letters and Sciences, Royal
  Commission on, (Ottawa) 1951,
  31-33
Atkey, Ronald G., 17, 50-51
Atlantic Development Board, 131
Atlantic Province Adjustment Grants,
  131

"Balance Theory" discussed, 84-92
Barker, Clarence L., 126
Berry, Glyn R., 151
Bennett, R. B., 68, 195
  "New Deal" legislation
  invalidated, 68
Bennett, W. A. C., 71, 108
Bergeron, Léandre, 222
Biculturalism. see Bilingualism and
  biculturalism.
Bilingualism and biculturalism,
  190-191
  in B.N.A. Act, 162
  in Constitutional Conference, 1968,
  42
  in Official Languages Act, 172
  in Reports of Royal Commission on,
  42, 180, 193
  in "Victoria Charter", 46
Bill of Rights, Canadian,
  as outlined in B.N.A. Act, 16
  regulation of emergency powers, 12
Black, Edwin R., 95-96, 226
Blackman, W., 114
B.N.A. Act, 193
  amendment of, 7-9, 40-52
  bilingualism in, 162

as codified constitution, 1-2
  division of legislative powers in,
  3-6, 26-30
  education, 30-34
  federal spending power outlined,
  28
  judicial review of, 18-26
  repatriation of amending power,
  7-11
  taxation, responsibility for, 27
Bourassa, Robert, 44, 175
  effect of his election on
  constitutional review, 44
Breton, Raymond, 192
Brewis, T. N., 123, 131
Browne, G. P., 21
Brunet, Michel, 164
Bucovetsky, M. S., 203

Cairns, Alan C., 23, 51
Cameron, David, 221
Canada Assistance Plan, 1966, 73,
  135, 138
Canada Pension Plan, 1965, 122
Canadian-American relations,
  185-189
Canadian Federation of Mayors and
  Municipalities, (CFMM), 67
Canadian Labour Congress, (CLC),
  204
Canadian Union of Students, (CUS),
  203-204
Cannon, J., 16
Careless, J.M.S., 161
Carter Report, 1966, 142
Civil Rights, Royal Commission of
  Inquiry, Report of, 17-18
Colonial Laws Validity Act, 1865,
  18-19
Communications policy, 177
Comparative federalism, 83-84
Confederal party systems, 85
Confederation for Tomorrow
  Conference, 1967, 40-41
Confederation of National Trade
  Unions, 204
Conference of Prime Ministers and
  Premiers, 58, 64, 75, 109
Conservative party, relations between
  federal and provincial wings, 95-96

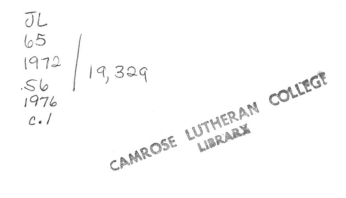